# Transition and Continuity in School Literacy Development

Also available from Bloomsbury

*Content Knowledge in English Language Teacher Education: International Experiences*, Dario Luis Banegas

*Children's Transitions in Everyday Life and Institutions*, edited by Mariane Hedegaard and Marilyn Fleer

*Language Education in the School Curriculum: Issues of Access and Equity*, Ken Cruickshank, Stephen Black, Honglin Chen, Linda Tsung and Jan Wright

*Researching Power and Identity in Literacy Practices in Malawi*, Ahmmardouh Mjaya

*Research Methods for Early Childhood Education*, Rosie Flewitt and Lynn Ang

*Subject Literacy in Culturally Diverse Secondary Schools: Supporting EAL Learners*, Esther Daborn, Sally Zacharias and Hazel Crichton

# Transition and Continuity in School Literacy Development

Edited by
Pauline Jones, Erika Matruglio and
Christine Edwards-Groves

BLOOMSBURY ACADEMIC
LONDON • NEW YORK • OXFORD • NEW DELHI • SYDNEY

BLOOMSBURY ACADEMIC
Bloomsbury Publishing Plc
50 Bedford Square, London, WC1B 3DP, UK
1385 Broadway, New York, NY 10018, USA
29 Earlsfort Terrace, Dublin 2, Ireland

BLOOMSBURY, BLOOMSBURY ACADEMIC and the Diana logo are trademarks of
Bloomsbury Publishing Plc

First published in Great Britain 2022
This paperback edition published in 2023

Copyright © Pauline Jones, Erika Matruglio, Christine Edwards-Groves and
Bloomsbury, 2022

Pauline Jones, Erika Matruglio, Christine Edwards-Groves and Bloomsbury
have asserted their right under the Copyright, Designs and Patents Act, 1988,
to be identified as Author of this work.

For legal purposes the Acknowledgements on p. xx constitute an extension
of this copyright page.

Cover image: © Wavebreakmedia/ iStock

All rights reserved. No part of this publication may be reproduced or transmitted
in any form or by any means, electronic or mechanical, including photocopying,
recording, or any information storage or retrieval system, without prior permission
in writing from the publishers.

Bloomsbury Publishing Plc does not have any control over, or responsibility for, any
third-party websites referred to or in this book. All internet addresses given in this
book were correct at the time of going to press. The author and publisher regret any
inconvenience caused if addresses have changed or sites have ceased to exist, but can
accept no responsibility for any such changes.

A catalogue record for this book is available from the British Library.

Library of Congress Cataloging-in-Publication Data

Names: Jones, Pauline, 1958- editor. | Matruglio, Erika, editor. |
Edwards-Groves, Christine, editor.
Title: Transition and continuity in school literacy development / Edited by
Pauline Jones, Erika Matruglio and Christine Edwards-Groves.
Description: London; New York: Bloomsbury Academic, 2022. |
Includes bibliographical references and index.
Identifiers: LCCN 2021027052 (print) | LCCN 2021027053 (ebook) |
ISBN 9781350148826 (hardback) | ISBN 9781350259744 (paperback) |
ISBN 9781350148857 (pdf) | ISBN 9781350148864 (epub)
Subjects: LCSH: Literacy–Study and teaching. | Curriculum planning. |
English language–Study and teaching.
Classification: LCC LC149.T72 2022 (print) | LCC LC149 (ebook) | DDC 370.117/5–dc23
LC record available at https://lccn.loc.gov/2021027052
LC ebook record available at https://lccn.loc.gov/2021027053

ISBN: HB: 978-1-3501-4882-6
PB: 978-1-3502-5974-4
ePDF: 978-1-3501-4885-7
eBook: 978-1-3501-4886-4

Typeset by Newgen KnowledgeWorks Pvt. Ltd., Chennai, India

To find out more about our authors and books visit www.bloomsbury.com
and sign up for our newsletters.

# Contents

| | |
|---|---|
| List of Illustrations | vii |
| Notes on Contributors | xi |
| Foreword *Debra Myhill* | xvii |
| Acknowledgements | xx |

Part I   Theory, Curriculum and Practice in Transition

1  Rethinking School Literacy Progressions   3
   *Pauline Jones and Christine Edwards-Groves*

2  A Review of the Literature around Literacy Transition   15
   *Trish Weekes*

3  Representing Writing Development: Research and Policy   29
   *Beverly Derewianka*

4  Transitions in School Literacy: Co-opting Everyday Rationalities   55
   *Björn Kindenberg and Peter Freebody*

Envoi to Part I: Literacy Transitions as Distributed, Participatory Practice   71
   *Jennifer Rowsell*

Part II   Investigating the Conditions for Literacy Learning and Teaching in Transition

5  Transition from Preschool to School: Spaces, Time, Interactions and Resources   77
   *Lisa Kervin and Jessica Mantei*

6  Transitions in Literacy and Classroom Interaction across the School Years   95
   *Christine Edwards-Groves, Stephanie Garoni and Peter Freebody*

## Contents

7  Understanding Literacy Transitions: Pedagogic Practices in
   Primary Writing Classrooms  119
   *Honglin Chen, Helen Lewis and David Rose*

8  Investigating Pedagogic Discourse in Late Primary and Junior
   Secondary English  145
   *Pauline Jones, Erika Matruglio and David Rose*

9  Exploring Multimodal Meaning Making in Science at the
   Transition to High School  169
   *Annette Turney and Emma Rutherford Vale*

10 Categories, Appraisals and Progress in Literacy Transitions  191
   *Erika Matruglio*

Envoi to Part II: Explicating Transitions between Hidden Literacy
   Curricula  209
   *Adam Lefstein*

### Part III  Horizons of Consequence: Accounting for Transition

11 Literate Identities in the Early Years of Primary School  215
   *Jessica Mantei and Lisa Kervin*

12 Articulating Education with Primary Students  233
   *Christine Edwards-Groves and Peter Freebody*

13 Transitioning from Primary to High School  253
   *Emma Rutherford Vale, Helen Lewis, Honglin Chen
   and Pauline Jones*

Envoi to Part III: Literacies for Successfully Navigating Transitions at
   School and Beyond  273
   *Elizabeth Birr Moje*

Epilogue: Ways to Transition Forward  281
*Pauline Jones, Erika Matruglio and Christine Edwards-Groves*

Appendix: Transcription Conventions  289
Notes  291
References  295
Index  331

# Illustrations

## Figures

| | | |
|---|---|---|
| 7.1 | Structuring of pedagogic activity | 133 |
| 8.1 | Curriculum genres configure two registers together | 149 |
| 9.1a | Analytical image | 175 |
| 9.1b | Classifying image | 176 |
| 9.2 | Sage's poster | 177 |
| 9.3 | Jack's Earthquake Explanation | 181 |
| 9.4 | Becka's sequential explanation | 184 |
| 9.5a | Zane's explanation 1 | 187 |
| 9.5b | Zane's explanation 2 | 187 |

## Tables

| | | |
|---|---|---|
| 3.1 | Organisation of Content in the Focus Syllabuses | 31 |
| 3.2 | Common Strands Relating to Writing in the Syllabus Documents | 32 |
| 3.3 | Components of the Text Creation Process as Represented in the Focus Syllabuses | 32 |
| 3.4 | Synthesis of References to *Audience* in the Focus Syllabuses | 34 |
| 3.5 | Synthesis of References to *Purposes for Writing* in the Focus Syllabuses | 36 |
| 3.6 | Synthesis of References to *Generating Ideas* in the Focus Syllabuses | 38 |
| 3.7 | Synthesis of References to *Researching* in the Focus Syllabuses | 40 |
| 3.8 | Synthesis of References to *Organising Ideas* in the Focus Syllabuses | 42 |
| 3.9 | Synthesis of References to *Drafting* in the Focus Syllabuses | 44 |
| 3.10 | Differences in the Reviewing Process between Inexperienced and More Experienced Writers | 45 |

| | | |
|---|---|---|
| 3.11 | Synthesis of References to *Reviewing and Revising* in the Focus Syllabuses | 46 |
| 3.12 | Synthesis of References to *Publishing and Sharing* in the Focus Syllabuses | 49 |
| 6.1 | Exhibit 1a – Read Me Your Story Ronnie | 99 |
| 6.2 | Exhibit 1b – Show Us Your Writing Ronnie | 99 |
| 6.3 | Excerpt 2a – Huge Is Bigger Than Large | 103 |
| 6.4 | Excerpt 2b – The Closing Activity: Alphabetical Order, Syllables, Brackets | 105 |
| 6.5 | Excerpt 3a – Remember It Is Fictional | 106 |
| 6.6 | Excerpt 3b – It's Not My Story | 107 |
| 6.7 | Excerpt 3c – Still Looking for Those Descriptive Words | 109 |
| 6.8 | Excerpt 4a – How Do We Test This Source? | 111 |
| 6.9 | Excerpt 4b – What Sort of Person Is Ho Chi Minh? | 112 |
| 7.1 | Exchange Orienting Matter to Curriculum Field: Garnering Ideas (Stage II Reviewing the Field) | 126 |
| 7.2 | Exchange Orienting Matter to Curriculum Field: Developing Ideas (Stage III Modelling Drawing) | 129 |
| 7.3 | Exchange Orienting Matter to Pedagogic Activity (Stage III Modelling Drawing) | 130 |
| 7.4 | Exchange Orienting Matter to Pedagogic Modality: Knowledge about Grammar (Stage V Modelling Writing) | 131 |
| 7.5 | W.A.L.T. – Characterisation | 132 |
| 7.6 | Exchange Modelling Describing the Setting | 134 |
| 7.7 | Exchange Modelling Characterisation | 137 |
| 8.1 | Examining Poetry in Upper Primary School (Year 6) | 150 |
| 8.2 | Preparing and Reading the Poem | 150 |
| 8.3 | What Do You Think the Poem Is About? | 152 |
| 8.4 | Elaborating Metalanguage: 'And the Rose … Might Symbolise That?' | 153 |
| 8.5 | Preparing to Write Responses to the Poem | 154 |
| 8.6 | Negotiating Everyday and the Abstract Meanings | 156 |
| 8.7 | Clarifying the Writing Task | 156 |
| 8.8 | Examining Poetry in Lower Secondary School (Year 8) | 157 |
| 8.9 | Identifying the Theme of the Poem | 159 |

| | | |
|---|---|---|
| 8.10 | Preparing and Reading the Poem | 160 |
| 8.11 | Elaborating with the Metalanguage during Joint Close Reading | 161 |
| 8.12 | 'Like the Weather Isn't Really the Weather' | 162 |
| 8.13 | Detailed Reading | 167 |
| 9.1 | Science Inquiry Skills in the Australian Curriculum | 170 |
| 9.2 | Sage's Information Report on Hourglass Dolphins | 179 |
| 9.3 | Jack's Earthquake Explanation | 182 |
| 9.4 | Becka's Sequential Explanation | 185 |
| 9.5 | Zane's Causal Explanation of Seasons | 188 |
| P.II.1 | A Generic Model of Teaching | 212 |
| 12.1 | Excerpt 1.1 – Year 3 Reading: We Were Going to Read about Whales | 234 |
| 12.2 | Excerpt 2.1 – You Can Tell from the Words and Pictures What's Happening | 239 |
| 12.3 | Excerpt 2.2 – Some Things You Don't Know How to Write | 239 |
| 12.4 | Excerpt 2.3 – If You See a Book You Like You Get to Take It | 241 |
| 12.5 | Excerpt 3.1 – Reading Things Like Story Treehouse Books | 244 |
| 12.6 | Excerpt 3.2 – We Normally Have to *Do* Things | 244 |
| 12.7 | Excerpt 3.3 – Set Your Brain Up for Reading | 245 |
| 12.8 | Excerpt 3.4 – If You Write for a Long Time It Hurts Your Hand | 246 |
| 12.9 | Excerpt 4.1 – After a Bit, I Just Put a Paragraph | 247 |
| 12.10 | Excerpt 4.2 – For Us to Actually Like What We're Writing | 248 |
| 13.1 | Development of Language for School Knowledge | 256 |
| 13.2 | Student Interview Data Sources | 256 |
| 13.3 | Gaps in Curriculum Experiences | 260 |
| 13.4 | Tracy, School B, Interview 2 | 263 |
| 13.5 | Tarni, School C, Interview 1 | 265 |
| 13.6 | Alice, School C, Year 7, Interview 1 | 266 |

# Contributors

**Elizabeth Birr Moje** is Dean, George Herbert Mead Collegiate Professor of Education, and an Arthur F. Thurnau Professor of Literacy, Language, and Culture in the School of Education at the University of Michigan, USA. A former high school history and biology teacher, Moje's research examines young people's navigations of cultures, identities and literacy learning in and out of school in Detroit, Michigan. Moje has published five books and numerous articles in journals such as *Science, Harvard Educational Review, Teachers College Record, Reading Research Quarterly, Journal of Literacy Research, Review of Education Research, Journal of Research in Science Teaching* and *Science Education*.

**Honglin Chen** is Associate Professor of TESOL in the School of Education at the University of Wollongong, Australia. Her research focuses primarily on learning and teaching of speaking and writing across a range of school and tertiary contexts. She has a keen interest in the roles of dialogic pedagogy, talking about writing, thinking and reasoning, and intersubjectivity in promoting language development.

**Beverly Derewianka** is Professor Emerita in the School of Education at the University of Wollongong, Australia. Her research interests include the shift from 'knowledge telling' to creative knowledge transformation, particularly in the context of learners' literacy development. She has published on embedding a language and literacy focus in the design of challenging units of instruction. Her most recent publications are *Teaching Language in Context* (2016, 2nd edn with Pauline Jones) and *Exploring How Texts Work* (2020, 2nd edn).

**Christine Edwards-Groves** is Professor (Literacy and Professional Practice) Australian Catholic University, Australia. She researches and publishes in the field of literacy pedagogy, classroom interaction and professional practice. Edwards-Groves is a key researcher in the International Pedagogy Education and Praxis network (PEP). Her most recent books are *Becoming a Meaning*

*Maker: Talk and Interaction in the Dialogic Classroom* (2017); *Middle Leadership in Schools: A Practical Guide for Leading Learning* (2020); and *Generative Leadership: Rescripting the Promise of Action Research* (2021).

**Peter Freebody** is Honorary Professional Fellow in the School of Education at the University of Wollongong, Australia, and a fellow of the Academy of the Social Sciences in Australia. His research interests are in literacy education, classroom interaction and, in particular, how these relate to equity in educational provision. He has served on Australian state and national advisory groups and has been chair of the International Literacy Research Panel.

**Stephanie Garoni** is Lecturer in the School of Education at La Trobe University, Australia. She is interested in the practices of schooling and how these practices are held together. She has many years of experience as a classroom teacher, teacher librarian, learning support teacher, enrichment coordinator, literacy and numeracy advisor and deputy principal in both Australian and overseas schools. She now lives and works in regional Victoria. Her current role is in the Nexus program as the academic coordinator.

**Pauline Jones** is Associate Professor of Language in Education in the School of Education at the University of Wollongong, Australia. Her research and teaching focus on educational linguistics/semiotics which she applies to studies of pedagogic dialogue, advanced literacy skills and teacher development. In addition to the study of literacy transitions (TRANSLIT) that is the focus of this volume, her current research includes a study of digital explanations in tertiary science classrooms, investigations of discipline-based creativity and of the nature of disciplinarity in secondary students' writing in science, history and English.

**Lisa Kervin** is Professor of Language and Literacy in the School of Education at the University of Wollongong, Australia. She currently serves as Associate Dean Research in the Faculty of Arts, Social Sciences and Humanities. She has published more than seventy journal articles and thirty book chapters focusing on adult and child interactions when using technology, young children and writing, transition and digital play. As co-leader of the Educated program and UOW node leader (including UOW Children's Technology Play Space) for the *ARC Centre of the Digital Child*, Kervin guides how technologies may be used to support and promote meaningful childhood experiences.

**Björn Kindenberg** is Licentiate in Language Education in the Department of Language Education at Stockholm University, Sweden, and a history and language teacher at a post-secondary level. He has coordinated several research-based professional development initiatives in Stockholm schools aimed at promoting content-based language approaches to literacy education and has also authored and edited publications on this topic. His thesis explores genre-based approaches in history education and how teachers can fine-tune the level of scaffolding offered by genres to meet the needs of individual students.

**Adam Lefstein** is Shane Family Professor of Education and chair of the Department of Education at the Ben-Gurion University of the Negev, Israel. His research and teaching focus on pedagogy, classroom interaction, teacher learning and educational change. His current and recent research includes a study of Israeli culture and primary pedagogy, an investigation of video-based dialogic debrief conversations, a design-based implementation study of teacher leadership and professional discourse, an experimental study of academically productive talk in primary language classrooms and an ethnographic investigation of language, class and classroom participation.

**Helen Lewis** is Researcher and Sessional Teacher in the School of Education at the University of Wollongong, Australia. Her research interest focuses on students' literacy development at primary, secondary and tertiary levels, and the associated pedagogic practices and teacher knowledge that support this development. She has a particular interest in analysing students' textual competence, drawing on analytical tools informed by Systemic Functional Linguistics. Along with Professors Honglin Chen and Debra Myhill, she recently contributed to and edited a volume on *Developing Writers across the Primary and Secondary Years: Growing into Writing* (2020).

**Jessica Mantei** is Associate Professor at the University of Wollongong, Australia, specialising in Language and Literacy research and teaching. As a member of the Play, Pedagogy and Curriculum Early Start research group, her interests include pedagogies for literacy learning across educational settings, young children as consumers and creators of text as they explore and respond to the messages they are exposed to, and those they convey in their own work, and teacher reflective capacities for the development of professional identities that inform teaching.

**Erika Matruglio** is Senior Lecturer in the School of Education at the University of Wollongong, Australia. Her research explores the complexities of the connections between language, knowledge and values and is driven by the need to understand how these connections differ according to discipline. Her publications and research draw on complementary theories of Systemic Functional Linguistics and Legitimation Code Theory in order to explore the nature of literacy practices in schooling. Her publications engage with topics such as the nature of classroom discourse, conditions which enable cumulative knowledge building, disciplinarity and the demands of writing in the disciplines.

**Debra Myhill** is Professor of Education at the University of Exeter, UK. Her research has focused particularly on the interrelationship between metalinguistic understanding and writing; the talk–writing interface; young people's composing processes and their metacognitive awareness of them; and the teaching of writing. She is director of the Centre for Research in Writing, which promotes interdisciplinary research, drawing on psychological, sociocultural and linguistic perspectives on writing.

**David Rose** is Director of Reading to Learn, an international literacy programme that trains teachers across school and university sectors (www.readingtolearn.com.au). He is an honorary associate of the University of Sydney, Australia. His research interests include literacy teaching practices, teacher professional learning, analysis and design of classroom discourse, language typology and social semiotic theory. His books include *The Western Desert Code: An Australian Cryptogrammar* (2001), and with J. R. Martin, *Working with Discourse* (2007), *Genre Relations* (2008) and *Learning to Write, Reading to Learn: Genre, Knowledge and Pedagogy in the Sydney School* (2012).

**Jennifer Rowsell** is Professor of Literacies and Social Innovation in the School of Education at the University of Bristol, UK. Her scholarship focuses on multimodal, makerspace and arts-based research with young people; digital literacies research; digital divide work; and applying post-humanist and affect approaches to literacy research. She is currently conducting research on intergenerational digital and analogue literacy practices during the pandemic. She is co-author of *Living Literacies: Literacy for Social Change* (with Kate Pahl) and co-editor of *Maker Literacies and Maker Identities in the Digital*

*Age: Learning and Playing through Modes and Media* (with Cheryl McLean). She co-edited the *Routledge Expanding Literacies in Education* book series with Carmen Medina.

**Emma Rutherford Vale** is a PhD candidate in the School of Education at the University of Wollongong, Australia. Her doctoral research focuses on indicators of writing development in science at the transition from primary to high school, and she is an experienced ESL teacher, literacy consultant and teacher educator in TESOL and English language and literacy. Her research interests include writing pedagogy and the role of metalanguage in classroom instruction.

**Annette Turney** is a PhD student in the School of Education at the University of Wollongong, Australia. Her PhD project focuses on the exploration of student-generated digital media in tertiary science using systemic functional theory. Her research interests include educational semiotics, multimodal assessment and disciplinary literacies. She is currently investigating writing improvement and the nature of creativity in curriculum disciplines.

**Trish Weekes** is a literacy consultant, publisher and researcher at Literacy Works, Australia. Her research interests include disciplinary literacy, Systemic Functional Linguistics and Sydney School genre pedagogy. She is the author of the Literacy Works range of literacy resources for secondary school subject areas.

# Foreword

## Debra Myhill

Underpinning and resonating throughout this book is the *Transforming Literacy Outcomes* (TRANSLIT) research project, a study exploring literacy development from preschool to junior secondary school. The project was a partnership with the New South Wales Department of Education and Training, Big Fat Smile Community preschools and the Catholic Education Office (Wollongong), and involved over thirty educators from across the Illawarra and South-West Sydney. It had a particular focus on key points of educational transition: from preschool to lower primary; from early to mid-primary; from upper primary to lower secondary; and from lower secondary to senior secondary, thus including students from ages five to fifteen. Principally through classroom observation and interviews, the project has spotlighted students' experience of literacy at these transition points, mapping the changing nature of literacy they experienced, and generating both a panoramic and individual view of literacy, which challenges educational orthodoxies regarding transition. It is this sense of challenge, and the corresponding potential to transform literacy outcomes, which permeates through every contribution in this book.

So how does it achieve this?

Firstly, the notion of transition is viewed as a complex concept with multiple strands, going beyond the more traditional and rather simplistic view of transition as a movement from one educational phase to another. While retaining an eye on these key transition points, the book explores developmental trajectories in oral language learning, reading and writing in terms of how individuals transition from novice to expert as they move through school and across disciplinary subjects. It also focuses sharply on learning and the experience of teaching and being taught, looking at the movement from being a more dependent learner to being a more independent learner. A particularly innovative aspect is the consideration of how transition is represented in curriculum documentation, focusing on writing, and how growth in mastery of the writing process, and managing audience and purpose are addressed. As a consequence, transition is presented as disorderly, difficult and differentiated, challenging more monocular views of transition as concerned with institutional shifts and psychosocial changes.

Secondly, the book considers literacy and transition through a strong theoretical framing which lends rigour and authority to its claims and conclusions. It adopts a sociocultural lens which recognises the situatedness of learning, the complexity of being a learner and the importance of context. At the core of the book and its focus on literacy is a Hallidayan conceptualisation of language as social semiotic, a way of making meaning in context. Halliday recognised that language and meaning are socially constructed, and that, in turn, language is a key tool of social reproduction, typically ensuring that the privileged remain privileged and the disadvantaged remain disadvantaged. Becoming literate is a process of development shaped by social and educational contexts within which language represents a system of choices for making meaning. The particularised context of school subjects gives rise to disciplinary discourses, where meanings are encoded in words, phrases and text structures in particular ways, which differ from more everyday ways of speaking and writing. Thus, students have to learn the semiotic resources through which knowledge is constructed in each subject.

Halliday's positioning of language as deeply rooted in social contexts aligns well with Bernstein's more general thinking about the structures of knowledge, a theoretical perspective which informs this book's interpretation of transition, and particularly the nature of transition from everyday to disciplinary discourses. Bernstein distinguished between everyday, common-sense knowledge which is context-dependent and specialised formal educational knowledge which is context-independent. Learners access everyday knowledge through their social and community encounters both inside and out of school, and that knowledge extends horizontally with experience. But, Bernstein argues, the specialised educational knowledge is vertically organised, with different vertical structures for different forms of knowledge. Thus, growth in literacy demands an expansion in understanding of the semiotic resources used to communicate socially and epistemically: students transition in their individual literacy journeys from reliance on everyday knowledge to an expansion of their epistemic repertoires to include the formalised knowledge and discourses across the disciplines.

Significantly, the methodological design of TRANSLIT has allowed for the generation of data which are richly grounded in the complexity of literacy transitions. Drawing on Garfinkle's ethno-methodological approaches which seek to observe and interpret how people act and think in their day-to-day social worlds, the study brings in insights gleaned from classroom observation of enacted literacy, literacy as it occurs in real time and space. This allows for a deeply contextualised and nuanced understanding of literacy practices in classroom across ages, phases and disciplinary subjects. This is complemented by interview data which elicit teachers' pedagogical understanding and espoused practice in the teaching of literacy. By also including interviews with students, we hear the voices of learners, illustrating their own lived experience of becoming and being literate.

As a consequence of these theoretical and methodological decisions, we are offered a thoughtfully interpreted sequence of understandings of the literacy journey and its multiplicity of transition points. To misuse a Hallidayan concept, it offers a trinocular perspective of literacy transitions: from the perspective of research and the curriculum; from the perspective of the contexts of different classrooms; and from the voiced perspectives of participants, both teachers and learners. In this way, the various insights presented through the book challenge conventional orthodoxies of literacy transition and emphasise the multifaceted, pluri-dimensional nature of literacy development. Through this rich and nuanced exploration, the reader can see ahead a pathway which genuinely offers the possibility of transforming literacy outcomes.

# Acknowledgements

This volume is the result of the contributions of many individuals and the editors are thankful for their expertise, labour and enthusiasm for the TRANSLIT project.

Particularly, we wish to especially acknowledge the participation of the teachers and students who joined the project, who generously let us into their classrooms, took time to talk with us and to share their experiences in order that we might better understand the complexities of literacy development.

We also recognise the generous contributions of Debra Myhill, Jennifer Rowsell, Adam Lefstein and Elizabeth Birr Moje – all of whom took time out of their busy scholarly lives in a difficult year to read and respond to chapters, provoking us and extending the dialogue on this most challenging matter of literacy transition.

Finally, we are very grateful to Jan Turbill for the hours she spent attending to the finer details of each contribution, discussing the messages emerging from the project and ensuring we had a coherent manuscript. Thank you, Jan.

# Part I

# Theory, Curriculum and Practice in Transition

# 1

# Rethinking School Literacy Progressions

Pauline Jones and Christine Edwards-Groves

## Introduction

Australia, like many other countries, is witnessing a widening gap between its high- and low-achieving students' schooling outcomes (Gonski et al., 2018; Goss, Sonnemann & Emslie, 2018; OECD, 2018), an issue closely linked to educational disadvantage, particularly among students from low-socio-economic, linguistically diverse and indigenous backgrounds. It is clear that many students are not well served by their school literacy experiences, that the pathways through the increasingly complex literacy demands of the school curriculum are fraught for many.

The work presented in this book contrasts with many decades of educational research and policy formation in which generic literacy skills – ideally acquired in the early school years and regarded as applicable across the various curricula domains – have been the principal focus. Instead, the language and literacy researchers contributing to this volume are interested in how each curriculum discipline puts literacy to work, and in how each shapes up a trajectory for literacy learning. Such a shift turns attention to changes that students experience over the school years, changes in the patterns of the pedagogic interactions in which they participate, in the developmental continuities and transitions reported by teachers at key junctures, and evolving modes of evaluating what has been said, read and written.

Contemporary curriculum provides an official rate of progress, stressing the cumulative nature of learning, and offers descriptions of what students should achieve at particular stages, in particular domains of knowledge in which literacy demands become increasingly specialised. In reality, however, the curriculum is a narrative about some students only; for others, it is an invisible timetable into which they must fit. For these students, the pathway is an uneven one with bumps which are either smoothed over or exacerbated by pedagogy. The task of operationalising this 'road map' falls to teachers who must select and sequence content, all the while anticipating and bridging gaps between points, prior to and beyond transitions between stages in schooling. However, this book is not about evaluating pedagogy; rather, it opens up questions of how teachers and students experience changing literacy demands over the years of schooling, and of how students come to be positioned as more or less successful literacy learners.

The book problematises literacy development, prompting such questions as: What constitutes literacy development? How is literacy development experienced by children and young people? How is it understood by teachers? Is it possible to identify key transition points for literacy development, points that are riskier than others, that require the attention of researchers, educators and policymakers?

## The Problem of Transition

Current conceptions of transition focus on institutional shifts such as that from prior-to-school to school settings, primary to high school, and senior secondary school to post-school settings such as work and university. Research and policy tend to address these shifts from the perspectives of organisational differences around such matters as teacher–student ratios and timetables, and the psychosocial changes associated with the increased demands for independence and maturational differences that accompany adolescence (Bowles, Dobson, Fisher & McPhail, 2011; Evangelou et al., 2008; Perry, Dockett & Petriwskyj, 2014). Few researchers have investigated the issue of transition from the perspective of the changing nature of literacy demands across the years of schooling and fewer still have explored the pedagogic practices through which learners are enculturated into increasingly specialised curricula domains. The contributions to this volume confirm the importance of attending to these identified transition points; for many students they are messy, risky and even cataclysmic for some. But acknowledging this alone is not enough, there is an urgent need to better understand the nature of these risks, how individuals are varyingly affected, and of the extent and duration of the transitions.

Yet there is a problem in studying teaching, learning and literacy development. This book is about the daily work of schools, so one problem is that these are very familiar topics for most people, including educators. For the researcher, that means teaching and learning are taken for granted (even pre-theorised), in particular on matters related to reading and writing, the 'obvious' gateways to educational knowledge. Professional educators, along with everyone else in society, can expound at length and with confidence on what is right and wrong for education, and what should and should not be done – in many cases without having recent experience of the classroom. Educational researchers can also talk about the rights and wrongs of educational practice without having examined the details of actual, everyday classroom work, or the curricular programmes and policy documents to which that work is accountable; and researchers can critique educational policies without attending to or documenting the everyday practices and processes by which those policies are initiated, contested, finalised, transmitted, implemented, assessed for their efficacy and revised.

Thus, a first task for researchers is to outline the concepts that form the foundation of their approach, and to operate with a sense of the connections among teaching, learning, reading and writing. As well, researchers need to make clear their assumptions about connections across time spans, across sites and communities, and across the set of knowledges that structure the work of teachers and students.

A second task is to apply a suite of descriptive and analytic procedures that allow the potentially integral features of the field – classroom interactions, curricular texts, assessments – to emerge and be examined, for the particular effects they have on supporting or changing teaching and learning. Finally, researchers need to outline clearly methodological approaches that can document the various participants' orientations to and understanding of the work at hand, without pre-emptively evaluating those decisions at the point of data collection.

## Theoretical Underpinnings of the Research

There are many ways to approach learning development and the organisation of school curricula. One of the most pervasive influences on curriculum design is Bloom's taxonomy (Anderson & Krathwohl, 2001; Bloom, Engelhart, Furst, Hill & Krathwohl, 1956), with the result that content is frequently organised into hierarchies of complexity (e.g. 'the Year 3 curriculum'). In contrast, Montessori curriculum is driven by the growth patterns of individual children, recognising that there are multiple pathways and that learning takes place as a result of the learner's agency in a carefully designed, facilitated environment (Feez, 2010; Orem, 1966). More recent approaches to curricula (e.g. 'The New Basics') draw on Dewey's (1964) notion of learner growth through problem-solving projects requiring inquiry, synthesis and critique.

In contrast to these approaches, Halliday (1991, 1993) saw learning as a semiotic process whether an individual is learning to read and write, or learning science or mathematics, or learning the processes of inquiry and synthesis. Such tasks require the learner to interpret and construct text in a particular context of situation (the activity or ideas, social relations and modalities in play), to link it to other texts and situations encountered in the classroom and, in doing so, acquire the literacy-knowledge patterns of the particular curriculum domain. From this perspective, successful school transitions require students to master the meaning-making practices of increasingly diverse and complex contexts: contexts marked by the changing nature of activities and ideas (Field), varying social relations (Tenor) and differing materials and modalities (Mode). Christie and Derewianka (2008) describe such changing semiotic demands from the perspective of writing development, offering a finely drawn picture of the language demands of successful writing in the curriculum areas of English, History and Science from early primary, through to late adolescence. Drawing inspiration from this work and taking Tenor as a starting point, the research reported on in this volume approaches literacy transition in terms of changing interactional patterns as a result of the nature of knowledge and the epistemological trajectory of different curricula fields, together with the increasing specialisation of semiotic resources. In doing so, a number of the contributors employ tools deriving from systemic functional theory (Berry, 1981; Halliday & Matthiessen, 2014; Martin & Rose, 2007; Rose & Martin, 2012) to explore the connections across these three situational variables.

Complementary to the Hallidayan perspective, Bernstein's sociology of education offers insights into the effects of different forms of pedagogy on individual consciousness, and hence pedagogy is implicated in the reproduction of social inequality. In particular, a number of contributors draw on the construct of pedagogic discourse (Bernstein, 1996) to describe how institutional and idealogically oriented teaching and learning designs have consequences for the types of transitions experienced by groups of learners at different points in time. In addition, Bernstein's later work on the structuring of different forms of knowledge provides a means of describing the disciplinary distinct uses of language observed across the years of schooling.

Other contributors draw on Garfinkel (1967) to (a) provide a more nuanced perspective of different forms of knowledge and how learners engage with curriculum fields and (b) understand how the project participants (learners, teachers and researchers) accomplish their everyday work. In particular, ethnomethodology (EM) (Garfinkel, 1967) is used to consider the observable practical action and practical reasoning of people as they participate in their everyday social worlds, in this case the world of schooling. Critical to EM is the analytic method conversation analysis (CA) developed by Sacks (1972) and collaborators (especially Sacks, Schegloff & Jefferson, 1974) that focuses on the speech-exchange system, particularly with respect to the orders, structures, rules and arrangements of turns and turn taking. This method reveals what is relevant (but often taken-for-granted) to interactive participants' (both hearers and speakers, e.g. teachers and students) meaning making at the time, and in school lessons delineates how institutional goals and identities are accomplished through the talk that shapes their everyday practice. When considering the issue of literacy transitions, EMCA provides a unique take on the practices of accomplishing transitions – both across the years of schooling and within the lessons themselves.

Through the theoretical lenses described above and the analytical purchase they afford, contributors are able to pay attention to the changing features of pedagogy across the school years. Pedagogy is a topic that has attracted extensive attention over recent decades, and one thing this attention has shown is that the term 'pedagogy' refers not only to observable act of teaching. Alexander, for instance, distilled his wide-ranging programmes of research and theory on the topic of pedagogy, and what it is taken to mean across different educational communities into the definition of 'the observable act of teaching together with the purposes, values, ideas, assumptions, theories and beliefs that inform, shape and seek to justify it' (Alexander, 2020: 47). In this manner, the contributors considered both the observable acts of teaching, and the attendant discourses as construed in the moment-by-moment unfolding of lessons, and as available through participant accounts and documentary evidence.

## The Research Project

Transforming Literacy Outcomes (TRANSLIT) (Jones et al., 2014–18) sought to address the gap in students' school outcomes from the perspective of language and literacy. Responding to the idea that literacy is the 'ultimate transformative technology' (Freebody, 2013), the contributors undertook to investigate the changing nature of literacy demands across the primary and secondary school years. The project explored the accepted transition points – preschool to school, middle to upper primary, upper primary to lower secondary, junior to senior secondary – in terms of the language and literacy demands experienced by students.

**The Research Questions**

The following overarching research question framed the study: *What is the nature of students' literacy experiences at critical transition points in schooling?* This question was operationalised by several sub-questions:

- What are the literacy demands at critical transition points? In other words: What literacy demands are evident in curriculum? How do teachers perceive these demands? What literacy practices are evident in classroom practice?
- How do students experience the literacy demands at critical transition points? In other words: How do students perceive these demands? How do students respond to these demands?
- What contextual factors are involved in teachers' and students' responses to these demands?

**The Research Design**

The project design comprised (a) a contextual study to describe the literacy teaching practices in classrooms (and curriculum) in three different school communities and (b) case studies of students to provide descriptive data on how students experience and interpret the teaching and learning of literacy in classrooms. The school communities comprised preschool, primary and secondary school sites in which observations of literacy pedagogy at the key transition points took place in the first half and second half of each year for three years. In all, more than fifty hours of observations were video recorded from twelve preschool and school sites. These observations were supplemented by sixty interviews with thirty-nine teachers across those sites. Case study students were recruited at the end of preschool, at middle and upper primary, and middle secondary (Year 9) and were subsequently interviewed at the beginning and end of the next three years. During that time over 150 interviews with 73 children and young people were recorded. In addition, over 150 student work samples were collected together with curriculum and planning documents.

## Overview of the Book

### Part I: Theory, Research and Practice in Transition

Part I describes the context for the research in terms of its theoretical positioning, and the relevant research and curriculum environments. It makes a strong case for further research into literacy development, identifying the worrying disjuncture between research and curriculum, and undoing any suggestions that literacy development is linear or universal. It does so amidst concern for declining student achievement levels, questions about the content of literacy curriculum in the twenty-first century and the nature of schooling in future-oriented societies. Some contemporary debates are old arguments that find new air in uncertain times (e.g. the 'phonics' debate) while others are particular to contemporary life and the knowledge required by citizens (e.g. the so-called 'soft skills'). Irrespective of their origins, such discussions are symptomatic of a general concern with the role of literacy in the aspirations of contemporary nations in terms of social and economic transformation as well as individual citizens' life chances.

In Chapter 2, Trish Weekes reviews literature related to school literacy development, confirming attention to three main transition points between stages of literacy development: for young children between prior to school settings and school, in the middle years of primary school (Year 4) and in the transition from primary to secondary school. She concludes that while researchers agree that the early years before school are critical for language development, there are many areas where the research needs to be strengthened, including our understanding of the connections between aspects of literacy (e.g. between oral language development and reading or writing), our knowledge of how groups of students move from one 'stage' of reading or writing development to the next, and the need for more robust theorisation of aspects of literacy and their component skills.

Chapter 3 explores how the trajectory of writing (or creating texts) is characterised in curriculum documents from a range of international jurisdictions. In doing so, Beverly Derewianka notes that there is often no clearly defined progression across the years nor much evidence of key transition points, with the result that they do not offer a well-defined, theoretically coherent developmental pathway to support teachers and their students. She concludes that although much teaching and assessment rely on this, it may well prove elusive because of the complex and recursive nature of literacy development.

In Chapter 4, Björn Kindenberg and Peter Freebody disassemble the myth that literacy development requires a gradual replacement of common-sense or everyday knowledge with specialised educational knowledge, arguing that this is not necessarily what is meant by the literacy learning trajectory such as that mapped by Christie and Derewianka (2008). Instead, they rework the dichotomous common-sense/uncommon-sense relationship with notions of interplay between everyday and specialised rationalities with a convincing analysis of texts drawn from across the learning trajectory.

## Part II: Investigating the Conditions for Literacy Transitions

Part II focuses on observations of literacy learning and teaching practices conducted across the key transition points. Chapters in this section draw on data gathered in literacy lessons conducted in preschool, primary and secondary classrooms. The contributors employ ethnographic, systemic functional semiotics, and analysis of exchange and participation structures to explore how teachers and students generate, manage and negotiate classroom settings – including their enabling and constraining features – within which literacy education takes place.

The perspectives taken in these chapters offer a unique multidimensional account of how students, via the patterns of classroom life, experience interactional events that can smooth or disrupt their progress in learning literacy.

Complementary analyses of observational data collected over three years, both across and within specific curriculum areas, show how instances of smooth or irregular progressions in literacy learning are made evident in:

(i) the design of the single- and multiparty language and other semiotic resources that are relied on and explicitly targeted in lessons;
(ii) the formal literacy demands of curriculum domains to which teachers are accountable, their realisation in specific activities and texts;
(iii) the particular ways in which physical space and time are organised in literacy learning events; and
(iv) the development of agency and diversity in teacher–student roles and relationships, and in assessment practices.

These complementary analyses share an interest in discourse and practice and offer views of the complexity of literacy transitions that are distinctive and potentially useful to teachers and teacher educators.

The contributors examine how transition is experienced, enacted and accomplished via moment-by-moment, fine-grained analysis within a particular sequence of interactions and via coarser-grained analyses of how literacy demands are delineated in the curriculum – in reading/viewing, writing/composing tasks, print and digital texts. Describing and explaining transition in these ways reveals how the coherence and consistency of learning trajectories have significant consequences for students.

In Chapter 5, Lisa Kervin and Jessica Mantei demonstrate that while literacy activities in the preschool and early school settings are similarly labelled, the pedagogies through which they are enacted vary considerably as the loosely framed, tacit practices negotiated by children give way to more strongly framed, explicit instruction of the first year of school. They argue that the skills, dispositions and agency that children develop as a result of negotiating a relatively invisible preschool curriculum need to be recognised and built upon in the early school years.

Chapter 6 considers lesson exchanges from three grade levels across schooling: Years 1/2, 5/6 and 11 to demonstrate how transition points are negotiated via the social and epistemic structures of literacy lessons. Using CA, Christine Edwards-Groves, Stephanie Garoni and Peter Freebody show ways that transitions are interactionally accomplished in-the-moment in lessons, challenging more orthodox understandings of what it means to transition across the years of schooling. Their analysis reveals shifts in that nature of literacy knowings, from managing sequences to activities, to engaging in epistemic exchanges and on toward textual forms of knowledge. Implications for pedagogies of literacy transition are revealed.

Chapters 7 and 8 also examine classroom interactions closely using pedagogic register analysis to better understand how literacy transitions are accomplished as learners participate in classroom activities. Honglin Chen, Helen Lewis and David Rose take a closer look at writing pedagogy at Kindergarten and middle primary classrooms as it is enacted in classroom talk, noting changes in the nature of the knowledge under focus, the demands of learning activities and the semiotic modes that support learning. Pauline Jones, Erika Matruglio and David Rose examine poetry appreciation in upper primary and junior secondary lessons, identifying ways in which students learn to respond to literature through their participation in classroom interactions. Their close analysis demonstrates how these interactions differ across time and between students, and thus how that a more inclusive, visible pedagogy is required if all students are to be successful English students.

In Chapter 9, Annette Turney and Emma Rutherford Vale examine how transition between primary and secondary schools is realised in the literacy of the science curriculum. Drawing on a corpus of students' texts, the key semiotic resources used by students as they shift into more technical understandings necessary for knowledge building in school science are described with meticulous detail. In doing so, they identify the shifts in demands in terms of linguistic resources as well as other representational forms such as diagrams and mathematical symbols.

## PartIII: Horizons of Consequence – Accounting for Transition

Part III complements the previous section, focusing on participants' accounts of changes in literacy demands from preschool through primary and secondary schooling. Drawing on data gathered in over two hundred interviews conducted with teachers and students, the chapters present 'exhibits' that capture participants' experiences of literacy transitions (i) at the preschool to school transition point, (ii) as they traverse primary school and (iii) as they then move into the secondary years. Recognising that curriculum accounts of literacy transitions are necessarily abstract, these exhibits are presented to enable depth treatment from each of the three theoretical perspectives – ethnographic, social semiotic and interactional perspectives. These analyses of interview data collected over three years show how participants nominate and/ or assume literacy learning progressions and the nature of such progressions. As with Part II, four dimensions can be articulated about these exhibits as follows:

(i) Participants' accounts of changes in salient interactional practices at key transition points
(ii) Teacher and students' observations of shifts in the curriculum-specific literacy demands across including texts and activities
(iii) Their experiences of the ways in which physical space and time are organised to support literacy learning events at key transition points
(iv) Participants' construals of agency and diversity in teacher–student roles and relationships, and in assessment practices

These analyses provide further evidence of the complex nature of literacy transitions, and of how students come to be categorised as particular kinds of literacy learners.

In Chapter 10, Erika Matruglio reports on how teachers in their interview accounts describe, evaluate and account for the literacy demands of schooling and the ensuing implications for students, and for their own pedagogic practice. Key themes emerging from the analysis include the need for increasing student independence, the diversity of students' needs, capabilities and backgrounds, the tensions between freedom and constraint, and the varying 'horizons of consequence' with which teachers work.

Chapter 11 returns readers to the early years of primacy school as Jessica Mantei and Lisa Kervin consider the ways in which learners are positioned as readers and writers, and their accounts of their literate identities. They prompt us to think about the ways in which teachers' professional identities are threatened by a myriad of policy, curricula and commercial imperatives with the result that their pedagogic practices and own beliefs about what it means to be literate are compromised.

In Chapter 12, Christine Edwards-Groves and Peter Freebody diverge from the interviews with teachers and learners about transition to take a macro-view of the research project by investigating a number of researcher-learner interviews from the project. These young respondents perceived their experiences of 'schooled' literacy as variously a set of institutional procedures, as distinct domains within curriculum, and as skills and knowledge put to work in different ways within different curricula. This chapter highlights the methodological challenges of interviewing young learners and its conclusions have much to offer literacy researchers seeking to include young learners in their endeavours.

In Chapter 13, Emma Rutherford Vale, Helen Lewis, Honglin Chen and Pauline Jones examine students' accounts of their experiences as they move from the primary school into the more strongly bounded curricula of the secondary years. Despite the aspirations of the national curriculum for cumulative learning within the curriculum disciplines, the authors identify significant differences in the curriculum content across the primary–secondary transition point as well as differences in learners' repertoires for responding to these differences. They argue for closer collaborations between primary and secondary schools so that programmes and pedagogies articulate across this crucial transition point.

# 2

# A Review of the Literature around Literacy Transition

Trish Weekes

## Introduction

Literacy development is of ongoing interest to educational researchers, policymakers and teachers. Literacy involves 'listening to, reading, viewing, speaking, writing and creating oral, print, visual and digital texts, and using and modifying language for different purposes in a range of contexts' within and beyond schooling (ACARA, 2013). It is widely understood that there is a sequence of social, emotional, learning and developmental stages as a baby grows from a child to an adolescent to an adult. In terms of literacy, a body of research has aimed to identify what children typically can do or should be able to do at various developmental ages or stages, with respect to oral language, reading, writing, vocabulary and other aspects of literacy. This endeavour is of critical importance to literacy researchers and educators, particularly in an era of curriculum reform and increased pressure to improve literacy achievement for all learners.

This review analyses research on literacy development from Anglophone countries, based on a collection of over two hundred original research articles, meta-analyses and review papers. The first section of the review addresses approaches and theories to literacy research, which contextualise the research review that follows. Next, the chapter will review aspects of literacy development which have received the most research attention: oral language, reading and writing. Major longitudinal studies and meta-analyses will be examined that identify sequences of learning and development in literacy, stages of development and transition points between stages. Research on relationships between aspects of literacy will also receive attention. The review will conclude with a brief survey of evidence on individual variation in literacy development and a summary of areas of agreement and debate in the literature.

# Review

## Approaches and Theories of Literacy

Historically, concepts of literacy and literacy development have inspired several different theoretical approaches. Each approach favours theories, methodologies, conceptualisations of literacy and component skills, and notions of learning and development. One way of making sense of these approaches, based on work by de Silva Joyce and Feez (2016), is to group them into three categories, based on ideas about literacy as coding and skills practice, literacy as individual practice or literacy as sociocultural practice.

Literacy as coding and skills practice focuses on the importance of learning to read by recognising letters of words and relating them to sounds. This approach, developed by structural linguists (e.g. Bloomfield, [1914] 1933) and informed by behaviourist psychology (Skinner, 1974), led to a focus on teaching of phonics where students practise recognising and reading consonant and vowel combinations and combining them into words (Flesch, 1955). The assumption behind this theory is that if students practise drills of matching letter patterns to sounds, in a prescribed sequence of patterns, they can learn to read simple words, then more complex words and then longer texts.

A contrasting approach considers literacy as individual practice. As a reaction against the systematic teaching of phonics, psycholinguists such as Goodman (1967) advocated a whole language approach, where children are immersed in reading and writing and predict the meaning of words. This approach is underpinned by learning theories by Piaget (1970) who considered the development of a child to be a natural process that occurs without excessive intervention from teachers or experts. Process writing emerged from this approach, where children write whatever they like, however they like, as a creative and individual act (Graves, 1983). Research in this arena tends to have a focus on the internal cognitive and psychological processes and capabilities of learners.

Other researchers from sociocultural approaches to literacy have considered literacy as a social and semiotic practice of meaning-making. This approach draws on a research base in psycholinguistics (Vygotsky, [1934] 1978), sociology (Bernstein, 1975), and sociolinguistics (Halliday, 1975, [1993] 2004). Halliday's sociolinguistic approach relates language use to social contexts and provides a 'language-based theory of learning' (Halliday, [1993] 2004). Children are explicitly taught to understand different purposes for communicating and writing in various social contexts and genres (or social purposes of texts) and their language features are taught explicitly (Martin & Rose, 2008). Teaching and learning unfold in a process of scaffolding (Gibbons, 2009) whereby teachers gradually reduce support for students as they learn and master linguistic features of written texts (Rose & Martin, 2012).

These approaches have differentially informed curriculum development and teaching practice over time in different locations. Debate on these issues has become known as the 'reading wars' (Kim, 2008). A 'balanced approach' to literacy incorporates many approaches, but there is still disagreement over the relative weighting of phonics or text-based learning and the sequence of when and how and if different features of language and components of literacy should be taught (Castles, Rastle & Nation, 2018).

In light of these approaches, the literature on literacy development will now be reviewed, starting with oral language development, followed by reading research then studies focusing on writing.

## Oral Language Development

Much of the research base on oral language (speaking and listening) concerns the early years before schooling and in the first few years of schooling. The main area of agreement is that the early years are a critical time for language development (Foorman et al. 2016; Fricke, Bowyer-Crane, Haley, Hulme & Snowling, 2013; Lee, Mikesell, Joaquin, Mates & Schumann, 2009). Oral language is widely considered to be a foundational skill that supports learning to read as well as comprehend and write. Oral language ability in young children predicts reading and comprehension in the first years of school (Lepola,

Lynch, Kiuru, Laakkonen & Niemi, 2016) and also predicts later reading comprehension (Hulme, Bowyer-Crane, Carroll, Duff & Snowling, 2012; Language and Reading Research Consortium & Logan, 2017; Loban, 1976).

Oral language continues to develop throughout the years of schooling and into adulthood. Loban (1976) conducted a landmark longitudinal study of 211 children from Kindergarten to grade 12 and monitored their oral language and writing development. Factors that characterised language development included the use of longer T-units (sentences), movement from concrete to abstract lexis, gradual growth in understanding of morphology and relations between words (e.g. synonyms), use of longer sentences and more complex syntax. Loban found that oral language skills in Kindergarten predicted reading and writing achievement in grade 6. In terms of development stages, his landmark study also found that steady growth of oral language in elementary school tended to slow or plateau in grades 4, 8 and 9. Oral and written language seemed to develop in parallel, although trends observed in written language also occurred in oral language and were observed around one year earlier in oral language. Many of these findings have been confirmed in subsequent research (Funnell, Hughes & Woodcock, 2006; Nippold, Mansfield & Billow, 2007; Owens, 2012; Westerveld & Moran, 2011).

Detailed socio-semantic accounts of the development of oral language from birth to the early years show how children's communication builds from protolanguage to a complex system of meaning-making through oral language (Halliday, 1975; Painter, 1984). A large body of sociocultural research has also highlighted the importance of classroom talk for learning, as students interact with the teacher through oral language (R. Alexander, 2008; Freebody, 2013; Koole, 2011; Mercer & Howe, 2012).

The body of research into oral language has highlighted the critical importance of the early years before schooling which has influenced government policy in early years education programmes. However, there is a notable paucity of research in oral language beyond the early years. Cognitive psychology perspectives have informed research by speech pathologists and researchers in language disorders to try to establish norms against which children with disorders can be evaluated (Miller, Andriacchi & Nockerts, 2016; Scott & Windsor, 2000), although these criteria have not been universally adopted. The literature acknowledges that individual variation is significant and that children start schooling with a wide range of literacy knowledge including oral language abilities (Meiers et al., 2006).

In summary, the literature demonstrates that oral language is foundational for learning to read and write as well as to learn throughout the years of schooling, yet only some links between oral language development and other aspects of literacy are understood. Further, oral language development continues from early years to adulthood, with growing complexity, length of sentences and abstraction, with significant individual variation.

## Reading Development

The literature on reading development is vast, with the majority of studies in literacy focusing on learning to read in the early years. There is general agreement in the literature that home and school environments are predictors of reading achievement and academic attainment in schooling (Hill, Comber, Louden, Rivalland & Reid, 2002). Longitudinal studies of children's reading have found that children display a wide range of knowledge about literacy and reading when they enter school (Meiers et al., 2006). Socio-economic status emerges as a predictor of reading achievement in the early years, as better readers tend to have been read to extensively at home, as is common in middle-class households (Parsons, Schoon, Rush & Law, 2011) and reading ability in Year 4 can be predicted by the number of books in the home (Thomson et al., 2012).

Initial reading difficulties are exacerbated as the years progress. Disadvantaged students continue to struggle while middle-class students experience reading growth (Walberg & Tsai, 1983). The widening achievement gap is a phenomenon known as the 'Matthew effect' (Stanovich, 1986). While disadvantage is a predictor of reading achievement, longitudinal studies have shown that paths of reading development are highly variable among individuals (Hill et al., 2002; Meiers et al., 2006; Parsons et al., 2011).

Understanding of stages of reading development have been widely influenced by seminal research by Jeanne Chall (1967, 1983), who identified six stages of reading development. Stage 0 (up to the age of six years) is a pre-reading stage where children grow in knowledge and use of spoken language and understanding of sound structures of words. Stages 1–2 are the 'learning to read' stage which involves mostly narrative or story texts. In Stage 1 (while at school in grades 1–2), children learn to decode letters of the alphabet and sound–letter correspondence, which are best learned through direct teaching of phonics. Stage 2 (grades 2–3) is the 'ungluing from print' stage where children become familiar with commonly used words and learn to read more complex words, gaining fluency and speed in their reading. Beyond Stage 2, children can recognise most words automatically. Stages 3–6 involve 'reading to learn'. Stage 3 (from grades 4 to 9) engages children in reading increasingly complex texts from subject areas, predominantly factual texts, where they must begin to analyse and be critical of what they read. Stage 4 is in high school (grades 10–12) where students learn to deal with multiple viewpoints, competing theories and multiple interpretations in their reading. The final stage is Stage 5 (aged eighteen and above) when readers analyse, synthesise and make judgements about what they read. Chall's study found that learning the alphabetic code is foundational for learning to read, but she also recognised the importance of connecting to children's prior knowledge and experience in making sense of their reading, especially in later years, and the importance of effective teaching.

The notion of 'reading' and identification of its component skills is contested in the literature. Much of the research has settled on 'the big 5' components of reading instruction: phonemic awareness (knowledge that words are made up of individual sounds), phonics (the relationship between a specific letter and its sound), fluency (the ability to read text accurately and fluently), vocabulary (making sense of written words and learning new words) and text comprehension (the intentional thinking process that occurs during reading) (National Reading Panel, 2000). Five different skills that predict reading achievement were identified by the National Early Literacy Panel (2008). In addition to alphabet knowledge and phonemic awareness, the authors identified the ability to rapidly and automatically name letters and objects/colours as predictors of reading, as well as the ability to write one's own name and to remember spoken information.

As a consequence of this varied conceptualisation of reading, and the acknowledged difficulty of measuring reading skills, research tends to focus on one aspect of reading at a time, such as phonics knowledge or vocabulary. Of all the dimensions of reading, code-based research on phonics dominates the literature. Building on Chall's models, detailed models of stages or phases of letter and word recognition in emergent and early reading have been proposed by Frith (1985) and Ehri (1999), progressing from pre-letter recognition to full word recognition. Meta-analyses on reading development reveal that code-related skills (i.e. phonemic awareness and phonics skills) predict the largest variance in reading achievement in early years (Paratore, Cassano & Schickedanz, 2010), and, on this basis, systematic teaching of phonics is advocated by many researchers as the best way to teach reading in the early years (Buckingham, Wheldall & Beaman-Wheldall, 2013; J. Rose, 2006; Snow, Griffin & Burns, 2005; Stanovich, 1986).

While phonics is no doubt important, there is a substantial body of research that shows it should not be taught in isolation from other reading comprehension and literacy skills, even in the early years (Chambers, Cheung & Slavin, 2016; Whitehurst & Lonigan, 1998; Xue & Meisels, 2004). Recent phonics-based meta-analyses about learning to read have identified that, in addition to phonics instruction, learning to read effectively depends on student knowledge of sound–letter correspondence, comprehension, vocabulary knowledge and context knowledge and also relies on the student's working memory and individual experience (Castles et al., 2018; Ehri et al., 2001). It has been argued that effective teaching of reading requires phonics instruction combined with fluency, vocabulary development and reading comprehension.

The literature base supports the idea that learning to read involves multiple skills including decoding skills. Even researchers from a cognitive and code-based tradition acknowledge that teaching of reading should include all of the aspects of reading, not just phonics alone. The 'four resources model', which incorporates multiple approaches to reading, has become influential in literacy research and teaching (Freebody & Luke, 1990). Nevertheless, the 'reading wars' persist in public debate, with phonics pitched against text-based or 'balanced' programmes for learning to read, a situation which is seen by many as a false dichotomy (Christie, 2010).

Also informing this debate is the theoretical conceptualisation by Paris (2005) about constrained and unconstrained skills. Constrained skills are easily mastered, such as recognising the alphabet, while unconstrained skills, such as vocabulary, continue to develop over many years, even into adulthood. Unconstrained skills tend to vary greatly between people and develop at different rates. This conceptualisation has added weight to arguments against a 'phonics-only' approach to teaching and the push for standardised testing based on code-based skills alone (Paris & Luo, 2010).

Another theme in the research on learning to read is the grade 4 slump. Following Chall's research, subsequent research has often found a decline or plateau in reading achievement around the age of ten years. As noted by Chall, the nature of reading changes around this time to become more fact-based and, at the same time, the curriculum tends to be more specialised and disciplinary, which may account for this phenomenon (Kucan & Sullivan Palincsar, 2010; Sanacore & Palumbo, 2008; Snow et al., 2005).

Multiple interactions between reading and other aspects of literacy have been explored in some research, but the knowledge base is not extensive in this area. Reading fluency and vocabulary have received relatively little research attention. Vocabulary research tends to map the number of words needed for reading comprehension (Coltheart & Prior, 2007; Coxhead, 2012; Nagy & Anderson, 1984; Nation & Snowling, 2004). One model of vocabulary development has three tiers of words (Beck, McKeown & Kucan, 2013). Tier 1 words are basic words that are commonly used and relatively easy to understand. Tier 2 words are more complex, frequently occurring words that are understood by mature language users. Tier 3 words are low-frequency words used in specific disciplines or domains. Various instruction models have been proposed that use or adapt this model and suggest a teaching sequence for these tiers of words, with Tier 1 used in the early years, then various Tier 2 and 3 words being introduced in the middle years (Flanigan & Greenwood, 2007). Little of the research has addressed the ways vocabulary knowledge interacts with comprehension of texts or other reading and writing skills.

Relationships between reading and writing development have been explored in some research. Shanahan and Lomax (1986) evaluated the relationships between reading and writing for students in Years 2 to 5. They found evidence to support an 'interactive model' whereby reading knowledge informs the development of writing, and writing can influence reading development. The nature of this interaction is strongly dependent on the type of instruction in school and amount of teaching time spent on these aspects of literacy. Other research has found that meaning-based activities with texts (including writing) are essential aspects of learning to read in Kindergarten and first grade (Morris, Bloodgood, Lomax & Perney, 2003), along with text-level discussions and sentence-level explanations (Louden, Rohl & Hopkins, 2008). From the sociocultural perspective, learning of reading and vocabulary occurs in the context of authentic texts and reading and writing activities (Rose & Martin, 2012).

The research base in literacy is dominated by a focus on the development of reading in the early years, particularly in phonics-based approaches to decoding. The sequence of learning to read in the early years has been quite clearly mapped from a number of different research approaches, yet when schooling begins, the research base on development of reading fractures and becomes less coherent, especially regarding the middle years and secondary schooling when disciplinary literacies come into play. The complexity of learning to read is acknowledged in the literature, yet relatively few studies have addressed the relations between aspects of reading, such as comprehension and vocabulary, or between reading and other aspects of literacy such as writing. Researchers acknowledge the need for more research to more robustly conceptualise balanced approaches to reaching reading, including 'instructional regimens' that are 'most effective at particular points in development' (Castles et al., 2018: 39).

## Writing Development

The literature on writing research is less extensive than in oral language or reading. Even though many children are not proficient writers, there are relatively few studies on writing (De La Paz & Graham, 2002). Meta-analyses report very few experimental studies on writing with robust methodologies (Donovan & Smolkin, 2008; Myhill & Watson, 2014). For example, the What Works Clearinghouse writing summary reviewed 3,400 pieces of research on writing but only 15 qualified for inclusion in their synthesis (Graham et al., 2016). Further, there is little research on the effect of instruction on writing (Donovan & Smolkin, 2008) and relatively little understanding of writing development (Kent & Wanzek, 2016; Wray & Medwell, 2006).

Concepts of writing are also contested in the literature. There is a lack of agreement of what writing quality means (Applebee, 2000; Myhill & Jones, 2006). Writing has been conceptualised in several different ways which makes it hard to compare and contrast areas of research. Research from the perspective of literacy as an individual practice considers the cognitive and affective aspects of writing (Wilkinson, Barnsley, Hanna & Swan, 1980). Writing is a kind of problem that can be solved through 'strategies' of writing (i.e. planning goal setting, revaluating, revising, editing) and processes of writing (e.g. considering the purpose and audience, and reflecting after writing) (Bereiter & Scardamalia, 2013; De La Paz & Graham, 2002; Graham & Perin, 2007; Graham et al., 2016). These approaches have been critiqued for not incorporating concepts of writing quality and inadequately considering the demands of academic writing in subject areas, particularly in secondary schooling (Smagorinsky, 1987; Smith & Elley, 1998). Other research has examined component skills of writing, including transcription fluency, language-based skills (word choice and grammatical sentence) and punctuation, or on predictors of writing achievement including spelling, reading and oral language (Kent & Wanzek, 2016). From the sociocultural semiotic view, writing is considered to be a highly valued form of meaning-making in schooling contexts, with a focus on identifying types of texts and patterns of language use as tools for making meaning (Christie & Derewianka, 2008; Humphrey, 2017; Martin & Rose, 2008).

Regarding writing development, researchers agree on the changing nature of writing over the years of schooling and the growing complexity of writing in the later years. There is also consensus that written language is different from spoken language and that spoken casual language and written academic language become more different as the years of schooling progress. In early years, writing involves a limited range of writing genres, dominated by narratives (Donovan & Smolkin, 2008) while in later years a wider range of factual genres are taught, starting usually in the middle years (Langer, 1986).

Major studies of writing development have been conducted by Britton and colleagues, Perera, and Christie and Derewianka. Britton and colleagues studied 2,122 pieces of writing from 65 schools in the UK (Britton, Burgess, Martin, McLeod & Rosen, 1975). They determined three main functions of writing: transactional, expressive and poetic, and they also examined different orientations of the writer to the audience. This study has been critiqued for not differentiating between writing for various subject areas (Applebee, 2000) and considering the instruction children received before doing the task (Donovan & Smolkin, 2008).

Perera's research (1984) identified four stages of writing development. The first is preparation, when children learn the basic mechanics of handwriting and spelling. The second stage is consolidation at around age six to seven years, when children start to express in writing what they can already express in spoken language. The third stage is differentiation when writing becomes automatic and diverges from speech. The final stage is integration when children control both oral and written language and can control language choices appropriately.

Christie and Derewianka (2008) also identified four stages in writing development. In the first stage, children six to eight years of age tend to write about everyday knowledge and express simple attitudes using grammatical resources that are based on concrete experience. In Stage 2, at the age of nine to twelve years, students learn to elaborate on everyday experience with some technicality and they expand the range of attitudes they express with more sophisticated grammatical choices. In Stage 3, aged thirteen to fifteen years, knowledge is represented and expressed in an increasingly specialised and abstract way and grammatical resources are more subject-specific. In the fourth stage, students aged sixteen to eighteen years write about specialised knowledge and make informed judgements using high levels of abstraction and technicality. From the socio-semiotic perspective, a pedagogy for writing involves making the language features of texts explicit for students, through modelling and language-based activities on the kinds of texts that students are required to write in different contexts. Writing practice occurs regularly with the teacher and then with peers and, finally, independently (Martin & Rose, 2008).

Other studies from a range of perspectives examine component features of writing, such as syntactic complexity. One common finding is that as children get older, syntactic complexity increases and there is greater use of subordination (Harpin, 1976; Loban, 1976; Myhill & Jones, 2006; Nippold, Ward-Lonergan & Fanning, 2005; Perera, 1984). This is true of speech and writing (Beers & Nagy, 2009; Loban, 1976; Perera, 1985). Loban's research (1976) focused on oral and written syntactic development. He identified that between grades 3 and 12, writing development takes the form of longer

T-units, greater elaboration, more embedding, increased use of adjectival dependent clauses and dependent clauses of all kinds, greater variety and depth of vocabulary and more use of language expressing tentativeness.

Other writing research identifies development of resources of coherence, including development of connectors (Struthers, Lapadat & MacMillan, 2013). Nippold and colleagues (2005) have also conducted studies on the features of persuasive writing at ages eleven, seventeen and twenty-one and found that adolescents and adults write longer texts, use greater subordination, use more relative clauses, more 'late developing connectors' (e.g. otherwise, therefore) and 'metaverbs' (e.g. assert, conceded, predict).

The area of grammar research is contested. Many studies strongly argue that teaching grammar has no impact on the quality of writing (Andrews et al., 2006) or that it even has a deleterious effect (Graham & Perin, 2007). However, as these studies are based on traditional grammar, they have been challenged by socio-semiotic researchers who view grammar as a tool for meaning-making (Love, Macken-Horarik & Horarik, 2015; Myhill & Watson, 2014). When grammar (as meaning-making) is taught in the context of writing, positive effects on writing quality have been found (Jones, Myhill & Bailey, 2013; Myhill, Jones, Watson & Lines, 2013) and metalinguistic understanding of grammar leads to deeper understandings of meaning choices in writing (Chen & Myhill, 2016).

Research in writing development has been shaped by the theoretical approaches that inform particular methodologies and objects of study, whether processes of writing, components of writing or written texts and their features. In general, stages of writing development have been identified that reveal growing grammatical complexity, technicality and abstraction over the years of schooling.

## Transition Points in Literacy Development

The literature on literacy development tends to focus on three main transition points: for young children between home and school, in the middle years of primary school and in the transition from primary to secondary school. Research on literacy education and development is dominated by early years literacies, a time when young children move from home to school and start to learn reading. As explained above, the early years are widely acknowledged to be critical for language and literacy development (Fricke et al., 2013; Hill et al., 2002; Krakouer, Mitchell, Trevitt & Kochanoff, 2017). Beyond early years, another transition point has achieved prominence: 'the fourth-grade slump' (Chall, 1983; Sanacore & Palumbo, 2008), characterised by a plateau or decline in reading achievement at around the age of nine years. Recent research has challenged the inevitability of this from a neuroscientific basis (Coch, 2017), and other researchers have looked to curriculum change as possible causes of reading challenges. Another literacy transition point identified is when students move from primary school to secondary school (Dinham & Rowe, 2008), which is at around twelve years of age. In Australia, national test scores show declining writing achievement for students between Year 5 and Year 7, and also between Year 7 and Year 9 (ACARA, 2019). Adolescents tend to lose interest in reading (P. A. Alexander & Fox, 2010) at a time when writing becomes increasingly important for school learning and assessment tasks (Christie & Derewianka, 2008; De La Paz & Graham, 2002; Langer, 2001; Luke et al., 2003). Much of the literature around the transition to secondary school, however, focuses on psychosocial aspects and does not refer to literacy achievement in any specific way (e.g. Hanewald, 2013). In secondary school, subject area discourses become more specialised, and one growing strand of literacy literature from the sociocultural approach involves mapping these disciplinary literacies (Brisk, 2015; Christie & Derewianka, 2008; Fang & Schleppegrell, 2010; Humphrey, 2017; Moje, 2008; Shanahan & Shanahan, 2008).

Researchers also acknowledge individual variation in literacy development. While there may be typical patterns of development, individuals and groups of students can move through stages at different paces and at different ages (Konza & Michael, 2010). Socio-economic disadvantage has long been recognised as a predictor of low literacy achievement (Stanovich, 1986), yet there is limited large-scale evidence of successful policies or pedagogical interventions to redress this situation. Other reasons for differentiated literacy trajectories include gender (Cole, Jane, Suggett & Wardlaw, 2016), disabilities and/or learning difficulties (Elliott & Grigorenko, 2014; Pugh & McCardle, 2009; Scott & Windsor, 2000), cultural backgrounds (e.g. Purdie, Reid, Frigo, Stone & Kleinhenz, 2011), whether or not the students are English language learners (Cummins, 2008; Hammer et al., 2014; Thomas & Collier, 1997) and whether students have experienced literacy interventions to try to address deficits or build skills (Hill et al., 2002). Much of the literature on individual variation notes the interplay of multiple social, cognitive, emotional, cultural and educational factors that influence a child's literacy development.

## Discussion and Conclusion

Traditionally, schooling is organised in year levels, with students of the same age progressing to the next grade together, regardless of their achievement. The literature on literacy development appears to provide little support for such a model of schooling. Stages of literacy development in reading and writing reviewed in this chapter tend to cover time periods of two to three years. In addition, the research acknowledges the diversity of individual rates of progress in one area such as reading or multiple aspects of literacy. The mismatch between schooling organised in year levels and literacy stages that encompass multiple years calls into question the notion of transition in schooling, whether from one year to another or from one phase to another (i.e. preschool to primary/elementary or secondary schooling). These schooling stages could perhaps be considered as 'artificial constructs' that do not serve student needs for learning in a 'continuous and seamless process' (Masters, 2019: 2, 91). In light of anxiety over declining academic achievement in standardised testing, and curriculum reviews in many countries, clear guidance from research is particularly important. However, as briefly described in this chapter, the research base on literacy development is far from conclusive about the fine detail of the stages of literacy development, the relationships between modes of literacy (e.g. oral language and reading and writing) and the best way for teachers to support all students in their literacy development.

# 3

# Representing Writing Development: Research and Policy

Beverly Derewianka

## Introduction

The aim of this chapter is to identify how effectively a selection of international syllabus documents represent writing development across the years of schooling. With a focus on the writing process in particular, the chapter will examine such documents to ascertain:

- whether a progression in writing development is evident;
- if so, how such development might be characterised;
- whether there are identifiable transition points from stage to stage.

Of further interest is the relationship between how writing development is depicted in these documents compared to how such growth is construed in the research literature. Bernstein (1990) views this relationship as one of recontextualisation, where research findings in the academic sphere are taken up, interpreted and transformed by policy designers, textbook writers, teacher educators and assessment authorities. The process of recontextualisation is a site of contestation, where different theories and ideologies jostle for attention and where policy designers make decisions based on pragmatic and often political considerations.

Throughout the chapter, an analysis is presented of the developmental trajectory of each element of the writing process in the international syllabuses. A comparison is then drawn between these trajectories and how writing development is described in the research literature – often revealing tensions and discrepancies.

## Analysis of the Syllabus Documents

The analysis of various syllabus documents was undertaken as part of the TRANSLIT project that was investigating key transition points in students' literacy development (see Chapter 1 for details). For the purpose of this chapter, a selection of syllabus documents has been made on the basis of certain common attributes. For practical reasons, it was decided to focus on major Anglophone countries, though for interest, Singapore was included as an example of a multilingual country with English as the medium of instruction and which is a high performer in international literacy assessment programmes. In some cases, a national English syllabus was available (Australian Curriculum: English (ACE), National Curriculum in England (NCE), The Singapore English Language Syllabus). In the United States, the Common Core State Standards in English Language Arts (CCSS ELA), while neither national nor a 'syllabus', have currently been adopted by around 41 states. Canada has no national English syllabus, so Ontario (The Ontario Curriculum: Language) was selected as it provided a detailed description of expectations across the years. In the New Zealand Curriculum: English, the levels of achievement are not sufficiently differentiated to enable an analysis of development.

Differences were apparent in terms of how the documents chose to organise the content, as illustrated in Table 3.1. Due to the limited scope of the chapter, only the writing element has been focused on.

The intention of this part of the project was not to make comparisons between the various syllabuses. Rather, the interest was in determining what was common to the syllabuses in relation to writing. This proved challenging as the various aspects of writing were dispersed through various strands of the syllabuses, despite the fact that they were organised around the macroskills (except for Australia). As a first step, every descriptor related to aspects of writing was identified. Those descriptors that occurred more than a couple of times were then collated into a framework representing the common key elements of writing in the documents (Table 3.2).

Although these common elements were all analysed in terms of developmental sequences in the documents, only the area of 'creating text' has been focused on here given space limitations. This element was selected as it implicates most of the other elements in the process of text creation.

**Table 3.1** Organisation of Content in the Focus Syllabuses

| Australia | England | Ontario | Singapore | United States |
|---|---|---|---|---|
| *Language* <br>• Language variation and change <br>• Language for interaction <br>• Text structure and organisation <br>• Expressing and developing ideas <br>• Phonics and word knowledge <br><br>*Literature* <br>• Literature and context <br>• Responding to literature <br>• Examining literature <br>• Creating literature <br><br>*Literacy* <br>• Texts in context <br>• Interacting with others <br>• Interpreting, analysing, evaluating <br>• Creating texts | *Spoken Language* <br><br>*Reading* <br>• Word reading <br>• Comprehension (listening and reading) <br><br>*Writing* <br>• Transcription/spelling <br>• Handwriting <br>• Composition (in speech and writing) <br>• Vocabulary, grammar and punctuation <br><br>*Appendices* | *Oral Communication* <br>• Listening to understand <br>• Speaking to communicate <br>• Reflecting <br><br>*Reading* <br>• Reading for meaning <br>• Form and style <br>• Reading with fluency <br>• Reflecting <br><br>*Writing* <br>• Developing and organising content <br>• Form and style <br>• Language conventions (spelling, punctuation, vocabulary, grammar, presentation) <br>• Reflection <br><br>*Media Literacy* <br>• Understanding media texts <br>• Understanding media forms, conventions and techniques <br>• Creating media texts <br>• Reflecting | *Listening and Viewing* <br>• Disposition <br>• Skills and strategies <br>• Extensive listening and viewing <br><br>*Reading and Viewing* <br>• Comprehension skills, strategies and attitudes <br>• Reading different types of rich texts <br>• Extensive reading <br><br>*Speaking and Representing* <br>• Features of spoken language <br>• Skills and strategies <br>• Types of spoken texts <br><br>*Writing and Representing* <br>• Mechanics of writing <br>• Skills and strategies <br>• Types of texts <br><br>*Grammar* <br>• Terminology <br>• Word, phrase, sentence level <br>• Text level <br><br>*Vocabulary* <br>• Terminology <br>• Development of rich vocabulary <br>• Use of vocabulary <br><br>*Appendices* | *Reading* for literature and informational texts <br>• Key ideas and details <br>• Craft and structure <br>• Integration of knowledge and ideas <br>• Range of reading <br>• Foundational skills (print concepts, phonological awareness, phonics, fluency) <br><br>*Writing* <br>• Text types and purposes <br>• Production and distribution of writing <br>• Research to build knowledge <br>• Range of writing <br><br>*Speaking and Listening* <br>• Comprehension and collaboration <br>• Presentation of knowledge and ideas <br><br>*Language* <br>• Conventions of Standard English <br>• Knowledge of language <br>• Vocabulary |

**Table 3.2** Common Strands Relating to Writing in the Syllabus Documents

| Kinder/Yr 1 | Yr 2 | Yr 3 | Yr 4 | Yr 5 | Yr 6 | Yr 7 | Yr 8 | Yr 9 | Yr 10 |
|---|---|---|---|---|---|---|---|---|---|
| | | | Spelling and Phonics | | | | | | |
| | | | Grammar and Punctuation | | | | | | |
| | | | Vocabulary | | | | | | |
| | | | Creating Texts | | | | | | |
| | | | Genre/Text types | | | | | | |
| | | | Text Structure | | | | | | |
| | | | Interpersonal Strategies | | | | | | |

**Table 3.3** Components of the Text Creation Process as Represented in the Focus Syllabuses

| Context | | | | | | |
|---|---|---|---|---|---|---|
| Audience | | | | Purpose | | |
| (Topic and task tend to be subsumed in sections of the composing process) | | | | | | |
| **Composing Processes** | | | | | | |
| Planning | | | Translation | | Reviewing | |
| Generating ideas | Researching | Organising ideas | Drafting | Reviewing and revising | Editing and proofreading | Publishing and sharing |

## Creating text

Research into the process of writing is dominated by cognitive models of text generation, exploring the factors that govern the internal decisions individual writers make as they write. The most influential research was the early work of Hayes and Flower (1980), extended and refined over the years. This approach modelled writing in terms of the task environment (rhetorical problem, task specifications, topic, audience, purpose for writing and the evolving text) and the subprocesses in the act of composing a text (planning, translating/drafting and reviewing). To a certain extent, this view of the writing process is reflected in the content of the various focus syllabuses (Table 3.3), which acknowledge the role of context (primarily in terms of audience and purpose) and composing processes. This chapter will deal with each of these components in turn.

While Hayes and Flower saw the subprocesses as a hierarchical system of resources to be drawn on recursively as needed during the act of writing, this is not evident in the presentation of the subprocesses in the syllabuses, where they are represented (perhaps inevitably) as a linear sequence.

## Responding to Context

### *Audience*

The notion of audience is notoriously elusive and controversial (Hyland, 2001). For some, audience is actual people, providing a real-world 'target' for the writer. Social interactive theory (Nystrand, 1989), on the other hand, would see audience as a more reciprocal concept, viewing writing as the dialogic negotiation of meaning between author and reader, with the text mediating their respective interests. From this perspective, writing development might be conceived of in terms of the degree to which the writer is able to 'construct' the reader, becoming sensitive to the needs, expectations and purposes of the putative audience – particularly when the task doesn't specify a readership. This is less likely in the primary years, where students are considered to have a less developed social cognition. A more nuanced engagement with the audience can be observed, however, from early secondary onwards, as students are expected to become increasingly familiar with the imagined discourse community to which the reader might belong (or not), anticipating interpersonal concerns and reactions as opposed to simply elaborating their own positions (Hyland, 2001; Myhill & Chen, 2020; Wray & Medwell, 2006). This requires:

> a highly refined understanding of social relationships, roles and interactions of discourse communities and rhetorical situations and how these would play into the ability to understand writing tasks, address rhetorical problems and reach the writer's rhetorical goals. (Andrews & Smith, 2011: 80)

A synthesis of the syllabus references to audience (Table 3.4) reveals that students are expected to write for a widening range of audiences, with a gradual (though uneven) developmental progression from family and friends, to familiar peers (the class), to a class of less familiar students, to a known adult (the teacher, the principal), to the school population, to the local community, to a generic unknown readership. The audience is thus portrayed for the most part as particular people, ranging from known readers to the less familiar,

Table 3.4 Synthesis of References to *Audience* in the Focus Syllabuses

### Audience

| Kindergarten–Year 2 | Years 3–4 | Years 5–6 | Years 7–8 | Years 9–10 |
|---|---|---|---|---|
| Identify the audience for writing, considering the impact on familiar and some less familiar audiences<br>– to share with family or friends<br>– to share findings with a group<br>– to inform the class<br>– to entertain another class | Write for a widening range of audiences<br>– for a class presentation<br>– for a peer group<br>– to contribute to a student poetry anthology for the school library<br>– to accompany a biography for a class collection | Identify the audience for writing<br>– letter to the teacher<br>– for an online student encyclopaedia<br>– to share with the class<br>– argument to the principal<br>– for a mock television broadcast for a general audience | Consider how their writing reflects the audiences for which it was intended<br>– a rap poem to express a personal view to the class<br>– for a community newspaper<br>– to share with classmates, family, and friends at graduation<br>– for a youth magazine, web page, blog, or zine<br>– to promote a candidate for school government | Adapt their writing for a wide range of audiences, considering appealing to your principal audience<br>– for peers<br>– for fellow students<br>– for the school newspaper<br>– for the teacher<br>– for the class yearbook<br>– for new students<br>– for a community newspaper |

with little consideration of what it means to 'bring the reader into the text' (Hyland, 2001).

In terms of key transition points, there is a shift from simply 'identifying the audience' in the primary years to 'considering how their writing reflects the audience for which it was intended' in secondary school. We can discern, therefore, a (relatively weak) transition point between primary and secondary in terms of a more reflective consideration of the reader – though this is also found in early primary in one of the syllabuses ('considering the impact on familiar and less familiar audiences').

## *Purpose*

Despite the relatively recent surge of research into purposes for writing – from Britton, Burgess, Martin, McLeod and Rosen (1975) and Applebee (1981) through to ongoing work in Australia (e.g. Martin, 2009) and North America (e.g. Bazerman, 2004) – there is little evidence in the syllabuses of the influence of this depth of scholarship. Australian researchers in particular have undertaken extensive analyses of student writing in response to curriculum demands in all learning areas from the early primary years through to senior secondary and beyond (e.g. Christie & Derewianka, 2008), making explicit the wide range of purposes for which students are expected to write in order to successfully achieve the academic outcomes outlined in the various stages of schooling.

From Table 3.5, we can observe that students are expected to compose a range of genres in each year. While there is an emphasis on traditional literary and persuasive genres (referred to variously as imaginative, narrative, creative, argument, and personal expression), there is only cursory acknowledgement of informative/explanatory purposes for writing – more so in the primary years than secondary. (Greater elaboration on academic genres is typically found in other areas of the syllabus or in accompanying documents.) There is, however, little indication of what constitutes increasing complexity across the years. The 'narrative' thread, for example, proposes 'fairy tales' in early primary, 'original fables' in mid-primary, 'narratives' in late primary, 'stories' in early secondary and 'rite-of-passage narratives' in later secondary. Apart from late primary, where features such as characters, setting, atmosphere and dialogue are specified, there is nothing to indicate how these genres differ in terms of increasing challenge.

Table 3.5 Synthesis of References to *Purposes for Writing* in the Focus Syllabuses

**Purpose**

| Kindergarten–Year 2 | Years 3–4 | Years 5–6 | Years 7–8 | Years 9–10 |
|---|---|---|---|---|
| Writing for different purposes | Writing literary or informational topics of increasing complexity appropriate to task | Writing for a range of purposes | Considering how their writing reflects the purpose for which it was intended | Adapting their writing for a wide range of purposes |
| Imaginative/narrative/creative<br>– a fairy tale<br>– poetry | Imaginative/narrative/creative<br>– an original fable<br>– a cinquain or shape poem | Imaginative/narrative/creative<br>– narratives, considering how authors have developed characters, settings, atmosphere and dialogue<br>– a poem or song on a social issue | Imaginative/narrative/creative<br>– stories, scripts, poetry and other imaginative writing<br>– a rap poem or jingle | Imaginative/narrative/creative<br>– a rite-of-passage narrative<br>– a narrative poem; a ballad |
| Informative/explanatory<br>– labels and captions for a pictograph<br>– a sequence of instructions<br>– a report (e.g. the seasons)<br>– science observations | Informative/explanatory<br>– a scientific explanation<br>– a procedure for an experiment<br>– a labelled map with a legend<br>– a timeline of significant events in the writer's life | Informative/explanatory<br>– an explanation of the water cycle including a flowchart<br>– a procedure for constructing a three-dimensional model<br>– a script on a topic of current interest | Informative/explanatory<br>– a report on a topic of current interest in the style of a newspaper article, including headlines | Informative/explanatory<br>– an account of an important event in Aboriginal history<br>– a speech about an Aboriginal leader or role model |
| Persuasive/arguments<br>– persuade the reader to accept the writer's point of view<br>– express opinions about a book or movie | Persuasive/arguments<br>None identified | Persuasive/arguments<br>– a formal letter outlining their opinion on a school issue | Persuasive/arguments<br>– raise issues and advance opinions<br>– formal expository essays, raising issues and advancing opinions<br>– supporting ideas and arguments with factual detail | Persuasive/arguments<br>– a review of a book or film<br>– an expository essay explaining a character's development<br>– a movie review to encourage others to see the movie<br>– an academic essay examining a theme in one of Shakespeare's plays<br>– an article on a local issue |
| Personal expression<br>– narratives about personal experiences and those of others (real and fictional)<br>– a personal recount of a past experience, including pictures | Personal expression<br>– reflecting on past experiences/events and ideas (e.g. through journaling) | Personal expression<br>– an original poem about a topic of personal interest | – a campaign flyer or brochure<br>Personal expression<br>– an autobiography<br>– a personal memoir | Personal expression<br>– a narrative about a significant personal moment in their own experience |

Taking the purpose of 'explaining', for example, one might track development from a simple sequential or cyclical explanation, to a causal relationship, an implication sequence, a system explanation, an explanation of the multiple causes or multiple consequences of a phenomenon (or a combination thereof), through to a complex theoretical explanation or perhaps a hybrid genre (Derewianka & Jones, 2016). While such a sequence isn't necessarily tied to student age groupings, it does provide at least a relatively systematic indication of how we might characterise increasing complexity across the years.

As with 'audience', the strand on purposes for writing suggests a minor shift between the primary years ('writing for a range of purposes') and a more intentional approach in secondary ('considering how their writing reflects the purpose for which it was intended'), but with no other clearly defined transition points.

## Composing Processes

### *Generating Ideas*

As part of the planning process, students are encouraged to gather information and ideas. From a psychological perspective, the generation of ideas is modelled as a cognitive process involving an initial mental representation of the assignment, taking into account the content knowledge and discourse knowledge expected. Ideas are then generated by constructing memory probes and using these to retrieve content from memory. The retrieved content is tested for appropriateness and the mental representation is constantly updated (Bereiter & Scardamalia, 1987).

In terms of development, Bereiter (1980) notes that children have not experienced the broad range of text structures, genres and topic knowledge to which older students have access. They are therefore constrained in terms of the ability to generate ideas from long-term memory.

The generation of ideas is only fleetingly mentioned in most of the syllabuses (e.g. 'discussing and recording ideas', 'writing down ideas') with the exception of Ontario – though only with elaborations in early primary and Years 9–10, as seen in Table 3.6. There is little guidance for teachers in terms of how the generation of ideas increases in complexity across the years or any evident transition points.

Table 3.6 Synthesis of References to *Generating Ideas* in the Focus Syllabuses

**Generating Ideas**

| Kindergarten–Year 2 | Years 3–4 | Years 5–6 | Years 7–8 | Years 9–10 |
|---|---|---|---|---|
| • Generate ideas about a potential topic (e.g. personal experiences, prior knowledge, familiar persons and objects) through listening to stories told by family members, sharing with a peer and observations<br>• Explore, record and report ideas and real events, drawing on their discussions about it and from their wider experiences<br>• Ask and answer questions about the topic<br>• Use visuals and realia as stimuli<br>• Brainstorm and describe personal feelings, past experiences/events, points of view and ideas on self-selected topics, using selected emotive/sensory details | Generate ideas about a potential topic, using a variety of strategies and resources (e.g. formulate and ask questions to identify personal experiences, prior knowledge, and information needs and to guide searches for information; brainstorm and record ideas on the topic) | Generate ideas about a potential topic and identify those most appropriate for the purpose | Generate ideas about more challenging topics | Generate, expand and focus ideas for potential writing tasks (e.g. complete a K-W-L chart to focus an enquiry about an identified topic; participate in a small group discussion to generate ideas for an opinion piece; use different types of questions – prediction, probability, possibility, and speculation – to deepen understanding of a specific topic; identify and rank focus questions for further investigation; summarise and paraphrase ideas in point-form notes; use formal debate strategies to explore ideas prior to research) |

## Researching

Although the process literature (e.g. Hayes & Flower, 1980) tends not to differentiate to any extent between generating ideas and researching, it is interesting that the syllabuses see these as distinct processes, shifting from what can be accessed from the student's current long-term memory to new information located in external sources (see Table 3.7). It is here that we observe much greater detail in each stage of schooling and a greater sense of progression from year to year. In the early primary years, students gather information from a variety of readily available sources. In later years, however, they are expected to read like a writer – conducting research to strategically select, organise and evaluate information with increasing sophistication.

Little indication is given, however, as to how the information gathering processes vary depending on the nature of the task, the topic and discipline area, the genre, the length of text and the time available or needed.

## Organising Ideas

Organising ideas involves selecting the most useful of the materials gathered from the generating and researching processes and developing a plan to guide their writing (Hayes & Flower, 1980). Students might seek patterns such as identifying an umbrella idea under which to cluster related ideas or ordering events chronologically. With regard to planning and goal setting, research indicates that young writers have greater difficulties in this regard (Flower & Hayes, 1981). They often entertain a single goal, whereas older writers will develop structural, rhetorical and stylistic goals. Only in the middle years of schooling do novice writers' think-aloud protocols begin to reveal abstract planning processes. The writing of sixth graders apparently benefits from learning to use specific planning cues to come up with new ideas, improve them and state their goals and main point (Scardamalia & Bereiter, 1985), but ten-year-olds do not benefit from such instruction (Burtis, Bereiter, Scardamalia & Tetroe, 1983).

While this is one of the less elaborated elements of the Hayes and Flower model, the focus syllabuses have fleshed it out with practical suggestions for organising ideas, including the use of visual scaffolds, model texts and technologies such as concept-mapping software. In this component, we find a

**Table 3.7** Synthesis of References to *Researching* in the Focus Syllabuses

### Researching

| Kindergarten–Year 2 | Years 3–4 | Years 5–6 | Years 7–8 | Years 9–10 |
|---|---|---|---|---|
| • Gather information to support ideas from a variety of sources (e.g. from listening to stories told by family members; from paired sharing with a peer; from observations; from various texts, including teacher read-alouds, provided sources, mentor texts, and shared, guided and independent reading texts; and media texts)<br>• Gather new material if necessary (e.g. use a graphic organiser to explain their material to a classmate and ask for feedback to identify gaps) | • Conduct short research projects that build knowledge about different aspects of a topic<br>• Gather information to support ideas using a variety of strategies and oral, print and electronic sources (e.g. identify key words to help narrow their searches; take notes; cluster ideas; develop a plan for locating information; scan texts for specific information from reference texts)<br>• Determine whether the ideas and information they have gathered are relevant and adequate for the purpose, and gather new material if necessary | • Conduct short research projects that use several sources to build knowledge through investigation of different aspects of a topic and refocusing the inquiry when appropriate<br>• Gather relevant information from multiple print and digital sources; assess the credibility of each source; and quote or paraphrase the data and conclusions of others while avoiding plagiarism and providing a list of resources and basic bibliographic information for sources used and information gathered; identify the steps required to gather information<br>• Interview people with knowledge of the topic; identify and use graphic and multimedia sources; keep a record of sources | • Conduct short research projects to answer a question (including a self-generated question), generating additional related, focused questions for further research and investigation and that allow for multiple avenues of exploration<br>• Gather information to support ideas for writing, using a variety of strategies and a wide range of print and electronic resources (e.g. produce a plan and a timeline to organise research tasks; record sources used and information gathered in a form that makes it easy to understand and retrieve)<br>• Assess the credibility and accuracy of each source; and quote or paraphrase the data and conclusions of others while avoiding plagiarism and following a standard format for citation | • Conduct short as well as more sustained research projects to answer a question (including a self-generated question) or solve a problem<br>• Narrow or broaden the inquiry when appropriate<br>• Create a research plan and track progress using a research portfolio<br>• Use key word searches and other browsing strategies to guide electronic research<br>• Locate a range of periodical and e-book information in online databases<br>• Gather relevant information from multiple authoritative print and digital sources, using advanced searches effectively<br>• Conduct interviews with community members, experts on a topic or witnesses to an event<br>• Use criteria developed in small groups to select appropriate information<br>• Use a detailed template to evaluate sources and information for reliability, usefulness, currency and accuracy in answering the research question |

stronger sense of progression, ranging from using basic organisational patterns (e.g. beginning-middle-end) in early primary through to patterns of cause/effect, compare/contrast, class/subclass and main idea/supporting details in later years (Table 3.8). Whereas in early years the students are supported, directed and provided with categories, in subsequent years they are expected to independently view issues from different perspectives, make connections, see different combinations, manipulate information, determine relevance, check for omissions, experiment with different patterns, synthesise multiple sources and undertake textual analysis.

## *Drafting*

The function of the translation process is to convert ideas into visible language, taking material from memory and transforming it into acceptable sentences (Hayes & Flower, 1980). In terms of writing development, cognitive theory suggests that in the early years of schooling, lower level skills of handwriting and spelling consume most cognitive resources in the translation process. From around ten years of age, however, transcription gradually starts to automatise, allowing for compositional fluency and creating space for the implementation of higher level metacognitive and metalinguistic skills, resulting in a more mature text (Alamargot & Fayol, 2009).

Along similar lines, Bereiter and Scardamalia's (1987) studies observed that novice writers have limited goals and tend to stay close to their current knowledge structures and experience without close attention to conceptual content or linguistic form, linking ideas together in a sequence with minimal planning and revision ('knowledge telling'). From around age twelve, experienced writers more consciously set goals, reflect on the task and reconfigure content and linguistic expression, reintegrating material at a different level with greater attention to audience and text coherence ('knowledge transformation'). Flower and Hayes (1981) identified a key distinction between novice and experienced writers as the ability to monitor their writing, knowing when to transition between different subprocesses of the writing act.

The syllabuses tend to focus on the content, language and structure of the emergent text rather than on the drafting process itself and how this might change across the levels of schooling, particularly in terms of increasingly

**Table 3.8** Synthesis of References to *Organising Ideas* in the Focus Syllabuses

**Organising Ideas**

| Kindergarten–Year 2 | Years 3–4 | Years 5–6 | Years 7–8 | Years 9–10 |
|---|---|---|---|---|
| • Sort ideas and information for their writing in a variety of ways (e.g. by using pictures, labels, key words, hand-drawn or computer graphics, or simple graphic organisers such as a web, a list, or a five-W's framework: who, what, when, where, why; a Venn diagram; a story ladder; sequence chart)<br>• Use graphics for succinct presentation of information<br>• Follow simple organisational patterns (e.g. time order: first, then, next, finally; order of importance; beginning, middle, and end; problem, solution)<br>• Determine, after consultation with the teacher and peers, whether the ideas and information they have gathered are suitable for the purpose | • Sort ideas in a variety of ways (e.g. by using graphs, charts, tables, diagrams, webs, outlines or lists; by underlining key words and phrases; by using graphic and print organisers such as mind maps, concept maps, storyboards, timelines, flowcharts, jot notes, bulleted lists)<br>• Follow simple organisational patterns (e.g. generalisation with supporting information, cause and effect, compare and contrast, categorise and classify)<br>• Take brief notes on sources and sort evidence into provided categories<br>• Plan their writing by discussing writing/models similar to that which they are planning to write in order to learn from its structure, vocabulary and grammar | • Sort and classify information in a variety of ways that allow them to view information from different perspectives and make connections between ideas (e.g by using a graphic organiser such as a fishbone chart, a T-chart or an 'Agree/Disagree' chart)<br>• Identify and order main ideas and supporting details and group them into units that could be used to develop several linked paragraphs or a structured, multi-paragraph piece of writing<br>• Plan their writing by:<br>– selecting the appropriate form and using other similar writing as models for their own<br>– noting and developing initial ideas<br>– selecting appropriate grammar and vocabulary, understanding how such choices can change and enhance meaning | • Sort ideas and information for their writing in a variety of ways that allow them to manipulate information and see different combinations and relationships in their data (e.g. by using electronic graphic organisers, tables, charts)<br>• Determine whether the ideas and information they have gathered are relevant, appropriate and sufficiently specific for the purpose, and do more research if necessary (e.g. check for depth of coverage of the topic and for errors or omissions in information using a T-chart) | • Identify, sort and order main ideas and supporting details (e.g. use a clear statement of topic or thesis to highlight the main points they plan in a persuasive argument; identify appropriate classification categories; use a cause-and-effect chart to organise causal relationships; develop an extended metaphor as a prompt for writing a poem; use a timeline to trace the development of a tragic hero)<br>• Work with several classmates to develop headings and group data for a textual analysis; use a concept-mapping software to move from a concept map to a writing outline; experiment with one or more organisational patterns to connect and order free associated images for a poem<br>• Synthesise multiple sources on the subject, demonstrating understanding of the subject under investigation<br>• Determine whether the ideas and information gathered are relevant to the topic, sufficient for the purpose, accurate, complete and meet the requirements of the writing task (e.g. verify information in another source; review supporting quotations to ensure that they accurately illustrate the intended point; use a checklist to ensure that all main points are adequately supported) |

sophisticated metalinguistic and metacognitive processes. As we can see from Table 3.9, there is little evident development from year to year, particularly no indication of a shift from knowledge-telling to knowledge-transformation in late primary nor any explicit acknowledgement of the constraints placed on drafting by transcription processes in early-mid primary. There are, however, differing expectations in terms of text length: short texts in early primary to a minimum of one page in a single sitting in mid-primary, a minimum of two–three pages in upper primary and writing at length in secondary.

In both the process literature and the syllabuses, there appears to be an assumption that composing refers to the creation of paper-based linear prose. The syllabuses don't incorporate multimodal resources (maps, diagrams, graphs, illustrations, animations, video, sound, and so on) into the process of meaning-making above. And although some adaptations of the Hayes and Flower model include 'composing medium' or 'tools' in the task environment, Haas (2013) observes that technology is virtually invisible – or at least over-simplified – in cognitive theories of writing, where drafting is treated exclusively as a mental operation. And yet, the composing process itself is dramatically changed with the affordances provided by electronic media – the ability to easily add, delete or rearrange text, to create and integrate multimodal elements, to collaboratively compose texts, to receive timely feedback, to access information on the fly and to benefit from heuristic prompts, planning software, spellchecks, genre-specific graphic organisers and so on.

## *Reviewing and Revising*

Reviewing involves the ability to detect a problem, diagnose the nature of the problem and know how to address it. From a developmental perspective, the cognitive operations that guide the experienced writer's methods of revision are believed to be not well understood, but it is surmised that they are too complex for use by primary schoolchildren's limited mental processing capacities (Case 1985). The literature (e.g. Berninger, 1996; Sitko, 1998) identifies the following tendencies (Table 3.10) as inexperienced students transition into more experienced writers:

Research suggests that particularly significant in the revising processes of nine- to thirteen-year-olds is the close relationship between metacognition and the development of compositional expertise in terms of reflexive

Table 3.9 Synthesis of References to *Drafting* in the Focus Syllabuses

## Drafting

| Kindergarten–Year 2 | Years 3–4 | Years 5–6 | Years 7–8 | Years 9–10 |
|---|---|---|---|---|
| • Write sentences by:<br>  – saying out loud what they are going to write about<br>  – composing a sentence orally before writing it<br>  – writing down ideas and/or key words, including new vocabulary<br>• Develop characterisation in a narrative using literary techniques (e.g. direct speech)<br>• Select and use language for effect to describe experiences/events/topics and/or persuade the reader to accept the writer's point of view/proposed action<br>• Use appropriate cohesive devices (e.g. connectors, pronouns, repetition of vocabulary or grammatical structures) to indicate relations between paragraphs/sentences and between the main idea of a paragraph and the key message of a text | • Develop increasing control over text structures:<br>  – in narratives, creating settings, characters and plot (e.g. series of events building towards the complication and resolution)<br>  – in non-narrative material, using simple organisational devices (e.g. headings and subheadings)<br>  – organising paragraphs around a theme<br>• Draw evidence from literary or informational texts to support analysis, reflection and research | • Distinguish between the language of speech and writing and choose the appropriate register<br>• Elaborate on, explain and/or justify the main idea of a paragraph by providing relevant factual, descriptive, emotive or sensory details and/or examples<br>• Choosing and experimenting with text structures, language features, images, sound and digital resources appropriate to purpose and audience<br>  – using a wide range of devices to build cohesion within and across paragraphs<br>  – using further organisational and presentational devices to structure text and to guide the reader (e.g. headings, bullet points, underlining)<br>• Use figurative language such as similes, personification and rhetorical devices such as exaggeration to achieve particular effects | • Select appropriate language, visual, digital and audio features<br>• Apply their growing knowledge of vocabulary and grammar to their writing<br>• Draw on knowledge of literary and rhetorical devices from their reading and listening to enhance the impact of their writing<br>• Apply their growing knowledge of text structure to their writing and selecting the appropriate form<br>• Use patterns such as repetition of key phrases for emphasis | • Draft and write fluently and at length for pleasure and information, including using information provided by others<br>• Produce clear and coherent writing in which the development, organisation and style are appropriate to task, purpose and audience<br>• Cite evidence and quotations effectively from primary and secondary sources<br>• Use judiciously structural and organisational features to reflect audience, purpose and context |

**Table 3.10** Differences in the Reviewing Process between Inexperienced and More Experienced Writers

| Inexperienced writers ... | More experienced writers ... |
| --- | --- |
| are typically satisfied with their first draft, lacking the skills to recognise when their texts need revision | set rhetorical goals and devote considerable time to monitoring the adequacy of their writing |
| leave any revision until the text is complete | incorporate online revision into every aspect of the writing process during the process of drafting |
| revise at the level of surface features such as spelling and grammatical errors | attend to both global and local aspects of the text |
| tend to assume that the text is clear and the reader will understand their intended meaning | are sensitive to the needs of a distant, unfamiliar readership |
| lack experience with reading and writing | have a large repository of past reading and writing experiences to draw on |

analysis, reasoning, the link between intention and text production, and the management and coordination of writing processes (Alamargot & Fayol, 2009). Younger students (eight-year-olds) were found to be less able to reflect on strategies used in their own writing, implying a growing meta-awareness of writing strategies with age (Langer, 1986).

Flower and Hayes's (1981) comparison of the processes used by expert and novice writers revealed that more experienced writers approached writing tasks as problem-solving activities that require strategic thinking and reviewing, while less experienced writers devoted little time to revising, satisfied to simply retrieve content from memory and write it down as it comes to mind.

The focus syllabuses don't resonate, however, with the research findings on the reviewing process. Even from early primary there is an expectation that children will identify problems with their writing at macro- and micro-levels and will rectify them, echoing Jacobs's (2004) observation that very young children are capable of metacognitive thinking about their writing. In fact, several of the features listed in early primary are also found in grades 9 and 10, such as providing revised drafts demonstrating clarity of expression, relevance, organisation, style, reordering of events, content, interest, emotive details and using connecting/linking words (Table 3.11). While not explicitly stated, the difference in challenge between early primary and the secondary years might be the degree of teacher scaffolding, from heavy support in primary to autonomy in secondary.

**Table 3.11** Synthesis of References to *Reviewing and Revising* in the Focus Syllabuses

**Reviewing and Revising**

| Kindergarten–Year 2 | Years 3–4 | Years 5–6 | Years 7–8 | Years 9–10 |
|---|---|---|---|---|
| • Reread what they have written to check that it makes sense<br>• Identify elements of their writing that need improvement, including content, clarity in expression of meaning, relevance, focus, interest, organisation, word choice, emotive/descriptive details and style, using feedback from the teacher and peers<br>• Make simple additions, revisions and corrections to their own writing (e.g. cut out words or sentences and reorder them to improve clarity; insert words from oral vocabulary and the class word wall or word webs to clarify meaning and/or add interest; | • Reread and edit texts for meaning and appropriate structure (e.g. by improving the coherence, reordering sentences, adding, deleting or moving words or word groups, removing repetition or unnecessary information, changing the sequence of ideas, adding material needed to clarify meaning, substituting words to increase interest, adding linking/transition words or phrases to highlight connections between ideas and improve the flow of writing, employing words from other subject areas or thesaurus, using gender-neutral language as appropriate, checking for and removing negative stereotypes, as appropriate) | • Edit for meaning and clarity (e.g. sentence length/complexity/diversity, words and phrases that would make the writing more vivid)<br>• Check that language is inclusive and non-discriminatory. Selectively use feedback from the teacher and peers to focus on specific features such as effective use of precise language, support of main idea<br>• Review information critically with a friend using a concept map, checklist or flowchart<br>• Meet identified criteria based on the expectations (e.g. adequate development of information and ideas, logical organisation, appropriate use of form and style, appropriate use of conventions) | • Identify elements in their writing that need improvement, selectively using feedback from the teacher and peers, with a focus on voice, diction, expression of feelings, figurative language or rhetorical devices (e.g. understatement, analogy), appropriateness of tone (e.g. sincerity, humour, horror, irony, pathos), creation of suspense and an effective beginning and ending | • Reflect on whether their draft achieves the intended impact<br>• Restructure their writing to improve content, organisation, clarity, coherence, consistency, style and overall effectiveness (e.g. add examples and evidence to support the main idea; remove irrelevant or confusing details; insert appropriate connecting words at the beginning of paragraphs in a series to signal continuity of thought and relationships between ideas; reorder events to emphasise the most important facts and ideas, identify a single controlling idea that unifies the text; reinforce a mood or feeling by sharpening the focus of |

- reordering sentences to present information in a more logical sequence; add linking words to connect ideas; replace general words with concrete, specific words/phrases)
- Proofread for errors in grammar, spelling, capitals, full stops using a simple checklist for reference
- Produce revised draft pieces of writing
- Meet criteria identified by the teacher, based on the expectations

- Using feedback from peers and teacher, evaluate specific features by assessing the effectiveness of their text and suggesting improvements (e.g. logical organisation, clarity of main idea, strong opening, depth of content)
- Propose changes to grammar and vocabulary to improve consistency
- Compare their material to the content of similar texts
- Proofread for grammatical choices, spelling and punctuation errors (e.g. using guidelines/checklist developed with teacher/peers)
- Meet identified criteria based on the expectations related to content, organisation, style and use of conventions

- Experiment with text structures and language features to refine and clarify ideas to improve the fluency and effectiveness of students' own texts
- Improve overall effectiveness and coherence (e.g. using an editing checklist specific to the writing task)
- Check for depth and breadth of coverage of the topic

the imagery and other rhetorical devices in a poem or short story; identify and remove redundancies and clarify or expand supporting details; rearrange ideas to improve parallel structure in a comparison and contrast essay; clearly identify your thesis in an argument; carefully select and cite supporting quotations)
- Proofread and correct their writing, using guidelines developed with the teacher and peers (e.g. consult print and electronic references to check spelling; develop and use a checklist specific to the writing task)
- Produce revised drafts of both simple and complex texts written to meet criteria identified by the teacher, based on the curriculum expectations
- Understand the role of an editor

### Publishing and Sharing

While early process models don't recognise a final publication and sharing stage, the focus syllabuses do include this option, influenced by such educationists as Donald Graves (1983) who view writing as a more collaborative act. From Table 3.12, we can observe that there is little sense of development from year to year, however, apart from a mention of using citation conventions in secondary.

Of particular interest is the reference to multimodal and digital modes of meaning-making – as if these appeared only as an afterthought rather than as an integral part of the composing process. Apart from issues of layout and handwriting, we find typographical resources (font, size, colour) and graphics (drawings, photographs, illustrations, diagrams, tables, maps, timelines, computer graphics).

## Discussion

With regard to the question as to whether the syllabus documents provide teachers with a principled, systematic account of writing development across the years, our analysis has shown that this is not necessarily the case. Although the present discussion deals with only one element (the writing process) of a limited number of English syllabuses, the observations below reflect similar trends in other areas of the syllabuses (such as vocabulary, grammar, punctuation, genre and text structure).

In many instances, there is little or no evidence of progression from one year to the next (though with a keen eye, one might be able to infer progression from some of the examples provided). In most of the syllabuses, it is hard to identify coherent threads within each element that pursue 'throughlines' consistently across the years, making it difficult for teachers to guide students through increasing expectations in relation to a selected feature. A thread relating to 'using appropriate cohesive devices' in the Drafting element, for example, starts in early primary but virtually disappears in subsequent years. Or an item such as 'Check that language is inclusive and non-discriminatory' appears randomly in late primary but is not mentioned elsewhere. By way of contrast, the two elements of 'Researching' and 'Organising Ideas' stood out for their substantial content and considered progression across the stages.

**Table 3.12** Synthesis of References to *Publishing and Sharing* in the Focus Syllabuses

**Publishing and Sharing**

| Kindergarten–Year 2 | Years 3–4 | Years 5–6 | Years 7–8 | Years 9–10 |
|---|---|---|---|---|
| • Use some appropriate elements of effective presentation and layout in the finished product, such as different print size, different fonts, indentation where appropriate, title, headings and subheadings, bullets, margins, colour for emphasis and graphics (e.g. use drawings, photographs, illustrations, a simple labelled diagram, a caption for a photograph)<br>• Print legibly, leave spaces between words and paragraphs, margins | • Use some appropriate elements of effective presentation in the finished product, including script, different fonts, graphics and layout<br>• Use legible printing and some cursive writing<br>• Use proper paragraph form including spacing and margins<br>• Read aloud their own writing to a group or the whole class, using appropriate intonation and controlling the tone and volume so that the meaning is clear | • Use a range of appropriate elements of effective presentation (e.g. include a labelled diagram, photographs, a beginning table of contents, glossary and index; formal letter layout, photographs or magazine pictures and a map in a travel brochure)<br>• Perform their own compositions, using appropriate intonation, volume, and movement so that meaning is clear | Use a wide range of appropriate elements of effective presentation in the finished product (e.g. a timeline; captions and text boxes to accompany the photographs in a photo essay; a bulleted or point-form layout in a summary of key points for a debate, an imaginative text layout, a spreadsheet to display detailed specific information) | • Use several different presentation features to improve the clarity and coherence of their written work and to engage their audience (e.g. select striking computer graphics and fonts to heighten the impact of a news article; select images or unusual fonts or other design features for a title page to reflect or foreshadow the content of a story; use design elements such as columns, headlines and visuals to create an arresting front page for a class newspaper; use different fonts to suggest a story's principal theme or mood; design an eye-catching layout for the front and back covers of a teen magazine)<br>• Accurately record all sources of information (and page references) in a list of works cited or references, observing conventions for proper documentation of full sources and extracts, in recognition of the need to credit original authors and promote academic honesty |

As for identifying distinctive transition points, the only one that can be observed is the movement in some elements from primary into secondary schooling – typically in terms of a shift from 'doing' to 'reflecting'. Even in the constrained skills such as spelling, phonics and punctuation, where one might expect more evidence-based consensus, there is little agreement about potential transition points. The Singapore syllabus, for example, expects most of the constrained skills to have been mastered by mid-primary, while other syllabuses stretch these out over the years of schooling.

Because there is typically no accompanying documentation of the theoretical rationale and construct of writing informing the syllabus, it is hard to know why certain decisions have been made, why certain perspectives and values have been privileged and how development is construed.

Overall, the syllabuses have to wrestle with the fact that writing is complex and multidimensional, involving not only mastery of the 'basic skills' but also engagement with the various curriculum topics and tasks, knowledge of the discipline and its genres, deployment of multimodal and digital technologies, interpersonal sensitivities, linguistic and metalinguistic knowledge, as well as cognitive and metacognitive strategies such as planning, researching, organising, reflecting, evaluating and revising. All these dimensions are brought together in each writing event but they develop at different rates. The challenge for policy developers is to guide teachers and students through this complexity in a way that orchestrates all these dimensions with integrity and without falling back on simplistic constructs of writing.

## Conclusion

If there is a certain lack of coherence and consistency in terms of what development might look like in an English syllabus, we can't necessarily turn to the research domain for an all-encompassing developmental trajectory that corresponds directly with the exigencies of policy designers. Garcia-Debanc and Fayol (2013) caution that the interests of researchers might not coincide with those of the syllabus designer/teacher and note that models of writing development are forever evolving, partial, complex, provisional and refutable – not intended to be prescriptive – while policy and teaching favour a stable, definitive, accessible inventory of components in a linear sequence apportioned into grades or stages.

Although most syllabus documents claim to be 'evidence-based', the link between the research base and the writing sequences proposed in the syllabuses is somewhat tenuous. So how does the literature characterise the development of composing processes across the years? And how is this reflected (or not) in the syllabuses?

Compared to the research into reading, research into writing is limited (Myhill & Chen, 2020). Very little deals with development across the years, tending to focus on specific age groups rather than longitudinal studies, and predominantly on skills in childhood rather than adolescence (Myhill, 2009; Perera, 1984; Wray & Medwell, 2006). Studies tend to be small scale, dealing with the emergence of a particular feature of writing, such as spelling or sentence structure (Alamargot & Fayol, 2009; Andrews, Hoffman & Wyse, 2010). Hyland (2011) points out that models are hampered by often contradictory studies and the difficulties of accessing unconscious processing. Furthermore, much of the research effort is concerned with specific student populations such as those with literacy difficulties or those from language backgrounds other than English. As Bazerman et al. (2017) acknowledge, studies on writing development remain fragmented along lines of theory, method and age ranges or populations studied.

The implications of this for syllabus development is noted by Christie (2010: 147):

> The research has rarely addressed writing ability in terms of the developmental trajectory from early childhood, when children enter school aged six or seven, until they conclude their schooling in late adolescence, aged 17 or 18. The issue is an important one, not least because control of writing is critical to control of school learning generally, while a principled account of the ontogenesis of writing in children and adolescents should inform pedagogy and design of the writing curriculum for all the years of schooling.

In terms of development, the cognitive literature tends to talk about 'novice'/'immature'/'inexperienced' writers versus 'expert'/'mature'/'experienced' writers – not necessarily related to age. There is general agreement that older writers have the benefit of maturation and experiential histories accumulated in long-term memory, along with greater facility with writing technologies (e.g. handwriting), competence with the basic skills (e.g. spelling and punctuation) and a more extensive linguistic repertoire, leaving space for higher order thinking and greater access to knowledge transforming strategies (Alamargot & Fayol, 2009). Along the pathway between novice and experienced writers, however, there is generally little evidence of fine gradations of development as required by syllabus designers, who need to distribute such composing skills incrementally along a year-by-year continuum according to age – even though in reality, progress in writing is a complex process involving fluctuations, regressions and surges, depending on the individual student and the language demands of the task.

At odds with the cognitive research, the syllabuses in the early years assume that young children are capable of producing aspects of written texts well beyond expectations. This might be explained by the relative absence of the teacher from the model – apart from providing feedback during conferencing. Alamargot and Fayol (2009) argue that, alongside maturation, explicit instruction and related practice play a central role in the learning and development of written production. Similarly, Andrews and Smith (2011: 80) make the point that 'cognitive models characterise development as "naturally" occurring as one gets older. The role of instruction is often lost in such models.' They conjecture whether the writing produced by young children is a function of their capacity or of the learning context, including the role of the teacher and the nature of the learning task. They also suggest that because process-based theories do not consider writing development in the medium to long term, they are not suitable for curriculum design.

Overall, there is a way to go before we have sufficient research evidence describing a more coherent developmental pathway that can inform policy design and classroom practice. Wray and Medwell (2006) point out that while it is obvious that the writing of fourteen-year-olds is likely to show developments from the writing of eleven-year-olds, which in turn will show developments from that of seven-year-olds, the nature of these developments is only imprecisely known. Along similar lines, Andrews and Smith (2011) contend that we do not yet have a model of research data to map reliably trends across time that could inform curriculum design – and that such an endeavour might be a misguided goal, as writing processes are always shifting rhetorically, situationally and from person to person. Alamargot and Fayol (2009) maintain that a fully formed model of the development of written composition is currently beyond our reach. Andrews, Hoffman and Wyse (2010) make a plea for longitudinal studies to address the lack of a coherent theory of writing development, and in particular, they lament the dearth of research into writing development in the secondary years. And Bazerman et al. (2017) concur that educators have no coherent, well-substantiated picture of what writing development across the lifespan looks like. They caution that without an integrated framework to understand development of writing abilities in all its variation, high-stakes decisions about curriculum, instruction and assessment are often made in unsystematic ways that may fail to support the development they are intended to facilitate.

As Beard, Myhill, Nystrand and Riley (2009: 3) counsel, 'more research needs to be done on what constitutes progression in writing and to conceptualise what that progression looks like'. In the meantime, books such as the current volume can facilitate a conversation between academics, syllabus designers and classroom teachers in coming to a better understanding of students' literacy development.

# 4

# Transitions in School Literacy: Co-opting Everyday Rationalities

Björn Kindenberg and Peter Freebody

## Introduction: Disorderly Transitions over the School Years

Contributors to this volume draw our attention to transitions in literacy development over the school years. Much of the research on literacy development, along with the theorising that supports it, has held fast to the doctrine of 'short-and-small', reporting on short-term interventions related to small, readily manageable aspects of either texts or learners' proficiencies. Less frequent are research projects addressing questions that take in a more distant horizon of consequence, with sufficient breadth and depth to afford sightings of the transitions that learners face daily in their reading and writing across the school years.

The project reported in Christie and Derewianka (2008) stands out as a departure from the 'short-and-small' tradition. By documenting the range of challenges presented to students over the span of the school years, these researchers advanced our understanding of the nature of literacy demands, and of how they vary over time and across curriculum areas. Applying Systemic Functional Linguistics (e.g. Halliday, 1993, 1999), Christie and Derewianka detailed the changing literacy demands on Australian students of history, science and English.[1] Focusing on lexico-grammatical patterns and text structures, they documented major linguistic changes and milestones along the way, within and across each curriculum area. They drew on Bernstein (1975: 218) to characterise this 'developmental trajectory' as both paralleling and helping to bring about a movement whereby 'simple "commonsense" knowledge' comes to be replaced by 'uncommonsense knowledge'.

With this trajectory Christie and Derewianka have put in place a substantial empirical baseline for our understanding of literacy development over the school years, signposting where and why students experience difficulties, and, in many cases, where they fail to progress on their way towards more abstract knowledge forms. Against this baseline, researchers, such as the contributors to this volume, can highlight difficult, even disorderly, literacy transitions that arise across a range of sites, such as exchange structures in classroom interaction or forms of complexity in images.

But one less noticed source of disorderly transitions may arise from fundamental changes in the quality of the learning work itself, rather than from the replacement of commonsense with uncommonsense. It may, in fact, be that the very assumption that commonsense is displaced presents some difficulties for our analysis of transitions in literacy. In this chapter we set out to examine and critique that assumption, reframing the underlying rationale of the developmental trajectory. Drawing on interpretive possibilities from philosophy and sociology, we aim to replace the idea of a decisive fissure between commonsense and uncommonsense with notions of interplay and evolution.

## Problems with Sense, Common and Otherwise

The centrepiece of Christie and Derewianka's (2008) contribution is a meticulous documentation of the phases of students' reading and writing in English, history and science curriculums, summarised in the form of a general developmental trajectory from early childhood through to late adolescence (p. 218 and pp. 219–37). They characterised the overall trajectory as comprising four milestones:

(i) early childhood: 'simple commonsense' knowledge is used in congruent grammatical forms, with simple expression of attitudes
(ii) mid-childhood to early adolescence: knowledge and attitude become elaborated with expanding grammatical resources
(iii) mid-adolescence: knowledge, attitude and evaluation become 'more uncommonsense' with the growth of grammatical resources
(iv) late adolescence: 'uncommonsense' is expressed in non-congruent grammar to express abstraction, generalisation, value judgement and opinion

Christie and Derewianka took these milestones (i.e. from congruent to increasingly non-congruent grammar) to parallel and enable a movement in knowledge from common to uncommonsense. They based the contrast between common-sense and uncommon-sense knowledge on Bernstein's (1975: 99) formulation of common-sense knowledge as 'everyday community knowledge, of the pupil, his [sic] family, and his peer group', contrasted with the uncommon-sense knowledge that is

> freed from the particular, the local, through the various languages of the sciences or forms of reflexiveness of the arts which make possible either the creation or the discovery of new realities.

Bernstein described common-sense knowledge in terms of its sources in categories of people, namely those in the 'community' around the learner – the family and peer group. But we find no specification of the qualities of the forms of knowledge that characterise commonsense. Instead, Bernstein named what 'uncommonsense knowledge' is 'freed from', the qualities it *no longer* displays: The journey away from 'the particular, the local' was described as a movement towards 'new realities'. Neither the forms of knowledge on which 'commonsensible' learners operate nor the categories of people in the 'community' that surrounds the 'un-commonsensible' learner were provided in this account.

We can draw out some unnecessarily troublesome implications of this definition of 'the uncommon' as a negation of 'the common sense'. First, practitioners of science and the arts are taken to be 'freed' from the particularities of the local circumstances in which they find themselves as practitioners; second, apparently it is not the community that surrounds them that accords them this freedom but rather 'various languages' and 'forms of reflexiveness'; and third, it is assumed that the local social settings in which individuals live cannot afford them access to appropriate, productive understandings about what might be going on in the arts or sciences.

These implications are uninformative if the primary interest is in educational theory and practice, and, at best, questionable if the primary interest is in the philosophy and sociology of knowledge, as found in a range of critiques (see Abbott, 2001; Biesta, 2014; Carlgren, 2020; Haack, 1993; Yates & Young, 2010). One critical question concerns the problematic break between commonsense and uncommonsense: How can utterly novel forms of uncommonsense, in fact 'new realities', emerge via a movement 'away' from the forms of knowing of our local families, peers and communities?

## Co-option – the Interplay of Everyday and the Scientific Rationalities

Here we attempt to address the problem of sense by smoothing the rupture connoted by Bernstein's (1975) dichotomy. For this purpose we turn to the work of philosophers of everyday knowledge (e.g. Husserl, [1900/1901] 2001; Ruggerone, 2013; Schütz, 1943, 1953), as well as to sociologists of 'the everyday' (Garfinkel, 1960, 1967; Sharrock, 2004) to draw attention to the relationship 'between the interests of everyday life and the interests of scientific theorising' (Garfinkel, 1960: 76).

Garfinkel was concerned with the study of rationalities in everyday and scientific activities. He complained that, within sociology, 'rationality' is often defined 'by selecting one or more features from among the properties of scientific activity as it is *ideally* described' (p. 72, emphasis added). This, Garfinkel argued, is an inadequate definition, equating scientific knowledge and procedures with 'rationality' in ways that relegate the 'effective, persistent, and stable' (p. 76) practices of persons in their everyday, practical and generally unnoticed activities to the domain of irrational behaviour, and, thereby, of no interest to formal social science. This relegation of everyday understanding, we argue, parallels conventional understandings of the relationship between common-sense and uncommon-sense knowledge and practice.

Garfinkel set out to circumvent this problem by first identifying a set of everyday reasoning practices, or 'rationalities', that serve *both* the interest of everyday life *and* of scientific theorising:

- categorising and comparing
- assessing the consequences of varying margins for error
- searching for the best means of proceeding
- analysing alternatives and their consequences
- assessing strategies for long- and short-term action

- taking account of timing
- predicting outcomes
- rules and conventions for distinguishing between, for example, facts, suppositions and conjectures
- determining whether or not there is a choice on the matter at hand and
- enumerating and evaluating different grounds for choice

Garfinkel next nominated a set of exclusively specialised 'scientific rationalities':

- compatibility of ends–means relationships with the principles of formal logic
- semantic clarity and distinctness in the use of key constructs, and the compatibility of the usage with socially established norms of usage
- semantic clarity and distinctness 'for its own sake' (p. 75) and
- compatibility of the definition of a situation with established scientific knowledge

Critical to our concerns, these four scientific rationalities Garfinkel took not to replace but to respecify the rationalities of 'everyday life'. Central to this distinction is that 'the practical theorist' achieves an ordering of events while seeking to retain and sanction the presupposition that the objects of the world are as they appear, while scientific theorising presupposes that any 'interpretation be conducted while holding a position of "official neutrality" toward the *belief* that the objects of the world are as they appear' (Garfinkel, 1960: 77).

We can apply this respecification of rationalities to Bernstein's (1975) dichotomy. When scientists and artists, or other 'specialists', are engaged in activities based on specialised theorising (in laboratories, factories, hospitals, workshops, courts of law, psychiatric clinics, classrooms, and so on; as in Lynch, 1993), they are not dispensing with 'everyday community knowledge' or forms of rationality (e.g. from their families and peer groups). Specialists, when acting as specialists, are not 'freed from the particular, the local' features at hand; rather, they are able to re-see, and reinterpret, those features as instances of more specialised rationalities – networks of facts, principles, activities and ethics of practice and communication that constitute the history of consensus among specialists in their field. As an alternative to 'freeing' themselves from the 'particular' and 'the local', on a bifurcated trajectory, we propose a sense of evolution and rationalities-at-interplay, whereby specialists can *more* purposefully attend to the local features at hand, using specialised resources to assess their immediate relevance and to act effectively.

To accommodate this sense of evolutionary and productive interplay between the rationalities of the everyday and of the specialised theorising, we suggest the term 'co-option'.[2] By using this term, we aim to reflect the application of an expanded set of accountabilities to which the rationalities of everyday 'sense' are held when the learning activities are in the interests of specialist theorising in the sciences, humanities, and the arts and crafts. The rationalities of everyday reasoning are co-opted and reworked into the rationalities of specialised theorising as the learner enters into activities that are gradually more fully organised by the history of consensus relating to those specialised interests.

## Co-opting the Everyday with the Theorised: Three Examples

Our discussion so far raises both conceptual and practical questions about how the relationship between everyday and specialised rationalities changes over the school years and beyond. How might we understand the notion of co-option in ways that expand the scope and utility of the developmental trajectory? Here we present three 'exhibits', selected examples of text from in- and out-of-school contexts,[3] all directly or indirectly concerned with scientific discoveries and knowledge-building. We discuss their linguistic development, their apparent common-sense-to-uncommon-sense movement, and 'co-option' in the everyday scientific interplay. Regarding linguistic development, these texts can be located at three points along the developmental trajectory: early childhood, mid-adolescence and late adolescence. We commence these analyses with an outline of each exhibit.

Exhibit 1, *Science news – Scientist drinks bacteria and wins the Nobel Prize!* (ACARA, n.d., a), is presented as a text written by a Year 5 school student (age about eleven years). It takes the form of a news report about the medical discoveries of the cause for stomach ulcers:

Barry Marshall is a doctor from Perth. He won the 2005 Nobel Prize with Robin Warren for finding out what causes stomach ulcers.

About 10% of adults get stomach ulcers. Stomach ulcers cause nausea and vomiting. Before Harry Marshall found out what caused stomach ulcers, lots of people actually died from them.

The text proceeds to describe how Marshall, who 'needed to get proof that his ideas were true', knowingly drank bacteria, got an ulcer and 'took a piece out of his own stomach' to examine it for evidence. This eventually enabled a successful treatment: 'people who get stomach ulcers can take antibiotics and get cured'.

Exhibit 2 is an expository text presented by a school student in Year 10 (ACARA, n.d., b). Accounting for variations and commonalities in astrophysicists' observations and discoveries, the text discusses their contribution to The Big Bang Theory:

> There are numerous theories and pieces of evidence that can possibly explain, that one moment there may have been nothing, and during and after that moment there was something: our universe. 'The Big Bang Theory' is a theory to explain what happened during and after that moment, of how our universe came about.

Following the introduction shown here, the text discusses the implications of Hubble's observations of redshift in electromagnetic waves and how this, together with the 'accidental' discovery of Cosmic Microwave Background Radiation by 'two young radio astronomers', fits into a larger theoretical puzzle relating to radiation in space. After a detailed account of the contributions of several scientists, the text concludes that The Big Bang Theory 'hasn't just been backed up by one person, being Edwin Hubble' and that 'if we hadn't come to discover these theories, even if they were proved wrong, or still remain a fact today, we wouldn't know what we know today about our Universe', a theory to which 'many others can relate their theories and evidence'.

Exhibit 3 is not a school text but a Swedish newspaper editorial: *'It's time for a more realist view on the climate issue'* (Värmby, 2020). It opens like this:

> Most researchers agree that the global climate is getting warmer and that this is caused by human impact. As to what extent, opinions differ.

In contrast to the consensus view, based on 'emotional arguments' that the rate of global warming correlates with increased consumption of fossil fuels, the author presents observations contradicting the consensus:

> A photo from the museum inside the mountain at glazier Kitzsteinhorn in Austria flickers past my mind. The photo shows that the glacier began melting as early as 1905. 'Before the really large carbon dioxide emissions took off', I think to myself. The Earth's climate has always varied significantly with ice ages and warmer periods. The 'Little Ice Age' ended about 1850. Since then, the average temperature has risen until the 1940's, without any major increase in carbon dioxide emissions.

The often-read 'alarming reports', the columnist says, 'come mainly from the UN climate agency IPCC', a 'politically governed organization' that tends to exaggerate the climate threat, something that has 'repeatedly damaged' its credibility. The author refers to 'well-known scientists', and 'climate scientists in the Nordic countries' with whom he has been in contact, to support these claims. Further, when observable facts are compared to modelled predictions, they speak against beliefs held by the IPCC, and the 'approximately 100 climate models' that have been applied have 'not been shown to be consistent with more recently measured, lower, temperatures'. The editorial concludes that 'instead of panicking that the world is going under, we should be focusing on more realistic and attainable measures'.

In turning our attention to linguistic aspects of these exhibits, we can initially note that they generally support the analytic trajectory presented in Christie and Derewianka's (2008) developmental model: Exhibit 1 (the late childhood–early adolescence phase) adequately reflects the grammatical tendencies to be expected from the trajectory – nascent expansion of nominal groups ('a doctor from Perth') and prepositional phrases ('out of his own stomach'); and some emergent use of abstract language (e.g. the nominalised 'vomiting'). Likewise, the author of Exhibit 2 exercises the linguistic competence appropriate for the mid-adolescence phase, including purposeful use of nominalisations and a generally appropriate control of the flow of information, thematically developed throughout large parts of the text (only hinted at in these short excerpts and quotations). Exhibit 3, here representing the trajectory's endpoint and beyond, bears the grammatical marks of an advanced text: The author demonstrates control of thematic development, control ranging from clause to whole-text level, for presenting an argument, given weight by nominalised processes (e.g. 'human impact', 'arguments', 'conclusions' and so on).

The differences among the texts signal increasing linguistic control at the *ideational* level of discourse, the experiential 'what-are-we-talking-about' level. The increased control is reflected in a movement from the ideationally concrete to the abstract, from scientists drinking bacteria to scientific knowledge about factors impacting climate. Does this movement also reflect an underlying epistemological shift from the world of 'commonsense' to that of 'uncommonsense'? It is unsatisfactory to attribute to the more or less overtly climate-denialist Exhibit 3 a high degree of 'uncommonsense knowledge' (if that is taken to be scientifically valued), while confining Exhibit 1 entirely to the realm of 'commonsense'.

The contrast between the texts is more productively explored by examining how the authors present 'facts of the matter', beyond the logical and causal relations found at the ideational level. In other words, how do these authors evaluate what they are talking about? This takes our analysis to the *interpersonal* level of discourse, the 'to-whom-am-I-talking' level, where we draw on Appraisal Theory (henceforth AT; Martin & White, 2005) to map lexico-grammatical differences between the texts. The developmental trajectory of Christie and Derewianka (2008) predicts increasing control of the lexis that authors make use of in order to orient to the topics of the texts (their *attitudinal positioning*, in the terminology of AT). Here we are interested not only in the level of control but also in how each author enacts interpersonal meanings that configure a distinct image of how science builds knowledge. For this part of our examination, we use a subset of the analytical repertoire of AT, its three types of attitudinal positioning: *affect*, concerned with emotional responses; *judgement*, concerned with assessment of human behaviour in reference to socially sanctioned norms of (in these cases, scientific) conduct; and *appreciation*: the assessment of form, impact and significance of a process or an individual.

We see immediately that all exhibits work with these resources for appraisal. As will become clear, however, the authors' differing images of scientific knowledge-building are contingent on the way everyday understanding is woven together with theorised knowledge. The nature of this interweaving can, we argue, be productively discussed in terms of co-option. To lay the ground for this discussion, we turn our attention to some marked differences in what is being appreciated (in AT terms) in the exhibits.

The author of Exhibit 1 tends to foreground the moral and ethical aspects of Marshall's person and conduct (the *propriety* of his behaviour, in AT judgement terms), such as his praiseworthy refusal to 'give people stomach ulcers on purpose'. The language for appraisal is not, however, exclusively directed at Marshall as an individual; the benefits of medical research for mankind are noted – stomach ulcers can now be cured.

In contrast Exhibit 2 (the Year 10 text) is less concerned with judgement or appreciation of individual behaviour. The attitudinal resources most evident are resources for *appreciation*, directed at (applying appreciation subcategories) the composition (the internal logic and the complexity) and valuation (the scientific interest) of the discoveries. The lexis for appreciation in Exhibit 2 reflects a recognition of both the discoveries and how they are integrated into the larger scientific process: 'many others can relate their theories and evidence [to the Big Bang theory]'.

Turning to Exhibit 3 (the editorial), a marked attitudinal difference is visible in terms of judgement and appreciation, here overwhelmingly negative in evaluating scientific findings, at least the ones pertaining to climate science. Attitudinally, the author advances the argument by constructing a dichotomy between 'emotion' and 'logic', claiming the former has distorted scientific knowledge in the public discourse. Positive evaluation of 'logic' is rarely stated in the text but rather, in AT terms, invoked. The evaluation is accomplished by the author's evident aim to position him- or herself as a neutral observer of facts, as opposed to public opinion and the IPPC. By detailing personal visits to glaciers, studying photos (the icons of 'truth') and reading reports, positive judgement is invoked as (AT categories are in parenthesis) accomplished (demonstrating *capacity*), meticulous (demonstrating *tenacity*), and honest and unassuming (demonstrating, respectively, *veracity* and *propriety*). We are invited to infer that the 'compiling' of 'alarming reports' (invoking negative *judgement* of the *capacity* of the politicised IPCC) contrasts with the author's calm approach. 'Compiles', in the context of the columnist's criticism, serves to reinforce negative appraisal, implying that the IPCC is being inappropriately selective and insistent in presenting its results. Equally subtle is the use of the word 'unfortunately', one of the few words in the text we have analysed as *affect*. In context ('unfortunately, this has repeatedly damaged the credibility of the IPCC'), this choice of wording implies simultaneous support for the IPCC and dismay at its self-damaging practices. The text, nonetheless, invests all the rhetorical and linguistic resources at its disposal in undermining the IPCC's credibility. And the reader is left with an impression that this stark criticism comes unwillingly from an observer who writes not just impartially, but from the heart.

The analyses cast some light on how these three authors, by attitudinal lexis, produce three distinct images of scientific knowledge-building. To summarise, key distinctions are: In Exhibit 1, individual scientists make new discoveries and render old theories and findings obsolete; in Exhibit 2, scientists are part of an integrated whole, where individual discoveries may find or lose their significance later, according to ongoing theory-building in the wider research community; in Exhibit 3, scientific discoveries are guided by observation of facts and critical reasoning, a process unfortunately undermined by political agenda.

In reference to the developmental trajectory, these texts would ideally reflect the movement from 'commonsense' to 'uncommonsense'. But there is something clearly missing, made even more apparent in analysis of attitudinal lexis, in the idea that Exhibit 3, although foregrounding critical reasoning, would constitute an example of 'uncommon-sense' scientific knowledge. Shifting our analytical framework to accommodate conceptualisations of 'everyday' and 'scientific' rationalities, we can re-examine how these exhibits use complementary sets of rationalities. Garfinkel (1960), for instance, took these rationalities to be properties of scientific and common-sense activities performed by individuals. Our re-examination uses AT to address how these properties are valued.

Re-examining Exhibit 1 this way, we see the young author foregrounding a range of everyday rationalities: *categorising and comparing* (when comparing different types of causes for ulcers), *analysis of alternatives and consequences*, and *rules of procedure* (evident in appraisal of the approach and ethical considerations involved in Marshall's self-experimentation). Exhibit 1 undeniably signals both a logic and what Garfinkel would term 'scientific grounds of choice'. These identified rationalities are all in the 'everyday' domain in Garfinkel's list of properties. They are, in this exhibit, brought to bear on the conduct of scientific research, something Garfinkel would find unsurprising, given his argument that scientific practices apply both sets of rationalities in interplay. We could observe that Exhibit 1, in presenting scientific knowledge-building as a process of hypothesising and experimenting, displays emerging signs, and thereby potential for interplay, of one of the 'scientific' rationalities: the *compatibility of the definition of a situation with scientific knowledge*.

Everyday rationalities are on display in Exhibit 2. We see *categorising and comparing* throughout the text (evident in the long original version, where the author compares, among other things, the properties of 'redshift' and 'blueshift' wavelengths), along with *analysis of alternatives and consequences* in the evaluation of the Hubble discoveries. But the text also displays notable 'scientific rationalities'. Meticulously defining and explaining terms and phenomena, it adheres to the principle of *semantic clarity and distinctness*.[4] The author is no less meticulous in trying to show that all the discoveries, observations and theory-development presented in the text gain their value not by being inherently 'groundbreaking' but by being subjected to the processes of scrutiny that have developed over the history of consensus within a scientific community. In other words, the rationale for *compatibility of the definition of a situation* (only hinted at in Exhibit 1) is in clear view here, lending additional scientific force to the everyday rationalities of comparing, contrasting and analysing consequences.

This productive interplay between the two sets of rationalities exemplifies what we mean by 'co-option'. The rationalities of the 'everyday' are 'repurposed', functioning as integral parts of, in these cases, an emergent specialised, scientific approach. Comparing Exhibits 1 and 2 we conclude that everyday rationalities have not been 'abandoned' in the latter, nor has the text moved into a world of 'uncommonsense'. Similarly, the young composer of Exhibit 1 does not seem trapped in the particularities of the 'commonsense community'. Rather, local everyday rationalities of comparing and contrasting can be seen as demonstrating critical moments of interplay, productively co-opted in instructional settings.

In Exhibit 3, discussing climate science, several everyday rationalities are found: The logic of *tolerable error* (the degree of fit between what is observed and what is expected) is applied in the author's observation of sea-level rise;

and in comparing these observations to research-predicted outcomes, the author is signalling an adherence to principles of *predictability* and *rule of procedure*. In this text these and other rationalities appear in an authoritative language that establishes the author as an arbiter of what constitutes scientific knowledge. While Exhibit 1 (implicitly) and Exhibit 2 (explicitly) seek to align their accounts of scientific knowledge-construction with the epistemological practices of science, Exhibit 3 evaluates scientific findings on the basis of whether they are supported by the IPCC or if they align with the views of certain researchers 'approved' (namely, those identified as 'well-known') by the author, as well as with the author's personal experiences.

In Garfinkel's (1960) language, the author's *rules of procedure* for determining valid knowledge seem 'tribal', rather than 'Cartesian'. Although everyday rationalities are not, per se, 'non-scientific', it is not clear that the author has employed any of the scientific rationalities that we view in Exhibits 1 and 2. Whereas Exhibit 2 is concerned with demonstrating that the production of numerous observations and theories adds to the strength of the scientific process, the author of Exhibit 3 implies that the sheer amount of the 'approximately 100 climate models' is in itself a basis for suspicion. To apply the notion of co-option, while the everyday rationalities of Exhibit 1 and 2 epistemologically orient towards a scientific position of 'official neutrality', the everyday rationalities of Exhibit 3 do not display this same co-option; rather, the observations and conclusions of this author detach themselves from 'compatibility with scientific knowledge'.

## Conclusion: A Curriculum for Co-opting and Repurposing the Everyday

Our metaphorical use of the evolution-based concept of 'co-option' is not meant to indicate that school learning is a process that lacks 'direction, purpose, or forethought' (as in McLennan's (2008) definition of evolutionary co-option). Rather, its intent is to call for an interpretation of literacy development that sees abilities and competencies not as a process of abandonment and replacement but rather as one of ongoing evolution and repurposing, coming to take on new functions for truth- and utility-value under the regimens of new, specialised circumstances. The 'co-option' metaphor emphasises the complex set of demands that institutionalised pedagogical practices present to *learners*. But from the perspective of those learners, co-option may even be more than metaphorical, if understood as a pedagogy that 'renders the tasks of understanding a curriculum that is beyond what they know, a curriculum they nonetheless can do' (Macbeth, 2011: 446). In terms of what young students know about the curriculum's plans for their knowledge and thought, co-options are likely unforeseen, and so may well reflect the original, literal description.

Bernstein's (1975) narrative for schooling is a process in which learners abandon what and how they know to gain entry to an idealised scientific and/ or artistic community – displaying freedom from the particular and the local features of everyday social and material life that seem to be all the 'family and peer group' can offer. As a complement to this view (sometimes presented as a contrast between 'horizontal' and 'vertical' discourse, see Bernstein, 1999), we have suggested a notion of non-mutually exclusive 'rationalities' (Garfinkel, 1960). What this view offers a learner who is a socially present agent, able to act rationally – thoughtfully, effectively, ethically – working with the particularities of the everyday world, while still open to a co-opting pedagogy that helps bring these rationalities, gradually, perhaps haltingly, into partnership with regime of specialised accountabilities.

The co-option metaphor presents some alternative interpretations of Christie and Derewianka's findings (2008). Their map of discernible linguistic changes along the developmental trajectory deepens our understanding of transitions across the landscape of school literacy. As our three exhibits illustrate, specialised vocabulary (non-congruent language, lexis for reasoned attitudes and so on) can afford specialised theorising, and, as Christie and Derewianka (2008: 218) commented, the expanded vocabulary 'parallels and makes possible the developments of knowledge'. Our comparisons of Exhibit 1, 2, and 3, however, point to a crucial difference between 'make possible' and 'make happen'. Congruent language (as in Exhibit 1) seems not to stand entirely in the way of scientific rationalities co-opting the everyday; while, inversely, the non-congruent language of Exhibit 3 does not, of itself, guarantee the co-option of these rationalities.

This observation has implications for schools, alerting us to the gradual, 'worked-up' nature of transitions – they are neither only taught nor only learned. Transitions call for closely observed, explicitly described teacher–learner reflections on how specialised truth-claims rework what is known from the everyday rationalities. Transitions can be realised in different forms, and at different developmental moments, under the interests of differing disciplines of inquiry (MacDonald, 1994). The interdependence of knowing and making claims about the truth – the ontology–epistemology relation – develops through enculturation into the consensus at work in each specialised domain of inquiry (Haack, 1993).

In that sense, transitions relate to Vygotsky's ([1934] 1978) view that certain functions become well enough developed that they gradually connect to and inform other functionalities, that it is this developmental work of inter-relating, repurposing linguistic, cognitive and social functionalities that the learner needs to perform under expert guidance and scaffolding. These work sites appear at different tempos, in different sequences and maybe at different moments. As a consequence a co-opting pedagogy can be associated with *learning activity* (derived from Vygotskyan theories by Davydov, see 2008) and the principle that school subjects should form their pedagogies around problems that students need to solve in order to 'reproduce the actual process whereby people have created concepts, images, values and norms' (Davydov, 2008: 121). We can see that this is a process characterised by 'the ascent from the abstract to the concrete' (p. 120) rather than the reverse.

In other words, the everyday rationalities of the 'Exhibit 1' student, the categorising and comparing, the analysing of alternatives, the predicting of outcomes and so on, need to be put to work in learning activities that reflect scientific process of inquiry (i.e. co-opted with the scientific rationalities). The integration of these rationalities into a more integrated scientific whole seems to be the feature that distinguishes the understandings of science shown in Exhibit 2 and Exhibit 3, rather than their differing levels of linguistic control.

Such co-opting learning activities take in the rationalities of everyday thought and activity, themselves 'abstractions', to make possible the access to specialised forms of curriculum and pedagogy. The apparent devaluation of these everyday modes of acting and knowing – indeed, their status as epistemological enclosures from which the learner needs to be 'freed' – may form part of an answer to questions about why and where we find 'disorderly' transitions in institutionalised literacy learning. We find these transitions not where they have been inadvertently left but precisely where we have put them – in the process of establishing grade levels, large classes, curriculum programs with fixed, 'normatively' legitimated tempos and sequences, standardised in spite of our recurring acknowledgement of the diverse needs and goals of learners, and of the varying histories and mores of the curriculum domains. In this sense we are behaving like Garfinkel's (1960: 77) practical theorists, 'seeking to retain and sanction the presupposition that the objects of the world are as they appear'. To put that another way, we educators – teachers, curriculum designers, researchers and the rest – act on a resolutely 'commonsensical' view of transitions in literacy learning, whereas the students may need us to act on conceptually well-grounded knowledge about when and how the various curriculum specialisations can productively co-opt, rather than replace, their understanding of the interests of everyday social activity.

# Envoi to Part I: Literacy Transitions as Distributed, Participatory Practice

Jennifer Rowsell

Transitions have steadily and insistently encroached on literacy theory and curriculum since the beginning of the century. Largely due to the ascendance of technologies, the increasing gap between home and school, and conceptual and theoretical efforts to move literacy through turns such as a spatial turn (Leander & Sheehy, 2004; Mills & Comber, 2015), a temporal turn (Compton-Lilly, 2016; Lemke, 2000), a post-human turn (Kuby, Gutshall Rucker & Kirchhofer, 2015; Kuby, Spector & Thiel, 2018) and an affect turn (Leander & Boldt, 2013; Leander & Ehret, 2019), transitions in literacy theory have been big and small but, without doubt, constant. Ushering literacy researchers, theorists and, most importantly, educators into the twenty-first century, transitions are necessary to move and transform literacy from twentieth-century book-ruled, word-driven literacy practices to screen-based, hybrid and multimodal communicational practices.

In the book, transitions cover discipline-specific literacy practices as well as broader, more socially, culturally, politically motivated literacy practices. The first section of the collection explores time-honoured literacy transitions as those profiled in the first chapter by Jones and Edwards-Groves such as cognitive transitions, constructivist transitions, pragmatic transitions that have resulted from seminal educational theory by Blooms, Montessori and Dewey to name a few. Weekes's chapter gives readers a landscape view of transitions within more conventional definitions of literacy and the core literacy strands of oral language, reading and writing. Stepping back to appreciate phonemic, semantic, grammatical and compositional transitions that are key to schooling also gives us pause to recognise a striking difference between schooled literacy and vernacular literacy practices. That is, these subtle transitions from sound to enunciations or from adverbial clauses to paragraph cohesion sit in contrast to the daunting task of reimagining what literacy is or should be in an age of social media, immersive worlds and touch-based reading. Derewianka's chapter dives deep into writing transitions moving from audience to purpose to composition to researching to the reviewing stages of writing. These movements and transitions through the writing process are unlikely to change much in the next twenty years, yet 'writing' in everyday lives has changed and calls on more modalities and rhetorical approaches that are no longer reliant solely on words and phrases, but instead on acumen with design and multiple modes (Cope & Kalantzis, 2000; Kress, 2010). Finally, Kindenberg and Freebody offer readers an intellectual lens on transitions in literacy theory and curriculum. Stepping back and drawing in developmental transitions from child to adult, Kindenberg and Freebody locate transitional pinch points over ages and stages, eloquently reminding readers that schooled literacy needs to form pedagogies around problems different age groups face to make schooling relevant, fulfilling and grounded in people's lives and lived experiences. As they say, it is a vision of transitions in literacy theory and curriculum that *moves from the abstract to the concrete.*

There is indeed a nostalgic feel to this first section in the book. What makes contemporary literacy theory and curriculum so confounding, and troubling, at the moment are the tremendous gaps between what schools regard as the problems facing age groups and how to craft curricula around them and what younger generations actually feel are the problems and issues they are facing and the ways that pedagogies respond to them. This is not the fault of teachers or schools in my view. This issue falls at the feet of international literacy policy and curricula developers. The simple truth at the moment is: schools are losing young people because of a clinging to anachronistic versions of literacy theory and curricula. I realise this is a dramatic statement, but it is not too far from what is increasingly featured in media, and Covid-19 has only increased transitional gaps and problems (Arreaza, Robertson & Ruben, 2020; Bloom, 2018; Jack, 2020). Renderings of literacy transitions that should be (more) present in formal schooling have to do not only with programmatic and pedagogic transitions but also with pedagogic time and space. That is, children and teenagers require different kinds of literacy pedagogy that speak directly to where their passions lie, which of course varies and is shaped around interests. Nevertheless, generally speaking, literacy should involve an account of varied modal and artistic forms including words, but with a much greater focus on words combined with other forms of expression and representations and the transitions that naturally ensue when combining photographs with written narratives or adding sound to moving image compositions (Rowsell, 2013, 2017). Transitions in literacy theory and curriculum should also collapse disciplinary silos so that literacy work sits comfortably alongside STEM work with young people making and building alongside each other (Marsh et al., 2017). Teachers need longer blocks of time to complete this kind of literacy/design work in pedagogic spaces. What is more, they need spaces equipped with software, tools and technologies to let students run free with ideas and with access to digital repository to curate information and to research as needed. What this means is moving from literacy as an isolated, solitary practice (e.g. reading a book at a desk or writing a five-paragraph essay) to a distributed, participatory practice involving a modular view of reading and writing (Kress, 2010). These types of literacy transitions are less about linear movements across pages in desks or at tables and instead studio and design transitions from laptops or desktops on tables to workspaces with tools and technologies back to digital texts and then to the editing table. Teaching in this reimagined sense of literacy transitions involves more cross-sector instruction between educators and professionals like graphic designers and more co-designing workshops as opposed to stand-and-deliver methods (Rowsell, 2013).

There is such wisdom in Kindenberg and Freebody's claim to shift focus from generational and developmental transitional pinch points and to focus on pedagogies that emerge from problems and ruling passions (Barton & Hamilton, 1998) of the young and the very young. Research needed now must attend to seismic changes and transitions in the world and this demands paradigm shifts away from book-led academic learning to learning that is participatory, action-oriented about issues that matter to young people and that are in the service of their problems and their provocations.

# Part II

# Investigating the Conditions for Literacy Learning and Teaching in Transition

# 5

# Transition from Preschool to School: Spaces, Time, Interactions and Resources

### Lisa Kervin and Jessica Mantei

## Introduction

The importance of literacy education in the early years is well documented and universally supported. The early childhood period prior to school entry is recognised as an important stage in which to establish the foundations for later literacy and numeracy (Zubrick, Taylor & Christensen, 2015). Therefore, the transition from prior-to-school settings to their first year of formal school is not only a major milestone for children but also a critical timepoint for literacy learning. In this chapter we examine literacy experiences offered in an early childhood setting and a classroom from the first year of compulsory, formal schooling from the perspective of the way learning space/s are used, the time for literacy learning, opportunities for interaction and use of resources. We consider these from the perspective of young children to more fully understand the complexities of transition to formal education. And we argue for an approach to teaching in the first years of formal school that embraces and capitalises on the experiences, beliefs and literacy dispositions of learners.

Depending on the Australian state or territory, the year before a child attends school may be referred to as preschool, preparatory, Kindergarten or transition. Attendance at any prior-to-school service is optional for Australian families. Prior-to-school services can be government run or privately owned. Some offer long day care while others replicate the timing of a 'school' day. Some children attend prior-to-school services from as early as six weeks old, while others may begin when they turn three or four.

This chapter reports on literacy learning in two settings in the Australian state of New South Wales (NSW). The first is a prior-to-school service where children aged between four and five years are in their final year before attending formal school. In NSW this is called preschool. The second is a setting where children are engaging in their first year of formal school. Again, depending on the state, the first year of formal school may be referred to as Kindergarten, reception, prep, pre-primary or foundation. In NSW, this is called Kindergarten[1] and children are between four and six years old.

Regardless of the educational context, the literacy experiences offered to children will reflect their educators' beliefs about literacy. Specifically, these experiences reflect the educators' beliefs about what it means to be a reader and a writer, and what it means to communicate in our society. These beliefs and subsequent decisions are impacted by cultural, historical, political and social discourses that contextualise educators' work. In the Australian curriculum, for example, children are expected to become proficient readers and writers as a result of their first years at school. Indeed, many children in prior-to-school services (and their families as well) also believe they will learn to read in their first year of school. These beliefs are based on values emerging from social contexts and histories of schools and learning. Immediately central to these beliefs is the way literacy is defined and, ultimately, the perceived role of educational institutions in people's lives.

The implicit beliefs and ideologies held by educators, policymakers, educational leaders and society as a whole about literacy, and about learning and teaching inform the ways schools are organised including the pace, sequencing and structure of curriculum. Contexts within which children learn to be literate can vary considerably. While there are many models of instruction throughout Australia (e.g. traditional models of instruction and critical inquiry models), increased measures of accountability and standardised assessment (and earlier prevalence of these in primary grades) drive the literacy opportunities made available in schools.

Social interactions are an integral part of literacy experiences. Through conversation children are able to negotiate access to space and materials, explore social relationships among participants and make connections to their own personal experiences. Conversation provides access to the perspectives of others. The conversations that children have opportunity to engage with matter for literacy learning (Bloome & Katz, 1997). Opportunities for children to participate in meaningful interactions with peers and educators allow them to generate, test and refine their literacy knowledge through conversation, observation and experimentation.

Our research occurred during a time of considerable curriculum reform, both at national and state levels. From that time, early childhood settings have been guided by a National Quality Framework that was developed by the Australian and state and territory governments with input from the early childhood sector and early childhood academics (DEEWR, 2009). While there is no mandated curriculum associated with this national framework, and therefore no scope and sequence for the development of specific skills for developing proficiency in reading, writing, talking and listening, central to this document are principles, practices and outcomes to guide educators as they support children's learning from birth to five years of age, including their transition to school. Although the Early Years Learning Framework (DEEWR, 2009) was reasonably well established across the early childhood sector at the time of data collection, those working with children in the year prior to their transition to primary school were feeling the effects of changes in the primary sector.

Since 2010, all Kindergarten children in NSW have been administered the Best Start assessment within their first five weeks of attending school. It is administered by teachers with the intention to identify children's mastery of a set of literacy and numeracy skills (NSW Department of Education and Training, 2009). Campbell, Torr and Cologon (2012, 2014) note significant push-down on the prior-to-school sector for educators to utilise behaviourist principles of direct instruction to drill young children in so-called 'basic skills' such as phonics as many families and educators strive to ensure children are 'school ready'. Comber and Kamler (2004) remind us of the importance of connection in pedagogical practice. Given the push-down of skills, it is important to consider what this period of transition from preschool to the first terms of Kindergarten looks and feels like for a child.

For the purposes of this chapter, we identify a sample of literacy experiences that appear quite similar in purpose across the preschool and Kindergarten settings. We analyse each in terms of the ways learning space/s are used, the time for literacy learning, opportunities for interaction with both educators and children, and use of resources. We draw upon our observations, interview data and analysed video excerpts of literacy experiences to extract examples of practice. We engaged with each of the sites weekly (at the invitation of the educators) during the periods of October to December (in the prior-to-school setting) and the following February to April (in the school setting). Interviews were conducted before and after visits. While these experiences may appear comparable, the ways children are expected to navigate the different structures and processes are quite different. It is not our intention to critique the teaching practices. Instead, we aim to examine the nature of the children's literacy experiences from one setting to another and the implications of the different demands during this critical transition point.

The literacy experiences we draw upon are from two consecutive educational contexts – a preschool setting and a primary school Kindergarten classroom. Both are located in the inner-city suburb of a large Australian city.

## Literacy Learning Space/s

Broadly, we refer to space as the physical environment and its organisation where literacy learning occurs. We consider these spaces to be intricate social worlds where participants interact in nuanced ways with processes and materials that are determined by the ideologies of educators in interplay with the lives of children (Kervin, Comber & Baroutsis, 2019). We look to the structures and boundaries within these spaces that may be specialised, constructed and regulated as part of literacy pedagogies (Bernstein, [1996] 2000). As children move between educational spaces, there is a need to engage in a process of recontextualisation as they negotiate new practices across symbolic, social and ideological borders (Bauman & Briggs, 1990). Dyson (2001, p. 14) argues that 'children must stretch familiar resources from their communicative experiences into new social constellations if they are to participate meaningfully in the literacy practices of school'.

The participants in each of the spaces we draw from in this chapter work within 'rules'. We draw upon our earlier work (Mantei & Kervin, 2018) to show how these differ between contexts and can be ill-defined from the perspective of child participants. The weak classifications of invisible literacy pedagogies are often characterised by large spaces with flexible boundaries that allow freedom of movement and choice of activity. Conversely, the strongly classified spaces of visible literacy pedagogies are controlled by the educator and fixed in nature, such as a floor space in front of the teacher for the delivery of predetermined and specialised content. An examination of space, then, enables us to consider how pedagogies impact the social nature of learning.

The preschool space has two areas – the preschool classroom and the outside area. We observe the educators and children treat these spaces as one, as they all move freely between the areas.

In the Kindergarten classroom children were grouped according to their performance in assessments, this was represented in terms of space by the small groups they worked with and where they were physically asked to be (i.e. their place on the floor or the desk they worked at). In both of these contexts we see spaces and places where literacy experiences occur.

## Time for Literacy Learning

The ways educators choose to organise literacy time send clear messages to children about what is important. We focus on time at the macro-level to examine the ways time defines the broader literacy session through the sequencing and pacing of specific experiences (Bernstein, [1996] 2000). At the micro-level, literacy experiences are examined within the session that are bound by a specific focus and criteria. The way time features in the interactions between participants provides insight into the pedagogical decisions of the teacher and opportunities for children to demonstrate knowledge. The decision to use implicit time management of content, sequencing and personalised learning progression provides greater control in the experience to the child. However, explicit sequencing, demonstrated through careful time management and progression through content, provides the teacher with increased control over the experience (Mantei & Kervin, 2018).

Interview data from educators in the preschool revealed a position that literacy is a set of social practices through which relationships could be built and learning could occur within a play-based construct. One educator explained, 'Literacy is pretty much incorporated in everything we do.' The educators detailed the ways they plan for intentional literacy teaching that was differentiated for children across the day. These children's needs, interests and capacities formed the central focus of the planned experiences with the aim to model and extend language and to develop interpersonal skills through 'language and literacy-based experiences … singing songs … reading stories and sharing books together, finger plays, puppet stories, lots of different ways to expand and introduce children to language and make language seem exciting to them'. Alongside planned literacy learning experiences, the educators were also alert to spontaneous opportunities that presented themselves throughout the day upon which they could capitalise for literacy learning. In these instances, time loosely bound the opportunities for literacy learning, as the educators and children responded to each other.

Literacy was viewed as transferrable and flexible across time and space and used to meet a range of needs from the teachable moment to accommodating a larger group than could not be housed in the reading corner. In one example, the 'veggie patch' became an extended focus for literacy learning. Signs had been erected labelling the area as 'The Veggie Patch'. Small labels on sticks identified different seedlings as tomatoes and corn. A makeshift bookshelf containing picture books, brochures and magazines about planting and sowing vegetables was positioned next to a low bench where educators and children may spend time together or alone being part of the vegetable growing process. And an iPad was located nearby, allowing educators and children to capture changes and new events in this space.

For children identified as being in transition to Kindergarten, specific times were set aside for developing a particular set of literacies. The educators acknowledged the preference of some parents that their children spend time being taught specific skills such as writing letters, words and their name by including in their transition programme 'lots of opportunities to practise writing and drawing'. However, a greater focus was on the children's skills for interaction such as listening, clarity in speech and the confidence to share ideas in a group, along with independence and 'self-help skills' because 'there's one teacher to 30 kids'. The development of interpersonal skills and independence in preparation for the new setting of primary school appears to have been prioritised over the learning of individual items because 'they'll get enough of that later when they go to school'.

Once in Kindergarten – with its more formal curriculum – the children participate in the literacy session, a two-hour designated block of time each morning every day. This sustained block of time is dedicated to literacy instruction. The teacher schedules a series of mini-lessons within the literacy session with the aim of teaching components of reading, writing, talking and listening. During the literacy session, the teacher moves the children between whole-class teaching episodes, small group teaching and independent work. The different groupings are designed to scaffold different skills and processes of literacy learning related to developing proficiency in reading, writing, talking and listening. During our period of observations, literacy was bound by pockets of time for whole class 'read alouds'[2] with letter and word study, whole class fine motor exercises, small group teacher-led and independent activities, handwriting, modelled writing and independent writing.

In her follow-up interview the teacher described the immediate need to keep moving, describing the pace of the literacy session as 'full-on for the two hours. So, we're into one thing, then there's the next and it leads into each other.' She emphasised the importance of 'hands-on experiences' that included phonics games, morning routines including (somewhat unusually) 'visual learning' where the children interpreted a picture each day using the sentence starter, 'I infer …'.

From a broader time perspective, the teacher shared a belief that these short lessons were cumulative events contributing to children's development across days and weeks and even into the following year. The teacher perceived her role, in this trajectory, to 'know my stuff and [know] where I have to take the children … Children need to know where they are and where they need to go to next as well'. In attempting to ensure time well spent, she sent home rubrics that mapped out the children's expected development in the discrete areas of reading, writing, talking and listening 'so they were aware of what we want them to be [because] parents have got different expectations to what we as teachers know where they should be'.

But this movement along the continuum is not an individual endeavour; 'Learning intentions' and 'success criteria', and the scope and sequence document from the synthetic phonics programme, were also identified as important for tracking learning across time. Indeed, the teacher indicated that the scope and sequence document showed that following six weeks of learning about phonics and moving through programme content (CVCC words to CVCC words using graphemes to read polysyllabic words), the children were ready to move to the next set of words because 'they're able to blend graphemes together and sound out words much easier and faster'. While there is pressure to move quickly within the contexts of the literacy session, the children spend equal time learning each set in the commercial programme and they move through the programme as a class.

The need to move quickly, yet to move all together is a clear tension for this teacher and her intention to get the children 'where they should be', not only in the immediate context of Kindergarten but into the future as well. The teacher observed there to be 'a lot of [reading] levels to get through in Year 1' and so she tries to 'push them up more'. She described a series of reading strategies she developed with a focus on reading fluency, 'use the camera words, sound out, segmenting words and sounding them out, rather than just looking at pictures for the clues'. While the teacher observed that with these skills, the children 'seem to move a lot faster', there appeared to be no acknowledgement of individual children's developmental progress, their aptitude or ability to take on the concepts.

## Opportunities for Interactions

Literacy practices are socially and culturally constructed as children develop social relationships. Interactions have long been understood as integral to the learning process (e.g. Rowe, 1989). In educational settings, it is common for children and educators to read, write and interact with each other. How this happens presents important considerations for how literacy learning is positioned. The different opportunities children and educators have to respond, create meaning, demonstrate understanding and communicate matter. Children learn to be literate as they interact with others. Noticing what people do with literacy, with whom, when and how is central to literacy as a social practice (Taylor, 2019).

Social control is a feature of the interactions within any discourse (Bernstein, 1975), and it becomes evident through the interactions between participants. Interactions in this chapter refer to exchanges between and among the people in educational settings, allowing levels of control and use of power to be examined. We acknowledge the important role that patterns of talk and role relationships have on not only what children learn but also how they learn (Heap, 1985). An examination of the interactions between and among the teacher and children offers insights into the literacy demands of the learning experiences that teachers design and children participate in. That is, it allows us to consider the content and pedagogical knowledge required for planning and teaching literacy experiences and literacy expertise to complete these.

The important role of play in the lives of young children is well established. We were particularly interested to see how interactions through play were represented in the literacy experiences. In preschool, the children regularly engaged in imaginative play scenarios. One such instance we captured from an observation in a prior-to-school setting follows:

> A group of children have decided to play a game in the 'home corner' of the classroom. There are dress-up costumes, a large house structure, shelving with artefacts from home, dolls, table and table settings. One of the children brings some loose-leaf paper, markers and scissors to the space. The paper is folded in half and decorated. These become the 'tickets' to enter the space, issued to friends as they make costume selections. After some dancing and putting the babies to bed the play moves to a tea party as the table is set and much conversation and role play occurs as imaginary food and drink are consumed. None of this could have happened without being issued a ticket to enter.

Role-play and drama activities are important for literacy learning. Through our observations, we captured an instance of role-play in the Kindergarten class during a whole class read-aloud. In this instance drama was used to develop the children's understandings of the events of the story and to support vocabulary development as they described their response.

> During the read-aloud the teacher paused three times. Each time, she picks up on an event in the story and asks the children to stand and make a dramatic response. Each role play only takes 1-2 minutes as the children stand, express their understanding using the 'freeze frame' drama strategy and resume their place on the floor as the read-aloud continues. The teacher participates alongside the children, exaggerating her reactions to demonstrate to the children the connection between her feeling and action.

As the teacher looks across the class, she names the responses she can see, for example identifying someone who was 'frightened'.

The seamless movement between the indoor and outdoor areas at the preschool created a sense of flexibility in the ways space could be used for literacy learning and subsequent potential for interaction. For example:

An educator sits outside in the middle of the play area on a park bench, a group of ten children gather around. The educator has a pile of picture books beside her. Some are familiar to the children, others are new. They read a story and move onto another. The educator responds to requests from the children. Each new story begins with the educator identifying the author and illustrator. The educator says 'and [the author] made this story up so you could listen to it'. As the stories are read the group of children sit close to the educator. As the reading continues, other children join the reading. Some children are on a nearby climbing frame, listening. There are children running around the group, riding bikes, pushing wheeled toys, calling to each other. The reading continues without interruption. The educator invites children to point to details in the illustrations on the pages and to share their predictions and observations related to the stories. Four books are read consecutively during this time.

Reading stories is a daily experience for these preschool children. They read for enjoyment, discuss book conventions and choose to participate in the experience. Interactions are positive, fluid and while the educator orchestrates the experience, the children control their involvement.

The Kindergarten classroom, on the other hand, has a carpeted area at the front of the classroom where all twenty-two children can gather with their teacher. The children are instructed to move to the floor area close to the easel.

The teacher is seated on a swivel chair at the front of the space, she has a big book on an easel ready to read. She invites the children to move closer to the book saying, 'You know this story, so you're going to help me read it.' This is the story the children have read every morning for the past week. The teacher begins the reading with a commentary about people who create texts, keen to get the children to name the terms author and illustrator. The children appear familiar with this content and volunteer both terms. The teacher puts on a tiara, a signal to the children that no one may speak or call out during the reading. The story is read aloud, as each page is finished, the teacher asks questions directed to the content in the story. They talk about vocabulary and the meaning of the story.

Reading a big book is a daily experience for these Kindergarten children. A big book is selected each week and reread daily as the teacher identifies and builds on particular reading skills and knowledge. Reading the same text provides familiarity as they develop language and listening skills and build their understanding of the written word.

Drawing was valued across both prior-to-school and school contexts, although there was a shift in the purpose and audience for drawing. In the preschool classroom we saw children draw inside and outside using a range of available resources that could be transported wherever it is that they wanted to use them. We consistently observed a lot of talk around the drawing activities and drawings took a range of styles – everything from big, swiping marks, to spirals and scribbles and more densely coloured shapes. What was important though was the meanings the children attributed to their creations and the representation of what the drawing meant, often connected to life experience.

While drawing also featured in the Kindergarten class, it was more structured and controlled. For example, we captured the following example from practice:

> The teacher has stopped reading a familiar text just before its ending. Each child is given an A5 piece of card on which to draw and/or write about the ending they would like for the story. Completed drawings are collated into a large box held by the teacher to be revealed one-by-one each day as they re-read the story and innovate on the ending.

These examples highlight how regular literacy experiences – an educator reading a book or the opportunity for a child to draw a picture – can indeed have quite different expectations across the contexts. For a child in transition, it is imperative that they learn that, while similar, these literacy events demand quite different processes. How it is that children become aware of what is expected of them, what is important with regard to literacy learning and how to meet their educator's purpose and expectations is of interest to us. The two contexts have different constraints and expectations which may or may not be made explicit and may or may not be understood. Literacy practices are not just about learning the skills (e.g. learning to read, drawing to communicate meaning) but also learning how to be socialised into the accepted social practices within these particular settings (Bloome & Katz, 1997; Taylor, 2019).

## Use of Resources

Resources are an integral part of the literacy learning environment. Much can be learned about the ways power and control feature in settings from an examination of who creates the resources, who chooses the resources, the purpose for which they are chosen and the ways they are used (Mantei & Kervin, 2018). While the term 'resources' is broad and includes those that are human, material, emotional and social, to name a few, in this chapter, we look to physical resources and the ways these materials are integrated into learning spaces during literacy time. These may include books (where the quantity and quality are important), printed matter (e.g. signs, newspapers, magazines, other types of community texts), writing tools and supplies (e.g. paper, pencils), technologies (e.g. computers and mobile devices) and print-bearing objects (e.g. charts, games).

An examination of the resources these teachers chose and utilised as being supportive of their teaching focus (and, by extension, the children's learning) provides insights into the ways the selected resources impact, enhance and/or inhibit literacy learning.

There were many common resources used during literacy activities that existed across the two spaces. These resources included books, paper for writing, paint, scissors and props for literacy learning. However, our data revealed that the same resource was often used in quite different ways with different levels of control. The following example of practice was captured in the preschool setting:

> It is after story time. Along the back fence of the preschool space, next to the chook shed, two children are crouched down busily working on a wooden bench. The children are painting a large rock. They have a palette of different paint colours. They work on different ends of the rock and paint illustrations on the top surface of the rock. The children work for about 15 minutes, until they feel they have finished their painting. There is no discussion. Each has

their own agenda. An educator monitors the area and replenishes the paint on the palette as needed.

And in the Kindergarten classroom:

> It is after the whole class reading of the big book. The children move to small groups where they are working on knowledge about letters, high frequency words and fine motor control. One group of four children are provided with individual packs of blue paint sealed into a zip lock bag flattened out for children to individually use as a slate for carving the high frequency words into the paint. High frequency words stored in their own ziplock bags are laminated onto cards to be used as models for 'writing' in the paint. We notice children respond in different ways to the task. One child holds the bag with one hand and carves into the paint with a finger on the other hand. For the others, they attempt to 'write' into the paint and find the task more difficult than anticipated and use the task time to manipulate the paint inside the bag. After 10 minutes a timer sounds, signalling an activity change.

What is interesting here is that both examples of practice followed from the reading of a story, and both utilised paint, but the demands and processes for engaging with the tasks are quite different. In both contexts the children were encouraged to make marks as they learned to write. Both the preschool and Kindergarten environments had paper and pencils available for the children and encouraged them to engage in writing each day. In the preschool classroom we noticed that most 'writing' opportunities were open-ended and taken up by the children as they made use of single sheets of paper available (sometimes recycled paper), pencils, markers and scissors to create their messages. In the main, the children determined the purpose and audience for their created texts.

We also observed a number of game-based resources during literacy experiences. As we watched these unfold in each context we were particularly struck by the nature of the game: who had created the game and for what purpose. While there were commercial games available (e.g. board games) in the preschool we saw more instances of children creating their own games with their own rules and selection of resources, and we also saw children create their own 'rules' for the commercially packaged games.

> Two girls, dressed in school uniforms from the dress up cupboard play a matching game with cards depicting items from a rural setting, e.g. tractor,

rabbit, carrot, dog, motorbike and so on. The cards are spread face up on the floor and the girls each hold a card that they must match with one on the floor. The game is designed to match like cards, e.g. carrot with carrot. However, these girls are delighted to generate their own categories, proudly showing the educators their match of the carrot with the rabbit and the tractor with the motorbike.

In the Kindergarten class we observed a number of teacher-created games at play. These were completed in small groups and during our observations always had a focus on letters and words. One example we captured was of a matching game:

> A small group is assembled on the floor area. The teacher has pre-prepared A4 laminated cards. Each card displays an image with a CVC word underneath (e.g. fan, bun, lip, dog). The letters of each word are sufficiently spaced so the teacher could cut each lengthwise into three parts. The children are to sort through these parts to reassemble the picture parts and individual letters to recreate the words. The children are expected to blend the word as they articulate individual sounds to combine them (blend) and read the word. There is a lot of activity amongst the group members. Some children quickly match a number of cards and arrange them outside the group area. Others find the task more demanding, finding some pieces and then taking time to search for the remaining piece. A timer signals the end of the 10 minutes for this game.

While there were many games to choose from, what struck us was how the different intent and conceptualisations for the play led to quite different activities and levels of creativity. When we consider resources for literacy activities, there are understandable differences between what a child creates (e.g. tickets to enter in the previously described imaginative play scenario) compared to what a teacher creates (cut up words), but each results in quite different literate activities and perhaps even what it means to play a game.

For children transitioning across contexts, the types of resources offered, and the ways children are expected to use these, are not without tension. For the children in the preschool context, their use of resources was connected to purposes they (in the most) determined themselves to facilitate their play scenarios and communicate their own meanings. These were often connected to the life experiences of the children. In the Kindergarten classroom these same resources were used as bound exercises defined by the teacher. These were often conducted individually, whereby learning to read and write letters and words was the priority. There were specific standards and skills that the children were expected to master.

## Discussion and Conclusion

While there are similar literacy experiences across the settings (e.g. read-alouds, role-play, opportunities to draw and write and play games) these were most often bounded by relatively invisible practices in the early childhood preschool settings with practices more visible in the first year of schooling (Bernstein, 1975; Kervin, Turbill & Harden-Thew, 2017; Mantei & Kervin, 2018). While this could be expected, our analysis does pose some important considerations for educators as they support children transitioning between the contexts.

Literacy practices are not neutral; they are the result of ideologies and values. Educators make decisions about how literacy activities should be organised and operate. These decisions may be intrinsically driven (the personal beliefs and knowledge of the educator) or may be influenced by external stakeholders (curriculum, system expectations, school policies) or a combination of both. Either way, the ways the learning experiences are designed and facilitated, the resources used to support the learning, the ways time and the spaces are used to control the type and extent of the experience, and the opportunities for interactions between and among participants convey much about what it means to be literate in the company of this community (Dyson, 2001). And while the power of the external stakeholders is strong, it is through the personal beliefs and knowledge of educators that learning becomes contextualised for this learner, at this time, in this setting.

A significant difference between these settings is the ways time features in literacy learning. Evident in the Kindergarten setting is a view of literacy narrowed both in terms of skills (reading, writing, talking and listening) and the time of day when literacy is 'done'. Conversely, the broadened definition of literacy held by the preschool educators generates multiple opportunities for children to engage in diverse literate events and for educators to teach through them. It must be acknowledged that the absence of a mandated curriculum in the play-based Early Years Learning Framework (DEEWR, 2009) reduces educators' accountability for formal teaching of the skills and strategies for reading and writing. However, the option of being literate across the day, across disciplines and across interests challenges Kindergarten teachers (Mantei & Kervin, 2018) to take seriously the literacy experiences, beliefs and expectations of a child in transition to their classroom.

The children in both settings are engaged in literacy experiences that appear quite similar. However, it is the differences that cause discontinuities in transition for the early development of a child as they transition to formal school (Kervin et al., 2019). One example relates to the mandated teaching and assessment of literacy skills such as phonemic awareness, phonics, fluency, vocabulary and comprehension in the NSW English syllabus (2012). The sense of urgency with which children are expected to accumulate this knowledge in the Kindergarten classroom is in stark contrast to the choice and autonomy of children in transition from preschool (Heap, 1985). It is the role of teachers welcoming children into the formal setting of school to ensure they have an understanding about the purposes and expectations (social and literacy based) of different lessons, as well as time to adapt to this skills-focused environment.

Literacy resources in the prior-to-school setting included those generated at the preschool centre and others introduced by the children and families. While standard forms of reading and writing such as writing on paper, reading picture books or playing card games were common in the literacy experiences, as ideas developed and understandings emerged, a rock or the concrete could become a canvas for a story, and puzzle pieces could become the characters in imaginative play (Dyson, 2001). The fluidity of the resources was observed to support literacy learning as it emerged. The freedom to adopt different authorial positions supported creativity and opportunities to pursue personal interests.

Conversely, literacy resources used in primary school classrooms are often purpose-built to align with the institutional nature of school and its focus on the components of reading and writing. In the Kindergarten classroom in this study, many of the resources were commercial products that focused on an important but relatively narrow range of early literacy skills such as letter–sound relationships. These resources were used to support learning across a series of literacy tasks with the common focus on learning: for instance, Set 2 graphemes. While contrived texts such as basal readers and word-based activities are frequently used to develop early literacy concepts, the risk of a steady diet of 'school'-style resources (Comber & Kamler, 2004) is that children may struggle to connect these classroom-based literacies with resources and experiences from their preschools, homes and communities, preventing the development of understanding about the function and power of literacy skills beyond the classroom.

Spaces for literacy learning are not neutral or static. Rather, literacy learning is enhanced when spaces are negotiated by the participants within (Bauman & Briggs, 1990). We have shown a number of examples that illustrate how children choose to engage with the learning environments and also how educators can anticipate and provide for literacy learning needs. While we can only speculate, it does appear that some are more supportive of a child in transition with clarity around the 'rules' (Bernstein, [1996] 2000) to participate and connect to the purpose of the experience.

Literacy learning is the result of complex and fluid ways time, space, resources and participants interact with each other. In this complex process children are learning to relate to each other, their teacher, the recontextualising rules in play (i.e. the what and the how of literacy in this setting) as they learn the rules of the setting. Specifically, these rules are the expectations and new ways of interacting with experiences that may look similar from one context to another but are actually quite different. To understand what transition means for these young children we need to understand what children do within a communicative space, the forms of agency children exercise and the materials they themselves deem relevant to the social action at hand. The sheer complexity of the transition from preschool to Kindergarten indicates how much young learners need to manage when they move from one setting to another. There is a need for greater permeability between these contexts. Rather than a push-down, there needs to be a push-up as we draw on children's existing literacies to support them in the transition to the literacies of formal school.

# 6

# Transitions in Literacy and Classroom Interaction across the School Years

Christine Edwards-Groves, Stephanie Garoni and Peter Freebody

## Introduction: Transition, Interaction and Practices

Examining the nature, timing and consequences of transitions in literacy education draws attention to those points that appear to present opportunities and challenges to long- or mid-term coherence and cumulativeness in the work of teachers and students. In this chapter the nature of transition and the different kinds of transitions students experience in their day-to-day literacy learning activity *and* as they progress year-by-year through the grades from primary to secondary school are discussed.

The discussion is situated within a body of well-recognised indicators of potential developmental discontinuities in language, thought and forms of knowledge provided in formal curriculum statements; in analyses of the texts that students encounter and are expected to produce; and in the informal 'guild-knowledge' that classroom teachers share. To add to these more typical formulations, we contend that an additional, distinctive view of transition is provided by detailed documentations of how students and teachers coordinate their literacy activities, moment-by-moment in their lesson talk and interactions (Edwards-Groves & Grootenboer, 2017; Freebody, 2013; Heap, 1985; ten Have, 2007). It is at turning points in classroom interaction practices that we examine students' participation in literacy learning as noticed, promoted or hindered (Edwards-Groves, 2017). This conceptualisation views the pedagogy of transition as interactionally accomplished (Garoni, 2019), 'brought off' in the practical work of coordinating literacy instruction through participant exchanges in lessons.

In this chapter, close analyses of lesson exchanges frame the discussion of how teachers and students negotiate transitions across the years of schooling. Lesson segments from three grade levels – Years 1/2 (an early stage of primary school), 5/6 (the last years of primary school before secondary education) and Year 11 (an upper senior secondary year level) – illustrate contrasts in how literacy pedagogy both shapes and is shaped by interaction patterns experienced in classroom lessons. We apply Conversation Analysis (CA) to see if certain orders of activity within lessons overtly connect to transitions, discontinuities and/or to the successful negotiation of literacy pathways across grade levels.

To preview, analysis of lessons in the three specific school-years provides 'telling cases' of how *knowing doing, knowing literacy* and *knowing disciplinary literacy* are set within particular *activity sequence management, epistemic exchange development* and *textual mediation*; and how these are configured and reconfigured over the school years. Specifically, these particular forms of *literacy knowings* emerge as an underlying core intent of many lessons as students progress through the grades – for example, from managing sequences of activity, to engaging in epistemic exchanges and on toward mediating textual forms of knowledge. We conclude with 'three-tasks-for-literacy' and 'three-tasks-for-pedagogy' that emerge amidst some official, professional and folk narratives about literacy development that surface in the ongoing activity and exchange structures that teachers and students use to organise the social and epistemic structures of their literacy lessons.

## Lessons as Socially Accomplished in Practices

Our first assumption in considering how students and teachers negotiate their literacy learning across the school years concerns the centrality of social interaction:

> Social interaction is the primordial means through which the business of the social world is transacted, the identities of the participants are affirmed or denied, and its cultures are transmitted, renewed, and modified. (Goodwin & Heritage, 1990: 283)

For the classroom this means that interactions are the 'primordial means' by which teachers and students, in lessons, conduct the 'business' of education-in-school. These lessons are evolving interactive events – sites of practical, social and cultural work-in-progress (Edwards-Groves, 2017).[1] The appropriate empirical centre of this inquiry is therefore the study of naturally occurring classroom activities, not, by themselves, substitutes such as what researchers code in lesson observations, or what teachers bring to bear in describing or evaluating lessons, or how a particular theory of teaching or learning pre-empts the nature and quality of pedagogical practices. We take it that, in using these proxy methods alone, 'the specific details of naturally situated interactional conduct are irretrievably lost and are replaced by idealizations about how interaction works' (Heritage, 1984: 236).

Further, we take it that on any given occasion, how an utterance is heard and responded to is available to the participants (and thereby to the researcher), while the intentions of speakers are not. Here the focus is on the work an utterance is taken to do, then and there. In determining even basic, apparently grammatically available interactional functions, such as 'questioning', what needs to be documented is how the participants proceed to display what they understand to be going on *in that instance*. Documenting this occasioned interactional work provides baseline information about what transitions in literacy learning are for these participants and how literacy learning is produced or encountered, dealt with or ignored.

## Talk-in-Interaction: An Analytic Approach for Understanding Lessons

We draw on CA,[2] an analytic method within ethnomethodology (Garfinkel, 1967; Sacks, 1992; Schegloff, 2007), to focus on interactional phenomena found to carry prominence in classrooms. Specifically, there are potentially multiple participants to the talk, and teachers confront potentially variable familiarity with the topic at hand. CA considers:

i. how participants in classroom talk-in-interaction manage the allocation and timing of turn-taking;

ii. the exchange structures via which they organise sequences of activities; and
iii. how they work with often extended and complex expansions around certain basic conversational structures (e.g. questioning–answering) to secure the attention of all participants and the substantive educational focus of that attention (Koole, 2012).

CA provides two features critical to analysing these three aspects of classroom interaction. First, in interactions, a participant takes a 'turn', and a turn is made up of one or more components called turn-constructional-units (TCUs). These generally comprise lexico-grammatical features, realisations in prosodics (tempo, pitch, loudness, intonation, etc), and recognisable contextual actions (visible acknowledgement at this point, in this episode, with these participants, in this place).[3] In classroom talk, it is observed that teachers' (T's) turns are often comprised of multiple TCUs, in this instance, four:

**Teacher:** (i) It's a sad story (ii) I think Ronnie should come to me later and tell me all about his dogs. (iii) I'd really like to hear it (iv) Lina?

Second, the core of any exchange is made up of turns organised as adjacency pairs – at least two turns, by different speakers, located one after the other in a culturally recognisable order. Adjacency pairs are a basic turn-taking 'resource for organizing sequences' (Schegloff, 2007: 13–14). In classrooms, adjacency pairs generally contain a teacher's *initiation* turn followed by a student's *response*:

**Teacher:** Would you like to show us your writing?
**Ronnie:** ((shows book to students))

Any adjacency pair is rarely rigid or isolated; and it is versatile and robust in its relevance and organisational affordances across interaction sequences. It can be split by intervening talk (including interruptions and insertions), take more than one turn each to complete, and become surrounded and intermixed with pre-, insert- and post-expansion turns from any participant aimed at, for example, clarifying, maximising clarifying, repairing misunderstandings. Or,

**Table 6.1** Exhibit 1a – Read Me Your Story Ronnie

| 1. | T | Ronnie^ read me the story that's on your book …. |
|---|---|---|
| 2 | Ron | ((reading aloud)) MY DOG DIED$^V$ |

**Table 6.2** Exhibit 1b – Show Us Your Writing Ronnie

| 1 | T | (i) Ronnie^ read me the story that's on your book (ii) the lovely idea you had that you wrote down in your story |
|---|---|---|
| 2 | Ron | ((reading aloud)) MY DOG DIEDV |
| 3 | T | (i) good^ boyV (ii) would you like to show us your writing^ |
| 4 | Ron | ((show book to students)) (0.2) |
| 5 | T | (i) lovelyV (ii) words-all-with-spacesV (iii) good boyV |
| 6 | Ss+T | ((applause)) (0.3) |
| 7 | T | (i) it's a sad story (ii) I think Ronnie should come to me later and tell me all about his dogs (iii) I'd really like to hear it (0.2) (iv) Lina^ |

in this next case, increasing the chances of a preferred response, with what is described as an insert-expansion (italicised):

**Teacher:** Ronnie, read me the story that's on your book, *the lovely idea you had that you wrote down in your story*

**Ronnie:** ((reading)) MY DOG DIED

Exhibit 1a (Table 6.1) shows just the adjacency pair[4] from a segment of a Year 2 writing lesson, and Exhibit 1b (Table 6.2) shows the full exchange as it occurred.

Turn by turn, we see:

i. T's insert-expansion between the initiation-request (1*i*) an insert (1*ii*) hearable as an encouragement
ii. Ronnie's response with the text of his story (2)
iii. T's post-expansion (3*i*), and her new request for a display of the written story (3*ii*), and Ronnie's compliance (4)
iv. T's post-expansion on the display, with 5*ii* warranting the display of the story
v. a confirming reaction from the students (6)
vi. a closing turn with two post-expansions from T (7*i* and *ii*) followed by her nomination a new speaker (7*iv*).

## What to Make of These Moves with Regard to Teaching and Learning Literacy?

It is useful here to recall James Heap's landmark studies of early reading and writing lessons in school, and his observations about what makes such lessons noteworthy:

> In order to read, consciousness passes through the document to the text, a passage which does not allow the document to be noticed, though it must be seen ... the importance of the written word as a phenomenon lies not in the written word itself, nor in its sense, but rather in the shift of attention performed to read it. (Heap, 1977: 105)

It is notable that in 3*ii* T asks Ronnie to show the written story even though the group has already heard the text, thereby directing attention to its features as a material document – 'show us your writing'. T's expansion following the display of the book (turns 5*i–iii*) further confirmed Ronnie's work and directed specific attention to the features of his 'story' as a document, a result of Ronnie's 'lovely' handwriting. In T's turn 7*i–iii* she nominated his 'story' as a recognisable *cultural-object-of-interest* – its sadness and that she would like to discuss Ronnie's dogs further.

In this approximately thirty seconds of teaching, this group has heard Ronnie's story as a *text*, observed the 'words-all-with-spaces' in his *document*, rewarded him as a group and heard that T thinks this *story* is 'lovely' but also 'sad' so that 'Ronnie should' talk with her later, declaring that the *text+document* is, further, an object of *cultural interest*. That is, there is learning to be had about handwriting, the nature of stories and the potential significance of their (in this case, emotional) content – seeing a reading–writing 'moment' as, at the one time, about the document, the text and the object of cultural significance.

Heap describes these as 'shifts of attention,' brought off in a short time and managed by T's versatile use of expansions. Such shifts in lessons about the interpretation and production of written texts call up, in turn, complex layers of expanding and revisiting generally found in and around the adjacency pair. These

> allow students to appreciate the text as within the culture ... the point of the comprehension phase is to bring the student within the culture as well. To conceive the point merely to be the transmission of knowledge is to miss altogether the acculturation work displayed in lessons. (Heap, 1985: 266)

In lessons, we may observe this regular, ongoing shuttling of attention in teachers' and students' closer-than-average monitoring of understanding, along material (what we use), cognitive (what we know) and cultural (how we know) lines. Such shuttling is located, in Exhibit 1b, in a complex, extended set of insertion moves all built around a three-word story. Notable also is that, after more than two years of formal schooling, these students show familiarity and proficiency with this routine; a routine that simultaneously generates the acculturation work required to be literate.

The regularity with which post-expansions on the basic adjacency pair have been observed in documentations of classroom talk has resulted in some analysts adding a 'third part' to the base 'pair' when describing classroom exchanges. This three-part-turn pattern has been commonly called 'Teacher-Initiation-Student-Response-Teacher-Feedback/Evaluation' exchange cycle[5] or IRF/IRE. The third-turn teacher feedback/evaluation move is made to evaluate the correctness or otherwise of a student's response and provides a 'vast array of interpretive works and contingent methods of actions' (Lee, 2007: 202), epistemic and procedural moves where

> the teacher carries out complex analytic work, estimating what students know and what they do not know, discovering particular identities of their students and their problems, finding and repairing what becomes problematic in the second turns, steering the discourse in particular directions.

Similarly, in their response moves, students are heard as demonstrating their analytic competencies, showing how they have understood prior turns (Edwards-Groves & Davidson, 2017). But it is the teacher's 'third turn', the immediate post-expansion, which indicates the teacher's public analysis of the zone between the students' evident understanding and knowledge, and the demands of the topic. That is, the 'R' turn can be heard as an indicator of where the key, active workspace, lies at that moment.

Through growing familiarity with the specific patterns of exchange organisation, students become acculturated in the participatory routines that afford their learning, without necessarily knowing much about the propositional content of the learning itself. As Macbeth (2011) showed, students are in a perpetual 'practicum' space in which they work up their entree into bodies of (literacy) knowledge via increasingly competent forms of participation in talk-in-interaction.

## Exchanges across the School Years: Literacy in Talk-in-Interaction

We next draw on lessons from three stages of schooling considered key transition educational points to show the kinds of literacy experiences these cohorts might typically encounter: early years (Year 1/2), primary (Year 5/6) and senior secondary (Year 11). The purpose is to de-familiarise the classroom lesson, to reset our disposition to know-already what the participants' interactive moves are and how well they might conform to external norms about 'good literacy teaching'. To preview, analysis of the selected exhibits reveals the contrasting triad of *knowing doing, doing literacy* and *doing literacy in disciplinary epistemics*. The shift to a focus on the interactive accomplishment of lessons aims to unsettle resistant undercurrents of classroom discourse patterns and points to particular transition-related challenges for literacy education.

### Exhibit 2: Literacy Groups in Year 1/2

In Exhibit 2 we present two excerpts from a transcribed classroom recording of the whole class activity of a Year 1/2 literacy lesson in the third week of school. Two teachers are standing on either side of the task management board in front of students seated on the floor. A worksheet outlines the required 'must do' activities, to which both teachers referred – itemised spelling, word meanings, syllables, brackets and alphabetisation. Excerpt 2a (Table 6.3) formed part of a six-minute teacher 'run down' of the spelling-vocabulary worksheet. The sequence begins with T1's pre-expansion (turn 1) directing students to the task demands to 'tell [her] something that's huge'.

T1's turn (1) comprised three TCUs: the first was a pre-formulation *(i)*, '<u>huge,</u> *that* means something that's, really bigger than <u>large</u>^', orienting to the meanings of specified vocabulary (the words 'huge' and 'large'); the second *(ii)* 'isn't it$^V$' called for agreement from the cohort; the third *(iii)*, '*tell me*

**Table 6.3** Excerpt 2a – Huge Is Bigger Than Large

| | | |
|---|---|---|
| 1 | T1 | (*i*)huge (.) that means something that's (.) really bigger than large^ (*ii*)isn't it^V (.)(*iii*)tell me something that's huge |
| 2 | S1 | oh oh ((hand raised)) |
| 3 | T1 | ((points to S1)) |
| 4 | S1 | um the Eiffel Tower^ |
| 5 | T1 | oh [fanta]stic ((points to S2 with hand up)) |
| 6 | T2 | [mm:m] ((nodding)) |
| 7 | S2 | school^ |
| 8 | T1 | a school is huge (.) good^ (.) anything else^ ((points to S3 with hand up)) |
| 9 | S3 | Sydney Harbour Bridge^ |
| 10 | T1 | excellent ((points to S4 with hand up)) |
| 11 | S4 | I werz:z um no no the Opera House^V |
| 12 | T1 | Opera House that is huge ((points to S5 with hand up)) |
| 13 | S5 | the sun^ |
| 14 | T1 | ooh that's the one I had in my head good boy (.) the sun is huge (2) anything else^ ((points to S6 with raised hand)) |
| 15 | S6 | °the ground^ is huge° |
| 16 | T1 | the ground^ (.) yes if [you're looking at all of the]earth good girl |
| 17 | T2 | [the earth (.)we call it earth] |
| 18 | T1 | ((points to S7 with hand up)) |
| 19 | S7 | Jupiter^V |
| 20 | T1 | Jupiter is definitely huge excellent ((looks at activity sheet)) |

*something that's huge'* was for students to provide candidate responses for assessment (Pomerantz, 1988). This move sets the routine IRF/E in motion, displayed as T1's turn-allocation (through pointing to the next speaker) and student-bidding (indicated by 'oh oh' and hand raising – turns 2, 5, 8, 10, 18). Throughout the sequence, student answers are provisional, indicated by an upward inflexion (^) (turns 4, 7, 9), illustrative of the teacher's right to evaluate and to close the exchange (Edwards-Groves, Anstey & Bull, 2014).

The breadth of acceptability of the students' responses about largeness – 'a school' and 'Jupiter' are accepted as *huge* – suggests that it is not word meanings that mattered most here. Rather, the turn-taking system for participating, the attentiveness to teachers' reactions to responses and the regulation of a sequence of tasks by reference to a public document formed the main workspace. Students are adeptly demonstrating procedural interactional knowledge – that is, participating in *knowing doing*, by practising their participatory responses in that doing.

The lesson continues (Table 6.4, Excerpt 2b) as teachers continued offering participation opportunities for collective response gathering.

The initial stretch of talk on 'syllables' opened with an adjacency pair (turn 86*ii* teacher question *'what are syllables?'*; turn 87 student response *'word chunks'*), which came with the insert expansion (86*iii*) *'sort of like chunks that you hear in a word'*. An extensive post-expansion demonstration of the nature of syllables followed, and how their number can be worked out (to turn 98*i*). Turn 87 was the only individual student response sought and successfully received in this 2.5-minute exhibit. So, the talk here almost exclusively managed the contributions of the students as a cohort.

A second part of the main 'lesson' was that the worksheet may require translation, clarified via a series of physical demonstrations – in this case, clapping or holding up fingers (turns 88*ii*–98*i*) or bouncing a tennis ball (turn 109) for each word chunk. An authorised schism that diverts the topic from syllables and alphabetical order (turn 100*ii*) was inserted as an additional 'lesson' on brackets is signalled by T1 (turns 100*iii*–105).

In summary, Exhibit 2 draws out the alphabet, syllables, brackets and word lists as relevant cultural objects worthy of attention, providing specific literacy learning that assembled four features of both texts and documents: what the words *large, huge* and *gigantic* mean, that syllables are chunks of sound in words, that incomplete circles are brackets and that if two words start with the same letter, to alphabetise them go to letter number two (as *'practised on Tuesday'*). What these teachers and students worked on was constructing the exchange management systems that can afford a response to these variable literacy demands involving:

> sustained and practical interest in how indeed their lessons are made to work, as recitations, demonstrations, spectacle, turn taking, and other practical orders of activity. (Macbeth, 2000: 59)

A notable feature here is that the vast majority of exchanges invited and received responses from the cohort and showed ways these students know how to *do* literacy lessons. Group chorusing is found to be a common practice in the early school years (McHoul, 1978); the entire cohort learns to answer as 'one participant', offering students who do not believe they know the answer both anonymity and the opportunity to witness the chorusing of those who

**Table 6.4** Excerpt 2b – The Closing Activity: Alphabetical Order, Syllables, Brackets

| 86 | T1 | (*i*) ((holds up paper and looks at it)) and the lucky last um part of that activity (.) ooh <u>write</u> these words in alphabetical <u>or</u>der (.) and state the number of <u>syllables</u>$^V$ (.) (*ii*) now syllables is (.) who can tell me (.) what are syllables ((leans forward, looking around)) shh (2) (*iii*) °they're sort of like chunks that you hear in a word° ((points to S1 with hand up)) |
|---|---|---|
| 87 | S1 | word chunks |
| 88 | T1 | (*i*) wor-word chunks so (.) (*ii*) what about the word <u>or</u>ange (.) clap it out (.) how many syllables^ ((raises hands, poised to clap)) |
| 89 | Ss+Ts | [((many students clapping twice))] |
| 90 | T1 | [<u>or</u> (.) <u>an</u>gel] ((clapping)) |
| 91 | T1 | great (.) how many (.) hold it up in your (.) with your fingers^ |
| 92 | Ss+Ts | ((many Ss holding up two fingers)) |
| 93 | T1 | two (.) well done (.) what about the word (.) gi (.) gan (.) <u>tic</u> (.) |
| 94 | Ss+Ts | [((clapping three times))] |
| 95 | Ss+Ts | [gi (.) gan (.) tic] |
| 96 | T1 | how many^ |
| 97 | Ss+Ts | ((holding up three fingers)) |
| 98 | T1 | (*i*) <three> (.) well done$^V$ (*ii*) ((holds up paper and looks at it)) so these words over here ((points to words on paper))= |
| 99 | T2 | =in the box |
| 100 | T1 | (*i*) cage (.) orange (.) age (.) gentle (.) gigantic (.) and large$^V$ (*ii*) all of those words we would like you to put into <u>al</u>phabetical order (.) (*iii*) and then there is ((stands up holding paper to the class)) (*iv*) what we call <u>brack</u>ets at the side there (.) (*v*) can you all see those^ |
| 101 | Ss | Yes:s |
| 102 | T1 | yes can you see those <u>Liam</u>^ |
| 103 | T2 | looking Brian^ ((raises eyebrows at student)) |
| 104 | Ss | Yes:s |
| 105 | T1 | the brackets (.) what does a <u>circle</u>^ ((makes circles with finger)) but the circle isn't complete at the top or the bottom (.) inside those brackets is you you put how many <u>syllables</u> [the word has]^ |
| 106 | T2 | [when you clap it out] ((claps hands)) |
| 107 | T1 | when you <u>clap</u> it out you could get a tennis ball maybe Ms Mayham ((turns to T2 and back to class)) and they could [try] |
| 108 | T2 | [mm] ((nodding head)) |
| 109 | T1 | doing <u>the</u> ((uses hand to act out bouncing a ball)) bouncing with a <u>tennis</u> ball like you do with your spelling words= |
| 110 | T2 | =or just clap it out |
| 111 | T1 | ((nodding)) or you clap it (.) ((points to paper)) and you need to write them in alphabetical order as well$^V$ |
| 112 | T2 | now [remember] |
| 113 | T1 | [we'll be] moving around the room to help you with this sheet as [well] ((looks towards T2)) |
| 114 | T2 | [re]member (.) if there's a word that starts with the same letter we practised this on Tuesday (.) you need to go to letter number two (0.3) ((T1 bends over to touch S5)) to see which one = |
| 115 | T1 | =((nodding))goes first |

respond acceptably. Thus chorusing and cohorting represent a recognition of heterogeneity among students that combines 'sympathy' and practicality, and show how lesson interaction practices dominate what literacy learning is enabled in the here-and-now of participation. We also note that students have become enculturated into the type of exchange management work that is continued across grade levels and that the protocol for classroom participation internalised by students is a prerequisite for work to proceed in an orderly fashion in later school years.

## Exhibit 3: Literacy in Year 5/6 writing

Exhibit 3 explores literacy learning in a Year 5/6 writing lesson. The teacher and students shuttle between everyday cultural logic, fiction writing and scientific knowledge (of galaxies, gravity, velocity). Participants' orientation was to the comprehension when producing a narrative text as a cultural object and the negotiable latitude offered in the fictional genre. This contrasts with the participation structures in sequences of activities relating to a particular document, as we saw previously. The sequence begins (Table 6.5, Excerpt 3a) with the teacher facilitating a whole class discussion about composing a narrative text on a space adventure. Several students are nominated by the teacher to share their creative plot ideas; the first was about an astronaut on the moon.

Table 6.5  Excerpt 3a – Remember It Is Fictional

| 1  | T   | Beth^ |
|----|-----|-------|
| 2  | Bet | [ar:r] he's on the moo:::n (0.2) <u>and</u> he decides (.) he wants to see if he can >jump off the moon< so he run:::s to the end of the moon an' jumps off |
| 3  | T   | okay^ so like a space run^ |
| 4  | Bet | yer:rh |
| 5  | S2  | but how would you <u>get</u>(.) how would you get to the end of the moon when it's like (.) |
| 6  | S3  | [circle] |
| 7  | S2  | [circle^] |
| 8  | S3  | how can you(.) <u>run</u> off the <u>edge</u> of the moon^ anyway [Isn't it goin'] |
| 9  | S2  | [>It's like](.) you can't (.) it's like<= |
| 10 | T   | =<u>RE</u>member it is^ it is^ (0.5) fic:::tio:::nal <as well> |

*Transitions in Literacy and Classroom Interaction* 107

The sequence started with T nominating a speaker, Beth, whose response demonstrated her knowledge of how a story can proceed, finishing with '*he runs to the end of the moon an jumps off*' (turn 2). S2 produced an unsolicited clarification '*how would you get to the end, if it's like a circle*' (turns 5, 7), indicating his orientation to something other than the textual knowledge required to write a narrative, challenging the validity of Beth's idea. By interjecting with '*How can you, run off the edge of the moon?*' (turn 8), S3 put to use his everyday commonsense knowledge of moons to initiate generalised repair (Drew, 1997). S2 demonstrated alignment with S3's response with, '*you can't*' (turn 9). This point, where the talk shifts from the textual features to content knowledge about space, drew a reorienting response from T (turn 10). Here T negotiated this exchange-transition by reminding students of the collective cultural logic (or mutual assumption) guiding how narrative texts are written: '*fic::tio::nal*' (turn 10). This move reinstated the textual focus of the lesson's literacy focus unhindered by scientific 'facts' raised by some students. This 'fact-based' scientific focus persists (Table 6.6, Excerpt 3b.

Here S4 moved to return to the scientific dilemma and expand the sequence with *You tryin* (turn 11). At this point the teacher interrupted to retain speaking rights but concedes to the evolving matter of establishing knowledge that '*gravity would be a thing*' (turn 12). This turn drew into relevance the need for explicit technical scientific terminology (and repeated by S3 turn

**Table 6.6** Excerpt 3b – It's Not My Story

| | | |
|---|---|---|
| 11 | S4 | [you tryin'] |
| 12 | T | [>there] needs to be< some factor there like (0.2) so you would need to think of (.) >like the< gravity would be a thing (.) the moon (.) you know (.)= |
| 13 | S3 | =if gravity is there$^V$ |
| 14 | S4 | the end of the moon (.) all those sorts of things |
| 15 | T | [the idea is good though$^V$ (.) I like]= |
| 16 | S3 | [you can't just jump off earth] |
| 17 | T | =the idea |
| 18 | S3 | you can't just jump off earth$^V$ |
| 19 | T | no(.) you need a spaceship to take you out |
| 20 | S5 | ye:ah (.) so (.) wouldn't that be the same [as the moon^] |
| 21 | T | [well(.) they might be] walking across the moon >I don't know< it's not my story (1.0) |

13) but reframed as a '*good idea*' (turn 15). S3 re-entered the conversation by overlapping T's talk and blurting out the response, '*You can't just jump off earth*' (turns 16, 18). In subsequent turns (18–21), the teacher and her students worked together to co-produce the disciplinary logic required to support the textual logic of the literacy task. Then T (turn 21) again moved to close the sequence with a hedge '*Well, they might be walking across the moon*, followed by a deflection *I don't know. It's not my story*'. In this way, she expressed her intention to move on from the scientific debate in favour of reinstating the literacy focus – narrative writing.

In the next excerpt, the teacher leads students to expand their story premises, drawing on their personal 'space knowledge'. Daisy talks about an encounter with aliens, and S7 used his interpretation of what came before to present his own scientific knowledge (turn 36). S7 proceeds to propose, it appears, a solution to the gravity problem and resolution of the narrative trouble (Table 6.7, Excerpt 3c).

The capacity of a 'story' to interleave scientific knowledge with 'weird,' fantastical elements is displayed here. T's first five turns (32, 34, 37, 39 and 41) indicate her encouragement of this interleaving but only when the scientific knowledge is reallocated to the literary discipline; that is, being about 'good ideas' and 'imagery' (implied), evidenced by her use of terms like 'descriptive' or 'exciting words' (turn 43). This implicit 'genre recognition' could be considered a form of disciplinary (literary) epistemology. Furthermore, it could be argued that the much-ignored factual knowledge of S7 is an illustrative example of 'unnoticed' literacy transition discontinuity. To conclude, a successful return to the textual literacy component of the task followed on from multiple redoings of the scientific dilemma 'how would you get to the end of the moon?' (made earlier in turn 5).

This shuttling back and forth between everyday cultural logic, the textual aspects of writing a narrative and scientific knowledge characterised *knowing literacy* in how teacher and students coordinated the business of accomplishing narrative writing in this Year 5/6 lesson. The exhibit shows shifts in the treatment of literacy as students are nearing the formal transition from primary to secondary school. These detailed analyses assist us to consider how literacy trajectories are intricately linked to interaction. For instance, students' turns are longer and comprised of

**Table 6.7** Excerpt 3c – Still Looking for Those Descriptive Words

| 30 | T | (hhh)Dais^ |
|---|---|---|
| 31 | Dai | um:m(0.2)well^(.)the one that I thought of(.)was that(.) the::e(.)astronaut went to Mars or some(.) or some weird place like that(.) and (hhh)he founds ali^ens and then they ate him |
| 32 | T | of course you^ would think of aliens= |
| 33 | Dai | =Yes! |
| 34 | T | I was waiting for someone to bring up aliens or Mar::s (hhh) |
| 35 | T | (1.0) |
| 36 | S7 | um:m (0.2) because like(.)the um earth's escape velocity is really high it takes a lot of energy like to get out of it because it um:m(0.2)because of its gravitational pull= |
| 37 | T | =gravity is pulling it back this way [and] |
| 38 | S7 | [yea:ah]>it's trying to go against gravity (.) but< uh-oh(.) I was thinking is that the:: um rocket ship didn't have enough fuel in it^ and it only just got out of its gravitational pull (.) and then yeah umm(.) the(.) fuel to make it keep on going out into space just stopped so (0.2) then umm (0.2) they started going into like overheating cause it didn't have enough fuel to keep it^ cool |
| 39 | T | okay(.) so >sort of like< stranded in that midway [point](.) |
| 40 | S7 | [yea:ah] |
| 41 | T | so you're sort of in the same direction as Connor |
| 42 | S7 | yea:ah= |
| 43 | T | =stuck in that(.) that midway point(.) alright^ (0.2) don't forget though in your story(.)I'm still looking for those descriptive words (.) still looking for those exciting words |

more student-initiated and expanded contributions that, at the same time, demonstrate a stronger hold on the more complex aspects of literacy and its relation to disciplinary work expected as this stage of their schooling – like more sophisticated scientific fictional writing with more descriptive vocabulary.

Although these interactions seem to be mostly concerned with knowing literacy (constructing a narrative), the teacher's de-valuation of the relevance of S7's scientific knowledge appears to be a missed teaching opportunity on issues of 'realism' versus 'fiction' in the sci-fi genre. Thus, it could be argued that the classroom discourse left implicit what could have been a shift towards a more advanced literary discussion (about the negotiation of scientific facts in the sci-fi genre). Such reconfigurations, when consciously executed, may productively smooth transitions to higher grade levels (where this type of literary specialisation is increasingly expected).

110    *Transition and Continuity in School Literacy Development*

## Exhibit 4: Literacy in and for Year 11 History

The segments in this section formed part of a term-long unit of study on European colonisation. In previous lessons, the motivations for colonisation of different countries (e.g. Belgium, Russia) were explored, and the next phase of the unit, parts of which we examine below, concerned the French presence in Indo-China/Vietnam. Excerpts are midway through the lesson after T initiated an extended exercise in leading students on from the set homework task exploring the impact of French colonisation. T's turns invited students' everyday reasoning about colonisation, towards the 'cultural logic' necessary to understand the questions for this lesson: 'what were they doing there? why were they colonizing? what's the motivation?' Such exchanges were structured as a teacher-led questioning series, reminding students that the issue 'for today' related to ideas covered earlier and reapplied here. Immediately prior to the exchanges in Excerpt 4a (Table 6.8), T (turn 179) had called for student 'guesses' as to whether Indo-China/Vietnam '*is gonna be similar to that or different*' from cases studied previously.

These exchanges oriented to both textual features (reading the novel extract as a source) and cultural logic (reading with corroborating primary sources). To arrive at the sequence closing, S2 provided multiple provisional attempts as possible answers (indicated by the upward inflections finishing turns 382 '*comradorie corroborie*' and 384 '*comradorie*') and addressed immediately by T who provides the preferred *great word* (turn 389) '*corroborate*' (turn 385). Notably, the salient lesson in these exchanges concerns the text as a cultural object, but located within a specialist historian culture. Consensus and collaboration are specialised literacy practices, in this case, whereby the text needs to be located within a congruent collection of other 'primary' historical texts.

Here specific texts, textual orientations and literacy activities, allied with particular technical skills required in the discipline of history, were explored as students and T jointly co-produced meanings related to testing and legitimising sources by: comparing with 'primary' sources (turn 380–1), corroborating (turns 385–9), getting all the sources (turn 390), piecing them together (turn 391), testing the source (turn 391) and in summary seeing if 'it is reliable' (turns 391–3). In this sequence, and in Excerpt 4b, literacy was put to work in an extended exercise that brought the students into the 'disciplinary logic'

**Table 6.8** Excerpt 4a – How Do We Test This Source?

| 179 | T | … let's see if you're right (.) shall we^ (5) okay$^v$ (6) now (.) rather bizarrely^ I'm going to give you an extract from a novel to look at ((T hands papers out, occasional chat))(2.4) okay$^v$ (.) we're going to start by having a look at a novel$^v$ I'm gonna shush up for a bit^ (.) what I'd like you to do is to have a read of that^ (1) and then (.) just generally talking we'll just answer the first few questions 'cause they're pretty easy then there's some (.) meaty ones underneath which I want you to have a bit more of a look at later (.) so^ (.) can you have a read through thanks^ … ((students reading the extract from the distributed sheet)) |
|---|---|---|
| 379 | T | alright$^v$ (.) so:o (3) what do we think, do we think I mean how do we test this source how do we:e (1) how do we:e^ say yes this is (.) this is legitimate$^v$ no it's not (.) how do we do that^ ((points to S1)) |
| 380 | S1 | compare it to primary sources^ |
| 381 | T | a:ah^ we actually gotta find some primary sources (.) correct$^v$ |
| 382 | S1 | comradorie^ corroborie^ |
| 383 | T | m:m^ |
| 384 | S1 | comradorie (.) would that work^ |
| 385 | T | corroborate (.) that's the one$^v$ |
| 386 | S1 | oh |
| 387 | T | cor:rob:or:ate((said slowly)) |
| 388 | Ss | ((laughs)) |
| 389 | T | okay (.) we corroborate (0.2) our primary sources$^v$ and we corroborate all our sources okay$^v$ (.) now it's a great word (.) what does it mean$^v$ |
| 390 | S2 | it's like (.) get all the sources and= |
| 391 | T | =piece them together okay^ (.)so what do we really need to do to test the source (0.1) in <u>summary</u> what do we need to do$^v$ |
| 392 | S3 | see if it's (.) sort of (reliable^) |
| 393 | T | see if it's reliable okay$^v$ |

necessary to understand and do history (Allender & Freebody, 2016); the text has been consulted and the need for it to be corroborated has been recognised, both part of reading and writing as an historian-in-Year-11.

## Excerpt 4b: What Sort of Person Is Ho Chi Minh?

Soon after Excerpt 4a, T selected a student to read from the Ho Chi Minh text. 4b (Table 6.9) shows how that reading provided a setting for T to intervene with relevant background knowledge and inferences. This 'joint reading' amounts to the gaps T assumes might exist in some students' knowledge that are necessary for interpreting the text, as well as for its interest as a cultural logic in the setting of this unit of study.

**Table 6.9** Excerpt 4b – What Sort of Person Is Ho Chi Minh?

| 426 | Cor | ((Corinne reading)) AT THAT TIME I SUPPORTED THE OCTOBER REVOLUTION ONLY INSTINCTIVELY= |
|---|---|---|
| 427 | T | =stop (.) October revolution meaning^ what^v |
| 428 | S1 | the Russian^// |
| 429 | T | //the Russian revolution-which-occurred in October 1917^v thank you^v ((points to Corinne)) |
| 430 | Cor | ((continues reading aloud)) um:m (.)NOT YET GRASPING ALL ITS HISTORIC IMPORTANCE, I LOVED AND ADMIRED LENIN BECAUSE HE WAS A GREAT PATRIOT WHO LIBERATED HIS COMPATRIOTS// |
| 431 | T | //what's a compatriot^ not a communist patriot(.)no^ |
| 432 | Ss+T | ((laughter)) |
| 433 | T | what's a compatriot^ (0.2) okay so Lenin here (.) he says there i:is (.) a great patriot who liberated his compatriots (.) his fello:ow (.) Russians^v (.) okay^ (0.2) until then^ ((points to Corinne)) |
| 434 | Cor | UNTIL THEN I HAD READ NONE OF HIS BOOKS= |
| 435 | T | =okay (.) so he's vaguely aware of the October revolution^v you couldn't be^v in the world in 1917 and not be aware of the October revolution^v (0.2) however he hasn't really grasped the full (.) sort of (0.1) significance of it (.) until^ (.) Lauren^ |
| 436 | Lau | ((Lauren takes on the *Round-Robin* reading)) THE REASON FOR MY JOINING THE FRENCH SOCIALIST PARTY WAS THAT THESE LADIES AND GENTLEMEN, AS I CALLED MY COMRADES AT THAT MOMENT, HAD SHOWN THEIR SYMPATHY TOWARDS ME, TOWARDS THE STRUGGLE OF THE OPPRESSED PEOPLES, BUT I UNDERSTOOD NEITHER WHAT WAS A PARTY, A TRADE UNION, NOR WHAT WAS SOCIALISM OR COMMUNISM, A COMRADE GAVE ME LENIN'S THESIS ON THE NATIONAL AND COLONIAL QUESTIONS PUBLISHED BY (0.3) L:L 'L'HUMANITE' TO READ |
| 437 | T | okay^v so (0.2) just stop there for a tick what sort of person does Ho Chi Minh seem to be:e^v what^ circles is he moving in^ what is he doing^ |
| 438 | S2 | getting into communism^ |
| 439 | T | okay^v he's starting to be interested in communism-ye:es but (.) in terms of a (.) sort of (.) person^v what is he^ |
| 440 | S3 | political^ |
| 441 | T | he's political^ is he:e (.)educated^ |
| 442 | Ss | [no] ((various answers called out)) [not really] |
| 443 | S4 | [he's trying] to be^v |
| 444 | T | so not completely (.) he:e he:e is aware of stuff but (.) feels like he needs to read more about it so (.) I guess (.)y-know (.) he's educated in other ways (.) I guess is p'haps the way (.) we need to phrase this (.) he's (0.1) he is interested enough to want to know more and he has the opportunity to actually find (.) to know more^v to go and grab a book and read stuff (.) OK^v |

For the most part, this sequence attended to textual meanings – of 'historical' terms, concepts and of the substantive content of the Ho Chi Minh text. Turns 427, 431, 435, 437 are instances of T's insertions into the round-robin-reading (of Corinne and Lauren), evidenced as interruptions [//] and signalled by *'stop'*, *'OK'*, *'so just stop there for a tick'*. Here insert-expansions structured the IRF/E-based 'understanding checks', displayed as a straightforward form of text consultation plus the provision of additional and implied information, for instance, in a three-part TCU (turn 437) (*i*) the sort of person Ho Chi Minh seems to be, (*ii*) the circles Ho Chi Minh is moving in and (*iii*) what Ho Chi Minh is doing; and later (turns 441, 444) Ho Chi Minh's level of education. Here T and Ss publicly 'co-discovered' the best characterisation of Ho Chi Minh as educated enough to become politically motivated. Analysis shows ways Ss demonstrate *knowing literacy within the disciplinary epistemics* of history. Interactionally, it is an IRE/F formation with attendant expansions drawing on everyday rationalities all brought into the students' historical account of Ho Chi Minh's role in the Vietnam war.

This exhibit directs us to more precise disciplinary-epistemics-literacy knowing, although the Ho Chi Minh text seems to be used to demonstrate corroboration of sources rather mechanically (*Can we trust this text? Yes, there is another source who says the same thing*). Here, the discontinuity might be that the type of literacy work of corroborating-sources that the interaction is about might well have been initiated in earlier grades.

# Conclusions

### Three Tasks for Literacy in School

What is borne out in these exhibits is Heap's point: that literacy's appearances often take the form of teachers' and students' ongoing shifting of attention and monitoring of understanding along *material*, *social* and *cultural* lines. We see that the nature, extent and intensity of focus of this shifting-in-practice vary across stages of schooling and learning areas. But our analyses show that a fourth element of attention to literacy is discernible – disciplinary epistemics. This relates to the specialised or technical disciplinary-specific knowledge of, for example, science-informed narratives or history (as in Exhibits 3 and 4). Thus, it was no longer culture-held-in-common that provided the specialised logic of literacy as it is encountered in the disciplines – in these cases, science and history. So we observe discipline-specific shuttling occupying the work space: pre-, insert- and post-expansions specifically designed to manage the *material-textual-cultural-specialised* interplay required for developing, accomplishing and using literacy (see also Kindenberg & Freebody, this volume).

Our exhibits suggest that pedagogical moves, accomplished in talk-in-interaction, emphasise different aspects of knowing literacy across the three stages of schooling presented. We show ways the pedagogy of literacy across grades functions essentially to transition students from knowing doing, towards knowing the doing of literacy, and knowing literacy in disciplinary epistemics. What is 'knowable' is embedded in social interactions, noting that along with a teacher's 'epistemic primacy' (Drew, 2018) is a teacher's sense of accountability to putting literacy to work in the business of:

i.  mastering schooling, evidenced as knowing doing,
ii. mastering basic textual aspects of reading and writing, evidenced as knowing literacy and
iii. mastering textual demands as they are reshaped by disciplinary epistemologies, evidenced as knowing literacy in disciplinary epistemics.

*Mastering schooling*, as in the case of children in the early years of school (Exhibits 1 and 2), initially privileges *knowing doing*, and the participatory rights and opportunities in that doing. This practice foregrounds everyday shared-in-common orientations, with some gradually increasing annotations to and from the textual. Literacy is recruited routinely into initiations and rehearsals of interactive displays of activities that turned out to be only loosely related to literacy, strictly defined. For example, we saw the topics and challenges presented by sounds, words, syllables and the alphabet as settings primarily for the 'acquisition of the organizational requirements of schooling' (Austin, Dwyer & Freebody, 2003). Here, the fundamental rationale of prioritising the 'craft' of being a learner in institutionalised education emerged as the work site, rather than progressing in literacy.

*Mastering basic textual aspects of reading and writing*, presented in Exhibit 3 from upper primary grades, shows a gradual shift in the nature of textual annotations from the everyday to account for cohesions across multidimensional aspects of literacy in relation to the code, comprehension, genre and critique (as in the four roles of a reader; Freebody & Luke, 1990; Freebody, 2019). This feature transitions towards *knowing the doing of literacy* with a gradual orientation to (other) disciplinary relevances and applications. We see from Exhibit 3, for example, that students and teacher drew on general world knowledge as they explicated scientific disciplinary knowledge in their orientations to one another and to the narrative writing task at hand. Here, there seems to be the beginnings of an observable shift towards literacy's business as constitutive of work in the curriculum disciplines.

*Mastering textual demands*, evident in Exhibit 4 presenting literacy in senior secondary, involves reshaping reading and writing practices as gradually accountable to the epistemics of the discipline, the privileging of the specialised and the technical across the textual-cultural space, with decreasing reliance on the known-in-common. Literacy accompanies and facilitates the discipline (in this case, history) by being put to use in distinctive ways, shaping a specialised cultural logic within a disciplinary orientation. When negotiating disciplinarity, interactions reveal ways *knowing literacy in particular disciplinary epistemics*, evidenced as Ss shift between epistemic (literacy-history) stances (Drew, 2018). In Heap's terms, the participants bring the textual to bear in consulting a series of epistemically and culturally relevant exchanges. This aligns with the point, argued by Pomerantz (1980), that students have access to what is knowable 'by virtue of the knowings being occasioned', that is, what is on for offer for knowing, then and there, by what one has seen or heard or been told.

## Three Tasks for Pedagogy

Understanding literacy in terms of 'transition' and 'pedagogy' means recognising the practices and contexts by which these are brought to life in largely unremarked ways. Exhibits show us three distinct, but somewhat overlapping, views of the role that teachers' pedagogical practices play in learners' development of knowledge, and their ability to display, in recognisable culturally acceptable forms, *that* knowledge in formal and informal settings. These views concern:

i. the management of sequences of activity,
ii. the development of epistemic exchanges around reading and writing and
iii. the mediating of textual representations of knowledge.

We may take the essential role of pedagogy to be setting up and guiding students through a 'series of activities', perhaps delivered via 'packages'. That successfully completing these activities, both individually and as a sequence, helps students construct literacy knowledge in ways related to the curriculum, and thereby amenable to valid assessment.

Or, we may instead regard pedagogy as primarily about producing interactionally specific, exchange-managed events that present participatory demands that, in turn, may indirectly enculturate students into literate forms of relevant knowledge, skills, dispositions and so on. Namely, classroom exchanges present significant 'epistemic' functions, partially or otherwise, with distinctive epistemological and dispositional challenges, regardless of how evidently those challenges mimic demands at the levels of literacy, knowledge, curriculum or assessment.

Alternatively, we may regard the fundamental purpose of pedagogy to mediate the state of students' knowledge and the textual demands that they face, in which case we need a conceptual framework that connects talk with discipline-specialised forms of knowledge, and both of these in turn with textual representation.

These contrasting views of the functions of pedagogy represent different ways of taking account of changes in the nature, intensity and sequencing of curricular demands. Distinctively, our data show how official narratives about literacy development might be reflected in the generally unremarked exchange structures that, in turn, organise the social and epistemic patterning of lessons; findings which extend Edwards-Groves's (2017) definition of lessons to be evolving interactive events, sites of practical, social, epistemic and cultural work-in-progress.

## Reconceptualising Literacy Transitions as Interactional Work

In this chapter we set out to show how studying the details of classroom talk affords a distinctive view of the empirical 'business' of the work of literacy. We can see how literacy is practised in the day-to-day, moment-by-moment organisation of classroom practices across the school years, and in the process, it becomes clear that literacy education is not always, all or only about literacy. This view supplements Christie and Derewianka's (2008) study of literacy discourses in schooling and leaves us with scope to respecify literacy transitions as social accomplishments (Garoni, 2019), opportunities and accountabilities that can be renegotiated, revisited and reworked with a view to better aligning changing student capabilities with particular reading and writing demands.

To point to a 'transition in literacy learning' is to refer to a discernible phase that seems to present, to both teachers and students, a consequential discontinuity in language, thought and/or forms of knowledge. Discontinuities may be negotiated smoothly or clumsily, they may afford productive prospects for new learning or turn into stumbling blocks, and they may pass unremarked and apparently unnoticed, or made overt. What they end up doing on any given occasion is, we argue, only available via an inspection of patterns of interactions constituting pedagogical practices. Our exhibits display a gradual reconfiguration of doing-knowing-disciplinary where the 'three tasks for literacy' tenuously correspond to the 'three tasks for pedagogy'. These might even be considered to be the seeds of a 'pedagogy of transition', whereby teachers might be given opportunities to compare pedagogies, literacy demands and curriculums across the school years (Tables 6.1 and 6.2).

# Understanding Literacy Transitions: Pedagogic Practices in Primary Writing Classrooms

Honglin Chen, Helen Lewis and David Rose

## Introduction

International concerns about standards of achievement in writing by school age children, particularly the lack of sustained growth of expertise, remain prevalent. In Australia, for example, the most recent NAPLAN (National Assessment Program – Literacy and Numeracy) National Report 2019 suggests that 2 per cent of Year 3 students across all states and territories are struggling with writing skills. This increases to 5.6 per cent for Year 5 and 9 per cent for Year 7 students (ACARA 2019). In Year 9, the number has nearly doubled reaching 15.8 per cent, that is, nearly one in six Year 9 students across Australia performed below the national minimum standard. In the United States, National data from NAEP (National Assessment of Educational Progress) (NCES, 2017) suggest a similar pattern of lower performance in writing by 4th and 8th graders. In England, data from national testing show that students' writing development lags behind that in reading at age seven and eleven (DfE, 2017). The lack of sustained progress in literacy is concerning, given an ability to write effectively is critical to progress and achievement in learning in all subject areas across all stages of schooling and subsequent success in future jobs (Myhill & Chen, 2020).

Reflected in this persistent decline in literacy performance is the so-called '4th Grade slump' described as the slowing down of progress in literacy development beginning with the fourth year of primary schooling (Chall & Jacobs, 2003). This period is now widely acknowledged as a significant literacy transition point, one that is brought about by 'shifts in focus and pedagogy relating to literacy and the curriculum' (McNaughton, 2020: 34). These changes include the increasing technicality and abstraction of knowledge presented in the curriculum (Christie & Derewianka, 2008) and an increase in complexity in school discourse (Painter, Derewianka & Torr, 2007). This requires advanced literacy skills – skills that are necessary to deal with the increasing demands of the curriculum (Humphrey, 2017). While previous research into transitions has examined strategies with which to assist students to cope with the social and emotional adjustments (e.g. Noyes, 2006), there is a paucity of understanding of how literacy transitions are supported in the primary writing classrooms.

Previous research into transitions has highlighted the importance of a learning curriculum – a learning environment that can 'steer students towards or away from developing the attributes of effective learning' (Claxton & Carr, 2004: 88). This chapter examines some of the ways in which the learning curriculum is enacted in writing classrooms in which students are inducted into the writing of narrative texts in one Kindergarten and one Year 3/4 classroom.

The data informing this chapter comprise classroom observation and interview data collected as part of a larger longitudinal project. Drawing on the Systemic Functional Linguistics (SFL) framework of pedagogic register analysis (Rose, 2014, 2018), we identify examples of pedagogic practice that teachers employ to develop knowledge and foster repertoires of participation central to the learning and teaching of writing. The findings contribute to the understanding of pedagogic practice related to teachers' knowledge of transition as children learn to write across different years of primary schooling.

## Effective Pedagogic Practice in Writing

The focus on pedagogic practice in this chapter recognises an ongoing call for a more systematic and compelling account of children's school literacy experiences (Baker & Luke, 1991). Corroborating this repeated call for more empirical evidence, research into literacy development has demonstrated that forms of pedagogic practice are largely responsive to 'the kinds of performance and dispositional outcomes' in literacy (Freebody, 1991: 254). This is because what teachers perceive to be writing and successful writers is inevitably enacted in pedagogies adopted by teachers to support learning to write.

However, how best to foster and enable development of competent writers has been much debated in the field of writing research. There are three major approaches to teaching writing – cognitive, process and text-based. Each approach has its own assumptions about writing processes and development, and each expresses a different view on effective writing pedagogies. Approaching writing as a process of discovery, the cognitive approach conceives of effective writing as involving a series of thinking processes orchestrated by writers during the act of writing (Flower & Hayes, 1981). In a similar vein, the process approach gives primacy to the process of composing texts and privileges pedagogic practices that incorporate the writing process of planning, drafting, revising and publishing (Graves, 1983).

The text-based approach draws on a sociocultural and semiotic approach to writing (Martin & Rose, 2008; Rose & Martin, 2012). From this perspective, developing confident writers involves expert assistance provided within the context of social interaction and shared experience. Combined with a social semiotic theory of language as a meaning-making resource (Halliday, 1978), this approach offers an explicit writing pedagogy aimed towards developing understandings of language choices through a teaching and learning cycle of modelling, guided practice and independent writing (Derewianka & Jones, 2016). The modelling stage explicitly teaches about the stages of a text and language choices of a selected mentor text. Guided practice comprises a distinct stage of teacher-guided collaborative writing often referred to as joint construction of a similar text. This chapter draws on this social semiotic approach to writing in order to present and apply an integrated understanding of pedagogic practice that facilitates literacy transitions in primary writing classrooms.

## Analysing Pedagogic Practice – a Social Semiotic Perspective

Examining pedagogic practice entails analysis of classroom episodes where writing is explicitly taught and modelled. Christie's (1995) conception of pedagogic discourse (a sociological term after Bernstein, 1990) as curriculum genres provides a powerful tool for describing how children are apprenticed into cultural ways of understanding and knowledge. Rose (2014, 2018) expands this conception to include two intersecting registers: a curriculum register of knowledge and values, and a pedagogic register of activities, social relations and modalities, corresponding to the social basis of semiosis: the experiential, the interpersonal and the textual. Pedagogic activities are structured around learning tasks undertaken by learners, which teachers may prepare, focus, evaluate and elaborate. At the scale of teacher/learner interactions, learners' tasks may be active – proposing meanings, or identifying meaning in texts or images, or receptive – receiving spoken meanings or perceiving them in images.

The social relations between teachers and learners comprise pedagogic relations, which are enacted between teachers and learners. These relations also include those between authors of texts and learners, and between learners' texts produced for evaluation and teachers' spoken and written evaluations. Notably, Rose's pedagogic register analysis goes beyond the traditional description of social relations as hierarchies of authority between teachers and learners. It offers tools to identify choices teachers make in engaging learners in a series of conscious acts in the forms of, among others, attention, perception, knowledge (i.e. acts of knowing, including memory). These conscious acts are negotiated by interactions through which the teacher may, for example, invite attention, approve perception and model or impart knowledge.

Pedagogic modalities represent the mode through which the pedagogic activities are presented. These include the actual knowledge resources, including a variety of spoken, written and multimodal resources, that are drawn from the environment, verbal and visual records, and the knowledge of teachers and learners to convey meanings, along with the way they are accessed. Learning cycles are realised in discourse as exchanges of knowledge or action, in which speakers take primary or secondary roles (Martin & Rose, 2007). In a pedagogic register, the teacher is usually the primary knower in a knowledge exchange, and learners are secondary knowers.

Together the configuration of pedagogic activities, relations and modalities provides a way of illuminating differences in the ways in which knowledge and values are exchanged, negotiated and developed in the writing classroom

(Rose, 2014, 2018, 2019). We draw on this pedagogic register analysis to identify possible shifts that can elucidate the nature of the transition in learning to write evident in the classroom. Although Christie's (1995: 221) early work provides evidence of 'significant shifts' in the nature of classroom talk, an analysis of shifts in writing pedagogic practice is lacking. The analysis will contribute to an integrated understanding of the pedagogic practice across early and middle primary years.

## Context of the Study

This chapter reports on part of the Transforming Literacy Outcomes (TRANSLIT 2014–17) project that investigated how literacy develops across the years of schooling by examining the notion of critical literacy transitions – from preschool to primary school to high school. The data included in this chapter were taken from two case study schools – Beachside Primary School and Portside Primary School – in a regional city in New South Wales (NSW), Australia. Beachside Primary School is in a fairly stable, socio-economically even area. It has 60 per cent of students in the middle quartiles for socio-educational advantage (2019, myschool.edu.au). It has few Indigenous students (2%), and 93 per cent of the children speak only English at home[1] (Australian Bureau of Statistics).

Portside Primary School is a multicultural public school located in a low socio-economic setting with approximately 75 per cent of students in the lowest quartile for socio-educational advantage, 38 per cent of the students coming from non-English-speaking backgrounds and 19 per cent from Indigenous backgrounds (2019, myschool.edu.au). Portside was an Early Action for Success (EAfS) school under the NSW Literacy and Numeracy Action Plan 2012–16 developed to improve literacy and numeracy learning outcomes in disadvantaged schools. As part of this EAfS initiative, a dedicated instructional leader was appointed to Portside whose role was to work alongside the teachers in early primary (Kindergarten to Year 2) years to model and mentor effective teaching practice in literacy and numeracy (Chen & Vale, 2020).

The overall TRANSLIT project employed qualitative and ethnographic research methods combined with linguistic analysis to examine contexts as constructed by teachers and students. Data gathered include lesson observations, interviews with teachers and students, curriculum documents and students' writing samples. Reported in this chapter are observation data collected from two literacy lessons: Beachside Kindergarten (2016) and Portside Years 3/4 (2016). Each of the selected lessons had an explicit focus on writing. The teachers are named Lesley (Kindergarten) and Kate (Years 3/4).[2]

# Findings

## Learning to Write Description: Kindergarten Classroom

In the first of the two case studies presented here, we look at the pedagogical practices of Lesley in a Kindergarten lesson and see how her varying pedagogic register enables students to construe the knowledge embedded in the lesson. This lesson was the final in a lesson sequence, the culmination of several readings of the chosen book 'The Magnificent Tree' by Nick Bland and Steven Michael King. The objective of this lesson was for the children to write a description of a tree of their own design, which they would first draw as a plan for the task, producing a knowledge source for them to refer to while independently writing their descriptions. Thus, the children would produce both an illustrated plan and a finished written text.

### *Learning Intentions*

An interview with Lesley showed her to be committed to explicit knowledge exchange, showing the children exactly what she wants them to do:

> In terms of how we [cope with challenges at transition points], it is the way we explain things, it's the way we model things, how we're explicit with the children … you really have to take a big step back and … have high expectations but model what you expect them to do, and if you model well and show them what they need to do and what you expect, then you're going to get the best out of the kids.

This pedagogical intent was evident in the structuring of Lesley's writing lessons and will be discussed in the ensuing sections.

### Structuring of Lesley's Pedagogic Register

Six discernible lesson stages shape the lesson: an introduction specifying for the children the intent of the lesson, a review of the field (revisiting the story book), teacher-modelled drawing (at the front of the class, with children participating while grouped on the mat), independent drawing (with children returned to their desks), teacher-modelled writing (again together as a group) and independent writing (again back at their desks). The lesson activities are carefully crafted and, in the learning cycles, the minutiae of interactions and interchanges of the lesson can be examined to particularise the classroom exchanges configured in the three register systems – pedagogic activities, pedagogic relations and pedagogic modalities.

We look at four exchanges of Lesley's Kindergarten lesson. The first two illustrate knowledge exchange in the curriculum field. The third exchange focuses on the pedagogic activity of the lesson, and the fourth illustrates the incorporation of a 'grammar moment', each exchange showing instances of the explicit approach to presenting matter in this Kindergarten classroom.

### Note on Presentation of Data

The selected classroom exchanges are presented in tables. The first column from the left numbers the learning cycles within the exchanges for easy reference and the second keeps track of whether the **speaker** is the teacher or student/s. The transcript of the lesson appears in the third column. The fourth column indicates the **role** that the speaker is playing in the exchange: the teacher is typically primary knower (K1), but she sometimes delays the confirmation of the knowledge with a question (dK1); students are typically secondary knowers (K2); occasionally, the participants are primary or secondary actors (A1/A2). The next column shows the phases of each learning cycle and their matter. The final two columns indicate either the sourcing of meanings or interacts between teacher and learners.

### Consideration of Character

In the first lesson stage (review of the field), Lesley guides the students to consider the nature of the two protagonists in the book and their corresponding concepts of trees. The illustrative exchange (Table 7.1) occurs towards the

**Table 7.1** Exchange Orienting Matter to Curriculum Field: Garnering Ideas (Stage II Reviewing the Field)

|   |   | Transcript | Role | Phases | Sourcing |
|---|---|---|---|---|---|
| 1 | T | [turning to next page] | | | |
|   |   | So here we are – here's Bonnie – | K1 | Prepare character | locate image |
|   |   | Her ideas were clear and simple and just, just lovely. | | | rephrase text |
|   |   | [turning to next page] | | | |
|   |   | But Pop, | | | |
|   |   | what did he like? | dK1 | Focus character | |
|   |   | He liked things a little bit, that were a little bit different. | K1 | Prepare character | recast image |
|   |   | He liked things that were big and grey | | | |
|   |   | And what did he like? | dK1 | Focus character | |
|   |   | [pointing to Pop's idea in book] | | | point image |
|   |   | Things that were …? | dK1 | focus quality | remind prior lesson |
|   | S | sticking out … | K2 | propose quality | recall prior lesson |
|   | T | Sticking out [nodding]. | K1 | affirm | |
|   |   | Things that were sticking out. | | elaborate quality | |
| 3 |   | [turning to next page] | | | |
|   | T | And they needed to come up with an idea. | K1 | Prepare story | rephrase text |
|   |   | And their idea was that the birds kept flying away, | | | |
|   |   | [turning to next page] | | | |
|   |   | *flying away* [gesture with open palm], | | | |
|   |   | and they didn't know how to get the birds back to stay. | | | |
|   |   | [turning to next page] | | | |
|   | T | So, they had to come up with an idea to build a magnificent tree | | | |
| 4 |   | [turns several pages] | | | |
|   | T | So, here's Pop, here he is, coming up with his ideas. | K1 | prepare character | locate image |
|   |   | And what did Pop like to do? | dK1 | focus activity | remind prior lesson |
|   |   | [pointing to Pop] | | | point image |

**Table 7.1** Exchange Orienting Matter to Curriculum Field: Garnering Ideas (Stage II Reviewing the Field) (continued)

|   |    | Transcript | Role | Phases | Sourcing |
|---|----|------------|------|--------|----------|
|   |    | *What did he like to do?* |      |        |          |
|   | S3 | *[one hand goes up]* | A2 |     |          |
|   | T  | *Rachel?* | A1 |     |          |
|   | S3 | *He um liked to make trees … that were um big um and metal and stuff* | K2 | propose quality | recall prior lesson |
|   | T  | *[nods]* | K1 | affirm |          |
|   |    | *He liked to make trees that were a little bit different.* |   | elaborate quality | recast image |
| 5 | T  | *How did you describe the tree, Sean?* *What did you think it was?* | dK1 | focus quality | remind prior move |
|   | S4 | *it had all bits and bobs like a robot.* | K2 | propose quality | recall learner knowledge |
|   |    | *Bits and bobs, a bit like a robot.* | K1 | affirm |          |
|   | T  | *And he had to draw them, draw down his ideas* |   | elaborate activity | rephrase text |

end of an activity in which Lesley models how to skim the picture book for pertinent information to do with the nature of Pop and Bonnie and of the trees they made. Here we are interested in how meanings are sourced from the text, images and shared knowledge from prior lesson stages. As part of skimming through the book, Lesley flips quickly through the pages. As she turns to a pertinent page, she orients the students to the image by physically **pointing**, **rephrasing** the text and **recasting** the pictures. For example, in the first learning cycle (1), the teacher prepares the task by rephrasing and recasting what the text and images say about the characters of Bonnie and Pop. Her focus question then reminds them of a quality that Pop liked, which had been discussed in a prior lesson stage, *Things that were sticking out*.

This simple exchange is indicative of the whole 'review of the field' stage. Lesley carefully guides the children to comprehend the experiential matter that is required for the lesson – that is to say, the differences between Pop's and Bonnie's ideas, the problem of the birds not staying and the solution to build a tree. While considering the 'person' of each of the characters (Bonnie and Pop), she moves attention to their main pertinent characteristic (the sorts of things they liked) and then on to the manifestation of these characteristics (how they were reflected in their tree design). Lesley gently increases the difficulty of her prompts (see her dK1 moves): in cycle 2, the task is to **recall qualities** that Pop liked (and multiple children respond); in cycle 3, the task is to **recall qualities** of the trees that Pop made (Rachel responds); and in cycle 4, the task is to propose qualities of these from learner knowledge (Sean is called on to respond). Lesley finishes this exchange with an elaboration which foreshadows the next stages of the lesson, where students, like Pop, will *draw down [their] ideas*.

## Consideration of Environment

The second example of curriculum field knowledge (Table 7.2) occurs in the third lesson stage, teacher-modelled drawing. The exchange illustrates how Lesley prepares the pedagogic activity by creating engagement through praise and helping recall, then elaborates on the activity by modelling reasoning and conception to foster understanding of the activity.

Already armed with ideas from the picture book, Lesley encourages the children to **propose** choices for the features of their own trees. She **reminds** children of their own learner **knowledge** from an earlier chat and **inquires** of their **choices**, helping them to **recall** their ideas to share with class members. The focus is on the broad idea of the tree, rather than specific details. She moves quickly from student to student building up ideas, develops affirmation and again concludes with an **elaboration** on the lesson activity.

## Consideration of Activity and Language

The final two exchanges focus on pedagogic activity and knowledge about language. In the first exchange (Table 7.3), Lesley importantly reorients the students to the lesson activity – the students are to translate their acquired field knowledge into a drawing. Lesley reminds students of the practicalities of using their writing books, drawing on teacher and shared knowledge from prior lessons. By being extremely explicit here, she ensures as far as possible that every student is enabled for the lesson activity. This is a monologic exchange, where the students' task is to **receive** the **steps** of the activity as the teacher explains them, at the same time as **perceiving** as the points at the book. The exchange is bookended by directed activity, initially preparing the activity (*before we even start writing*) and finishing by elaborating on it (*Don't*

*Understanding Literacy Transitions* 129

**Table 7.2** Exchange Orienting Matter to Curriculum Field: Developing Ideas (Stage III Modelling Drawing)

| | | Transcript | Role | Phases | Sourcing |
|---|---|---|---|---|---|
| 1 | T | Now, you had some really good ideas before this. | K1 | prepare ped activity | remind learner knowledge |
| | | You thought of putting some … what … in your trees? | dK1 | focus thing | |
| | S1 | pillows | K2 | propose thing | recall learner knowledge |
| | T | You thought of some pillows, didn't you? | K1 | affirm | |
| | | so that they were soft. | | elaborate quality | remind learner knowledge |
| 2 | T | What did you think, Kristi? | dK1 | focus idea | remind learner knowledge |
| | S2 | Some soft stuff | K2 | propose quality | recall learner knowledge |
| | | so the baby chicks can hatch | | | |
| | T | Oh, that's a great idea. | K1 | affirm | |
| | | We had lots of those ideas. | | | |
| 3 | T | What did you think, Jasper? | dK1 | focus idea | remind learner knowledge |
| | S3 | a dome around the nest, | K2 | propose activity | recall learner knowledge |
| | | so if there's a storm they can be protected from the lightning | | | |
| | T | That's right, that was Sean's idea … | K1 | affirm | |
| | | He said he's going to have a tree, and then put like a shed around the tree | | elaborate activity | rephrase move |
| | | because if a tornado or a tsunami came along, then the tree would be protected for the birds to land there | | | |
| | | Because that's why we're designing this tree today – we're trying to attract the birds to come and be a part of it. | | elaborate ped activity | rephrase move |

start our writing yet because we're going to unpack our heads). The repeated **locating**-and-**pointing** is embedded in the teacher talk and provides strong scaffolding and clear instruction which develops to the final injunction when Lesley elaborates and segues to the next step in the lesson.

**Table 7.3** Exchange Orienting Matter to Pedagogic Activity (Stage III Modelling Drawing)

|   | Transcript | Role | Phases | Sourcing |
|---|---|---|---|---|
| T | So, before we even go and start writing, | K1 | prepare ped activity | new teacher knowledge |
|   | [takes up writing book sample from board] | | | point writing book |
|   | we've got our writing books which we've already got on our tables | | | locate writing book |
|   | and here is our planning page in our writing books. | | focus step | locate page |
|   | [opens book right out] | | | |
|   | This part, remember, is for drawing your plan, | | receive step | remind prior lesson |
|   | [indicates left portion] | | perceive step | point page |
|   | this side is for the teacher to help you, | | receive step | locate text |
|   | [indicates right portion] | | perceive step | point page |
|   | and then we start our writing. | | receive activity | remind prior lesson |
|   | [indicates bottom page] | | perceive step | point page |
|   | Don't start our writing yet, | | elaborate ped activity | new teacher knowledge |
|   | because we're going to unpack our head and get our ideas. | | | |

In the final exchange (Table 7.4), the knowledge exchange dips naturally into the language stratum, giving a grammar reinforcement in context of modelling writing. Lesley verbally **locates** the **text**, being explicit about *one more sentence*. She inquires of the children's knowledge (*what could we use?*). She then probes the students' **knowledge** of the use of pronouns. As she focuses and refocuses on the word, the students are required to **propose** answers and **display** their knowledge, Lesley **insists** on the correct **choice** and **elaborates** with the correct metalanguage.

## Learning to Write Description: Year 3/4 Classroom

The second case study we examine in this section draws on observational data from Kate's writing lesson, a composite Year 3/4 class. The class is learning about writing an introduction to a novel, focusing in this lesson on description of setting and characterisation.

**Table 7.4** Exchange Orienting Matter to Pedagogic Modality: Knowledge about Grammar (Stage V Modelling Writing)

| | Transcript | Role | Phases | Sourcing |
|---|---|---|---|---|
| T | *One more sentence* I'm going to think *of. Umm ...* | K1 | prepare ped activity | locate text |
| | *Instead of saying 'my tree, my tree, my tree',* | dK1 | focus word | remind prior move |
| | *what word could I use instead of that?* | | | |
| | *Instead of 'my special tree, my special tree, my special tree' ... it gets very boring ...* | | | remind prior lesson |
| | *what could we use?* | | | |
| S1 | *our tree* | K2 | propose word | recall learner knowledge |
| T | *Our tree? Well it's not your tree, it's still my tree.* | K1 | reject | |
| | *What could we use instead of '[(something)] tree'?* | dK1 | focus word | enquire prior move |
| Ss | *It. It* [chorus] | K2 | propose word | Infer prior lesson |
| T | *It! It! I'm going to use the word 'it'.* | K1 | affirm | |
| | *It's its plural, sorry (no), it's its pronoun: 'it', 'it'* | | elaborate metalanguage | restate prior lesson |

## *Learning Intentions*

As pointed out by Rose (2018), a cultural function of the pedagogic register is the exchange of knowledge and values between teachers and learners. Kate's interviews showed her to be concerned with the value of making the learning intentions explicit. When asked to elaborate on making her learning intentions visible, she responded:

> Making sure they know exactly what they're aiming for at the beginning of the lesson – that's important. Then from there, it's their individual goals, and each of my children either have it on their desk ... I have to be intentional on who I'm giving what piece of information. It's guiding each of them. Some of it I just keep in my head.

Kate's lesson had two aims, designed to interact with each other. She summed them up at the beginning of her lesson.

> Who thought their writing today was better than they've done for a little while? (most hands go up). Yeah, I thought it was too ... I thought you really

**Table 7.5** W.A.L.T. – Characterisation

| CHARACTERISATION |
| --- |
| In most stories characters seem to steer the events in the story. W.A.L.T. |

focussed on what you were asked to do – [pointing to W.A.L.T] 'We Are Learning To describe the character and to describe the place.'

There were four broad lesson stages that we could discern in Kate's writing lesson: lesson intent and reviewing the setting; teaching about characterisation; introducing the writing task; and independent writing (see Table 7.5). The data presented here focus on the first two lesson stages during which Kate guides students through a deconstruction and analysis of pertinent aspects of features of setting and characterisation.

Kate's emphasis throughout was less on explicit physical pen-in-hand modelling, but her concern was to demonstrate the thoughts and actions that go into creating a text. She provided a rich context for her students to experience a variety of models from which to choose for their own creations.

By far the main part of the lesson involved examining one exemplar – a WAGOLL (What A Good One Looks Like) – for features of description of the setting and character that could be emulated in the students' own writing. By this approach, they discover register features of an 'introduction'. For example, 'purpose' was examined through reminding them of a recently read text, *A File on Rose Moncrieff*. Kate and the children explored the sorts of information available at the opening of the novel, concluding:

> We found all that out because of the introductory paragraphs. The introductory paragraphs in every novel are really important.

### *Structuring of the Pedagogic Activity*

The curriculum goal of the lesson is the 'introduction' to a novel with a particular focus on characterisation. Similar to what we have observed in the Kindergarten classroom, Kate begins the lesson with reading of the introduction of *A File on Rose Moncrieff* followed by a close read of how the setting and characters are portrayed. She refers to earlier lesson moves to

Understanding Literacy Transitions   133

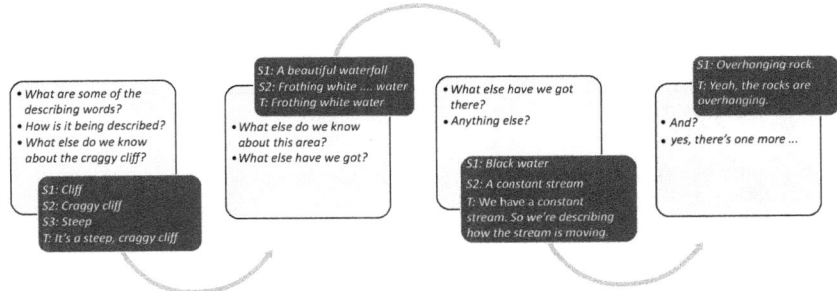

**Figure 7.1** Structuring of Pedagogic Activity

reference the unit theme of writing an introduction to a novel and quickly focuses on the lesson theme of setting.

Figure 7.1 provides an overview of how the pedagogic activity unfolds in four exchanges where the teacher and students work together to negotiate and co-construct their knowledge of the setting. The text is projected on the board so all can see. The learning tasks centre around identifying the elements of the setting as portrayed in the introduction to a novel: the cliff, waterfall, water/stream, rocks and their appearance: *the beautiful waterfall* and the *frothing white water, the black water, constant stream, overhanging rocks*. In each exchange, students are guided to complete the tasks at hand through focus questions including, for example: *How is it being described? What else do we know about this area? What else have we got there? And?* The teacher invites the students' contributions which are affirmed and elaborated with a refined explanation: *It's a steep, craggy cliff; Frothing white water; We have a constant stream; So, we're describing how the stream is moving; Yeah, the rocks are overhanging.*

The teacher concludes the learning cycles about the setting by reminding the class: *that first paragraph there tells us ... where it is and what it looks like.* The knowledge exchanged here is realised through lexical relations: the setting and its surrounds and their qualities (*a steep, craggy cliff; frothing white water; black water/a constant stream; overhanging rocks*).

In the Waterfall exchange presented in Table 7.6 students are guided to identify the qualities of the cliff. There are two fields of knowledge – place and character – which are revealed through the experiential analyses following

**Table 7.6** Exchange Modelling Describing the Setting

| | | Transcript | Role | Phases | Sourcing |
|---|---|---|---|---|---|
| 1 | T | Today we're going to be doing some writing, | K1 | prepare activity | |
| | | and the writing we're going to do today is going to focus on that introduction to writing a novel | | | |
| | | – the way authors do that – | | | |
| | | and we'll look at **characterisation**. | | focus metalanguage | |
| | | I'm going to read it and I want you to tell me **what this first paragraph is about**. | | focus topic | locate text |
| | | 'The pool was almost hidden by the early evening shadows. It sat in the back of the glade at the foot of the steep, craggy cliff. Behind some overhanging rocks, a beautiful waterfall was feeding into the pool's black water a constant stream of frothing white water. | | receive text | read text |
| 2 | T | What's it **about**? Laura? | dK1 | focus topic | |
| | S1 | the shadows on the pool | K2 | propose topic | recall learner |
| | T | [nodding] It's talking about that. | K1 | affirm | |
| 3 | T | [points to another student] | dK1 | | |
| | S2 | it's **about describing what the pool's like** | K2 | propose topic | recall learner |
| | T | It's all the **descriptions**, isn't it, | K1 | affirm | |
| | | so those, lots of **describing words** | | elaborate metalanguage | |
| 4 | | … | | | |
| 5 | | But what is it … **how is it being described?** | dK1 | focus quality | recast text |
| | | It is very …? | | focus word | |
| | | [arm gesture for craggy] | K1 | prepare quality | |
| | S4 | **craggy** | K2 | identify word | recall text |
| | T | Craggy | K1 | affirm | |
| | | [underlines on board] | | | mark text |
| | | It was a craggy cliff. | | elaborate wording | rephrase text |
| 6 | | It said **more about** that craggy cliff as well. | K1 | prepare quality | locate text |

*Understanding Literacy Transitions* 135

**Table 7.6** Exchange Modelling Describing the Setting (continued)

|  | Transcript | Role | Phases | Sourcing |
|---|---|---|---|---|
|  | *What else do we know about the craggy cliff?* | dK1 | focus quality | |
|  | *[points to student] It was …?* | | focus word | locate text |
| S5 | [indistinct] | K2 | … | |
| T | *hmmmm* | K1 | reject | |
| 7 | *[points to another]* | dK1 | | |
| S6 | *it's **steep**?* | K2 | identify word | recall text |
| T | *It's steep.* | K1 | affirm | |
|  | [underlines] | | | mark text |
|  | *So there's **two parts** to that. It's a steep, craggy cliff.* | | elaborate wording | |

Rose (2014). The teacher prepares the class for the lesson activity by referring to the knowledge of prior lessons using terms such as *introduction, authors, characterisation, first paragraph, descriptions* and *describing words*. The focus question in cycle 2 guides students to identify and locate the setting of the story (*e.g. What's it about?*). S1 (K2) proposes the *shadows on the pool*, which is affirmed by the teacher (K1) and elaborated by S2, *it's about describing what's the pool like*. Kate approves and repeats *It's all the descriptions, isn't it?* (C3/K1). She further elaborates the technical field by reinforcing the metalanguage: *lots of describing words*.

In the final cycles (5–7), the field (setting) is elaborated through the focus question (*How is it being described?*). The teacher guides the students towards a response by prompting (*It is very…?*) and arm-gesturing. S4 identifies the wording (*craggy*) which is affirmed and reformulated by the teacher: *It was a craggy cliff.* Kate inquires further about the qualities of the cliff by probing, *what else do we know about the craggy cliff?* (C6, dK1). The knowledge is exchanged and negotiated through two dK1^K2^K1 cycles (C6, C7) with an elaboration phase at the end to offer a more technical understanding: *So, there's two parts to that. It's a steep, craggy cliff.*

### Repertoires of Learner Participation

The main curriculum goal of the lesson is to describe characters. The pedagogic register analysis of Kate's lesson shows that modelling was woven into the fabric of the discussion, gently guiding the children from simply describing what they see in the text to making implications and interpreting actions of the characters under examination.

Pedagogic relations pertain to the interpersonal dimension of the pedagogic practice – how knowledge is negotiated and exchanged through the roles adopted by the teacher and students. Learner participation is enacted as teacher and learner roles through ways in which 'learners are addressed, speak, and are affirmed' (Rose, 2019: 255). In Table 7.7, we are interested in a crucial aspect of learner participation that is construed through conscious acts and interacts that are solicited from the students.

In the exchanges presented in Table 7.7, Kate moves on from examining the way the WAGOLL dealt with the setting to its portrayal of character, showing the children the importance of introducing the character's name very early on.

In cycle 1, the teacher prepares the activity by focusing on *a few things about Archie*, inviting students to identify wordings in the text that denote his character. The pedagogic function of the learning sequence is to identify attributes of Archie: *school kid (C3), hot and sticky (C4), an adventurer (C10), wonderous kid (C12)*. Throughout the learning cycles included in Table 7.7, Kate **models characterisation** by **inviting reasoning** through focus questions such as: *What do we know about Archie? (C1) What else?* She constantly **models reasoning**: *He could be worried (C7); People who wonder about things, they question things (C10)*. The teacher invites learner participation by **inquiring** their **perception** of the text (C2/dK1, C3/dK1, C5/dK1) and **reasoning** (C7/dK1, C8/dK1, C10/dK1).

There are many instances where the teacher **models conception** (C5) and **reasoning** (C3, C10, C12) for learners to emulate. Kate models and directs reasoning about the attributes of the character: *So, we know that he's a school kid (C3); He was very hot and sticky because he'd been doing something (C5)*. It is worth noting that only one instance of modelling appears in the Prepare phase (C5). In the remaining modelling moves the teacher **imparts knowledge** or **models reasoning** as an elaboration on students' contributions. This implicit modelling move may present challenges for some who are not attuned to the intention of the higher order elaborations (see Chapter 8).

There is an explicit shift in the nature of conscious acts that are requested from the students beginning from cycle 5. In cycle 5 the task shifts from **perceiving words** in the text to **conceiving connections** between elements

*Understanding Literacy Transitions* 137

**Table 7.7** Exchange Modelling Characterisation

|   |   | Transcript | Role | Phases | Interacts |
|---|---|---|---|---|---|
| 1 | T | So, what do we know about Archie? | dK1 | prepare activity | model reasoning |
|   |   | We've found out **a few things about Archie** from this text. [underlines words?]. | K1 | focus character focus wordings | |
| 2 |   | … | | | |
| 3 | T | What else? | dK1 | focus character | inquire perception |
|   | S2 | He's um xxxx in school | K2 | identify wording | display perception |
|   | T | Yes, he's a school kid. [underlines in school] So we know that he's a school kid | K1 | affirm elaborate character | repeat model reasoning |
| 4 | T | [pointing to another student] | A2 | | direct display |
|   | S3 | He's hot and sticky | K2 | identify wording | display perception |
|   | T | He was. [underlines hot and sticky] | K1 | affirm | repeat |
| 5 | T | He was very hot and sticky because he'd been *doing something*. What had he *been doing*? | K1 dK1 | prepare activity focus | model conception inquire perception |
|   | Ss | Running through the forest [chorus] | K2 | identify wording | display perception |
|   | T | Yeah, he's been going for a run. | K1 | affirm elaborate activity | |
| 6 | T | Yep? [pointing to another student] | A2 | | direct display |
|   | S4 | … wonder | K2 | identify wording | display perception |
|   | T | So … he does wonder about things. [circles wonder] | K1 | affirm | repeat |
| 7 | T | If he wonders about things, **what sort of person** do you think he is? If he wonders? | dK1 | focus character | inquire reasoning |
|   | S5 | um … he … [no answer] | K2 | … | |
|   | T | Is he just a blob, who doesn't bother doing anything? | dK1 | focus character | inquire reasoning |
|   | Ss | No [chorus] | K2 | | concur |

**Table 7.7** Exchange Modelling Characterisation (continued)

| | | Transcript | Role | Phases | Interacts |
|---|---|---|---|---|---|
| 8 | T | If he's wondering about something, he's …? | dK1 | focus character | inquire reasoning |
| | | [pointing to another student] | A2 | | direct display |
| | S6 | Worried about something? | K2 | propose quality | display perception |
| | T | He could be worried. | K1 | affirm | repeat |
| 9 | | … | | | |
| 10 | T | But what does that make him? It doesn't make him a blob, it makes him a …? | dK1 | focus character | inquire reasoning |
| | S8 | Adventurer? | K2 | propose character | display reasoning |
| | T | Oh, it could be an adventurer! | K1 | evaluate | model reasoning |
| 11 | S2 | A wonder'ous kid? | K2 | propose character | display reasoning |
| | T | Yes, someone who questions things. People who wonder about things, they question things. | K1 | affirm elaborate character | approve model reasoning |

of the text, that is, the quality *hot and sticky* and the activity *going for a run* (C5/K1). The focus thus moves away from the task of identifying wordings in the text to proposing an interpretation from prior knowledge. The kind of the relationship that is negotiated here is that between learners and the author of the text under study (Rose, 2014).

Such intertextual engagement is the focus of the tasks in cycles 7–8 where Kate continues to invite students to draw out inferences or **reason** about the qualities of the character: *if he wonders about things, what sort of person do you think he is if he wonders?* (C7/dK1). The shift to **propose quality** from knowledge presents some difficulties to learner participation as can be observed in cycle 7. The teacher's second dK1 attempt guides the class towards a desired response through an explicit prompt: *Is he just a blob, who doesn't bother doing anything?* This is not met with success, so Kate repeats the focus of the task in cycle 8: *If he's wondering about something, he's …?* S6 **proposes quality** – *worried about something* – which is affirmed and re-presented by the teacher: *He could be worried.*

The knowledge exchanged in these learning cycles is structured around the qualities of the character. Kate guides the negotiation of knowledge through directing attention to the relations between lexical items: *hot and sticky* and *going for a run*; *wondering about things* and *worried*. In cycles 10–12, Kate extends the knowledge about the qualities of the character by further inquiring about what could be generalised about the **character types**: *What does that make him?* The knowledge that is negotiated here is realised by a more complex lexical relation, classifying, requiring an ability to identify character types: adventurer (C10), thinker (C11), *a wonderous kid* (C12). Such a shift in the task demands would not have been revealed without the analysis of the deeper level of pedagogic relations.

## Discussion

This chapter sets out to examine pedagogic practices that can 'steer students towards … developing the attributes of effective learning' (Claxton & Carr, 2004: 88). In particular, it examines practices that support learning to describe place and characters in an early and middle primary classroom. The analysis identifies three shifts in ways that pedagogic practices are configured differently through a combination of pedagogic activity, pedagogic modalities, and teacher and learner relations.

### Increase in Complexity of Knowledge and Task Demands

From the perspective of field, the first shift is the increase in specialisation and complexity of knowledge that centres around place/setting and characterisation. In both lessons place or setting is a key subject matter that is explored and discussed as part of the pedagogic activities. In Lesley's lesson, the knowledge exchanged is realised mostly through lexical items. For example, the place comprises a tree which is construed as a **quality** (*bits and bobs like a robot* in Table 7.1; *a dome around the nest, some soft stuff* in Table 7.2). Learners were invited to draw their trees so as to attract birds to come. In the Year 3/4 lesson, the gaze was directed to the setting and its surrounds which are explored in terms of their appearance (*steep, craggy cliff,* *overhanging rocks*), colours (*frothing white water, black water*) and movement (*frothing white water, a constant stream*). The knowledge exchanged is much more complex and is realised through relations between lexical items (*steep – craggy – cliff; frothing – white – water; stream – moving*).

While the focus of the Kindergarten lesson was on 'place' (a tree), discussion of character was necessary in order to particularise the tree. Lesley's treatment of character focuses on identifying what particular things the characters as persons liked. The focus of Years 3/4 class is on characterisation – the ability to generalise about character types (*a thinker, an adventurer, a wonderous kid*). The knowledge exchanged is more abstract and complex – a shift away from everyday, common-sense understanding. Much of the pedagogic activity is structured around eliciting attributes of the characters in the story and the meaning of those choices. Students are requested to infer (reason) about the characters and understand the author's intention of those choices. The task demands an increase in complexity requiring appropriate responses from students' prior knowledge and values (Rose, 2014). These are the skills that are required for more advanced writing of the complex narrative texts.

## Shift in Modes of Meaning

The second shift is the increasing importance of learners' knowledge. Our lesson observations have identified a range of knowledge sources such as picture books, verbal and visual records, and the knowledge of teachers and learners. In the Kindergarten classroom, the sources shift frequently between visual images and picture book (Exchange 7.1), writing book and pages of the book (Exchange 7.3). The shared meanings are construed as a 'here and now' experience enacted through pointing and locating (Exchanges 7.1 and 7.3). These concrete meanings are brought into the pedagogic activity as the knowledge is negotiated and exchanged. Learners are further assisted through restating, recasting and reminding (Exchanges 7.2 and 7.4).

The Year 3/4 classroom draws predominantly on the model text and spoken sources of learners' and teacher's knowledge. The teacher's questions mostly inquire of students' perception or reasoning (Exchanges 7.6 and 7.7). Students infer answers from their prior knowledge which are affirmed and elaborated by the teacher. Sourcing of meaning shifts from identifying wordings from the text, facilitated by pointing and locating, to inferring and generalising from learners' prior knowledge. The construal of shared meanings draws largely from acts of enquiring, recasting, and restating (Exchange 7.6) and verbally enquiring, reminding, recalling, restating and recasting (Exchange 7.7).

## Shift in Repertoires of Learner Participation

A further shift is the increase in the cognitive demands required for classroom participation. Rose's pedagogic register analysis offers a rich means of analysing social relations exchanged between learners and teacher in the classroom, in particular, the cognitive engagement in learning tasks. In Lesley's lesson pedagogic relations are distinctly structured as **perceiving, receiving** and **attending** which predominate the repertoires of participation in Exchanges 7.1 and 7.3. The teacher is mostly **directing** and **modelling**.

There is a more varied use of interacts in creating repertoires of participation in the Year 3/4 writing classroom. The Exchanges in Tables 7.6 and 7.7 enact participatory repertoires through a distinct combination of interacts, ranging from **perceiving** in Exchange 7.6, and **reasoning** in Exchange 7.7. The instances where the learner's display of reasoning, perception and choice constitutes the learning to write activity are pedagogically significant given that pedagogic discourse plays a pivotal role in cultural reproduction and transformation (Rose, 2014, 2018). These enacted roles of learners and teachers manifest in unfolding pedagogic relations have consequential effects for 'the kinds of performance and dispositional outcomes of school experiences' (Freebody, 1991: 254).

There is a discernible shift in ways that learners are engaged in pedagogic relations. We see a move from a more directive role by the teacher in the Kindergarten classroom to a more demanding participatory role expected of learners in the Year 3/4 classroom, which is demonstrated by more cognitively and perceptively orientated interacts (reasoning, choosing and perceiving connections). While acts of **conceiving, perceiving** and **reasoning** are observable in both classrooms, the interacts differ substantially across the classrooms leading to configuration of different repertoires of participation. In the Kindergarten classroom students are appropriately guided to **perceive**,

**conceive** or **reason** through the teacher **directing perception** and **modelling conception** or **reasoning** (7.1–7.4). Guidance is also provided to facilitate learning in the Years 3/4 classroom (7.7). There are increased requests for **perceiving connections and reasoning** about ideas drawn from learners' knowledge (e.g. inquire conception, perception, reasoning, in 7.6). The varied participatory patterns identified in this study have important implications for more effective writing pedagogic design.

## Conclusion

This chapter has examined important changes at a crucial literacy transition point in the primary writing classrooms. The pedagogic register analysis enables an integrated understanding of how knowledge is negotiated, explained and modelled, and how this is supported by distinct patterns of participation and modes of meaning. Our analysis provides evidence of significant development which is marked by the increase in the complexity of knowledge, different expectations of learner participation and more abstract modes of meaning that support learning.

These changes point to the increased significance of teaching advanced literacy skills such as critical reasoning – the capacity to reason, infer and generalise (McNaughton, 2020). Yet policy recommendations for better performance have often attributed the decline in writing performance to simply an inability to compose well-structured sentences and use correct spelling and punctuation. This has given rise to policy recommendations stressing the importance of basic, introductory literacy skills (NESA, 2020). We would argue that one of the reasons for the decline in writing outcomes is that students are typically not explicitly taught the kinds of 'thinking skills' that increase in complexity across the school years and how such skills are integral to the quality of their writing.

Our analysis has also identified that the teacher relies on responses from a few capable students on which new knowledge is modelled, introduced and elaborated (see Rose, 2018, and Chapter 8 in this collection). However, the intention of this pedagogic practice may remain implicit and invisible to those who may not be attuned to the function of this implicit pedagogic discourse.

The inequitable access to this official pedagogic discourse may continue to widen the performance gap if the crucial transition is not supported explicitly and effectively.

# 8

# Investigating Pedagogic Discourse in Late Primary and Junior Secondary English

Pauline Jones, Erika Matruglio and David Rose

## Literary Studies in the English Curriculum

This chapter considers classroom discourse practices in late primary and junior secondary English lessons around the teaching of poetry. Subject English in the Australian curriculum comprises the study of language, literacy and literature from the first year of schooling through to the end of junior secondary school. With respect to literature or 'verbal art' (Hasan, 1985), students develop an appreciation of literary texts for their personal, social, cultural and aesthetic value and potential for enriching students' 'scope of experience' (ACARA, 2015). Developing such appreciation requires students to engage with two different but related layers of meaning: a first order of meanings construed directly by the wordings of a text and a second order of more abstract, thematic meanings that are symbolised by the text, to make a commentary or observation on some personal, social or natural condition (Austen, 1993). Hasan (1985) refers to the interface between first- and second-order meanings – where the language of the text becomes signs with deeper meaning – as an intermediate layer of *symbolic articulation* – in other words, where meanings have meanings. In the English curriculum, texts must be 'read as tokens of an underlying message or "theme": the text as a whole is treated as a kind of metaphor, with the story itself projecting a deeper level of meaning' (Martin, 1996: 127). This phenomenon of thematic meanings, with its emphasis on metaphorisation, marks verbal art from expository texts (Hasan, 1985) and makes subject English particularly challenging for many students without the means to access those abstract meanings.

The distinct nature of subject English resonates with research into disciplinary literacies that focuses on the ways in which disciplines and their curricula formations differ with respect to the beliefs they have about the nature of knowledge, core ideas and principles, inquiry and reasoning practices as well as discourse and language structures (Goldman et al., 2016; Moje, 2008). Christie (2005) describes the student as an apprentice; that is, 'one who is initiated into ways of behaving, of knowing and of thinking, ways of identifying and responding to issues, ways of addressing problems and ways of valuing' (2005: 162).[1] In this vein, the *Australian Curriculum: English* (2015) describes subject English as a cumulative body of knowledge to be acquired by students from early primary to senior secondary school. However, much of the research into the language demands associated with the increased abstraction and technicality of the curriculum has focused on students' writing (Christie & Derewianka, 2008). Few researchers have studied the development of subject-specific reading, with exceptions such as Shanahan and Shanahan (2014) and Rose and Martin (2012). Further, despite the sustained and increasing interest in classroom dialogue (e.g. Alexander, 2020; Edwards-Groves & Davidson, 2017; Mercer, Wegerif & Major, 2019; Resnick & Schantz, 2015; Thwaite, Jones & Simpson, 2020), fewer researchers still have studied the dialogic basis of disciplinarity,[2] that is, how students are enculturated over time into subject-specific ways of making meaning through classroom interactions.

English is the only compulsory curriculum subject taken by students in their final years of high school in the Australian state of NSW, yet for many students, success at English is elusive, perceived to be a matter of having 'a way with language', of having a certain 'gaze' or disposition rather than requiring specific skills or knowledge (Maton, 2014). By the time students reach senior secondary school, they are in effect 'sorted' into different streams of the English curriculum. Students who have internalised the required gaze are likely to study the 'Advanced' stream (~43%) while others take 'Standard' (52%) or reduced 'English Studies' (2%). These different 'levels' of English contribute significantly to students' university entrance ranking, as English is the only subject which makes a mandatory contribution to the Australian Tertiary Entrance Rank (ATAR). Only 9 per cent of students in the Advanced stream score less than 40 per cent, but 50 per cent of those in Standard and 96 per cent in English Studies scored under 40 per cent (Universities Admissions

Centre, 2020). These figures strongly suggest that streaming of subject English contributes to educational stratification in Australia (cf. Macken-Horarik, 2006). We were interested in how these differences in access and participation were realised across the primary/secondary transition. Our findings lead to a proposal for widening this access to more students.

## Learning to Appreciate Poetry

In this chapter we investigate the means by which students learn to appreciate literary texts in the form of poetry – a special case of aesthetic language in use. Students from the earliest years of school to senior secondary are expected to both appreciate and compose poetic texts.[3] Generally speaking, there is a move in the Australian curriculum from the study of poetry for pleasure in primary school to the study of poetry in its own right in secondary school. In the primary years, it is anticipated that students explore rhythms, rhymes, word patterns and play, and begin to consider sound devices and imagery, and point of view. In a space of two short years, however, such understandings are assumed, and emphasis in the curriculum shifts to semantics, issues of representation, intertextuality, the viewpoint of the text (cf. that of the responder) and to the examination of literary criticism itself (ACARA, 2015).

## The Data

The data at hand are drawn from a larger study of literacy transitions from the preschool to middle secondary school, TRANSLIT (see Chapter 1 this volume). The study included over fifty hours of observations of literacy learning across twelve preschool and school sites as well as case studies of approximately seventy students over three years.[4] The aim of the study was to explore how students' literacy experiences changed across the years of schooling. Observations in the secondary school setting were of lessons involving literacy in English, history and science. In order to explore the issue of cumulative learning in poetics, we examine two lessons – one observed in the final year of primary school, and another observed two years later in lower secondary.

## The Pedagogic Model

The model we deploy for analysis treats lessons as instances of *curriculum genres* (Christie, 2005). Genres more broadly are varieties of social activity recognised by members of a culture, or 'goal-oriented social processes' (Martin, 1992; Martin & Rose, 2008). Genres weave together three dimensions of meaning: *fields* of social activity, *tenor* of social relations and values, and *modes* of meaning making. Patterns of field, tenor and mode (collectively *register*) are realised as patterns of meaning in language. Poems are instances of *knowledge genres*, such as stories, descriptions or arguments. Knowledge genres configure fields of knowledge with social values, in spoken, written and visual modes. Poems differ from other instances of these genres, particularly in their modes of rhythm, rhyme, sound and word play. They tend to condense their fields and privilege thematic readings, to amplify affective, moral and aesthetic values.

Curriculum genres configure two registers together: a *curriculum register* of knowledge and values, with a *pedagogic register* of learning activities and relations between teachers and learners, using spoken, written and visual modalities. In any lesson, or lesson series, a curriculum register of knowledge and values is exchanged between teachers and learners, through a pedagogic register of activities, relations and modalities (Rose, 2016, 2018, 2019; Rose & Martin, 2012). Figure 8.1 summarises relations between these two registers.

Pedagogic *activities* are centred on learning tasks undertaken by learners. Learning tasks may be prepared and focused by teachers, who also usually evaluate them, and may elaborate on the learning. Learning tasks can be identified at three broad scales: of lessons and lesson series, of activities within each lesson and of teacher/learner interactions, where the task is often to respond to teacher questions. This tier of pedagogic activity has been termed *learning cycles*, as it often involves cycles of focus questions, responses and evaluations (widely known as 'initiation-response-feedback' or IRF cycles; following Sinclair & Coulthard, 1975; Mehan, 1979). Pedagogic *modalities* are the sources of meanings, including teachers' and learners' knowledge, recorded texts and images, and the environment, and the means of sourcing them into the classroom discourse, through speaking, gesturing, writing and drawing. Pedagogic *relations* negotiate the activities of learning, in which teachers and

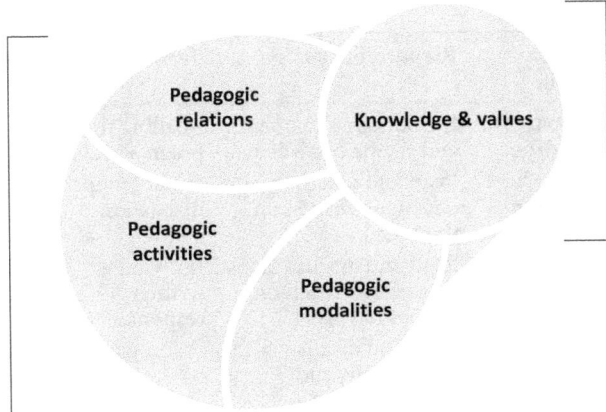

Figure 8.1 Curriculum genres configure two registers together

learners take complementary but asymmetric roles to co-construct curricular knowledge and values. Teachers' roles broadly include presenting knowledge, evaluating learners and directing activities, while learners display knowledge or receive it, and both teachers and learners may solicit knowledge and actions from each other (Rose, 2018, 2019).

## Analysis

### Lesson 1: Learning about Poetry in Upper Primary School

*The Rose That Grew from Concrete*, a poem by rapper Tupac Shakur, is the mediating text for this lesson. This brief poem is frequently used in school literature classes for exploring notions of resilience, of tenacity and of individual transformation. The lesson we focus on here is one in a series exploring literary devices and literature. The teacher's goals for this lesson are to do with exploring the poem's symbolism and interpreting the poem's themes. We identified four stages in the lesson: preparing for and reading the poem, identifying its themes through group discussion, individual writing of responses to the poem and individual writing of a new poem. Each stage included several activities that varied between whole class, small group and individual participation structures. Table 8.1 shows how activities in each

**Table 8.1** Examining Poetry in Upper Primary School (Year 6)

| Time | Lesson stage | Prepare/Focus | Task | Elaborate/Evaluate |
|---|---|---|---|---|
| 00:00–00:15 | Prepare for Reading | Introduction to poem and theme of resilience | Reading the poem aloud | |
| 00:15–34:05 | Joint Close Reading | Read and discuss focus questions written on the board | Small group discussion | Reporting back to the class |
| 14:00–34:05 | Individual Close Reading | Read and discuss focus questions written on the board | Individual written responses | Whole class sharing |
| 34:05–49:15 | Poetry Writing | Read and discuss instructions and success criteria | Writing poem | Assessment |

**Table 8.2** Preparing and Reading the Poem

| T | 'The Rose that Grew from Concrete' is a poem **about reaching our goals <u>despite the hardships and conflicts we face on the way</u>**. So there's a bit of **a hidden message** in this poem; as much as it's **about just a rose that's grown up through the ground**, the poem can be <u>highly inspirational</u> because **we can all realise <u>our dreams</u>** and make them <u>come true</u>, OK? <br> … <br> *Did you hear about the rose that grew* <br> *from a crack in the concrete?* <br> *Proving nature's law is wrong it* <br> *learned to walk without having feet.* <br> *Funny it seems, but by keeping its dreams,* . <br> *it learned to breathe fresh air.* <br> *Long live the rose that grew from concrete* <br> *when no one else ever cared.* |
|---|---|

stage are centred on a task, which is prepared, focused or elaborated by other activities.

The first stage of the lesson introduced the students to the poet, and to the teacher's interpretation of the poem's major theme as the importance of personal resilience. The teacher then read the poem[5] aloud while students followed on their individual copies. Table 8.2 presents a segment of this preparation and reading. Thematic meanings are highlighted in bold, and values are underlined. Here the teacher explicitly names the poem's themes as *a hidden message* and links this message of *reaching our goals* to countering negative values of *hardships and conflicts*, and promoting positive values of *inspiration* and *making dreams come true*.

The second stage of the lesson, Joint Close Reading, provides the data for our detailed analysis below. The students' task in this stage was to work in small groups to identify instances of the poem's personal growth message. This task was focused by reading and discussing the questions: *What is the poem about? What is its message? What do you visualise?* During the group discussions, the teacher visited groups of students to support their interpretations. The task was then elaborated by calling on several students to share their responses with the class.

In our analysis of talk during the group discussion and reporting phases, we were interested in how the students and teacher engage with the poem's themes – that is, reading beyond the literal meanings of the text to more universal, 'metaphorised' meanings – in these interactions. We investigated how this was achieved by using *pedagogic register analysis* (Rose, 2018, 2019), which applies the model of curriculum genres outlined above to the structuring of learning cycles.

Learning cycles are realised in discourse as exchanges between speakers, who take up complementary roles (Martin, 1992, 2006; Martin & Rose, 2005, 2007a; Rose & Martin, 2012). The obligatory role in an exchange of knowledge is that of providing authoritative knowledge, or *primary knower*, K1; other roles such as seeking knowledge are *secondary knower* roles, or K2. Table 8.3 illustrates these roles with a teacher/learner exchange from the group discussion task during Joint Close Reading. The teacher asks two boys, Isaac and Rafe, for the response they have been discussing to the focus question, '*What is the poem about?*' Each move in this exchange is analysed in three columns. The first labels the exchange *roles*, the second labels the *phases* in each learning cycle and the third labels types of pedagogic *interact* between teacher and learners.

In pedagogic exchanges such as this, the teacher is usually the primary knower (K1), either presenting knowledge or evaluating that of learners. Even though Isaac and Rafe display ideas here, the teacher has the final authority to evaluate them, as K1. The evaluation is expected by the learners' responses, which are therefore *secondary knower* roles (K2). The teacher's initial question delays this K1 evaluation, and is labelled dK1, for *delayed primary knower*.

**Table 8.3** What Do You Think the Poem Is About?

| Sp    |                                                                                          | Role | Phase         | Interact           |
|-------|------------------------------------------------------------------------------------------|------|---------------|--------------------|
| T     | *What do you reckon boys?*                                                               | dK1  | focus theme   | inquire conception |
| Isaac | *I reckon the story is about, like Rafe said, instead of the rose, it's the man.*        | K2   | propose theme | display conception |
| Rafe  | *Like you could replace it with a person.*                                               | K2   | propose theme | display conception |
| T     | *OK*                                                                                     | K1   | affirm        | approve            |

This is the exchange structure of the so-called 'IRF' pattern of classroom discourse. It functions to create an active learning task, a vocal response, that can be evaluated.

The *phase* and *interact* columns label the pedagogic functions of these exchange roles. In this learning cycle, the central task is to propose a thematic reading for *the rose* in Tupac's poem, labelled here as *theme*. The teacher's dK1 question focuses this task, and the K1 role affirms it. In terms of pedagogic relations, the learners' task is to display their conceptions of this figurative meaning, so they can be evaluated. The source in this case is the learners' own knowledge. The term *conception* denotes their recognition of the symbolic relation between literal and figurative meanings (*the rose* = 'a person'). This perspective reveals the pedagogic function of the ubiquitous dK1^K2^K1 discourse pattern in the 'shaping of consciousness' (Bernstein, 1990; Christie, 2005; Christie & Martin, 1997). Learning must be displayed to be evaluated, for the benefit of both learners and teacher. Hence the dK1 role solicits this display, and the K1 role evaluates it (Affirmations may *repeat, approve* or *praise* responses).

One exchange stood out among those occurring during the group discussion because the teacher's elaborating went beyond modelling the reasoning process. In the first cycle of Table 8.4, Sam displays her conception of the symbolism, 'saying what his life was like'. In the second cycle, the teacher asks what she means and she reasons that 'no-one else cared what he did but he still cared'. This interpretation of personal resilience is clearly what the teacher wanted to hear, as it is repeatedly approved as 'on the right track' and praised as 'excellent'. This very strong affirmation imbues the following elaboration

**Table 8.4** Elaborating Metalanguage: 'And the Rose … Might Symbolise That?'

| Sp | | Role | Phase | Interact |
|---|---|---|---|---|
| T | What do you reckon girls? | dk1 | focus theme | inquire conception |
| Sam | We've been trying kind of … [indistinct]. | K2 | | |
| | Like he's saying what his life was like | | propose theme | display conception |
| | except using a rose that grew from the concrete. | | | |
| T | Okay. | K1 | affirm | approve |
| T | So give me some more information | dk1 | focus theme | inquire reasoning |
| | What do you mean? | | | |
| Sam | Like he's saying that when he was growing up, | K2 | propose theme | display reasoning |
| | no-one else cared what he did but he still cared. | | | |
| T | All right. Yeah, I think so. | K1 | affirm | approve |
| | I think you could be on the right track, yeah. | | | approve |
| | Excellent | | | praise |
| | And the rose growing out of the concrete | | elaborate metalg | model conception |
| | might **symbolise** that. | | | |

with high affective value, to recast Sam's interpretation with the literary metalanguage of *symbolising*.

Reporting back from the small group task was a crucial phase in the lesson because it presented the interpretations that the teacher valued most highly, to prepare the rest of the class for their individual writing tasks. Table 8.5 is an extract of Rafe and Isaac's reporting and demonstrates the benefits of the preceding group discussion with the teacher's guidance. Here the teacher's dK1 questions focus on the discussion activity, 'What did you say? … Then what happened?', to which the students display their reasoning about relations between literal and thematic meanings.[6]

In the first two cycles of Table 8.5, Rafe reinterprets the poem's *rose* as 'a person' and *proving nature's law is wrong* as 'proving people wrong'. In cycle 3, Isaac reasons about the symbolism in three steps. First he recalls that Tupac 'grew up in a ghetto house' and compares it to more familiar experience of

Table 8.5 Preparing to Write Responses to the Poem

| | Sp | | Role | Phase | Interact |
|---|---|---|---|---|---|
| 1 | T | *Rafe, what did you say? You and Isaac?* | dK1 | focus ped activity | inquire reasoning |
| | Rafe | *Well we went and replaced the rose with like a person.* | K2 | propose theme | display reasoning |
| | T | *OK.* | K1 | affirm | approve |
| | | *Bianca, shhh, just listening because this might help you with your interpretation.* | A2 | | direct behaviour |
| | | *[Bianca stops talking]* | A1 | | |
| | | *So you replaced the rose with a person* | K1 | affirm | repeat |
| 2 | T | *And then what happened?* | dK1 | focus ped activity | inquire reasoning |
| | Rafe | *And then he's proving people wrong about what he can do.* | K2 | propose theme | display reasoning |
| | T | *Okay. Awesome.* | K1 | affirm | approve, praise |
| 3 | T | *So Isaac, what did you say?* | dK1 | focus activity | inquire reasoning |
| | Isaac | *Well like I said I told you, do you remember how you said he grew up in a ghetto house?* | K2 | propose theme | display reasoning |
| | T | *Yep, so like a ...* | K1 | affirm | approve |
| | Isaac | *Maybe he's like he went to a school and he was always teased, because he's just that person that was left out of everything.* | K2 | propose theme | display reasoning |
| | | *And maybe he was trying to say to people that he can still do what he wants, he can still do his dreams.* | | propose theme | |
| | | *And that's because it's really unusually for a rose to grow on concrete.* | | propose quality | |
| | T | *It is, isn't it? Yeah.* | K1 | affirm | approve |
| | | *It's not something you'd see every day. You'd see weeds and things growing out of concrete usually but not a rose which is quite spectacular.* | | elaborate quality | model reasoning |

hardship and conflict, being 'teased' and 'left out of everything'. Overcoming that hardship then becomes the inspirational message 'he can still do his dreams'. He then relates this message of personal growth to the symbolic power of the metaphor 'because it's really unusually for a rose to grow on concrete'. The teacher affirms and elaborates this symbolic value as 'quite spectacular'. This exchange thus ideally illustrates the functioning of a pedagogic register, as an exchange between teachers and learners, as they co-construct the knowledge and values of the curriculum register.

What does close examination of the classroom dialogue like this indicate of how students become successful students of subject English? To begin, we see something of the difficulties for eleven-year-olds in making a shift into the abstract, metaphorised meanings of literature. In the group discussion, the students offered a succession of ideas, often restating the teacher's preliminary interpretation or another student's contribution. Through guided learning cycles such as those described above, the students' interpretations became markedly more confident and closer to the idea of resilience when reporting back.

In Table 8.6, we see how the reporting back phase was rounded off with reference to the teacher's whiteboard notes. One student is asked to read the notes, which are then elaborated by the teacher in a series of moves which unpack the abstraction 'resilience' into more everyday wordings and first-order meanings and draw together this message with the students' preceding discussion of the metaphor.

The writing activity required the students to go further and to demonstrate their grasp of symbolism as well as reproduce this literary reading of the poem, by responding to the following questions: *What do you think this poem is about? What does the rose symbolise? What does the concrete symbolise? How is the image of the rose growing from concrete an example of resilience?* After a brief explanation by the teacher of the meaning of *symbolise*, 'it's a rose but it could also be talking about something else, couldn't it?', the students are directed to begin their writing activity. However, Rafe has a further question about the activity, negotiated in Table 8.7.

Rafe's question demonstrates a keen awareness that the distinction between literal and thematic meanings matters and suggests for this student at least, thematic readings of texts required in the secondary English classroom are

**Table 8.6** Negotiating Everyday and the Abstract Meanings

| Sp | | Role | Phase | Interact |
|---|---|---|---|---|
| T | Owen, please, the first two lines. | dK1 | focus text | direct perception |
| Owen | 'This poem is about resilience and being able to overcome challenges and hardships.' | K2 | identify sentence | display perception |
| T | OK | K1 | affirm | approve |
| | So there is a bit of an underlying message that if you're resilient, you keep going, you keep trying, you will be able to succeed. | | elaborate theme | model reasoning |
| | It would be very difficult for a rose to grow through concrete. | | | |
| | Concrete's often hard, it's walked on a lot, so for something to keep growing around in that kind of environment would be very difficult. | | | |

**Table 8.7** Clarifying the Writing Task

| Sp | | Role | Phase | Interact |
|---|---|---|---|---|
| Rafe | So we have to write what? | K2 | | inquire activity |
| | Is it what the poem's about or what we think it's about? | | | |
| T | All right. Yeah that's a good point. | K1 | | approve |
| T | So right. Okay. | K1 | focus ped activity | invite attention |
| | Rafe's just asked me, he said | | | |
| | 'Do we write what the poem is about when we read it | | | |
| | or what we think it's about?' | | | |
| | Can you write for me what you think it is about? | dK1 | focus theme | direct activity |
| | I should have made that a bit clearer. | K1 | | |
| | We all know that the poem is about a rose | | | |
| | growing up though concrete. | | | |
| | But tell us what you think it might be about. | dK1 | | |
| | Is there another meaning? | | | |

Table 8.8 Examining Poetry in Lower Secondary School (Year 8)

| Time | Lesson stage | Prepare/Focus | Task | Elaborate |
|---|---|---|---|---|
| 00:00–19:05 | **Prepare for Reading** | Review literary devices and importance of annotation | Reading the poem aloud | Discussion of poem's mood |
| 19:05–58:03 | **Joint Close Reading** | Refer poet and discuss his authority to write about immigrant experience | Stanza by stanza reading | |
| 58:03–1:00:08 | **Evaluation of Poem** | Focus questions for small group discussion | Individual written responses | |

within reach. He is well on the way to development of the disciplinary 'gaze' required for success in senior English. However, there is no such guarantee for all other students in this class. Their teacher is careful to actively engage as many as possible, by giving them tasks such as reading questions aloud from the board, but he relies on a handful of top students like Rafe to display conceptions and reasoning about thematic meanings, which can be affirmed and elaborated towards the curriculum goals of the lesson. Practising teachers we have worked with over many years report that such students generally number in the order of 10 per cent of any class (Nuthall, 2005; Rose & Martin, 2012). The exchange in Table 8.8 illustrates teachers' reliance on these students to co-construct the curriculum register for the rest of the class. Here Rafe prompts the teacher to redefine 'what you think it is about' as thematic meanings, for the benefit of not only himself but also his fellow students.

## Lesson 2: Poetry Appreciation in Year 8

Our second lesson took place approximately eighteen months later in a year 8 class. Some of the students in this lesson were participants in the first lesson, by now in their second year of studying secondary English (Matruglio & Jones, 2020). The poem, *Migrant Hostel* by Peter Skrzynecki, was the mediating text for the lesson which was one in a series focusing on representations of refugee and migrant experience in literature. Staging of this lesson is set out in Table 8.8.

The staging of the Year 8 and Year 6 poetry lessons is strikingly similar, both beginning with preparation and reading of the poem, followed by close reading with the whole class, then by group and individual reading and writing tasks. Given the strong boundaries between primary and secondary curricula and practice, this commonality suggests a curriculum genre of poetry appreciation that has evolved in the culture of schooling and is tacitly learnt and implemented by teachers.

On the other hand, there were significant differences between the two lessons in both curriculum and pedagogic registers. A key pedagogic difference in Year 8 was the absence of group discussion in Joint Close Reading; instead the teacher directly asked the class for thematic interpretations, to which a handful of students responded, and the class was directed to take notes from the discussion. The curricular point of departure for the lesson was literary metalanguage. The Prepare for Reading stage began with a brief reference to the poet, and the teacher then asked students to identify the theme from the poem's title. This was a relatively easy task given that migration is a sustained topic in this stage of the school curriculum. Here it highlights the poem's themes as if they are almost a backdrop to learning to use literary metalanguage.

Instances of literary metalanguage and its application in analysing thematic meanings are highlighted in bold in Table 8.9. The teacher first names these as 'the *theme* or the *idea* of the poem'. Student Gino uses the term '*alluding*' to conceptualise the hostel as a symbol of 'people on the move'. Gino recognises the function of thematic readings to make general observations from specific instances, as he offers 'a hostel is not permanent' as his evidence, which the teacher approves and elaborates more technically as 'the *symbolic nature* of using a hostel'. The teacher then models the pedagogic activity, 'using that type of *symbolic representation*', to interpret the significance of not only the hostel but 'our *persona*'. She recasts the act of interpretation as 'how we *pull out* some of these experiences'.

Following this preparatory analysis of the title, the task of reading the poem aloud was prepared with the contribution of punctuation to its reading. One student then read it out aloud while others followed on individual copies, abbreviated in Table 8.10.[7,8]

The lengthiest activity in the lesson was Joint Close Reading, stanza by stanza. Table 8.11 illustrates how the Year 8 students must now take responsibility for conception of thematic readings. In the first cycle, the

**Table 8.9** Identifying the Theme of the Poem

| Sp | | Role | Phase | Interact |
|---|---|---|---|---|
| T | *What about the title, Migrant Hostel,* | dK1 | focus theme | inquire conception |
| | *what could that tell us **about the theme or the idea** of the poem?* | | | |
| Gino | *They're ah at a hostel for migrants,* | K2 | propose theme | display conception |
| | *so he's **alluding to people like on the move**,* | | | |
| | *since a hostel is not permanent.* | | | |
| T | *Good* | K1 | affirm | approve |
| | *OK, so already the **symbolic nature of using** a hostel.* | | elaborate metalg | model conception |
| | ... | | | |
| | *Using the idea of a hostel is that this is not necessarily a permanent base, OK?* | | elaborate theme | model reasoning |
| | *Now think about the extension of **using that type of symbolic representation**,* | | elaborate ped activity | |
| | *where if this is ... if they're using hostel as somewhere that's not permanent,* | | | |
| | *they could also be talking about the fact that whoever **our character** or whoever **our persona** is,* | | elaborate theme | |
| | *is **also someone** who has not necessarily found a permanent place yet.* | | | |
| | *I think it does a very good job of telling us straight away **how we pull out** some of these experiences of refugee stories, OK?* | | elaborate ped activity | |

teacher focuses on the term 'partitioned off' in the second stanza, which Charys conceptualises as 'something dividing them'. In the second cycle, the teacher prepares with the term '*symbolic representation*' and asks what partition '*symbolises*', to which Stella offers 'isolation'. In the third cycle, Ava reasons further that it symbolises past and future lives of the migrants. The teacher elaborates this with the interpretive process 'looking at the two sides of a partition', but it is these students who have provided the thematic meanings.

**Table 8.10** Preparing and Reading the Poem

| Sp | | Role | Interact |
|---|---|---|---|
| T | Okay, let's read it, all right? | A2 | direct ped activity |
| | So when you read poetry, this is what I have to do. | K1 | impart knowledge |
| | You gotta make sure that you pay attention to wherever the full stops, wherever the commas are, wherever the dashes are, etcetera. OK? | | |
| | Who's a confident reader who wants to have a go? | dA1 | solicit display |
| Ss | [hands up] | A2 | invite evaluation |
| | Ella? Yeah. [nodding at Ella] | A1 | permit display |
| Ella | **Migrant Hostel, Parkes, 1949–51** | K2 | display perception |
| | No one kept count | | |
| | of all the comings and goings – | | |
| | arrivals of newcomers | | |
| | in busloads from the station, | | |
| | sudden departures from adjoining blocks | | |
| | that left us wondering | | |
| | who would be coming next? | | |
| | Nationalities sought | | |
| | each other out instinctively – | | |
| | like a homing pigeon | | |
| | circling to get its bearings; | | |
| | years and name-places | | |
| | recognised by accents, | | |
| | partitioned off at night | | |
| | by memories of hunger and hate.[25] | | |
| | ... | | |
| T | Beautiful. Well done. | K1 | praise |

The Year 8 teacher's focus on literary metalanguage was evident in her use of elaborating phases to recast students' interpretations in appropriate terms. In Table 8.12, the teacher prepares by abstracting from *weather* and *seasons* in the third stanza, to 'changes' in general. She then selects Gino, who names these abstractions as 'contrast' and 'metaphor', and offers his own interpretation of the contrast as 'moods and the different people every day' versus 'the bigger picture of what's happening around the world'. In this way, Gino demonstrates

**Table 8.11** Elaborating with the Metalanguage during Joint Close Reading

| | Sp | | Role | Phase | Interact |
|---|---|---|---|---|---|
| 1 | T | 'Years and name-places recognised by accents, partitioned off at night.' | K | focus line | direct perception |
| | | Does everyone know what it means by that? Partitioned off? | dK1 | focus wording | inquire knowledge |
| | Charys | Like there's something dividing them. | K2 | propose theme | display conception |
| | T | Yeah. Good. | K1 | affirm | approve |
| 2 | T | So I think this is where you can actually talk about the **symbolic representation** here, OK. | K1 | prepare metalg | model reasoning |
| | | Think about what does a partition, what does that **symbolise** in our story so far, in our poem so far? Stella? | dK1 | focus theme | direct reasoning |
| | Stella | Isolation [indistinct] | K2 | propose theme | display conception |
| | | Isolation? | K1 | | check |
| | | Good. | | affirm | approve |
| 3 | T | What else? | dK1 | focus theme | inquire reasoning |
| | Ava | Well I guess to me it kind of **symbolises** how they have two lives. One is what they've left behind and then another's what they're trying to start. | K2 | propose theme | display reasoning |
| | T | Good. So in other words looking at the two sides of a partition itself. Good, I think that's brilliant. | K1 | affirm elaborate theme affirm | approve model conception praise |

he has made a shift from offering the personal responses accepted in the earlier years towards the critical social analysis anticipated by the secondary curriculum. The teacher affirms him but then elaborates with the preferred metalanguage of 'symbolism', 'symbolic representation' and 'personas'. She does so because these terms are criterial for success with assessment tasks in junior secondary English, and increasingly towards senior literary studies.[9]

**Table 8.12** 'Like the Weather Isn't Really the Weather'

| Sp | | Role | Phase | Interact |
|---|---|---|---|---|
| T | So if he ... if Skrzynecki is talking about the weather and talking about the seasons in this instance, he's not only discussing like immediate changes that happen but also how this happens over time. | K1 | prepare theme | model conception |
| Gino | [hands up] | A2 | | invite evaluation |
| T | Gino? | A1 | | permit display |
| Gino | There's like **contrast** and **metaphor** in that because it ... like the weather isn't really the weather, it's about the moods and the different people every day or the seasons of like the bigger picture of what's happening around the world, what's causing it. | K2 | propose metalg propose theme | display reasoning |
| T | Yep. Good. And I would probably instead of **metaphor**, | K1 | affirm | approve qualify |
| | I'd actually probably use **symbolism** in this instance, OK? | | elaborate metalg | model knowledge |
| | I would use that this is **symbolic representation** of the immediate changes that our character or our **personas** have to go through and it's as well as the long-term effects. | | | |

## Discussion

In his definition of pedagogy below, Alexander poses a challenge for us to discern more abstract, general meanings that lie beyond 'the observable act of teaching', not unlike the interpretive challenges posed to students in the poetry lessons we have sampled here.

> Pedagogy is the practical and observable act of teaching together with the purposes, values, ideas, assumptions, theories and beliefs that inform, shape and seek to justify it. In acquiring this penumbra, pedagogy also connects teaching with the wider culture. (Alexander, 2020: 47)

In this contribution we have focussed on observable acts of teaching, to reason about how learners are apprenticed into the art of reading thematic meanings in literature, across the primary/secondary school divide. To bring some order to our own penumbra of interpretation, we approach the ensuing discussion from three perspectives: development as apprenticeship into thematic readings, qualitative differences in curriculum as it is enacted in the school's year levels and problems of equity associated with 'invisible pedagogies'. Finally, we argue for a visible and more inclusive pedagogy that can subvert such inequities.

## Apprenticeship into Thematic Reading

The nature of apprenticeship into subject English takes a distinct form. Through the exchanges we have seen, Rafe, Isaac, Gino, Charys, Stella and Ava perform their identities as 'good English students'; that is, students who recognise the nature of the task as one in which they must reconfigure the language of the text – its first-order meanings about the material world of the text – into signs with deeper, more abstract thematic meanings. For example, the description of the poet's migrant hostel experience must be reconstrued into generalisations about impermanence, resettlement and the displacement of people in a shifting world order.

Reading thematic meanings requires students to go beyond paraphrasing the language of the text, and to recognise the 'foregrounding and repatterning of first order meanings' (Hasan, 1985: 98). Such foregrounding is often achieved through value-laden contrasts with the norms of the text (Martin, 1996), for example, the fragile beauty of the rose against the gritty urban environment, the local specificities of the migrant hostel against the global mass movements of people. We suggest that the reasons some students develop the facility to accomplish these sophisticated readings more than others lie in the nature of the interactions about texts that they participate in over time. Those students who perform reliable readings for their primary teachers are increasingly called upon to do so for their peer audiences, so that by junior secondary school they have consolidated their authority and confidence with respect to the study of literary texts.

## Differences between Learners

The English curriculum as it is enacted in classrooms differs between year levels and among individual learners. Early literacy researchers such as

Williams (1995) have examined the shared reading practices of parents and children and linked these to social positioning, but we need look no further than the English lessons examined here for the consequential effect of different experiences. In Year 6, we noted that through the range of activities offered (small group, reporting back) more children had their contributions heard and affirmed than in the secondary class, where reading was a whole class activity with speaking turns apportioned to a small group of students. In Year 6, the opportunity to rehearse their interpretations of the poem through the small group activity brought some students' contributions closer to the kind of thematic reading expected by the teacher. However, not all contributions are of the order that will be valued in the secondary school, many students remain stranded in paraphrasing the first-order meanings of the poem. There are risks when students are encouraged to 'make connections between their own experiences and those of characters and events' as anticipated by the *Australian Curriculum: English* (ACARA, 2015). Such personal responses will not serve students well in secondary school, as Macken-Horarik (2006) finds for the grading of students' text responses in Year 10 English assessments.

## Problems with 'invisible pedagogies'

Beyond the lessons we have observed and analysed lies the matter of pedagogy more generally. The shift from personal response in Year 6 to acquiring the tools for literary criticism in Year 8, identified in our analyses, resonates with variant forms of pedagogy described by Bernstein (1990). The approach to poetry appreciation in the Year 6 class and in the official curriculum suggests a liberal progressivist pedagogy, one which emphasises a curriculum register of personal response, that valorises individual voice. Our analysis demonstrates that the transition to appreciating poetry in the secondary school demands that students engage in a different curriculum register, a critical one which uses literary tools to reflect upon the broader cultural and historical milieu and to interrogate relations between social groups such as migrants. With regard to pedagogic register, Bernstein interprets both progressivist and critical pedagogies as focused more on acquisition of dispositions, than on transmission of skills. Insofar as criteria for these dispositions are left implicit, both are termed 'invisible pedagogies'.

Our analyses show empirically how this plays out in the poetry appreciation curriculum genre. In the Prepare stage, teachers provide generalised cues for the reading task – the theme of resilience in Year 6, and symbolic representation in Year 8. Students are then asked to identify specific instances of thematic meanings in the poems, first with the whole class and then individually. Nowhere, however, are they shown explicitly *how* to identify or interpret these instances. To do so successfully without explicit modelling requires an orientation to interpreting written meanings that only some students are able to display. In the Joint Close Reading stage, the teachers depend on these students to model the task of interpreting instances, to prepare other students for their individual tasks. Clearly, then, they are working with a pedagogic model of scaffolding in which learners are prepared for tasks by modelling. But rather than the teacher directly modelling the tasks, the practice is to affirm the top students' responses, validating their authority for others to learn from, as Bella is admonished in Table 8.5: 'this might help you with your interpretation'. One reason for this absence of direct modelling may be an assumption that connections must be inferred by learners themselves, to develop a literary gaze;[10] another may be that teachers themselves are not trained in techniques for closely analysing instances of meanings in texts, and sharing them explicitly with students.

This implicitness of criteria contributes to the unequal participation found in our data, in which access to thematic readings – and thus to valued ways of knowing and valuing – is available to some students more than others. Inequality of access has powerful consequences as it contributes to the sorting of students into different streams of English and thence into different post-school opportunities. We flagged earlier that teachers generally find around 10 per cent of their students consistently responding actively in class discussions. When asked what other students are doing during these discussions, teachers generally agree that some are passively following the conversation, but that others are disengaged. This tripartite division of classrooms is strikingly reflected in proportions of students later enrolling in senior secondary English streams. It could be inferred that the 'advanced' stream is more likely to be taken by those who have benefitted passively from these conversations, while the disengaged group are destined for the 'standard' stream.

## Explicitly Scaffolding Second-Order Semiosis

If we wish to truly empower more students with respect to success in subject English, a more interventionist role of the teacher is needed. What might such a pedagogy look like? In this regard, Bernstein contrasts invisible pedagogies with visible ones, which are more concerned with transmission of skills and make criteria more explicit (Martin, 2006). However there are two challenges for teachers in applying explicit pedagogy to literary studies. On the one hand, teachers need tools for explicitly showing learners how to read second-order meanings in literature. On the other, they need modes of classroom interaction that can engage all students in actively reading and responding to questions about thematic meanings, rather than just a confident few. These intertwined issues are directly addressed in the scaffolded literacy activity known as *Detailed Reading*, which is designed to enable every student in a class to engage with higher order meanings in a text (Martin, 2006; Martin & Rose, 2007b; Rose, 2015; Rose & Martin, 2012). In Detailed Reading, learners' tasks are to identify wordings in each sentence of a short text. These identifying tasks are prepared and/or focused with meaning and location cues that provide sufficient support for any student to do each task successfully. Success and affirmation with the tasks ensure that all students then benefit from higher order elaborations.

This is an ideal practice for preparing the Joint Close Reading stage in these poetry appreciation lessons. Rather than expecting students to recognise thematic meanings from generalised focus cues like *What is the poem about?*, they can be supported to recognise specific instances in the text. This is illustrated here by designing a Detailed Reading of the first two lines of *The Rose*, as in Table 8.13. In this imagined example, the cues are figurative meanings, from which students identify the literal meanings that symbolise them. It starts by preparing the lines with their figurative meanings, and reading them aloud, and then identifying and elaborating each metaphor in turn. Meaning cues are in bold and sourcing cues underlined.

The first cycle here prepares students to recognise the figurative meanings as they read the literal wordings that symbolise them. Cycles 2 and 3 prepare them to identify each metaphor, from the same figurative cues. Cycles 4 and 5 then elaborate, guiding them to recognise the autobiographical inference of the metaphors. Tasks of reading and identifying are distributed by name,

**Table 8.13** Detailed Reading

|   | Sp |   | Role | Phase |
|---|----|---|------|-------|
| 1 | T | The first two lines are symbols of a child growing up in a harsh place. | K1 | prepare theme |
|   |   | S1, can you read those two lines for us? | dK1 | focus text |
|   | S1 | Did you hear about the rose that grew from a crack in the concrete? | K2 | identify text |
|   | T | Thanks, S1. | K1 | affirm |
| 2 | T | OK, can you see what symbolises the child growing up in the first line, S2? | dK1 | focus theme |
|   | S2 | The rose that grew? | K2 | identify wording |
|   | T | Exactly right. | K1 | affirm |
| 3 | T | Can you see symbol of a harsh place in the second line, S3? | dK1 | focus theme |
|   | S3 | A crack in the concrete. | K2 | identify wording |
|   | T | Yep. | K1 | affirm |
|   |   | So a crack in the concrete is a very harsh place for a rose to grow, isn't it? |  | elaborate theme |
| 4 | T | Do you remember the harsh place that Tupac grew up in? | dK1 | focus theme |
|   | Ss | [hands up] |  |  |
|   | T | S4? |  |  |
|   | S4 | A ghetto house. | K2 | propose theme |
|   | T | That's right. | K1 | affirm |
|   |   | That's what he is comparing to a crack in the concrete. |  | elaborate theme |
|   |   | That's what we call a metaphor. |  | elaborate metalg |
| 5 | T | So who do you think the rose symbolises? | dK1 | focus theme |
|   | Ss | Tupac | K2 | propose theme |
|   | T | Exactly | K1 | affirm |
|   |   | He is talking about himself growing up. |  | elaborate theme |

to engage and affirm all students in turn, while more challenging elaborating tasks may be solicited with traditional hands-up. Crucially, the sourcing of meanings is carefully controlled, from teacher's knowledge and reading the text in 1–3, then recalling shared knowledge in 4, to prompting students' own reasoning in 5. This practice provides sufficient support for all students to recognise this poem's patterns of metaphor and interpret their thematic meanings. Following such modelling for a few lines of the poem, they would be well prepared to continue the activity in small groups and to participate actively in the subsequent whole class discussion. The same principles for modelling the interpretive task could also be applied to the Year 8 reading, using literary metalanguage to prepare, focus and elaborate tasks of identifying its 'symbolic representations'.

## Conclusion

Teaching subject English is a key activity in facilitating smooth transitions across the primary and secondary divide, but one which demands attention to the discontinuities in curriculum and pedagogy, if we are to ensure that all students experience success. Official curriculum documents rarely specify pedagogy, but the personal, localised responses suggested by the primary curriculum and those which require analysing, interpreting and evaluating in the secondary years inflect particular ideologies – ideologies that have implications for what is taught and how it is taught. In this respect, we are reminded of Alexander's coupling of the 'observable act of teaching' with an ideological 'penumbra' that connects it with the 'wider culture' (2020: 47). Following Bernstein, we interpret the wider culture in terms of its distribution of resources, in particular the distribution of symbolic resources by the school (Rose, 2007). The capacity to interpret thematic meanings is a crucial resource for success in secondary English, and thence for access to further education. Our analyses illustrate how this resource is distributed in the English classroom, engaging and rewarding some students more than others. Such close observation of the act of teaching enables teachers to see how different forms of consciousness are shaped in the minute-by-minute unfolding of pedagogic dialogue. But it also offers a means to re-engineer pedagogy so that success in English is not so elusive but makes its ways of behaving, of knowing and valuing available to all.

# 9

# Exploring Multimodal Meaning Making in Science at the Transition to High School

Annette Turney and Emma Rutherford Vale

## Introduction

Learning how to make and understand scientific meanings is a significant element of teaching and learning in science classrooms. However, communicating scientific ideas can be challenging for learners as they first confront the specialised meaning-making practices of science. As learners progress through school, this challenge increases with greater disciplinary specificity entailed in science learning. In entering the middle years of schooling, learners encounter changing curriculum demands that implicate the development of a repertoire of meaning-making resources that are increasingly distinct to the knowledge under construction (Christie & Derewianka, 2008; Christie & Maton, 2011; Fang, Schleppegrell & Cox, 2006). Alongside the increasing specialisation of knowledge, learners face an expectation of greater independent engagement with multimodal texts for learning. Hence, control over a disciplinary-specific repertoire of literacy practices becomes critical to academic success at the transition to high school (Christie, 2012; Christie & Derewianka, 2008).

In the Australian curriculum, literacy in the disciplines is recognised as one of seven general capabilities that are woven into each learning area. In science, literacy is embedded in the science inquiry skills strand (Table 9.1). Learners are required to comprehend and compose texts in a range of genres, modes and representations in order to interpret and critically analyse information, to describe data and processes, to formulate hypotheses, and to construct

**Table 9.1** Science Inquiry Skills in the Australian Curriculum

| Science Inquiry Skill | Year 5 | Year 6 | Year 7 | Year 8 |
| --- | --- | --- | --- | --- |
| Processing and analysing data and information | Construct and use a range of representations, including *tables* and *graphs*, to *represent* and *describe observations*, patterns or relationships in data using digital technologies as appropriate (ACSIS090) | Construct and use a range of representations, including tables and graphs, to *represent* and *describe observations*, patterns or relationships in data using digital technologies as appropriate (ACSIS107) | Construct and use a range of representations, including graphs, *keys* and *models*, to *represent* and *analyse* patterns or relationships in data using digital technologies as appropriate (ACSIS129) | Construct and use a range of representations, including graphs, keys and models, to represent and analyse patterns or relationships in data using digital technologies as appropriate (ACSIS144) Summarise data, from students' own investigations and secondary sources, and use scientific understanding to identify relationships and draw conclusions based on evidence (ACSIS145) |
| Communicating | Communicate ideas, explanations and processes using scientific representations in a variety of ways, including multimodal texts (ACSIS093) | Communicate ideas, explanations and processes using scientific representations in a variety of ways, including multimodal texts (ACSIS093) | Communicate ideas, findings and evidence-based solutions to problems using scientific language, and representations, using digital technologies as appropriate (ACSIS133) | Communicate ideas, findings and evidence-based solutions to problems using scientific language, and representations, using digital technologies as appropriate (ACSIS148) |

evidence-based arguments (Australian Curriculum Assessment and Reporting Authority (ACARA, 2016)). By the end of Year 7, learners should be able to 'communicate ideas, findings and evidence-based solutions to problems *using scientific language, and representations*' (ACARA, 2016, p. 58). Significantly, the curriculum identifies using a range of semiotic (meaning-making) resources including language, diagrams, tables, charts, graphs, scientific symbols and models as essential science skills. Despite recognising the importance of these literacy practices in developing scientific inquiry skills and understanding scientific content, the discipline-specific ways of making meaning in science have not traditionally been a main focus in science classrooms (Tang, 2016). This lack of focus on the semiotic resources implicated in doing science at the transition is significant as the representational demands of curriculum content grow as students move into more abstract applied knowledge in the senior years.

In this chapter, we investigate how learners navigate changes in the representational demands of science at the transition from primary (Year 6) to secondary school (Year 7). Taking a social-semiotic approach to meaning making informed by Halliday's (1993) systemic functional approach to language and Kress and Van Leeuwen's (2006) visual grammar, we present the analysis of a selection of work samples produced by learners in Years 6 and 7 to explore multimodal literacy practices. In particular, we describe key semiotic resources used by learners as they move from common-sense understandings to more complex technical understandings necessary for knowledge-building in school science. Through this exploration we seek to better understand the semiotic repertoire required for success in science at the transition from primary to secondary school.

## Background

The development of scientific discourse is an essential element of apprenticeship into science disciplines at school. As learners transition from primary school to secondary school around the age of twelve they are increasingly expected to interpret and use the language of science. However, how learners develop control of the progressively specialised range of resources for making meanings in science is not well understood, with little research exploring how command of language resources develops across the years of schooling (Christie & Derewianka, 2008). The research literature shows that learners can struggle to bridge the gap between the use of language in everyday life and the concise and technical language of scientific texts (Fang & Schlepegrell, 2008; Feez & Quinn, 2017; Shanahan & Shanahan, 2008). Further, the language experience of many learners does not include a strong orientation to the characteristic structures of scientific English, including not only technical vocabulary and representational conventions but importantly the grammatical structures implicated in realising the meanings of scientific discourse (Halliday & Martin, 1993; Lemke, 1990). A key endeavour of science, for example, is to explain phenomena. In order to do this, scientific language has evolved distinctive linguistic resources that enable complex reasoning, which include nominalisation, condensation of technical meanings in the noun group and grammatical structures to realise causality (Halliday, 2004; Halliday & Martin, 1993; Hao, 2018). However, these language features can present challenges for learners and point to the need for explicit instruction to develop control of particular language resources to successfully engage in science learning.

A distinctive feature of scientific discourse is its use of multimodal resources (Lemke, 1998). As learners are apprenticed in ways of knowing and meaning in science, they need to master diagrams, graphs and scientific symbols to record, represent and reason scientifically. The importance of being able to interpret and express meanings multimodally in science classrooms has long been recognised by educationalists (Halliday & Martin, 1993; Kress, Jewitt, Ogborn & Tsatsarelis, 2001; Lemke, 1998). Despite such recognition, the teaching of science has tended to neglect an explicit focus on the multimodal construal of scientific ideas. Research work in the area has concentrated on describing how scientific meanings are made through the use of specific semiotic resources such as images (Doran, 2019; Ge, Unsworth, Wang & Chang, 2018), while other work has turned to explore how these resources might combine intersemiotically (e.g. in written language and images) in texts and practices in the science classroom (He & Forey, 2018; Unsworth, 2020). A limited focus on the multimodal construal of scientific meanings is potentially problematic as different semiotic modes have evolved to represent different kinds of meanings in science, for example, the use of images to show spatial relationships such as the proximity between entities, graphs to represent trends in data or linguistic resources to relate events temporally (Kress et al., 2001). Additionally, as learners progress through school, they need to be able to coordinate combinations of these resources in increasingly complex texts in disciplinary appropriate ways. Concern regarding learners' multimodal disciplinary literacy is further engendered by the frequent use of multimodal ensembles (where language and diagrams are interpolated (see Figure 2)) in science textbooks and in assessment materials (Bezemer & Kress, 2010; Danielsson & Selander, 2016; Unsworth, 2020).

## Context

The focus for this chapter is data drawn from a satellite cluster of the TRANSLIT project, gathered in Sydney as part of a study exploring the nature of writing development in science at the transition from primary to secondary school. Data come from three primary schools, selected to represent diversity according to size and the socio-educational positioning of learners, and one secondary school. Learner participants, consisting of four boys and seven girls in total, were selected by the classroom teachers in Year 6 to represent a range of literacy attainment levels from low average to high attainment. Sample texts were collected from in-class tasks in Year 6 and again in Year 7, including information reports and explanations. The texts explored here while not representative of all those produced in science classrooms across the transition from primary to secondary education are typical of those collected in this research.

## Theoretical Framework

Texts produced in science classrooms are filled with combinations of semiotic resources. To understand the purposes of these semiotic combinations in the texts explored here we have turned to Halliday's (1978) social semiotic theory. Halliday contended that texts' functional organisation is shaped by the meaning-making work they are used for and the social environment they are used in. In Systemic Functional Linguistics (SFL), the social environment is captured in three distinct contextual domains: field, tenor and mode. Field refers to the subject matter, tenor to the relationship enacted between social participants and mode to the channel of communication. These correspond to three generalised social functions, described as 'metafunctions' in SFL, that are enacted simultaneously in acts of meaning making. The ideational metafunction serves to construe our experience of the world and to make logical connections; the interpersonal metafunction enacts social experience and relationships; and the textual metafunction organises the message of the discourse. These domains shape how meanings are dispersed through a text. Although Halliday's theory is a linguistic one, presenting an account of how meanings are made in language, he recognised that language is only one of many semiotic systems (1978) and his theory has been used to consider semiotic systems outside of the linguistic (Kress & van Leeuwen, 2006). A systemic functional approach to multimodal meaning making recognises that different semiotic systems function differently, although the resources from these systems can be used collaboratively to make meanings in multimodal texts (Royce, 2002).

Multimodal texts are shaped by the social purposes for which they are used. This is to say that a text's form will differ according to the communicative work it is intended to do, such as to explain, describe or persuade. In 'Sydney School' approaches to SFL these forms are theorised as genres, 'staged, goal-oriented, social processes' (Martin, 1992; Rothery, 1989). They are recognised as configurations of meanings used to achieve particular communicative work, which through use have developed regularities that are recognised as distinctive within discourse communities (Martin & Rose, 2008). Typical genres encountered in school science are information reports, explanations and procedural texts, which serve the purposes of explaining and describing scientific phenomena, and enacting scientific practices and processes (Goldman et al., 2016; Halliday, 2004). These genres are identifiable by the social purposes they serve and through the distinctive ways that they configure meanings. Genres can be realised in verbal language but also through other semiotic modes or combinations of semiotic modes, and in a range of media.

The analytical work of this chapter focuses on how ideational (content), interpersonal and textual meanings are expressed multimodally. The analysis of the students' writing draws on SFL to explore how the learners represent entities and activities, how they connect ideas logically and how they condense technical meanings. The image analysis draws upon systemic functional semiotics (Halliday, 1978; Kress & van Leeuwen, 2006; Unsworth & Chan, 2009) to consider how scientific meanings are presented visually. The analysis looks at how images are used to represent entities and their properties, distinguishing between everyday images (like the photographs of dolphins in Figure 9.2) and technical images (like the scientific diagrams in Figure 9.4). Images can also show different relationships between entities with analytical images showing part/whole relationships and classifying images showing type/subtype relationships. Figure 9.1a presents an analytical image, where different stages of the frog's life are shown as part of a life cycle, whereas Figure 9.1b shows a classifying image depicting the eight moons as types of satellites orbiting Jupiter. Images are also used to show scientific activities,

**Figure 9.1a** Analytical image

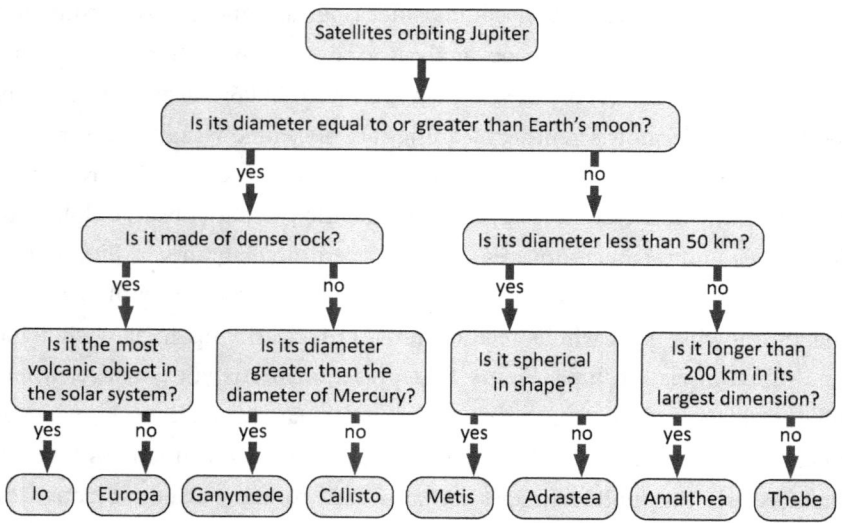

**Figure 9.1b** Classifying image

which in their simplest form are represented by vectors that depict motion or directionality (Doran, 2019) such as in Figure 9.5a where Earth's journey around the sun is represented by the arrows.

Many of the images in the dataset are presented with writing in 'multimodal ensembles'. To explore the interplay of images and language, we consider the 'commitment' of meaning. Commitment refers to the amount of meaning-making options taken up in the use of language or images (Hood, 2008). For example, a description of a dolphin as 'a striking black and white hourglass dolphin' carries more meaning than 'dolphin'; similarly, a full colour photograph of a dolphin swimming in a pod (Figure 9.2) carries more meaning than an outline sketch of a dolphin. The differences in meanings committed in images or in language can be useful in considering how particular texts communicate scientific meanings.

## Representing, Describing and Explaining Scientific Phenomena across the Transition

In this section we explore work produced by learners in Years 6 and 7 to consider the range of multimodal literacy practices in science at the transition. Significantly, learners' opportunity to engage with disciplinary science in the primary classroom varied considerably according to research site and classroom teacher, meaning that learners did not bring a consistent experience of the skills, knowledge and repertoires of science as a foundation for their transition into secondary school where the technicality of scientific content increases.

## Sage's Hourglass Dolphin Information Report (Year 6)

The hourglass dolphin report (Figure 9.2) describes the features and behaviours of an animal. It is broadly typical of the work of the biological sciences strand of the Australian curriculum where students describe the characteristics of living things including how changing physical conditions can impact animals. Sage's report unfolds through the expected stages of an information report, with the subject identified in the title and the central photographic image. The following stages of the report present a series of descriptions that focus on the dolphin's physical appearance, habitat, diet and behaviours. The order of the text stages is visually motivated, rather than following an expected reading path, with the bibliography, for example, positioned at the top centre and the reader encouraged to read left to right across columns. As a result, the organisation of Sage's poster makes it more difficult to relate the images and

**Figure 9.2** Sage's poster

the relevant verbal text (e.g. the map and its accompanying text segment on habitat). There are also some less typical choices of phasing in the written text with a general classification statement appearing at the end of the Description stage, 'and its classification is mammal'.

In comparing the meanings made in images and language, we can see clear differences in the types of meanings represented and the degree of meaning committed. Sage uses photographic images to depict the dolphin as a 'kind of' sea animal and to illustrate its appearance and actions, with the second image serving to show its behaviour, swimming in a pod. Sage's use of contextualised photographic images conveys a sense of her understanding that science involves the observation of real-world natural phenomena. This observational focus is mirrored in the Description stage of the report, where Sage describes the hourglass dolphin using precise and generally objective terms. She locates the dolphin in a taxonomy of things via relating clauses which describe its physical attributes including colour, size and weight. Movement into a written style is evident in the way Sage has condensed information into concise noun groups, for example, 'a striking black and white appearance resembling an hourglass'. The nominalisation 'appearance' (expressed in more common-sense terms as 'what it looks like') enables Sage to provide expanding information and to more precisely qualify aspects of appearance in a condensed form within the clause, allowing a comparative meaning 'resembling an hourglass'. Description of habitat and behaviours is realised by action and relating processes, 'these dolphins are extremely fast and swim just below the surface creating a large spray of water above'. Sage's written description is congruent with the visual representation of the pod of dolphins although additional meanings are realised in the written text regarding the conditions that the dolphins swim in, not only that they swim in pods (shown visually) but also that they swim with other creatures and face threats.

There are a number of features of Sage's poster that point to her developing a scientific stance. Verbally, Sage's use of passive voice in the Diet stage enables her to foreground the entity being described and also remove agency, construing an objective voice which is a critical step in scientific writing. Increasingly precise language choices to describe behaviours, 'navigate' and attributes 'echo-location' and 'long-finned cetaceans' are also evidence of Sage's developmental movement into a technical field. Signs of Sage's developing use

*Exploring Multimodal Meaning Making*      179

**Table 9.2** Sage's Information Report on Hourglass Dolphins

| Genre Stages | Image | Language |
|---|---|---|
| Phenomenon Identification | Colour photographic image of an hourglass dolphin jumping through the water. The shape and appearance and action are shown. | Named in the title, 'Hourglass Dolphins' |
| Description | Colour photographic image of an hourglass dolphin jumping through the water. The shape and appearance and action are shown. | Hourglass dolphin identified in the topic sentence and its appearance elaborated in a series of relating clauses and in the comparison of its shape to an hourglass. Additional information is supplied regarding the size and weight of the dolphin. The dolphin is classified as a mammal. |
| Diet | Not shown | Fish, squid and cetaceans are identified as the diet. The use of echolocation as a method for locating food is specified. |
| Habitat | World map with the dolphins' habitat represented by a broad blue band across the Southern Ocean | The accompanying text label identifies the blue band as the hourglass dolphins' habitat. The location is specified as the Antarctic and sub-Antarctic waters. Additional information is supplied regarding the number of dolphins. |
| Behaviours | Colour photographic image of a pod of hourglass dolphins jumping through the water | Elaborates the manner of the dolphin's behaviour: swimming fast and in a pod alongside other cetaceans. Threats to dolphins are also described. |

of scientific images is indicated by her use of the map (an analytical image). Across the map's lower quadrant, the location of the hourglass dolphin's habitat is symbolically represented by a turquoise band stretching across the Southern Ocean. In the accompanying key, the band is labelled 'hourglass dolphins', necessary as the meaning of the band is symbolic and only explicitly recoverable by making connections with the adjacent text segment on 'Habitat'. In contrast, Sage's use of water motifs, blue wavy underlining and water drops, and the visual and verbal duplication of 'hourglass' in the title present a common-sense rather than scientific view of phenomena. These visual references contextualise the information report, yet are more common features of story-telling genres and perhaps reveal Sage's concern with presenting her information attractively rather than recruiting visual resources to realise conceptual knowledge. Further concern to entertain and engage the reader is apparent in the use of attitudinal language, which is less usual for scientific genres, including a direct address to the reader, 'as you would expect'. By examining the use of semiotic resources, we can see that Sage is moving towards a scientific style although at this developmental point the scientific information load is carried predominantly by the written text, which is characterised by greater specificity and technicality (summarised in Table 9.2).

## Jack's Earthquake Consequential Explanation (Year 6)

The use of a range of canonical and non-canonical genres was typical of the tasks observed in the primary science classrooms. Such tasks are exemplified here by Jack's earthquake storyboard. Drawn from a sequence of lessons investigating the impacts of abrupt geological changes on the Earth's surface, the storyboard task has been used to elicit an explanation of the effects of an earthquake. The task is unusual in disciplinary science and could be argued to set up a tension between purposes of narrating the events of an earthquake, an everyday field, and explaining the consequences of an earthquake, a scientific field. The task does, though, offer a number of meaning-making opportunities that allow Jack to demonstrate understanding of the topic. The storyboard unfolds temporally over a sequence of four frames that explain the effects of an earthquake on the human and natural world. In representing his explanation as a storyboard, Jack is guided to depict processes of change from frame to frame which provides a useful step towards the way that temporal processes can be represented in sequential images in scientific diagrams. This step is significant as learners are expected to represent increasingly complex processes diagrammatically as they progress through the senior years of schooling (Unsworth, 2020). This temporal organisation is similarly marked in the accompanying captions by the use of temporal resources such as 'first', 'then' and 'after'. Such resources are more typical of a recount or sequential explanation, yet Jack maintains a focus on phenomenon and activity in general. This signals a developing understanding that science is interested in explaining observed phenomena in generalised ways, rather than recounting individual or personal instances (Figure 9.3).

*Exploring Multimodal Meaning Making* 181

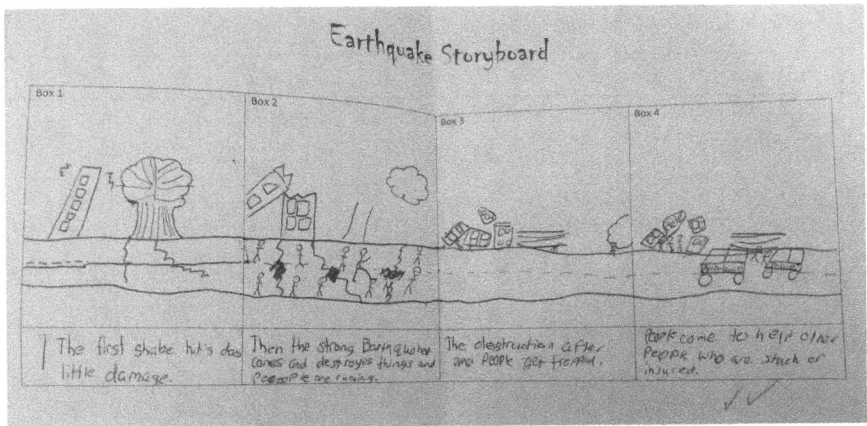

**Figure 9.3** Jack's Earthquake explanation

In comparing the meanings made in images and language, we can see considerable differences in the commitment of meaning. In the images, Jack depicts the effects naturalistically showing the real-world things affected by the earthquake; the apartment block, the tree and the people fleeing the scene. Meanwhile, in the verbal text, Jack condenses the depicted impacts, capturing them in condensed expression in the noun group, 'little damage' and the nominalisation 'destruction' as well as implicitly through activity, 'people are running'. It is in the images that Jack reveals the destruction in the broken building and the cracks in the road, the location of the trapped people (under the ruins or the tree) and those who came to help (the police and the ambulance in frame four). Verbally, more generalised meanings related to impact of the earthquake are construed, for example, 'destroys *things*' to describe the impact and adjectives used to qualify the force of the tremor, for example, 'the *strong* earthquake' or the extent of the damage, for example, '*little* damage'. These differences are summarised in Table 9.3.

Jack's representation is largely common sense in both modes. Construal of entities, for example, is via relatively everyday language choices such as 'shake' rather than 'tremor' and 'things' rather than 'buildings or infrastructure'. Similarly, his images do not yet depict a scientific reality, with limited attention paid to the relative size and scale of the participants, although the blank background and flat perspective may hint towards scientific diagrammatic norms. These verbal and visual choices are likely constrained by the storyboard

**Table 9.3** Jack's Earthquake Explanation

| Genre Stages | Image | Language |
|---|---|---|
| Phenomenon Identification | | Earthquake identified in the supplied title 'Earthquake storyboard' |
| Explanation Sequence: Consequences of light tremor | Multiple impacts of the tremor are depicted; listing apartment block accompanied by jagged lines to represent shaking; road shown with the result of the tremor depicted in the crack stretching across it. | The tremor is identified as the first of a number and the extent of the damage is captured in the noun group 'does little damage'. The use of material processes, 'hits' and 'does' conveys a sense of immediacy. |
| Consequences of severe tremor | Destruction depicted in the collapsed building, tree broken in half, multiple deep cracks shown in the road and multiple people standing in the road | 'The strong earthquake' construes a taxonomy of tremor size, 'destroys *things*' provides general information about damage 'and people running' implies the physical and emotional impacts of earthquakes. |
| Consequences overall | Final destruction is shown in the collapsed building. The impact on people with multiple figures shown trapped under buildings and under the tree. | 'The destruction after' directs the reader explicitly to the depiction of damage in frame 3 |
| Explanation Explains the human impact of the earthquake | Help is specified in the images of the ambulance and police car | 'People come to help' construes less typically science meanings to do with how humans respond to disasters. |

format which encourages brevity linguistically and visually and as noted sets up a tension between telling a story about an earthquake and describing the effects of earthquakes. The tension of the storyboard format is also apparent in the change of tense in the second frame with the writing moving from timeless present, typical of explanations, to present continuous tense which creates a sense of immediacy more typical of storytelling. In spite of this Jack's text shows signs of a developing movement into scientific meaning-making norms. In particular, the nominalisation in frame 3 'the destruction' serves a textual role to package up the preceding activity, enabling Jack to concisely progress the explanation sequence in ways typical of science writing. As we show here the task choice plays a significant role in affording particular semiotic opportunities. In this text although Jack shows understanding of the consequences of an earthquake, he is constrained by the typically storytelling use of storyboards. In its place a task that anticipated an explanation genre using diagrammatic images and interpolated text would offer greater opportunities to foster multimodal literacy practices for science.

## Becka's Explanation of How Light Reflects (Year 6)

During the primary school observations, few of the lessons employed textbooks to guide the scientific learning. An exception was Becka's classroom where the teacher made extensive use of the 'Primary Connections' teaching materials designed by the Australian Academy of Science (2012). Working from the physical sciences strand of the Australian curriculum, the learners conducted a series of hands-on investigations exploring how light can be reflected, absorbed and refracted. Becka's text (Figure 9.4) records the results of those investigations and unfolds as a series of short explanations of what she observed. Her text approximates the results section of a laboratory report, a genre typical of science learning in secondary school. Although the properties of light are not explicitly named as the focus of the report, this is recoverable from the series of teacher-provided prompts that structure the text. Interestingly, the stages of the explanation unfold either in language or in images, rather than in multimodal ensembles, with the explanation of how light travels and forms shadows presented linguistically and the explanation of how light reflects depicted diagrammatically (Table 9.4).

The task presents considerable meaning-making demands for learners as it requires a movement from the concrete contextually embedded goings-on of experimentation to the explanation of empirical phenomena independent of the context. When conducting an investigation, learners share hands-on experience and so can indicate elements including equipment and activity through the use of gestures and unspecific reference that points to the physical context of the experiment (e.g. that one), whereas in recording their results, learners cannot rely on elements of shared physical context and thus have to take up more explicit semiotic choices. This demand for explicitness requires considerable resources for condensation of meaning across modes. Visually, Becka employs a diagrammatic representation of how light reflects, depicting the key entities and processes clearly. The diagram shows light travelling

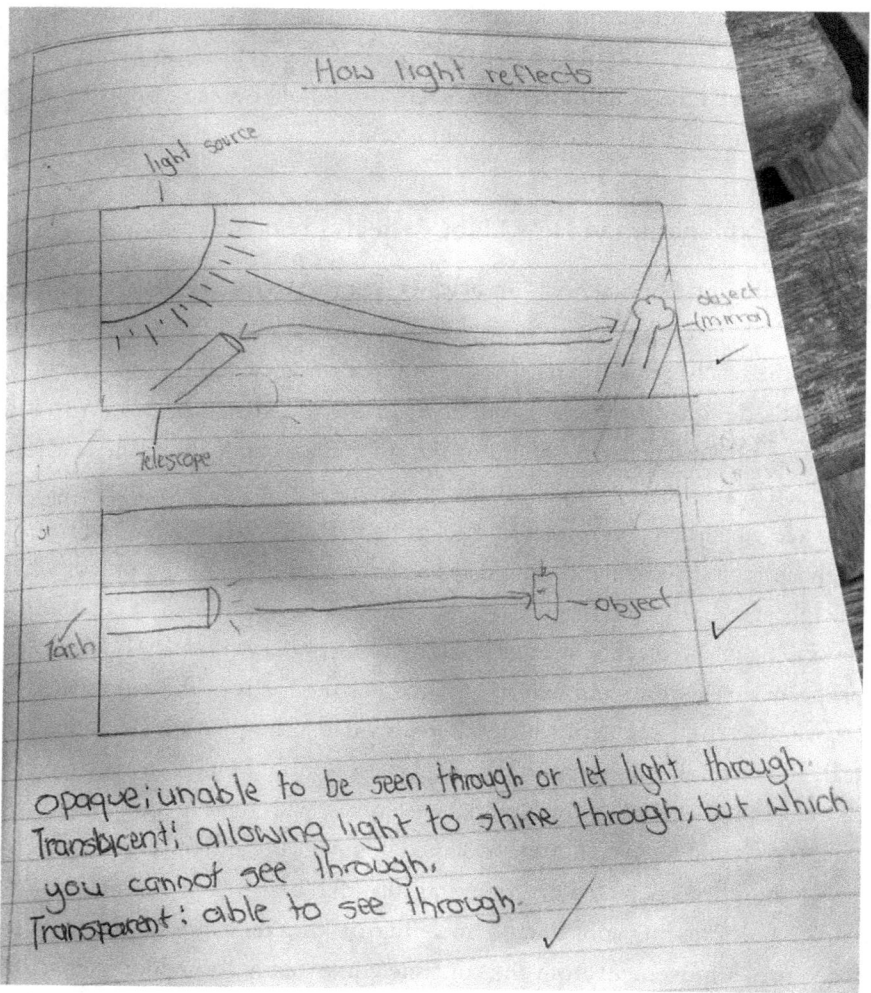

**Figure 9.4** Becka's sequential explanation

(represented by lined arrows) from a source (sun) to a reflective surface (mirror), from which light is then reflected to the telescope. To develop her diagram Becka could condense further science meaning by showing light travelling in a straight line rather than a wavy line which would represent light's properties with greater accuracy. The shift from the minimal explicitness of conducting the experiment, with context bearing much of the semantic load, to a need for maximal explicitness is further reflected in the use of verbal resources. Semantically this involves a shift to language for reflection, including a need to

**Table 9.4** Becka's Sequential Explanation

| Genre Stages | Image | Language |
|---|---|---|
| Phenomenon Identification | | Recoverable from the question prompts used in the investigations |
| Explanation sequence: how light forms shadows | Not shown | Precise description of the entity, 'a dark 2D shape'. Clause complexes express conditions that affect the size and shape of the shadow, 'when the shapes moves', 'when the object gets pulled away' |
| how light travels | Not shown | Some specialised entities indicating a movement towards technicality – 'light source'. Conditions that affect the investigations are indicated in the use of qualities, 'straight'. Passive voice maintains focus on the materials and activity 'when our light source was cut off'. |
| how light reflects | Key entities are represented schematically; the sun, telescope and reflective surface. The process 'light travels' represented visually. | Not explained |

logically connect the observed events. Logical connections between activities are expressed through clause complexes providing information about the conditions under which the phenomenon was observed (e.g. 'when the object gets pulled away from the light source'). This enables Becka to reason about the results and is a critical resource for explanations in science.

In Becka's work we can see clear development of the multimodal disciplinary literacy practices necessary for science in secondary education. Her diagrams show she is moving towards conventional representations of scientific content, using abstract schematic forms rather than naturalistic representations of the experiment she observed. Significant abstraction is apparent in her diagram with the removal of extraneous detail signalling the generalisability of the conditions shown, for example, light will always travel and be reflected in this manner in these empirical conditions. Her growing control of technicality is apparent in her careful lexical choices, for example, the use of 'light source' instead of light and the specification of the shadow as 'a dark 2D shape'. Becka also foregrounds activity and materials through the use of passive voice (e.g. 'When the telescope was bent *our light source was cut off.*), signalling a focus on activities and entities rather than human agency that is typical of scientific writing. Overall, there is a sense that Becka is developing an understanding of how to represent scientific ideas conventionally.

## Zane's 'Seasons' Explanation (Year 7)

As learners move into secondary education, they are apprenticed into the tools and activities of science as well as the conventions for representing scientific phenomena with an increasingly trained gaze. As the body of knowledge grows cumulatively across the school years, the science concepts that learners encounter grow in complexity and abstraction. In the Australian curriculum, Year 7 learners encounter phenomena that include complex systems, interactions and relationships (ACARA, 2016). To explain these phenomena learners are increasingly expected to read and produce multimodal texts where images and language are integrated. The explanation below produced by Zane is typical of the kinds of multimodal ensembles that learners are asked to produce at this level. Working from the Earth and space sciences strand of the Australian curriculum, the learners investigated the phenomenon of the seasons. After identifying the phenomenon in the image, title and opening topic sentence, Zane's text unfolds through a labelled diagram and an accompanying written implication sequence that elaborates the relationship between the seasons and the earth's orbit around the sun (Figure 9.5).

Central to explaining seasons is the need to represent the Earth's tilt on an axis and its passage around the sun. Zane uses simple abstract forms to represent Earth and its axis of rotation (shown symbolically) orbiting the sun placed at the centre of the diagram. Earth's orbit is shown symbolically through the use of a dotted line and reinforced by the central curved arrow. Zane further represents the series of activities involved through the recurrent images of the earth to explicate the impact of the planet's tilt on the Southern hemisphere's seasons. The complexity of the explanation sequence lends itself to diagramming where compositional features of the earth's hemispheres, the property of the tilt and the activity of orbiting the sun can be condensed effectively. Further meaning is committed in the accompanying text labels that

# Exploring Multimodal Meaning Making

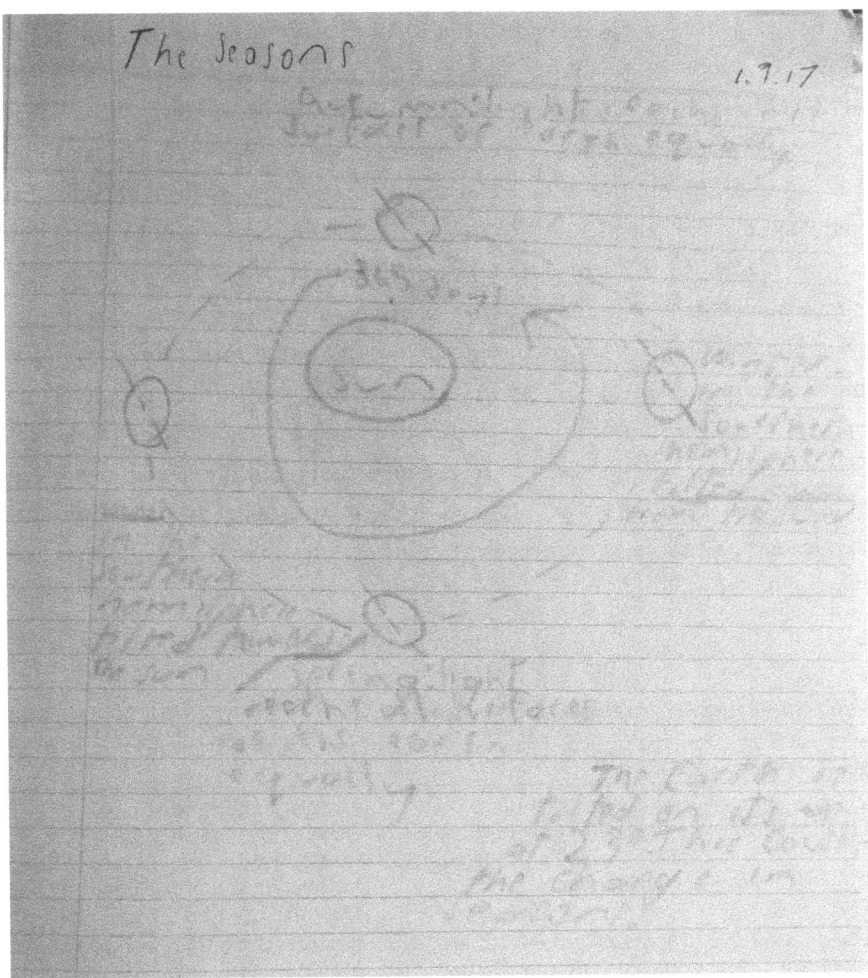

**Figure 9.5a** Zane's explanation 1

| |
|---|
| **Explain how the season on Earth are created. Try to use appropriate science terms we have been learning such as 'tilt' and 'rotate' to explain your ideas precisely.** |
| The Earth has seasons because of the tilt the planet is on. The tilt is 23° making Summer in Southern hemisphere [and] Winter in the northern hemisphere.<br><br>In Winter the poles get no sunlight and in Summer gets only sunlight. The winters are colder and summers are warmer in the Southern hemisphere as it is farther and closer respectively. |

**Figure 9.5b** Zane's explanation 2

explicitly identify the seasons and the Southern hemisphere and explain the impact of the tilt on the light received, for example, light reaches all surfaces of the earth equally. Turning to look at Zane's written explanation (Figure 9.5) we can see that he summarises key elements of his diagrammatic explanation. He specifies key entities entailed in the activity, for example, 'the southern hemisphere', 'the poles' and 'the sun', and identifies properties such as 'the tilt the planet is on'. He also uses resources for condensing meaning with a circumstance of reason realised by a dense noun group ('because of *the tilt [[the planet is on]]*'). This enables Zane to condense information that might more usually be expressed as an independent clause (e.g. 'because the planet is on a tilt'). The causal relationship between earth's tilt and the angle and amount of the sun's rays received by the hemispheres at different times is not explicitly stated, although it is implied in the final contrastive statements that explicate the relationship between the poles 'get no sunlight' in the winter and being colder (Table 9.5).

**Table 9.5** Zane's Causal Explanation of Seasons

| Genre Stages | Image | Language |
|---|---|---|
| Phenomenon Identification | The seasons is named in the title and the cause of the seasons is explicitly stated in the written label. | The cause of the seasons is explicitly identified in a relational attributive clause with a circumstance of reason in the text opener. |
| Explanation sequence | Properties of the earth are depicted symbolically, for example, the dotted line to show the tilt of the planet. The sequence of activities is represented by the repeated image of the Earth and accompanying season label. Earth's orbit's is represented symbolically by a dotted line and its passage of time reiterated in the curved arrow labelled 365 days. Relationship between the sun and the Earth is depicted conventionally. | Logical relations are realised implicitly, for example, the non-finite clause 'making summer in the southern hemisphere, winter in the northern hemisphere' implies a consequential relationship between the tilt and the different seasons in the hemispheres. Properties and dimensions of the earth are realised in noun groups, for example, as Thing in the noun group, for example, 'the tilt the planet is on' with composition realised by a Classifier^Thing structure in the noun group, for example, 'the southern hemisphere'. |

In high school learners are increasingly expected to read and produce such infographic texts where images and language are integrated. Such multimodal ensembles are common in textbooks and are important ways of assessing learning in test materials. Coupled with this multimodal shift is an increasing expectation that students represent scientific phenomena conventionally. Linguistically, this movement is characterised by a shift towards increasing technicality with students developing and using language to precisely name entities and describe their dimensions and properties. Circumstantial meanings describing when, how, where, in what manner and so on, both within and across clauses, become increasingly salient for accurately recording procedures and observations and for reasoning about observed activity. The move to increasing technical precision is mirrored visually with learners expected to utilise scientific diagramming, moving away from naturalistic depictions of scientific entities and activities towards greater abstraction by employing graphical elements (arrows, dotted lines), decontextualised forms and meaningful use of spatial composition. Further, learners are increasingly expected to use appropriate forms to succinctly express relationships between scientific phenomena and to show their properties.

## Discussion and Conclusion

This work reveals a considerable shift into discipline-specific forms of literacy as learners move from primary to secondary education. The shift is evident in the use of recognised science genres such as explanations and laboratory reports, as well as increasing technicality and condensation of meanings in both image and verbiage. Further evidence of this shift is apparent in the increasing use of 'infographic texts' where visual and linguistic resources are integrated in multimodal ensembles. Such texts present challenges for learners as they need to interpret the meanings packed within such ensembles and also produce them. Inherent to this challenge is the need for learners to understand the affordances of semiotic resources for communicating scientific meanings. The representational challenge of science is further compounded by the nature of the reality to be depicted, with learners needing to assume a scientific reality that involves the representation of elements not usually visible to the naked eye (Kress et al., 2001: 160), meaning that learners must learn to manage increasing demands for abstraction.

The effects for learners of this shift are considerable and are amplified by the broad interpretation of what it is to do and mean in primary science. Although each of the schools in this study presented learners with opportunities to engage with science learning, the broad conception of science combined with considerable variability in where, how and by whom it is taught resulted in learners bringing a range of experiences of doing and meaning in science that may not align well to disciplinary science practices of the secondary school. Learners' preparation for moving into the discipline is as a result highly variable. Further, the extent to which science teachers are able to model and instruct in the semiotic resources of their subject remains unclear, with primary teachers' confidence in teaching science identified as an ongoing concern (Harlen & Holroyd, 1997) and limited opportunities for the exchange of expertise available across the transition from primary to secondary education (Murphy, Neil & Beggs, 2007). Equally, high school teachers often feel poorly positioned and ill-prepared to apprentice students in the literacy practices entailed in disciplinary meaning making in their subject areas (Fang, 2014; Love, 2010).

The variability of student experiences of science is accompanied by significant differences in their linguistic repertoires for scientific meaning making at the transition to high school. Some learners showed evidence of a widening linguistic repertoire evidenced by expanded flexibility and control of language for describing and explaining with greater precision, technicality and conciseness. Others, meanwhile, demonstrated less precise and more common-sense language choices more characteristic of everyday spoken language, which indicated a less secure literacy foundation from which to transition to specialised learning of science. Such differences in student repertoires provide signposts to learners who may be at risk at the transition.

Better understanding of the range of semiotic resources which are most critical to the movement into abstract and technical learning in science should provide for a better transition into secondary science. Further, greater knowledge of the multimodal literacy practices that underpin successful science discourse can inform *curriculum development, classroom teacher expertise and more strategic teaching and assessment* to support cumulative learning across the transition to secondary science and beyond.

# 10

# Categories, Appraisals and Progress in Literacy Transitions

Erika Matruglio

## Introduction

The project on which this volume is based concerns youngsters' trajectories in their literacy learning across the school years. The TRANSLIT project (see Chapter 1 this volume) has collected data from a wide range of sources, including classroom observations, students' work samples and curriculum and policy documents. This chapter focuses on what teachers say in interviews about students' literacy development, how they account for – describe, evaluate and explain – the trajectories of literacy learning that their students face. Of interest for this chapter are the following: How do teachers specify the changing literacy demands on diverse groups of learners, in terms of the volume or qualities of those demands? When and why are there smooth and rough patches, jumps and dips? Are there any qualities that literacy learners must possess in order to successfully negotiate critical transitional points?

The assumption is that, if teachers observe their students experiencing transitional difficulties in literacy learning, some notion of a 'literacy trajectory' will make an appearance in teachers' accounts. An ensuing assumption is that exploring these accounts should be useful in building a better understanding of the nature of key transition phases and what the implications might be for pedagogy, differentiation, evaluation processes, and curriculum content and design (Fontana & Frey, 2000). So, classroom practitioners' accounts are key features of the context for this study, and coherent, detailed analytic work on these accounts has the potential to support ongoing reform in pre- and in-service programmes.

## Three Themes in Teachers' Commentary about Their Daily Work

Three recurring themes in the interviews with teachers are explored in this chapter. To preview, two of the themes concern the importance they ascribe to variations in their students' independence, and to variations in the diversity of their students' needs, capabilities and backgrounds. This chapter reports on how teachers implement concepts about independence and diversity, in ways that offer both rich examples and forceful explanations that together describe, evaluate and explain how the literacy demands of schooling can be addressed via more focused pedagogy. Using examples from interviews with teachers, the implications of these accounts for students' work and for teachers' daily classroom practice are explored.

The way teachers weigh up the value of independence and diversity for their classroom work (and for schooling more generally) has wide-ranging implications for a third theme in this project, what we term the 'horizons of consequence' that they attribute to their teaching – how far ahead they maintain they can and should look as they plan for their students' learning. In general, we found that if interviewees characterised independence and diversity as challenges to be overcome, then they tended also to describe an outlook that is of shorter term than those of their colleagues who characterised independence and diversity as presenting distinctive opportunities for learning.

This chapter demonstrates that how teachers talk about these three themes not only reflects an empirical map of their teaching but also establishes a warrant for the structures and contents of their lessons, and their own assessments of the adequacy of that warrant. That is, it explores how the teachers' accounts relate these themes to students' progress across the years of schooling, and how that both describes and justifies their own teaching practices.

Some observations need to be made about these interviews with teachers. Firstly, they are 'semi-structured'. While the interviewers have a set of prescribed questions, they are also instructed to leave the script to follow points that are unclear or of particular interest. Neither speaker knows how the direction of the interview will proceed or the particular emphases which may emerge (Langdridge, 2004). Secondly, the teachers knew in advance that the project of which this interview forms a part is about literacy, specifically about transitions in literacy learning between age and grade levels. This can explain the sometimes highly literacy-specific responses to very general prompts.

## Methodology

The data drawn on in this chapter consist of seven teacher interviews across schooling years spanning from the first year of school (called 'Kindergarten' in the Australian state of New South Wales) to Year 9. The seven interviews included one teacher from each of the following years: K, 2, 3, 6, 7 and two from Year 9. The primary teachers were located in schools which fed into the secondary teachers' high school. Interviews were focused on questions surrounding the particular literacy demands of the curriculum, the transition needs and challenges for students, and what students needed to be able to know, and to do by the end of the school year. APPRAISAL[1] analysis (Martin & White, 2005) from Systemic Functional Linguistics is used to analyse teachers' accounts of their students' learning. This type of linguistic analysis is particularly suited to understanding evaluative and attitudinal meanings. It can therefore provide an insight into how teachers evaluate curriculum demands, transition points and the impacts of these on their students and their own pedagogy.

The approach to the data included an initial analysis to establish emergent themes concerning the impact of student diversity and independence on literacy development. A systematic thematic analysis (Boyatziz, 1998; Cohen, Manion & Morrison, 2007) was then conducted, in which instances where teachers talked about these themes were coded on the interview transcripts. As part of this process, tables were developed (see Appendix A for an illustrative example) synthesising teachers' perspectives on these themes (e.g. diversity can be problematic for lesson planning, or classroom seating arrangements can be used to manage diversity) and illustrative quotes for each perspective were listed. APPRAISAL analyses were then carried out to gain further insight into teachers' attitudes towards diversity and independence.

APPRAISAL is a linguistic system which theorises the nature of the attitudes which are expressed in language (the system of ATTITUDE), how these are scaled up or toned down (GRADUATION) and how the attitudes are sourced, either originating from the speaker's own perspective or referencing the perspective of others (ENGAGEMENT). It can also account for the ways that certain attitudinal meanings are made explicitly (inscribed ATTITUDE) or implicitly (invoked ATTITUDE). Within the system of ATTITUDE, evaluations can be made about an individual's feelings (AFFECT), people's character and behaviour (JUDGEMENT), or about things (APPRECIATION) (Martin & White, 2005). The systems of AFFECT, JUDGEMENT and APPRECIATION can be further subcategorised; these more delicate options are explained and exemplified in the sections below, as they become relevant, and a simplified network drawing of the APPRAISAL system can be found in Appendix B. Following a detailed, manual APPRAISAL analysis of some illustrative and representative examples from the interview data, the results were used to confirm the systematic thematic analysis and to enrich the discussion of independence and diversity with respect to students' experience of literacy transitions.

## Independence and Diversity as Key Features of Students

In this section I focus on the themes of independence and diversity in an attempt to understand how these qualities relate to different 'horizons of consequence' both in teachers' planning and in their practical organisation of daily classroom practice. In particular, I draw out those moments of discord that are taken to create problematic transitions for students across the trajectory of their literacy development or of their schooling more generally.

While limitations of space prevent the use of extended excerpts from interview, discussion of each of the themes of independence and diversity begins with a snippet of teacher talk to provide a sense of how the interviews typically progressed. The excerpts selected are broadly representative of some of the issues connected to the broader themes of independence and diversity. Some initial observations on the unfolding of each excerpt are provided, and discussion then turns to a more thematic perspective, aided by the APPRAISAL analysis.

## Independence

The excerpt below shows an interview with an assistant principal, Macey,[2] who also taught a composite Year 1–2 class and who had spent thirteen years teaching across the Year 1–6 range. In prior sections of the interview the teacher has outlined her career as a teacher and a school leader and there has been some discussion about the nature of her class and the diversity of her students (a theme which is picked up again below). The interview now turns to a discussion of the project's aims via a general question about transition points. Text in square brackets ([]) provides explanatory insertions.

I:  What do you see as the big transition points, Macey, in um, school?

T:  I find the structure and routine of [Stage 1] is something that the children can quite get used to and obviously need. Stage 2 [School Years 3 and 4] is then a very different learning environment. The level of and expectation of independence is quite high, so for me as a Year 2 teacher I really try to promote that level of independence so that they're somewhat prepared, but I know that there's children who are ready for that, and there's other children who aren't.

So, something I feel our school can develop in is that seamless transition. So, I hope from the project that we will start to get insight into what's coming next so I can prepare them for that, but also that better understanding of where they're coming from. I think there is still a bit of divide between our Year 3 and our Year 2 teachers. I don't know that we do have quite enough dialogue at the moment. So, I think that knowing what kind of learning they're used to having and how they can bring that into where they need to be is a key point.

In terms of Stage 2 to Stage 3, I found the levels of development, when I got a Stage 3 child out of Stage 2, some were still very immature. They're still on the cusp of 'do they own their learning? Are they at that point where they feel it's their responsibility?' And that's a big thing. I mean if they're not motivated for themselves … so it's trying to promote that inner drive … 'who are you doing this for? Are you doing it for yourself and that sense of satisfaction and achievement when you do achieve and are successful?'

In this brief section the teacher provided an overall sequence of what she saw as adjustments and accommodations that teachers and students both need to make over the course of their schooling. A span of evolution for the students is presented from '*structure and routine*' to an '*expectation of independence*' and on to '*inner drive*'. In Stage 1 (Years 1–2) the focus is on coming to terms with the participation structures of the classroom; in Stage 2 (Years 3–4) on the development of personal engagement, and in Stage 3 (Years 5–6) on individual acceptance of responsibility and psychological commitment. The ability to participate effectively in the whole-group settings of the classroom is taken to provide a platform for internalising the learning programme and deriving satisfaction from progressing within that programme. Independence is construed as the students' capacity to do the work expected of them and to have positive feelings about their learning.

The APPRAISAL analysis of the teachers' discussion of independence revealed a preference for making judgements of students' *capacity*, describing independent students as those who are competent, capable, successful and prepared. Independent students are also reported as experiencing positive feelings of satisfaction towards their success.

> Who are you doing this for? Are you doing it for yourself and that sense of **satisfaction** (+ satisfaction) and **achievement** (+satisfaction) when you do **achieve** (+capacity) and are **successful** (+capacity)? (Macey, Year 2 teacher)

Independent students are also sometimes judged as *tenacious* or dependable, in that they take responsibility for their own learning.

> Another one could be **taking responsibility** (+ tenacity) for what they haven't got. And that's where, as well, **having the list of things that they need to study** (+tenacity), or **having the list of things they need to have** (+tenacity) that is important. (Dianne, Year 9 teacher)

While independence is spoken of in largely positive evaluative language, it is also represented as a double-edged concept by some teachers. On the one hand, it is something that teachers consciously try to develop in their students. Teachers understand increasing independence to be necessary for students' successful transition to the next stage of schooling, and so devote considerable time and effort into planning activities that will build student independence and prepare them for the increasing demands for self-regulation in their future. This is exemplified in the excerpt below, reproduced from the extended snippet above.

> Stage 2 is then a very different learning environment. The level and expectation of independence is quite high. So for me, as a Year 2 teacher, I really try to promote that level of independence so that they're somewhat prepared. (Macey, Year 2 teacher)

While independence is a goal of learning, it is also perceived as a challenge, and even sometimes as an attribute with negative connotations. In fact, independence itself is never explicitly described as something valuable in the data. Rather than using adjectives (for example) to characterise independence as 'good', 'important' or even 'necessary', the teachers take its value for granted and their talk strongly implies that developing student independence is something to be sought after.

> If you've got the good text there and you just manipulate that, again and again and again, eventually the doing it on their own comes a lot easier. (Macey, Year 2 teacher)

However, where independence is evaluated explicitly in the teachers' talk, it is construed as a challenge. This is especially the case if students' ability for self-regulation outpaces – or runs in a different direction from – the teacher's perception of their cognitive development. In the excerpt below, the teacher expresses her frustration when very young readers become increasingly competent at decoding the words on the page, but are, in her opinion, not sufficiently able to understand what it is they are 'reading'. In cases such as these, independence is not a goal to be pursued but a problem to solve.

> I find that **challenging** every day, because I guess their minds are still relatively young, so quite often when they become competent readers at a young age, the texts aren't appropriate for them that they're capable of reading, because the themes in the texts are beyond them, even though they're capable of reading them. (Macey, Year 2 teacher)

> Yeah, and then well here it's sort of it's been a **challenge** to sort of work out how to extend a lot of the kids because a lot of them can just do it straight away. (Andrew, Year 6 teacher)

Independence is also perceived to be linked to motivation, where a teacher wants students to be self-motivated rather than constantly driven by the teacher's explicit guidance. The ideal of intrinsic motivation appears as early as Stage 3 (age eleven) and is linked with ideas of maturity and responsibility. While students are expected to want to learn for their own sake, teachers also recognise that this is 'a big thing'.

> When I got a Stage 3 child out of Stage 2 some were still very immature. They're still on the cusp of – do they own their learning? Are they at that

point where they feel it's their responsibility? And that's a big thing. If they're not motivated for themselves ... I don't want them doing it for me. (Macey, Year 2 teacher)

Overall, a progression can be seen in the teachers' accounts of independence as lacking in students' early stages, and needing to be intentionally and explicitly developed so they can cope with the future increasing demands of their schooling. While independence can be seen as problematic if gained too early, by Stage 3 teachers aim for students not only to be able to work on specific tasks on their own but to be self-motivated and 'mature', working 'for themselves' and not for the teacher. This independence is seen as critical not only for students' transition to high school but also for their continued success in learning, as by the end of primary school they must have learned to read on their own so that they can read (on their own) to learn in secondary school (Rose & Martin, 2012).

## Diversity

Turning to the theme of diversity, I begin with an extended excerpt from the same teacher who began the section on independence.

T: So I went from Year 6 down to Kindergarten, so teaching children how to read and how to write and all the basics and then obviously I found, and I do still find in Stage 1 you get the biggest, spectrum of learners, because you do get the child coming in who, can already read, and you get the child who has no idea whatsoever.

So being able to differentiate the learning but also make it, I guess, meaningful in the way that everybody reaches their expectation at the end of the day. So, I find that I very much apply the concepts of the 'how to' to learning about now, so how to read. And then, OK, now in my classroom because of the fact that they are high achievers, most of them are close to or are independent readers. So now I've got to know well OK where to now with their learning? And then it really is about breaking down texts and looking at what components are there and why they're there, and what's the purpose of those texts. And so, I find that challenging every day.

In this excerpt, the teacher immediately attached salience to differentiating students in terms of their literacy capabilities commenting on the '*biggest spectrum*' of learners. She differentiated two categories of students: 'the child coming in who can already read' and 'the child who has no idea whatsoever'. This point about the biggest spectrum of learner at entry, however, was resolved by the teacher into an apparently satisfactory outcome: 'everybody reaches their expectation at the end of the day'.

She then marked a shift of perspective with 'OK' and proceeded to discuss the distinctive challenges applying to her current students. The categorisation at work from this point on is *high achievers*. The teacher contrasts their competence in reading with their 'young minds' and the fact that in more advanced texts the 'themes in the texts are beyond them'. This in turn called for the teacher to take a more analytic approach to her pedagogy around the varying components and purposes of texts. Her current students may be 'independent readers' but they nevertheless present challenges 'every day'.

Diversity is widely acknowledged as an unavoidable fact in modern education. While the New South Wales Department of Education (2020) supports inclusive education strategies through which 'all students can access and fully participate in learning, alongside their similar-aged peers, supported by reasonable adjustments and teaching strategies tailored to meet their individual needs', diversity in the classroom is perceived to be problematic by all the teachers interviewed. This is visible in the frequent couplings between judgements of students' varying capacities and negative appreciations of the diverse classroom context. Diversity resulting from children achieving both higher and lower than the majority of the cohort is construed by teachers as being a problem, as the following examples illustrate.

> It's sort of it's been **a challenge** (- appreciation) to sort of work out how to extend a lot of the kids because **a lot of them can just do it straight away** (+ capacity). (Andrew, Year 6 teacher)
>
> Children that often come in with **very low amounts of English** (-capacity), knowing where to start with those kids and what to do with them when the other kids are reading and writing is certainly **difficult** (- appreciation). (Catherine, Year 3 teacher)

Diversity is a factor that is understood by teachers to vary from school to school in quantity, and from stage to stage in consequences, with perhaps the biggest variations expected in the very early years of schooling, as Macey comments in the extended excerpt above.

Despite this apparent variation in diversity between schools and stages, teachers frequently used language resources of GRADUATION to upscale the extent of the problem of teaching students from diverse backgrounds and with differing support needs. They do this in several ways. They may quantify the amount of students or families affected ('we've got **quite a few** families that are from refugee backgrounds': Yasmine, K teacher), they may quantify the frequency with which the issue occurs ('children that **often** come in with very low amounts of English': Catherine, Year 3 teacher) or they may quantify the amount of energy required on the part of the teachers ('I'm **always** thinking about what I'm going to do with that top group, and what am I going to do with that bottom group': Catherine, Year 3 teacher).

This diversity leads to several implications for teachers, including the need to differentiate lessons for students and plan for each individual student's capabilities. Teachers appear to manage student diversity in the classroom in a number of ways. Some perceive group-work and whole class sharing as a useful way of scaffolding for less-able students, who, it is claimed, will be able to tell from the work of others what is expected of them.

> I think the sharing is quite good because some of those kids that don't sort of get it or know what's expected can sort of go oh that's what they've done. (Andrew, Year 6 teacher)

Other teachers seem to teach to the middle, perceiving both the higher- and lower-achieving students to be somewhat problematic. Some teachers claim to differentiate for each individual student in their class:

> I differentiate for all of my children ... they're not all on the same cluster. So I have to differentiate for everyone ... I don't teach for the middle group – I teach for everyone, so they're all individual. (Yasmine, Kindergarten teacher)

Different classroom groupings are also used to manage student diversity. Teachers use either seating patterns in the classroom, or withdraw particular groups, such as EAL/D (English as an Additional Language or Dialect) learners or learners struggling with literacy, for support outside the classroom. The excerpt from the teacher interview below illustrates how one teacher problematises diversity as something which she tries to solve using groupings in the classroom. It also indicates the frustration that she feels, and how it challenges her ability to effectively teach all students effectively at the same time.

> Well I guess because you can't meet their needs all at the same time. You're with one group and sometimes you can glance out of the corner of your eye, and you know that somebody needs something and you're just trying to balance that all the time. (Catherine, Year 3 teacher)

Teachers' talk about diversity also shows their tendency to be more circumspect in their language about students' capacities than when they were talking about independence. When they are discussing their diverse classrooms, teachers tended to state positive judgements about students' capacities overtly, describing students as 'bright', 'capable', 'advanced' and 'pretty good readers'. However, their negative judgements about students' capacities were often invoked, or stated indirectly. Teachers used constructions from which the listener is meant to interpret a judgement of negative capacity, for example, students who 'read word-by-word', students 'not engaged by the texts' or students 'having issues with sentence construction'.

In addition, explicitly stated positive judgements of students' capacities tended to be given as attributes of the child ('capable kids', 'they are bright') while the more negative assessments of their capacities are given as things they do or can't do ('reading word by word', 'need to verbalise it'). It is possible that this tendency to make more covert assessments of students' difficulties when talking about diversity results from an awareness of the more politicised or problematic nature of the discourse around diversity. That is, there may be a tension between diversity as 'fact' and mixed ability classrooms being both the norm and generally accepted as best practice (over ability streaming for example) and the difficulties teachers experience from it in the classroom and in their planning.

## Conclusions

The differing levels of independence and diversity encountered by teachers in their classrooms lead to different 'horizons of consequence' when teachers plan learning. While some teachers espoused a commitment to producing 'future focused learners' (Yasmine, Kindergarten teacher) and look ahead to the next stage of learning or beyond, some focus on only one school term ahead, while others feel only able to focus on what they want each student to be able to do in the even more immediate future.

> To be honest, getting them into Year 4 I haven't thought about too much. My class is so diverse. I feel like just getting them to their own next little goal is where to look to. (Catherine, Year 3 teacher)

These differing future orientations have the potential to result in widening gaps between students who are already performing well at or above expectations for stage level and those who are not. If a teacher's objective is to help the student advance to the next level 'for them' (as above, 'everybody reaches *their expectation* at the end of the day') and there is not an overarching orientation to also preparing them for the next stage of schooling they will encounter, the potential exists for the existing achievement gaps between students to be maintained across the schooling years rather than closed. The tension between the individual student's 'next little goal' and the more generalised expected stage outcomes could possibly result in particular transitional difficulties for some students and warrants further investigation (Masters, 2019).

This issue is especially visible in the talk of a Year 7 teacher in this study. She characterised her students as 'bright' but not entirely *prepared* for either their current or future literacy learning needs. Her focus then becomes to make sure her students learn how to be critical, something they will need for the remainder of their secondary school, positioning criticality as an 'end-point' in literacy growth and development.

> I mean, they're all very competent, but when you come to do those specific things of structuring your ideas so that you can analyse language and poetry and being able to really deconstruct the technique within it, that's where they start to struggle. That's not an easy thing for any kid, I don't think. And they don't come from primary school with that ability to write in that way either. In terms of their literacy, they use words well and, as I said yesterday, we did an activity: your favourite words – and some of the words … like they've obviously in primary school been taught … because they're bright … they have this enormous word bank. That's great but in high school when you come to that side in terms of being able to read and that understanding, that critical sense, rather than just being good with language in a creative

way, so ... I guess that's something that I'm going to have to really work on with them. (Caroline: Year 7 teacher)

As evident in the excerpt above, the interviews indicated that critical or analytical thinking looms large when teachers think about the future. Generally speaking, a trajectory though the schooling years seems to implicate a trajectory towards critical thinking as a marker of maturity in student learning and away from what teachers perceive as more 'basic' forms of thinking and writing.

## Horizons of Consequence: Towards Criticality

When teachers were asked what might be different about the demands of literacy in the years following where they were currently teaching, they often focused on the need for students to be more critical. This is particularly visible in the response of the Year 6 teacher, Andrew, when asked how Year 7 would be different in terms of literacy: 'I think, I guess the content they look at might be a bit more heavy in regards to inferred meanings and things like that, so it won't just be as black and white so to speak, I guess.' The issue of what critical thinking is though, and how it should be developed cannot be taken on face value and the relationship between criticality and pedagogies which foster it needs to be problematised (Cremin & Chappell, 2019). From the TRANSLIT project data, while teachers in primary school realise students will need critical and analytical thinking for Year 7, Year 7 teachers feel like students don't come to them with this ability. It would seem that this represents a particular transitional difficulty and warrants further investigation.

While some teachers, such as the Year 9 teacher Ben, saw creativity and critical thinking as inherently linked ('it's a high level of refinement and creativity and imagination that accompanies that ability to analyse something'), most of the time concepts of criticality or analysis were juxtaposed in the teacher's talk with either creativity or with 'lower order' ways of thinking ('moving beyond that just describing and recounting').

Importantly, while critical and analytical thinking were construed by the teachers as absolutely necessary for success in the HSC ('that's critical in high school and that's the HSC'), it was also presented as something not available equally to all students. Several teachers commented on students who 'just want the right answers' or who 'just take what they have been given in class', who are 'used to ... getting the information disseminated to them'. We can see here the complex interplay between notions of diversity, or *types of students*, independence, critical and analytical thinking and the teachers' struggle to prepare their students for the demands of their future education, their horizon of consequence:

> Yeah, a lot of sub-text as well. ... And there are kids that do it. There are students that are really, really bright, and they will understand and they won't need to ask. But for the ones that just want the answer here because they want to get on to ... and maybe it's got to do with its Year 9 as well – it's early Stage 5 where they don't really care about anything else other than themselves. (Diane, Year 9 teacher)

It is within the daily interplay between catering for diverse students of different 'types' and who are at different 'levels', who nevertheless all need to develop dispositions of independence and intrinsic motivation and who need to learn how to think critically and analytically, that teachers establish their warrants for the structure and the content of their lessons. Additionally, it seems from many of the interviews that teachers experience a certain level of frustration and/or difficulty that the reality of their classrooms is not what they would like it to be, as we have already seen in Catherine's assertion above that 'you can't meet their needs all at the same time'.

The teachers in the study endeavoured to make good use of the resources and tools they have available to them, such as ESL and gifted and talented withdrawal and programmes such as 'Getting Reading Right', with its associated mandated classroom seating plan in order to manage what they see as the 'challenge' of diversity. They also claim that the nature of their work is different, depending on school type and clientele. However, even in academically selective secondary schools, such as the high school in this study, teachers in Year 9 are still categorising students as differently able. This categorisation of students also appears to shift in focus from students' *capacities* in Year 7 to their *achievement* in formalised testing by Year 9. While the Year 7 teacher describes students as 'bright' or 'pretty good readers' or comments on the size of their vocabulary, the Year 9 teacher frequently describes them as 'bottom band' or 'upper band'. This reflects the marking and reporting scale for the end-of-school examination that students sit at the end of Year 12, in which performance is rated in bands 1–6. It appears that the end-of-school examination exerts an influence on teachers who begin to rank and categorise their students in the years leading up to the examination, almost predicting where certain types of students fit on a ranked scale. The difficulties experienced by some students at certain transition points would appear to reinforce these categories of students, leading to inequitable educational outcomes. There is therefore still an urgent need to better understand how disjunctive transition points are more problematic for some students than others.

In terms of the focus of contributions to this volume on the smoothness or otherwise of students' transitions across the grade levels, I conclude that teachers' ideas about the nature, timing and consequences of learners' transitions are shaped by their sense of the looming relevance of individual students' personal, social and, where relevant, cultural attributes. In particular for this chapter, how independent they are and how diverse they are matters.

APPRAISAL analysis of the teacher interviews has demonstrated that teachers evaluate their diverse classrooms as presenting particular challenges to their daily work. Teachers are constantly assessing their students in terms of their ability to access the curriculum, be independent and be prepared for future stages of learning, and in so doing, they categorise students into certain types (high achieving, low achieving, struggling, etc.). They then cater for multiple types of students in the classroom through the use of targeted pedagogic strategies (group work, seating arrangements, withdrawal). While they tend to make positive judgements of students more directly, describing attributes of the child, they rely more on implied attitudinal meanings expressing elements of diversity (EAL/D or refugee status or students without the right home environment) or talking about behaviours when they talk about students who are performing at lower levels. Teachers express the importance of both independence and critical thinking for students' continued educational success, but by Year 9 student types of more/less independent and more/less critical still exist.

The interviews with teachers reported here mirror other research data which emphasise the interplay of various factors on children's literacy development (Weekes, this volume) and the artificial assumption that progress through the school years is 'a continuous and seamless process' (Masters, 2019: 91). There is still much to be understood about the nature of literacy transition points through schooling; however, the teacher's accounts included here raise important implications for curriculum writers and policymakers and suggest valuable avenues for further research.

## Appendix A: Sample table developed synthesising teachers' perspectives on Independence

|  | Year 2 | Year 3 | Year 7 | Year 9 |
|---|---|---|---|---|
| Independence can be a problem | If they are independent it's hard to work out where next They can decode but not comprehend | | | |
| Independence is necessary due to diverse classrooms | | More capable kids can work independently while teacher works with other groups | | |
| Independence is necessary early in schooling | They need to be ready for Stage 2 Some Stage 3 children are too immature It's harder to develop intrinsic motivation in older students | | | |
| Independence is linked to intrinsic motivation/ love of learning | They need to be responsible for their own learning by Stage 3 | | | Taking responsibility for what they need to know and organising themselves is a skill students need Sometimes the teacher needs to check they have everything they need |

*Categories, Appraisals and Progress in Literacy Transitions*  207

|  | Year 2 | Year 3 | Year 7 | Year 9 |
|---|---|---|---|---|
| Students must analyse/interpret themselves and not be told the answers |  |  | Students need to develop the ability to be analytical about their own work | Facilitate students' interpretation not tell them Doing their own analysis leads to better grades |
| Repetition results in independence |  | Constant manipulation of text leads to the ability to do it on their own |  | Practise every year means by Stage 5 they can do it themselves |

*Note*: Columns for Kindergarten and Year 6 have been removed for reasons of layout.

## Appendix B: Appraisal System Network (Simplified)

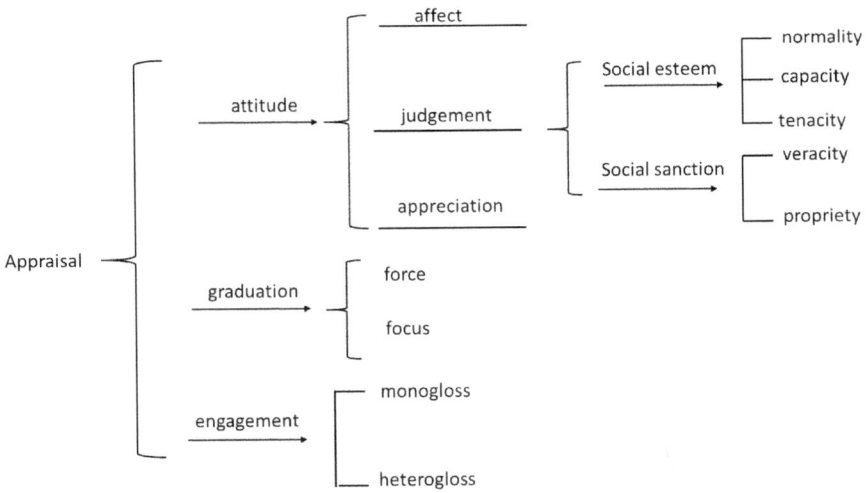

# Envoi to Part II: Explicating Transitions between Hidden Literacy Curricula

## Adam Lefstein

We learn in school both the knowledge prescribed by the formal curriculum, such as how to read and write, and also the hidden curriculum (Jackson, 1968), including, for example, how to be a student, which answers and behaviours are good or at least legitimate and which will likely get us in trouble, what counts as knowledge, who we are and what is our social position, and what goals are worth pursuing. The five chapters in this section of the book show that both the formal and hidden curricular contents and expectations shift as students move through the different stages of schooling. While these shifts are significant, they are not always made explicit, therefore posing the risk that some students will continue to act in accordance with the previous stage's expectations and therefore fail to perform in institutionally appropriate ways and/or learn the curricula. Hence, the research presented here about transitions between rules, pedagogies and literacies is critically important.

While the five chapters speak in different theoretical languages, employ different analytic methods, focus on different objects, stages and disciplinary spaces, they tell a relatively consistent story of discontinuities between educational stages vis-à-vis interactional norms, literacy expectations, textual genres and more. In Chapter 6, Edwards-Groves, Garoni and Freebody contrast three phases, each characterised by a different general orientation: early primary literacy lessons, in which the emphasis is on mastering the classroom interactional norms; late primary writing lessons, in which the emphasis is on mastering narrative conventions; and high school History lessons, in which students are initiated into the specialised literacy of reading as an historian, in order to construct historical knowledge.

The other chapters zero in on transitions between seemingly similar literate activities or texts across two different educational phases. Kervin and Mantei (Chapter 5) show how the move from preschool to Kindergarten involves a tightening of space – from flexible and free use of indoor and outdoor spaces to clearly divided learning groups; time – from flexible and fluid use of time to a dedicated two-hour morning literacy block; interaction – from free play, in which the children create their own rules, to teacher-prescribed tasks with strict guidelines; and expectations – from student choice to a sense of urgency to make curricular progress. Chen, Lewis and Rose (Chapter 7) compare the writing of description in Kindergarten and Year 3, noting that the transition to primary school involves an increase in task complexity, greater expectations for student reasoning, and a greater role for students' ideas and knowledge in making sense of the texts studied. Jones, Matruglio and Rose (Chapter 8) contrast poetry study in late primary and junior secondary English: while in primary school the emphasis is on literal comprehension, in secondary school students are expected to read between the lines and identify and reason about themes and interpretations. The authors note that reading practices that are valued in primary school, such as personal responses to literature, do not serve them well in secondary English, in which they are expected to engage critically and analytically with the text. Finally, Turney and Rutherford Vale (Chapter 9) contrast students' science texts in the transition between Year 6 and Year 7. The authors show that in high school students are expected to represent scientific phenomena through multimodal texts that integrate precise, technical scientific language with abstract visual diagrams.

Together, the chapters address or at least touch upon all the dimensions of Alexander's (2001) generic model of teaching: the lesson frame, including the organisation of space, time, students, curriculum and routines; and the acts that compose the lesson: tasks, activities, interaction and judgement.

They paint a particularly elaborate and insightful picture with regard to the types of texts students consume and produce, the tasks they are called upon to perform and their concomitant cognitive demands, and the discourse and social interaction through which teachers mediate students' engagement with these texts and tasks. I would like to know more about the organisation of students and about assessment practices. With regard to the organisation of students, Jones, Matruglio and Rose (Chapter 8) note that 'by the time students reach senior secondary school, they are in effect "sorted" into different streams of the English curriculum'. Similarly, in Chapter 5 we learn that in Kindergarten students are grouped according to their performance on literacy assessments. What happens between these two points in time? Are students also sorted into literacy sets or streams in primary and lower secondary schools? Transitions are likely critical junctures in this streaming process, when prior sorting decisions can be contested or ratified, and through which students' academic standing – and fate – is gradually solidified. In my own context (Israel), the move from primary to middle to secondary school is also a move from loosely or non-sorted classes, to differentiated groups within heterogeneous classrooms, to wholly separate streams. The questions of who gets streamed into which group, what forms of literacy and pedagogy they encounter there and what are the educational and occupational opportunities their assignment offers have critical social consequences. Moreover, students are not only sorted into streams within schools but are also sorted between schools: How do transitions vary between different types of schools and social contexts?

With regard to assessment, the chapters provide many examples of teacher judgement being passed on to students in classroom discourse; such interactions shape students' learning about what counts as an institutionally acceptable answer or interpretation. Yet, I was surprised that the authors do not discuss summative assessments, especially assessments that are administered at the end of one key stage as part of the transition to the next stage. Such assessments – often, high-stakes, standardised tests – are critical for communicating not only to students but also and especially to teachers' official expectations about which literacy practices are most valued.

These five chapters make it abundantly clear that literacy is not a single entity – Literacy 'with a big "L" and a single "y"' (Street, 1993) – but includes multiple practices involving multiple purposes, social contexts, text types, interpretive processes and interactional routines. The privileging of some literacy practices by schools and the delegitimising of others have social and political consequences. Who benefits and who loses when teachers and schools transition between literacies? In what ways do students – and teachers – resist and/or realise agency in navigating these transitions?

Finally, how can, do and should we as educators support students in coping with these transitions? Most of the authors write in praise of explicitness – explicating rules, processes and assessment criteria, and explicitly modelling expected practices. Do such practices indeed support more successful transitions? How are they and other pedagogies experienced by the students? What scope do they and their teachers have to exercise agency in shaping their literacies and literacy transitions?

**Table P.II.1** A Generic Model of Teaching

| Frame | Form | Act |
|---|---|---|
| Space |  | Task |
| Pupil organisation |  | Activity |
| Time | Lesson |  |
| Curriculum |  | Interaction |
| Routine, rule and ritual |  | Judgement |

Source: Alexander (2001a: 325).

Part III

# Horizons of Consequence: Accounting for Transition

# Literate Identities in the Early Years of Primary School

Jessica Mantei and Lisa Kervin

## Introduction

Our literate identity is formed by the ways we view ourselves as users of language and our roles as literate participants in society. The concept of a literate identity sits within a sociocultural paradigm that views identity as a social construct shaped by the beliefs and social practices of a community and developed through the experiences and relationships we have with others within those unique settings. An identity is shaped by context and experience and realised through practice (Compton-Lilly, 2006; Vasudevan, Schultz & Bateman, 2010). As such it is open to change in response to subsequent opportunities, experiences and relationships (Sumara, 1998) across time and place.

Early development of literate identities occurs within home and community settings where young children are inculcated into the values and ways of being literate in that group. These early days are spent connecting with family and community texts, popular culture and popular media including not only commercial texts and characters but also historical and institutional materials valued by the community (Dyson, 2003; Yoon, 2016). It is here a child develops emergent understandings about themselves as a literate person through what they observe and what they learn to be relevant (Buchholz, 2016). It is through purposeful participation (Yoon, 2016) within these early settings that children develop confidence about themselves within the context of their world, and they take control by positioning themselves in line with experiences they have had, and with those they imagine (Dyson, 2019; Kervin, 2016; Sumara, 1998). Literate identities are formed and realised in response to the stories we tell ourselves about what it means to be literate, the stories others tell about us and about what counts (Dyson, 2003; Harste, Woodward & Burke, 1984; Sfard & Prusak, 2005).

Therefore, educational contexts have much to work with as young children enter these new settings. Heath's (1983) seminal work alerted us to the ways educational settings shape and challenge the ways individuals, groups and indeed whole communities understand themselves as literate people. What is well established in research literature is that transitions to educational institutions are smoother for those whose cultural and social practices are complementary to the academic literacies of school (Dyson, 2019; Gee, 1990). It is in educational spaces that a new form of inculcation – what it means to be a reader and writer *here* – shapes new versions of an emerging literate identity (Compton-Lilly, 2006; Taylor, 2019), the identity of 'student'.

The educators' role, then, is not only to acknowledge the identities their students bring to school (Gee, 1990) but also to nurture and expand their capacities for literacy. Educators operate within a set of societal expectations related to their beliefs about the purposes of schools, particularly in those crucial early years. Yoon (2016: 66) notes that early years educators are often positioned as holders of knowledge who are tasked with the responsibility of preparing learners for their 'entire academic futures in Kindergarten'. Martens and Adamson (2001) observe the impact of the educator as an authoritative figure with significant influence over how a child will come to understand themselves as a literate person. And Dyson (2019: 80) identifies the 'official lens' of the educator as a barrier to understanding the nature of a learner. And so, the literate identities of the educator, that is, their beliefs about literacy learning and what it means to be literate, cannot be discounted as we consider the ways students learn to be literate within educational settings.

Our research occurred at a time of national and state-based curriculum reform. Literacy pedagogy in Australian primary schools was driven by the national formal school English curriculum (Australian Curriculum and Reporting Authority (ACARA, 2014)). Literacy definitions in that curriculum relate to the composition and comprehension of texts across semiotic modes with a focus on four types of knowledge: knowledge about text, about grammar, about words and visual knowledge (ACARA, 2014). And alongside this, the New South Wales (NSW) Education Standards Authority (formerly BOSTES) interpreted the National Curriculum for NSW teachers through the creation of its own syllabus.

During the time of our research, the primary teachers were in the very early stages of using this new state-based English syllabus (NESA, 2012). In 2015 the National Literacy and Numeracy Progressions (ACARA, 2018) were developed with the view to enabling teachers to identify specific behaviours of students that demonstrate literacy skills and understandings to help them plan teaching, assess, track and monitor student progress. From 2016 to 2017, ACARA and the NSW Department of Education led development of the National Literacy and Numeracy Progressions. This fifty-eight-page document itemises discrete skills within the 'elements' of: speaking and listening, reading and viewing, and writing. Within each element are 'sub-elements'. For example, the sub-elements of reading and viewing are understanding texts; phonological awareness; phonic knowledge and word recognition; and fluency. Within each sub-element are 'Levels and Indicators', which are 'grouped together to form developmental levels' or 'progression levels' (ACARA, 2018: 5). Teachers across the primary years of school are required to track their students' literacy development across the elements, sub-elements, levels and indicators and use them for the purposes of demonstrating student growth. To provide some insight into the extent of detail a teacher is required to undertake in mapping about each student's 'progress', one sub-element of reading, phonic knowledge and word recognition contains nine levels within each for a total of thirty-nine indicators of mastery. Given what we know about the ways literate identities are shaped by experiences and interactions, it is easy to see the potential for the early years of formal school to be a strong influence on the ways teachers and their students see themselves as literate individuals.

Alongside this, state-based initiatives contributed to the work of teachers as they navigated national reform. The development of the state-based Literacy and Numeracy Strategy 2017–20 was released during our research. It identified key elements for literacy teaching, including early intervention for students in the early years, explicit teaching and diagnostic assessments. In addition, many primary schools were required to undertake a district-wide programme (L3) targeting the teaching of reading and writing. L3 is a classroom intervention focused on systematic and explicit teaching during classroom-based daily literacy sessions. And further, the school at the focus of this chapter had also purchased a synthetic phonics programme for implementation across all grades. Its prominence in Kindergarten and Year 1 was clear in the planning and delivery of daily literacy learning opportunities offered. This multitude of policy change, mandates, frameworks, competing pedagogies and purchased packages made for a very busy time in the primary school for leaders, teachers and students alike.

This chapter presents data gathered from a primary school in the inner-city cluster of the TRANSLIT project, a school whose students came from backgrounds with diverse social and cultural histories. While some lived in this inner-city suburb, others travelled with their parents to attend the school near their workplace.

We draw upon case study data from the first two years of the formal primary school setting – Kindergarten and Year 1. In NSW, children in Kindergarten are categorised as 'Early Stage One' and Syllabus documents outline the Learning Outcomes that must be achieved throughout that year before they may move on to 'Stage 1' (Years 1 and 2). For literacy, this means mastering twelve literacy learning outcomes for each Stage focused on developing knowledge, skills and understandings in reading, writing, speaking and listening. Data shared in this chapter comprise classroom observations and subsequent semi-structured interviews with a Kindergarten and a Year 1 teacher from the contextual study of the TRANSLIT project, and semi-structured interviews and writing samples from three case study children who participated in regular interviews about the nature of their literacy learning experiences across the three years of the study. Teacher data were analysed deductively to provide insights into these teachers' literate identities in connection with: (1) their role as teachers, (2) the roles of the learners in their class, (3) the activities and resources they utilised for literacy teaching. Interview questions designed to elicit this information included: What do you believe your role to be as a teacher? What are your expectations of the learners? What do they need to be able to do in x grade (e.g. Kindergarten) and what will they need to be able to do in the following year? How do you support your learners for literacy learning? Coding of data occurred within our literate identity frame of analysis and was used to make insights into these teachers' literate identities at the time of the project.

Student data were analysed inductively, which afforded insights not only to their perspectives about themselves as learners but also to the ways they saw their teachers' practices as part of that identity. Interview questions focused on literacy (reading, writing, talking and listening) individually and together across the interview, and included: What are some ways you do reading/writing/talking and listening in your classroom? What are some important things in your class that you need to know about reading/writing/talking and listening? What does your teacher think about your reading/writing/talking and listening (how do you know)? What are things you think you will need to do when you're in [the next year of school] and how do you feel about that? Coded data were used then to draw out the ways these teachers and learners viewed literacy learning in this classroom. The findings include the voices of the participants through direct quotes selected as representations of the full data set. They are offered as insights into the views of the participants about their experiences within and in transition across these Kindergarten and Year 1 classrooms.

The chapter initially examines the expectations for literacy learning from the teachers' perspective. It then draws on case study data from individual children to examine what it means to be a literacy learner in Kindergarten and then following the transition to Year 1 at this school. We aim to explore the ways learners are positioned as readers and writers within the constructs of each classroom and how these children talk about their literate identities.

## Introducing the Teachers

Yasmine and Maddison (all names are pseudonyms) taught consecutive grades (Kindergarten and Year 1), held formal executive and literacy leadership positions in the school, and were friends. Both were experienced classroom teachers whose literacy leadership positions were connected with training they had undertaken in the delivery of a commercial programme focused on developing students' knowledge about letter–sound relationships. Both teachers self-nominated to participate in the research.

## Yasmine: Kindergarten Teacher

At the time of the project, Yasmine had been teaching at the school for approximately two years. She was an experienced classroom teacher with training in early years teaching and specialised reading teaching. Responding to what she identified as a 'big push' from the NSW Department of Education, she had introduced a commercially produced synthetic phonics programme to be delivered in all classrooms. While she acknowledged the programme would mainly be used with children in the first three years of school, Yasmine had arranged training for all staff in its delivery 'to bring them up to speed' with the teaching techniques. Her focus on bringing all teachers 'on board' included supervising their delivery and using a 'gentle pat on the shoulder' to remind them to teach 'this way, not that way', referring to the prescribed script and processes for delivering the phonics programme.

Yasmine expressed the need to generate in her students certain literacy dispositions, 'you've got to catch them in Kindergarten and get them on top of their love for learning, and then set them up so that they're successful'. Success in Yasmine's classroom was measured in a range of ways. The synthetic phonics programme included a scope and sequence for tracking the students' learning of sounds 'eight phonemes at a time so you're not learning them in isolation', and of spelling and vocabulary – 'camera words', 'crunchy words', 'WOW words' and words from the 'million dollar wall'. Teacher-selected 'learning intentions' and 'success criteria' were shared at the beginning and end of lessons. Learning intentions 'focus the children on the purpose of the task', while success criteria, expressed as 'I can' statements, allowed the children to identify their learning gains. Yasmine explained that she wanted the children to 'pick up' this language to talk about letters, words and learning for future use

> when my children that go to their Year 1 teacher next year will be able to say the 'I can' statements ... and as they go up during the years, they will become more complex in the way they can answer.

Yasmine explained that she used 'benchmarking' to set each student a 'reading goal', which, for most, was displayed on a wall in the classroom. But for children whose reading proficiency was lower than a 'level five', a different system was used to prevent them from 'becoming disheartened'.

> They'll have a special other area where they'll keep theirs in a folder. But they'll be working towards goals in their reading and then they've got to learn how they're going to get to the next level.

For writing, Yasmine explained that she wanted to see the students 'try to write a sentence' from sentences the teacher had constructed during the week as the modelled writing component of the synthetic phonics programme. Examples of these sentences included, *The cat sat on the mat; He can play the drum; She was at the party*. Yasmine also engaged students with writing through 'cut up stories' where the same stories from modelled writing were printed onto long cards and cut up into their individual words for subsequent reconstruction. As with reading, the students were benchmarked into levels and the 'cut up' task was differentiated. Some were required to sequence the cards with the support of the model sentence, while others reconstructed it from memory.

Yasmine described her job as a teacher is

> to do it all, to juggle it all. My job is to be the teacher and to look at the syllabus and look at the content, know my stuff and where I have to take the children … Children need to know where they are and where they need to go to next as well.

## Maddison: Year 1 Teacher

Maddison was, at the time of the project, an experienced teacher of approximately 13 years. Maddison explained that she had spent her full career at this one school, and that she had 'worked her way up' into a leadership position that involved delivering the school's purchased synthetic phonics programme and providing literacy leadership for staff, specifically in working with students identified as gifted and/or talented. Maddison shared that those early days in leadership were challenging because 'I was obviously younger than a lot of the people I was supervising' and therefore needed to show them that 'I know what I'm talking about'. Maddison believed that her 'learning in the gifted and talented field' was of benefit to the school when she brought 'those learnings into a Stage 1 context'.

Like Yasmine, Maddison shared the desire to 'promote that inner drive. And I find that's very hard, the older the child gets'. Maddison observed that 'the structure and routine of Stage 1 is something that the children get used to and obviously need'. And that, despite being immature when they reach Stage 2 (Years 3 and 4), these children will need to be independent readers and writers. As such, Maddison described the need to promote independence.

> From a young age I really try to push that. So – who are you doing this for? Are you doing it for yourself and that sense of satisfaction and achievement when you do achieve and are successful?

Maddison observed that early years teaching required a focus on 'the basics'. She explained that the need to differentiate the learning was acute in these early years because 'you get the biggest spectrum of learner, because you get the child coming in who can already read, and you get the child who has no idea whatsoever'. Maddison expressed concern that children can develop 'holes' in their understanding, which undermines their motivation. For this reason, Maddison wanted all teachers to be 'up to date', which meant being trained to teach the synthetic phonics programme. As in Kindergarten, learning in this Year 1 room was tracked using 'learning intentions' and 'success criteria'.

In reading, Maddison expressed the belief that good readers are 'those who read a lot' and that part of her role is to 'foster a love of reading'. In measuring reading proficiency, Maddison looked for evidence of children's knowledge about the strategies they use to read, 'I don't care if you can read that book and you can read it fluently, but if you can't tell me all the different comprehension keys, well you haven't got it there I'm not going to move you up [a reading level].' The comprehension keys Maddison referred to come from a programme the school had purchased focused on developing strategies for comprehension including 'monitoring understanding' and 'using fix up strategies'. Examples of 'comprehension keys' observed in Maddison's classroom included 'the 3-point retell', 'the 5-point retell' and 'two positives and something to work on'.

In writing, Maddison preferred children to write about 'simple topics' that represented 'real life to them', for example, the selection of a pet or the concept of homework. Maddison considered topics such as pollution and those with 'really strong political messages' to be too hard. Writers in Maddison's Year 1 class worked on developing understandings about the structural and language features of a range of 'text types'. These features were conveyed to Year 1 through learning intentions and success criteria, displayed for easy reference on the front wall of the classroom.

Maddison indicated the need to monitor learning:

> I've got to know, OK, where to now with their learning? … And so, I find that challenging every day, because I guess their minds are still relatively young.

She expressed concern about their ability to take on concepts, 'will they get it/won't they get it? And how engaged will they be or won't they be?'

Clear in both teachers' accounts is a sense of responsibility for the students' mastery of a range of skills perceived as important at each grade. These skills were carefully articulated to students and there was an expectation that they not only master the skill but articulate the strategy they used to get there. Evident in each teacher's view was the place of Kindergarten and Year 1 for developing foundational skills, and that failure in mastery would have long-term ramifications.

## Introducing the Students

The previous sections summarised literacy pedagogies and drivers for practice from the teachers' perspectives. Next are accounts from three case study students – Zada, Harry and Talika – across the years of Kindergarten and transition to Year 1. Evident in their accounts are the ways each child perceived their teachers' pedagogical practices and, subsequently, what it meant to 'do' literacy here.

### Zada

While Zada was quietly spoken during interviews, she demonstrated enthusiasm and a sense of engagement with the demands of literacy learning. Zada expressed an interest in craft-based literacy experiences, including the making of a 'peep' box with her mother, which she shared for class news. Zada identified a particular interest in the sharing of information through oral language, including news, 'because people stand up and you get to listen to what they're gonna say, and sometimes they might have a picture and you get to see what they drew'. Zada identified a key difference between school and her preschool was that her school has 'a whiteboard and preschool doesn't'.

As a reader, Zada expressed the view that the purpose of reading was to improve.

I: Why do you think your teacher wants you to read those words?

M: So we get better and better at them.

I: So why is it important to read?

M: Because you can get better and better at reading properly. You need to think about the start of the letter and then you might get it correct. You have to sound out the capital letter.

She explained that she reads 'camera words' and recited them from memory: 'I, are, she, was, to'. In Kindergarten her 'home reader' was a set of A4 pages stapled together with sentences created from the camera words and a checklist for tracking multiple readings printed on the cover. The cover of Zada's Kindergarten home reader indicated she had read it fourteen times. The 'story' read: *I sat. She sat. Pam sat.*

Zada observed that reading in Year 1 was different because 'we get to read real stories' and that her teacher 'tries to get us to read fluently and not like robots'. She had reached the Level 15 benchmark on the basal readers in the purchased reading programme, which meant her teacher 'sees what level you're on and then she puts that on you'.

In writing, Zada similarly focused on the development of skills, 'you get better at doing it … because you sound out the start of the letter'. She shared:

You can do handwriting and then you can write a sentence, and it's really good to write a sentence, because you can get better and better at writing.

She explained she had received an A+ for 'My story about a cat' (*The cat sat on the mat.*) and three stickers for another story about a snail. Zada shared one story from her Kindergarten writing book, which was a sentence from

Yasmine's modelled writing: *She was at the party*. While Zada's illustrations reflected her understanding of a party, 'balloons, party things, stars', she indicated that she didn't know who 'she' is in the story, 'That's just what Mrs Y (Yasmine) said to write.'

Writing in Year 1 for Zada followed a predictable pattern, 'Normally we write a story after it (hearing a story). And we've got to try and like do the same pattern as that story.' She indicated that it was important for a writer in Year 1 to monitor

> punctuation, capital letters, putting spaces in your words, making sure you don't do capital letters when it's in a sentence ... And with your title you have to do capitals.

When asked what she thought about when she was writing her story about a cat, Zada explained: 'You've gotta think about that it makes sense. And you know because you have to reread it.'

For Zada, reading and writing in Kindergarten required her to learn about letters and words using teacher-made resources. The transition to Year 1 introduced her to the basal readers believed to be 'real books', and opportunities to engage with the mechanics of writing with a view to constructing stories that 'make sense'. It seems Zada truly valued opportunities to glimpse the home lives of her peers and to share something of her own home experiences with them.

## Harry

Harry presented as confident and happy to share his insights into the ways literacy worked in his early years of primary school. Harry identified mathematics as his favourite subject and soccer as his preferred sport. During interviews, Harry's responses to questions were generally quick and focused; however, some revealed uncertainty about the purpose of a classroom task or what it was that he was 'supposed to do next'. Harry described literacy learning as 'lots of things' that included 'drawing, writing, reading and practising English', which he clarified as 'just like writing'. He explained that success in literacy was rewarded with a 'Wow', a reward system in the school where the accumulation of stickers and awards led to bronze, silver and gold awards. Harry proudly declared 'In Kindergarten, I got my gold.'

As a reader, Harry exclaimed that 'Reading is amazing!' He elaborated by observing that 'when you read you know more letters. And when you read you know more words to spell and you get like … you improve.' Harry explained why it is good to read: 'Well reading just teaches you like other words to spell and then you know what to do next.' In Kindergarten, Harry reported that his teacher told him to 'read fast' the words in his phonics booklet.

In Year 1, Harry believed that although his teacher would remind him to 'read fluently' at times and to 'think about what the writer's trying to do to you', his teacher liked his reading because 'I'm just quick at it'. He explained that his teacher used reading groups to work with short novels and that he was in Group 1: The Dolphins. While Harry wanted the Dolphins to read *Snow White*, his group was allocated *Eight* instead. Harry did not know why he was placed in the Dolphins group, what he had in common with the other students in the group or why his teacher had chosen *Eight* as their text.

· In writing, Harry explained that he was beginning to master 'running writing' and that he was able to connect the letter *u* to other letters. In Kindergarten, he described writing tasks as they related to the teacher-made 'phonics booklet' from the commercial synthetic phonics programme and he explained the benefit of paying attention: 'You've got to listen to the teacher, so you know what you're supposed to do.'

In Year 1, Harry indicated more than once that the purpose of writing was to 'persuade, inform and entertain'. He explained that it is important to 'think about what you have to do', to 'improve' and to 'get faster'. Harry identified that writers need to have a 'good story' or 'a good fact'. He explained the need to 'put lots of hooks. It could be an outrageous statement, anecdotes, stories.' And he focused on the place of punctuation, 'you need to make sure you put full stops and exclamation marks or question marks and commas'. Harry expressed the desire that literacy learning in Year 2 would provide him with 'more time' 'to put all my things in' because one challenge he faced in Year 1 was that 'You have to hurry'.

Reflected in Harry's talk appears to be his teacher's interpretation of syllabus documents and the school's use of phonics and comprehension programmes across Kindergarten and Year 1. His account of his experiences with literacy learning relate to speed and the need to complete a series of tasks quickly.

Harry's hopes for a slower pace that provides time to bring his 'things' together in Year 2 perhaps indicate some discomfort with this task-oriented approach.

## Talika

Talika participated in case study interviews with enthusiasm and a sense of wanting her listener to understand deeply the nature of literacy learning at her school. Talika shared her perspectives on classroom literacy experiences as 'doing' a range of things, including 'doing texts that inform', 'doing a planning page' and 'doing *The Enchanted Forest*'. Talika identified as one achievement her abilities with 'fancy writing and bubble writing', explaining 'I know how to do an "A" so far'. Talika was careful to clarify that neither fancy nor bubble writing were always appropriate for writing and should be reserved for 'something like a title'. Talika described literacy learning as 'reading, writing, drawing and probably talking too!'. Like Harry, Talika had also been the recipient in Kindergarten of a 'Wow' award for her writing.

In reading, Talika expressed a sense of doubt about her proficiency and the need to improve because 'I will need to read a lot when I've grown up'. She identified a preference for

> books that entertain, like about fairies or mermaids or something. I like to read something about make-believe.

She observed that reading required you to

> improve what you're doing. So, at the first [part] of the morning, there's rules – rules we have to achieve … what's your personal goal.

Reading for Talika involved engagement with resources including 'vocabulary suitcases', 'little charts' and 'reading level posters'. She expressed particular fondness for 'posters that tell us what to do, that's what I really like'.

In Kindergarten, Talika explained reading was hard because

> 'she didn't really know the words' and that she shouldn't 'look too close to the writing or maybe your eyes would hurt'.

She reported that her teacher asked her to 'talk a little louder' and to use her strategies and that 'if the teacher's busy, you should just go onto the next word'.

In Year 1, Talika reflected:

> I probably wasn't really looking that serious at the words in Kindergarten, but now I do, because I've learned so much, and now I can read properly.

She shared that in a recent 'test' she was 'reading *The Three Little Pigs* and I read so good I got level 16'. She identified the need to 'expand' on her reading, which, she explained, meant to 'do better on my reading, not to go too close onto the words or don't forget my glasses!'

Writing for Talika was focused on handwriting. She wondered, 'What would happen in the world if we all just scribbled?' She explained more than once 'you have to write neat' and that her teacher 'gives out Wows if it's really neat'. Talika identified strategies for achieving neatness when you 'do' writing:

> not pressing down too hard and the pencil will break, you have to think of doing it gently, but not real gently that means no one can see it. And you have to sharpen your pencil first then you can see it properly.

In Kindergarten, Talika shared that writing was hard for her because she 'forgot the sound she was writing' and her letters 'aren't clear'.

In Year 1, Talika was proud to discuss improvements in her handwriting:

> I'm getting close to make my writing neat. Yeah, because I'm in Year 1, I can make my writing fit into the lines, you have to write small. So not too big or not too short – just the right size.

Talika had adopted a new strategy for achieving neat writing,

> Sit up straight when you're in the chair, make sure you're holding the pencil close, and not too far and not too close, and making sure that your feet are on the ground and not wobbling or anything.

Talika shared that the purpose of writing at school is to entertain, inform and persuade, and that she wrote for her teacher because 'That's what I always do.' However, at home, Talika, stated that she wrote for her 'parents, my sisters or my brothers or my friends' and that she wrote 'about nice things, how kind, caring … how special they are'. Talika expressed excitement at the prospect of being in Year 2 where 'people do really cool, fancy writing, and I want to be just like them.'

Evident in Talika's talk is her sense of missing the mark in these early years of school. She is clear about her perceived shortcomings and the classroom routines and processes for remediation, acknowledging her growth from Kindergarten to Year 1, and her determination to meet the benchmarks. Despite the writing challenges identified at school, Talika's identity of herself as a writer prevailed through her home writing practices and desire to excel following her transition to Year 2.

## Discussion and Conclusion

A critical consideration for any educator is the experiences, beliefs and capacities that have shaped the literate identities of the learners entering their classrooms. The very young children in this study brought to their formal schooling years literate identities established through the experiences, interactions, stories and texts of their homes and communities (Dyson, 2003; Sfard & Prusak, 2005). There was little evidence, however, that these were part of the content of the classroom environment. For example, neither teacher spoke about the students' outside school experiences, and no field observations were made where the students were asked to draw on their own experience. The teachers in this study each expressed the desire to develop in Early Stage 1 and Stage 1 children a love of literacy and learning. However, teacher and student accounts of literacy learning in this data set reflected a more 'official teacher lens' (Dyson, 2019). Apart from Zada's reference to a home school connection through news, the pedagogical practices of these teachers were more closely aligned with operational practices than with the place of literacy beyond classroom tasks.

Of course, there is no question that the literate identities of four- and five-year-olds need to expand and grow (Gee, 1990; Sumara, 1998), and students need to learn the individual skills that make up reading and writing. They also need to develop new relationships and new stories about themselves as increasingly skilled and judicious users and creators of text (Compton-Lilly, 2006; Kervin, 2016). But heavily structured literacy sessions with specialised language and a focus on specific and isolated classroom-based aspects of literacy such as phonics or handwriting could potentially railroad rather than grow that identity. We saw Talika's doubts about being a neat enough writer who knows just the right amount of pressure to put on the tip of a pencil,

Harry's preoccupation with the accumulation of Wows, and Zada's real love of storytelling through the spoken word confined to weekly News. Accounts from these case study students suggest they are indeed developing new aspects to their literate identities, but are these the identities we want learners to take on as 'relevant' (Buchholz, 2016) at this time and in this community?

Literacy in these classrooms appeared to be the physical act of 'doing'. The teachers and students described *doing* text types, *doing* phonics, *doing* peep boxes, *doing* neat writing and so on. And this 'doing' appears to be a series of transactions with people and resources as opposed to engagement with experiences that grow literacy knowledge. There is considerable pressure for children not only to get things done but to be able to articulate the set of pre-identified strategies or 'rules' they used to get there. For example, being able to read aloud accurately and fluently was insufficient evidence for Maddison to 'move' a student 'up' to the next level in the commercial reading programme. More was required. We know the powerful role of the teacher in developing the literate identities of their learners (Martens & Adamson, 2001). What is the impact on the futures of young children who are led to believe that literacy is a series of classroom-based activities, items, resources, rules and strategies?

As established earlier in this chapter, our project was conducted during a period of considerable reform. It could be that new mandates in those documents, for example, the strict scope and sequence of the ACARA Literacy Progressions (2014b) with its multiple elements, sub-elements, level and indicators, have impacted these teachers' ability to engage children with rich and individualised literacy learning experiences that promote understandings about what it means to be literate across home, school and community settings. It could also be that greater levels of teacher accountability to demonstrate learning gains are generated through this reform, imposing on teachers increased demands for demonstrating student growth. But we propose a different view.

The purchase of commercial packages was observed in this study to narrow the curriculum so that the focus was not on meeting the nationally mandated ACARA Literacy progressions (2014b) or even the state-based K-6 English Syllabus (2012). Instead, evident in the ways these children described their classrooms was that learning is driven by the scope and sequence of the purchased programmes at the expense of learning opportunities focused on the rich language of quality literature (for example). In one programme, teachers worked through linear 'sets' of letters and words that were later printed onto A4 paper stapled together to create a 'book' containing 'stories' from those letters (*I sat. She sat. Pam sat.* etc.). The child's reading of that text was 'benchmarked' against the programme's scope and sequence and judgements made about reading proficiency. Programmes such as these promote a new language of literacy learning (wow words, crunchy words, etc.) that cannot transfer into the homes and communities of the learners or take into account students' experiences in prior-to-school educational contexts. Commercially produced resources are created by people who have never visited this school, these teachers or these students, and so, they can offer only one-size-fits-all approaches. As evidenced by Harry's sense of being rushed and Talika's sense of failure in Kindergarten, learning in these programmes cannot be individualised according to needs, interests, experiences and abilities when everyone is working with the same eight sounds at the same time.

Commercially produced programmes are expensive, and one purchased for this school consumed the full annual professional learning budget. Significant investment requires significant return, and significant buy in. The leadership of this school had purchased a package that required teachers to adopt narrowed pedagogies focused on a particular stance on learning. Teachers work with the resources and opportunities on offer, and decisions like these generate a new level of accountability – to the school budget. The risk for students as they transition across the school years, then, is that they continue to experience narrowed versions of what it means to be literate, potentially missing opportunities to develop increasingly sophisticated skills beyond spelling.

Yoon (2016) observed that it is easy to blame teachers, to advise them to adopt broadened versions of literacy and to implore them to teach what they know to be a true reflection of the ways literacy works in society. But that is inappropriate because the problem is bigger than that and largely outside of teachers' control. Teachers operate within hotly contested political climates that privilege so-called 'standard' forms of English language, written forms of communication and an increasingly narrowed curriculum driven by standardised assessment of individual skills. We also know that educators in the prior-to-school sector experience ever-increasing pressure to adopt skills-based explicit teaching approaches that drill phonics and phonemic awareness

(Campbell, 2019). Without supporting documents and sustained professional learning focused on new curricula, teachers and schools are forced to find that support elsewhere.

Like Maddison and Yasmine, teachers take seriously their responsibilities and strive to do the best job possible. They invest considerable time trying to ensure they meet the needs of their learners and the demands of the mandated curriculum. But the educational reforms occurring at the time of this project were introduced without funding for teacher professional development and without the provision of resources to support the facilitation of these new ways. Government underfunding of the curriculum reforms has left teachers vulnerable and in search of help. Commercial enterprises have filled this void with the creation of packages claiming alignment with syllabus documents, offering a way to track all learners, and the promise that all learners can succeed through the facilitation of their programme. But they can't respond to the complexity of the syllabus and what it means to be literate, nor can they respond to the nuances of a school community and the individual needs of each student. It is not enough for government institutions to mandate change without supporting teachers with quality professional development and resources. Because it is through this support that teachers can enact pedagogies that connect home, school and community literacies that value and grow student identities, and convey to learners a view of literacy as a complex and powerful act of making meaning.

# 12

# Articulating Education with Primary Students

Christine Edwards-Groves and Peter Freebody

## Introduction

Interviews with students and teachers about literacy learning and teaching formed an important part of the data collection and analysis for the TRANSLIT research project. In this chapter, we draw on interviews about literacy learning with three students at different transition points across the primary school. In their participation with teachers and their fellow students in lessons and other school activities, students display their practical interpretations of what is going on in their education. But they are not usually called on to do the specialised work of articulating these interpretations in the interactional setting of a research interview. In this chapter, we use Conversation Analysis (CA) to examine that specialised work in a selection of interviews about learning literacy with primary students at three typical 'transitional' points in primary school education, Kindergarten (the first year of formal schooling in New South Wales, Australia), Year 2 (the transition point into primary grades) and Year 6 (the last year of primary school before entering secondary school).

We document how these students drew on estimates of the recognisability and noteworthiness of their observations to accomplish the interview, including the goal of presenting themselves as 'adequate interviewees'. Two aspects of these interviews are highlighted: how fastidious is the moment-to-moment coordination that both parties displayed in sequencing the elements of the interview; and how students made apparent their interpretations of what they encounter in their literacy learning at school. Their perspectives revealed three distinct 'takes' on reading and writing for school: as a set of institutional procedures, as distinct domains within the curriculum, and as skills and knowledge put to work in different ways within different discipline areas. Implications for research are drawn out in relation to the meanings attributed to nature and conduct of interviews with young literacy learners at different points in time.

## Students' Displays of Practical Interpretation

We begin with a distinction between the interpretations of literacy learning as a practical, observed activity in classroom lessons and those that afford accounts for use in settings such as queries, quizzes and interviews. We aim to show how participating in an interview calls on a particular set of interpretive and reasoning processes that might, but do not necessarily, arise from successful participation in the activities that form the topics of the interview itself. Consider, for instance, the practical interpretive and reasoning processes that these eight-year-old learners display in Exhibit 1 (Table 12.1, Excerpt 1.1)[1] (next), a commonplace exchange in a Year 3 primary literacy lesson in which their teacher introduced the topic of the book he intends to read with the students.

**Table 12.1** Excerpt 1.1 – Year 3 Reading: We Were Going to Read about Whales

| 22 | Tch | remember I told you that we were going to read about whales today$^v$ |
| 23 | Ss | ye::es ((chorused)) |
| 24 | Tch | what's special about whales, Jeffrey^ |
| 25 | Jef | because they can't go, they've gotta go up to the top to breathe |
| 26 | Tch | that's <u>right</u>$^v$, why do they have to breathe Jeffrey^ |
| 27 | Jef | because >if-they-don't-then<, they'll <u>die</u>$^v$ |
| 28 | Tch | they'll die$^v$ that's right because they <u>aa::re</u>^= |
| 29 | Ss | =mammals ((chorused)) |
| 30 | Tch | they're mammals, that's right$^v$= |
| 31 | Ste | =<u>us</u>, <u>we</u> are mammals |
| 32 | Tch | yes, we're mammals, how do you know we're mammals Stewart^ |
| 33 | Ste | because, um, (1.5) you, you <u>think</u> about it// |
| 34 | Tch | //yeh, so, <u>what</u>^// |
| 35 | Ste | //we breathe |
| 36 | Tch | we breathe air$^v$ what else do we do that makes us a mammal (1.0) Jane^ |
| 37 | Jan | cos we are warm-blooded^ |
| 38 | Tch | we're warm-<u>blooded</u>$^v$, that's right$^v$ |

*Articulating Education with Primary Students*     235

From this forty-five-second glimpse, we can summarise a few of the features of their learning that these students show they understand:

- Teacher (Tch) asks some questions directed at the entire cohort of students (turns 22 and 28), and some directed at specific students (e.g. Jeffrey and Stewart). Presumably Tch asks questions for the cohort because he expects that most will provide a common answer, at the same time as allowing for those that do not know, or who are unsure, who will hear what Tch has judged to be 'common enough' knowledge – the 'moral sympathy' of cohorting (Macbeth, 2000).
- When an acceptable exchange with an individual student is completed, the exchange is almost never repeated with a different student, nor are alternative answers expected from other students.
- So the entire cohort is expected to learn from all of the exchanges with individual students, because when one student answers, and the answer resolves the exchange (indicated by a teacher evaluation turn like 'that's right' or 'yes'), the entire cohort (as the overhearing audience) can later be held accountable for hearing that exchange, including how Tch and student came to arrive at that resolution. So, what is said then, and so heard by the other students (as witnesses to the exchange), is to be taken as what is to be known and learned here-and-now in this part of the lesson.
- A two-part question–answer exchange (an instance of a 'base adjacency pair', see Schegloff, 2007) can be expanded prior to, during and/or after the pair (e.g. turns 24–31).
- Students can initiate exchanges (e.g. Stewart in turn 31), but these initiations can themselves be expanded by Tch's requests for a rationale (clarifications, addition of facts or expansions on why this matters in terms of the immediately prior base adjacency pair, e.g. turns 32–38 focusing on knowing mammals). Every student contribution, including Stewart's initiation in turn 31, is confirmed by Tch usually via repetition of the student speaker's words with a concluding downward inflection v, taken by the cohort as the resolution of the original base adjacency pair.
- Paralinguistic features (e.g. intonations, gestures) are interactional moves, potentially signalling crucial information such as who should take a turn at talk, how attention or the topic should shift, or the status of current base adjacency pair as either adequately completed (e.g. v in turns 30, 36, 38) or yet to be resolved (e.g. ^ in turns 24, 26).

- Teacher and students also know that students can and often will apply a conventionally questioning intonation (^) when they provide a response to a question from Tch, as in Jane's turn 37, and that this functions as a 'handing-back' of the speaking turn to Tch for comment on that response, a response that is only provisionally an 'answer' at that time.
- More generally, in this case, the topical exchanges prior to the reading of a book will relate to what and how that 'reading' will be; readers will be held accountable for knowing and applying 'what's special' about the contents of the prior talk to the reading event.

This teacher and his students displayed these and other practical understandings through the generally unnoticed patterns that recurred, untroubled, in their exchanges. As contributions elsewhere in this volume show, these understandings are either not evident or do not take place so smoothly in the transcripts of lessons with younger students; rather, they are acquired through common practice over time, coming to count as 'just what lessons are like'.

## Coordinating Authenticity in Students' Accounts

The chapter opened with a classroom transcript demonstrating the efficiency with which students participate and comply with the interactional demands of teacher–student question–answer sequences typically encountered in lessons. From this, it would seem understandable that answering questions in an interview setting with researchers, also experienced former classroom teachers, might be a seamless move for young learners well-accustomed with the similarly constructed question–answer exchange format of an interview.

In these next sections we set out to illustrate the argument that being interviewed does not simply afford an opportunity to speak authentically and comprehensively about one's experiences of literacy learning and their practical interpretations of them. Rather, it calls for figuring out what features of those experiences not only are shared with the interviewer but, at the same time, are also noteworthy, not so obvious and banal that they need or should not be mentioned. This applies to interviews in general, but as we set out to show here, interviewing students puts particular pressure on researchers' appreciation of students' developing understandings of 'shared-but-noteworthy' trade-offs in this distinctive interactional setting. It thereby cautions interview researchers about downgrading the responses of students by reference to their age-related naiveté *with regard to the topics* of their own education. As we see from Exhibit 1 (Table 12.1), and from decades of classroom interaction research (e.g. Edwards-Groves, 2003; Freiberg & Freebody, 1995; Gardner, 2019; Mehan, 1979), even young students show finely developed interactional competencies and practical interpretations of the workings of lessons (Edwards-Groves & Davidson, 2017).

Interest in students' views about their learning experiences in education settings is acknowledged as an important counterweight to the practice of relying predominantly on researchers' analyses of teachers' perceptions of students and educational processes more generally (Pires Pereira & González Riaño, 2018). In her comments on students' understandings as a researchable field, Groundwater-Smith (2005: 2) argued that students have been

> observed, surveyed, measured, interviewed and commented upon in order to inform a research agenda to which they have made little contribution. ... students are rarely recognised as active agents, who can not only be reliable informants, but also interpreters of their own lives. They are at worst silenced; at best patronised.

Positioning students as reliable informants and interesting participants in studies of everyday school life is a critical move towards resetting the scales of input into practice and policy. By enriching the relevance and credibility of research on topics such as the learning of literacy in school, the vast field shaped almost exclusively by what adults take to be its important and interesting contours can be reconceptualised. This resetting involves highlighting the assumptions and analytic strategies of researchers.

To expand this notion in a practical sense, we examine a small selection of interviews about literacy learning with students at three typical 'transitional' points in primary school education, Kindergarten, Year 2 and Year 6. The interviewers Philippa, Cheryl and Cate were all experienced former teachers who became university researchers.

## Being Interviewed

Most applications of interviews in applied settings such as schools take for granted a number of features of this apparently simple exchange format: the investigators' question followed, subsequently, by the respondent's answer. Most commonly overlooked are the demands on interviewees to account for – describe, formulate, evaluate and the rest – the practices in which they successfully participate in their everyday lives, in this case, their activities in school lessons that involve reading and writing. If the teacher and students who took part in Exhibit 1 (Table 12.1) above were interviewed immediately after this pre-reading episode, how would they recall, describe, explain and evaluate it? How would they outline their practical interpretations of, for example, exchange structures, intonation patterns or the educational value of pre-reading discussion? What features of these exchanges might they single out for positive or negative comment? What happened, why, with what effect and how might it have been clearer, more informative, more connected to the book reading that followed and so on?

We begin with an extended treatment of an interview with one of the youngest students in our study, one of the least experienced of our interviewees. We do this to highlight assumptions made about interviewees' access to knowledge about reading and writing, learning, being in school and, importantly, about themselves.

## Accounting for Literacy Learning in Interviews: Gina and Philippa

In **Exhibit 2** we highlight some of these assumptions by examining segments of an interview between interviewer Philippa (Phi) and Gina (Gin), a Kindergarten student aged five years. Below are three brief excerpts[2] taken from their much longer interview on the topics of reading and writing in school and at home. We aim to draw attention to how aspects of literacy learning are made salient in and drawn into relevance as the exchange systems unfold in the conduct of the interview itself (Edwards-Groves, 2017).

In this exchange (Table 12.2, Excerpt 2.1) Gina first indicated that what she 'loved' about reading is actually what it is – 'telling from the words and

**Table 12.2** Excerpt 2.1 – You Can Tell from the Words and Pictures What's Happening

| 70 | Phi | what do you love about reading^ |
|---|---|---|
| 71 | Gin | because you can tell from the words and pictures what's happening$^v$ |
| 72 | Phi | you're very clever aren't you$^v$ well done$^v$ and what do you not^ like about reading |
| 73 | Gin | nothing$^v$ |
| 74 | Phi | you love reading do you^ |
| 75 | Gin | ((nods)) |
| 76 | Phi | good girl$^v$ |

**Table 12.3** Excerpt 2.2 – Some Things You Don't Know How to Write

| 116 | Phi | do you go to the library at all^ |
|---|---|---|
| 117 | Gin | because some things, you don't know how to write$^v$ |
| 118 | Phi | yes$^v$ some things you don't know how to write$^v$= |
| 119 | Gin | =and with some books my mum needs her glasses |
| 120 | Phi | (1) does she^, that makes it hard too doesn't^ it |
| 121 | Gin | ((nods)) |
| 122 | Phi | (1) what's your favourite thing about writing^ |
| 123 | Gin | nothing really$^v$ |

pictures what is happening' (line 71). She does not hear the question as calling for singling out one aspect or outcome of reading or more specific content-focused discussion about reading or books (as was shown in the earlier classroom exhibit). Philippa left Gina's response unexamined, treated as a correct answer in a series of turns that for all intents and purposes evaluated her answer and closed off the sequence, but at the same time upgraded to an attribution of 'cleverness', and rewarded with Philippa's 'well done'. This pattern of upgraded, attributional evaluations of Gina's responses is repeated in turns 74–76, and elsewhere in the interview. Noting this interviewer's move might be considered at this point to be less about loving reading and more to do with encouraging Gina's participation in the interview.[3]

In Excerpt 2 (Table 12.3) Gina pointed out that what is 'hardest about writing' is when 'you don't know how to write' (line 117) or when you need glasses. As with what she loved about reading, what makes writing hard is what writing is, especially when you don't know how to do it. As in Segment 1, she did not hear the question as calling for reference to a particular aspect or outcome of writing or to some features of her own developing capabilities;

neither the task nor her competence in managing it was partitioned. Rather, Gina heard and responded to 'reading' and 'writing' in terms of what they signify as things, rather than what they present as a collection of distinguishable subcomponents. She went on to find nothing about (in the sense of 'within') reading to dislike, and nothing about writing that is her 'favourite'.

Most visibly, both the attractions and challenges presented by reading and writing were about when Gina cannot do them, rather than about some feature of writing such as orthography, spelling, vocabulary, and so on. If reading and writing are what they are, rather than a skill or knowledge-set for dealing with a collection of puzzles or predicaments, then to name something not to like or some 'favourite thing' about it would be to talk about some other thing.

The exchange in turns 119–120 is noteworthy. This, as Gina and Philippa both knew, was an interview as part of a project involving many other teachers and students. The paraphernalia of the interview was visible – the recorder, Philippa's notepad, the move to a separate, quiet room – but Gina nonetheless introduced a domestic peculiarity concerning her mother's need for glasses as an instance of something that makes writing hard. This, she presented as both shared-but-noteworthy and an answer to the base question, an answer perhaps offered in the interests of completeness. Interviewees are, usually tacitly, assumed to appreciate the distinction between idiosyncrasies (e.g. 'I happen to have trouble with apostrophes') and idiosyncrasies that cannot be extracted as 'data', not able to be generalised across respondents. Every response is taken to be at the one time noteworthy, both a look-inwards towards truthfulness and salience, and a look-outwards towards relevance across the data set. Gina's responses (turns 117 and 119) showed that she was not working with either of these vistas as she talked about what she found hard about writing.

In Excerpt 2.3 (Table 12.4) we see that Gina heard Philippa's 'how' questions (in turns 43, 45, 47 and 51) as indicating an interest in the formal, organisational procedures (rather than, say, the psychological or affective motivations) involved in a Kindergarten student's choice of a book to borrow from the school library. When pressed about what she 'looks at' – which was converted in turn 55 into 'look *for*' (from a procedural to a preferential question) – Gina uncoupled Philippa's turn 56 combination of 'like and want,' and gave an answer based on 'liking'. Philippa then capitalised on this connection of the procedural to the preferential features of the process (turn 51). It was Philippa

*Articulating Education with Primary Students*           241

**Table 12.4** Excerpt 2.3 – If You See a Book You Like You Get to Take It

| 39 | Phi | do you go to the library at all^ |
|---|---|---|
| 40 | Gin | yes, but just one day^v^ |
| 41 | Phi | just one day^, and what happens^ at the library |
| 42 | Gin | you borrow a book and take it home but I wasn't here to bring my library book, back, because my sister has broken her bone and she's here, and it's still broken |
| 43 | Phi | oh really^, the poor thing. when you go the library and you're asked to take a book home, how do you know what book^ to take |
| 44 | Gin | (0.9) because they are on the shelf or on the table |
| 45 | Phi | and how do you choose^ |
| 46 | Gin | because you look at a book and, if you see a book you like and you want (.) you get to take it >but-the-lady-scans-it-first< and you put it in your library bag |
| 47 | Phi | and how do you know it's a book that you like^ and want^ |
| 48 | Gin | because it's on the table^v^ |
| 49 | Phi | yeah// |
| 50 | Gin | //they're for kindergarten and they're on the table^v^ |
| 51 | Phi | and how do you know the one that you want (.) what do you look^ at |
| 52 | Gin | the cover |
| 53 | Phi | yeah (1) and what// |
| 54 | Gin | //and you have to look in the book first |
| 55 | Phi | oh, in the book (.) what are you looking for in the book^ |
| 56 | Gin | if you like the pages or not |
| 57 | Phi | a:ah, and so when you think >yes-I-like-the-pages< you can take that book can you^ |
| 58 | Gin | yeah^v^ |

who converted 'when you think *this*, you can do *that*' into a matter of personal preference.

We note that Philippa adapted her turns in light of the logic built up by Gina herself in the course of the interview. For instance, the 'book that you like and want' (turn 47) was reput as 'the one that you want' (turn 51), and Philippa's question (57) reput the matter in terms hearable as purely procedural – 'you can take that book'. Issues potentially about preferring and deciding were gradually reframed by Philippa in terms of Gina's orientation to the institutional customs and rules of the school library.

To summarise, Gina's answers are relevant, informative and, as far as we know, truthful, but we get some purchase on the matter of interviewing as specialised interaction when we consider why they also seem curious to the point of being eccentric.

## The Specialised Knowledge of the 'Good Interviewee'

Here are Philippa's questions across all of Exhibit 2: What do you love about reading? What do you not like about reading? How do you know what book to take? How do you choose? How do you know it's a book that you like and want? What do you find hardest about writing? What's your favourite thing about writing? We would likely predict that a interviewee more experienced in the ways of schooling and interviewing would have heard these questions as either odd ('How do I know what book to take out of the library?') or as being about her personal, potentially idiosyncratic dispositions and preferences, trading on an interest in possible distinctiveness of the answers she might give in relation to those of other individuals in similar settings (as opposed to, say, 'How does one know what book to take out of a library?'). A more experienced interviewee might assume that Philippa already knows, and does not need to be informed, about the rationale or the formal procedures for borrowing a book from a library, or about what reading is, or that not knowing how to read, or to see, can make it hard.

So some of Gina's contributions are heard as curious because she showed no inclination to personalise the questions by relating them to her strengths, weaknesses and preferences as a reader or writer, and to map those personalised observations onto the subcomponents of reading and writing, and, in turn, to compare, at least implicitly, the contours of that map with the accounts of other comparable respondents. She may well have chosen to hear Philippa's queries about *knowing, choosing, liking, wanting* and *loving* as calling on her to reflect on and articulate her own abilities and preferences, and further to nominate features of those that might cause her to engage in certain literacy activities more than others. And she would likely, for instance, be able to talk about *knowing, choosing, liking, wanting* and *loving* her favourite foods in more differentiated ways.

The quaintness of Gina's answers here arises from the mismatch between what we suspect the interviewer expected to hear, or needed to hear to produce a 'data point', and what Gina provided. This quaintness becomes a research problem only when that mismatch is mistaken for Gina's inadequate understanding of learning to read and write.

A further prediction would be that some categories of older interviewees might recognise that some of Philippa's questions are based on, and thus calling for, an acknowledgement of the multifaceted nature of 'reading' and 'writing'. For example, in terms of 'what's hard', maybe the vocabulary, or long sentences, or punctuation, or complicated storyline and so on. A terminology is assumed for naming the parts, the rewards and the challenges of 'reading' and 'writing'. The model interviewee might also bring that terminology to bear on a consideration of the development of literacy over time – questions about 'hard now' and 'easy later'. Clearly Gina is comfortable with it all, except for when she doesn't know things.

To summarise, in examining the following interview exhibits with students at different grade levels, our central task is to examine variations in the students' 'shared-but-noteworthy' trade-offs, and in what terms they provide interpretations that call up differing relationships between, on the one hand, what reading and writing for school involves and, on the other, their own practices, capabilities and preferences.

## Conducting Interviews with Older Students

### Exhibit 3: Harriet, Year 2

This next exhibit is drawn from an interview between interviewer Cheryl (Che) and Harriet (Har), a Year 2 student aged seven years.

Harriet's request for clarification (turn 11, Table 12.5, Excerpt 3.1) is an expansion on the base adjacency pair that also adds relevance to the home-school contrast to her answer in this interview setting, which she took to call for a distinction immediately before she could answer the question put to her (turn 10). Her answer (turn 12) consisted of categories of books, as examples ('things like'). She points directly to a knowledge shared with Cheryl of what these texts are like and how they would be relevant as school-reading materials. Noting, a list formation can: (i) collect categories of people or things, (ii) deliver typical categories or (iii) construct a sequence whose order is important in accumulating, or building a hierarchy of elements, or delivering an up- or down-grading in terms of some quality (Jayyusi, 1984). In Harriet's turn 13 her prefacing of the list with 'things like' indicates that the listing would deliver a recognisable shared collection, a common sense of the

**Table 12.5** Excerpt 3.1 – Reading Things Like Story Treehouse Books

| | | |
|---|---|---|
| 10 | Che | what are you reading at the moment^ |
| 11 | Har | well I'm reading things like (1) >at home^ or at school^< |
| 12 | Che | umm tell me at school^V^ first and then// |
| 13 | Har | //umm things like story treehouse books, and some chapter books and picture books^ |
| 14 | Che | right^V^ |

**Table 12.6** Excerpt 3.2 – We Normally Have to *Do* Things

| | | |
|---|---|---|
| 40 | Che | we've talked about some of the things you read in year 2^, do you do any reading in maths^, or science^, those other, subjects^ |
| 41 | Har | (2) not really, 'cause we normally have to do things |
| 42 | Che | so it's more experiments and// |
| 43 | Har | //yeah |
| 44 | Che | right, ok^V^ |

larger range of materials. Lists perform interactional functions that can operate both retro- and prospectively; in this case, the list retrospectively clarified the significance of Harriet's move in 11 to distinguish home from school reading materials and set up that distinction as potentially relevant to subsequent talk about Harriet's preferences, competences and so on.

We note another list in Cheryl's turn (40, Table 12.6, Excerpt 3.2); an 'etcetera procedure' inviting other locations for 'any reading'. Harriet shows she did not hear Cheryl's 'do you do any reading' as a question about the class as a whole and led to the distinction between reading and 'doing things'. Harriet interrupted the looming list (turn 42), indicating not only the broad reach of her earlier 'not really' but also the confidence she had in knowing what Cheryl was about to list. It accomplished a further avowal of the shared understanding she demonstrated above (turn 13). The close-knit structures of the exchange indicate and actively construct high levels of coordination and shared understanding.

In Excerpt 3.1 we saw Harriet draw an interactionally decisive distinction between home and school reading materials. Here she delineated relevant distinctions within school work, locating 'reading' as not-doing, perhaps contemplative as distinct from performative.

In turn 44 (Table 12.7, Excerpt 3.3), what is important for reading in the classroom was heard by Harriet in terms of the appropriate management of

**Table 12.7** Excerpt 3.3 – Set Your Brain Up for Reading

| 44 | Che | what are some of the things that you think are important when you read in the classroom$^V$ |
|---|---|---|
| 45 | Har | mm, maybe not to be too loud^ and maybe reading quietly, otherwise you could disturb other classes^ |
| 46 | Che | ok right$^V$, and what are some things your <u>teacher</u>^ thinks are important |
| 47 | Har | umm, that you should read lots of chapter books 'cause some picture books aren't that good// |
| 48 | Che | //uh huh// |
| 49 | Har | //like they don't have many words^, and things like, umm (1) some <u>dorky</u> ones they're not, they don't really set your brain up for reading much^ |
| 50 | Che | right ok$^V$ and do you know what would be a dorky book^ |
| 51 | Har | Dork Diaries^ and Diary of a Wimpy Kid^ |
| 52 | Che | ok$^V$ all right$^V$, they don't set your <u>brain</u>^ up, that's an interesting// |
| 53 | Har | //'cause my brother used to read them but he doesn't get much learning from them |
| 54 | Che | yeah, ok$^V$ |

classroom conduct, rather than as something significant about the nature of the reading to be done. As in Excerpt 3.2, 'you read' was heard as 'we read', noting the class cohorting as shown in Exhibit 1. For this speaker in this interview, the question was interpreted as an instance of the institutional procedures of schooling, within which the activity 'reading' takes place. In turns 46–52 we see expansions on the base adjacency pair about kinds of books (47), rationale for reading different books (49), two examples from the contrasting set (51) and a supporting anecdote (53).

Cheryl and Harriet together constructed a close-knit set of expansions that produced, effectively, an illustrative account. Via this account, Harriet directly made what is, across the sample of Year 2 students interviewed, the rare connection between the supposed cognitive effects arising from the reading experience and the contents of the reading materials – the words. It was not for her, in this instance, a case of reading of itself somehow being a good thing. It is more specifically the causal sequence that she specified: the inclusion of words is connected to 'setting up the brain for reading', which in turn affords for the getting of learning.

As with earlier examples, the question (turn 114, Table 12.8, Excerpt 3.4) did not draw out any orientation on Harriet's part to writing as a set of subcomponents or to her sense of her own skill set. Her answer (115) was

**Table 12.8** Excerpt 3.4 – If You Write for a Long Time It Hurts Your Hand

| | | |
|---|---|---|
| 114 | Che | is there anything you find, <u>hard</u> about writing at school^ |
| 115 | Har | umm maybe if you write for a long time it hurts your hand^ |
| 116 | Che | yeah$^v$, that's true, that's true$^v$, so:o what are some of the things that you think your <u>teacher</u> thinks are important^ about writing$^v$ |
| 117 | Har | umm (2) I'm not sure |
| 118 | Che | no^, ok$^v$, what does she encourage you to think about when you're writing^ |
| 119 | Har | ((shrugs)) |
| 120 | Che | ok$^v$, all right$^v$, that's fine$^v$ |

offered as provisional (^), as a question-back, asking for validation. Unlike Harriet's confident reply to the question in Excerpt 3.3 above, in which she related and illustrated with an example from her own family the teacher's priorities for reading, she was not prepared even to guess at her teacher's expectations about writing.

## Exhibit 4: Lee, Year 6

Exhibit 4 is an interview between interviewer Cate (Cat) and Lee (Lee), a Year 6 student aged twelve years. The following exchanges reference the reading and discussion of an example of his writing, a pastiche of fairy tales that he brought to the interview.

In turns 37–38 (Table 12.9, Excerpt 4.1) Cate raised the issue of paragraphing and received an acknowledgement from Lee that this is an aspect of his writing he would like to improve. In the remaining turns of the segment, via a series of insert expansions, Cate accounted for her inquiry (39), asked specifically about Lee's understanding of paragraphing (41) and put his response to the test (43). For his part in these moves by Cate, Lee produced a series of 'downgrades' first explaining why the paragraph marks were on the page (40), next indicating a vague grasp of paragraphing (42) and, finally, after a demurral and a substantial pause, acknowledged he did not really know (44).

Noticeable throughout this segment is, again, the close-knit nature of the exchanges, with many latched turns (= =) and interruptions (//). This invests the two pauses in this segment, in turns 41 and 44, with some significance. Closely knit turns indicate high levels of anticipation and thus shared

**Table 12.9** Excerpt 4.1 – After a Bit, I Just Put a Paragraph

| | | |
|---|---|---|
| 29 | Cat | what's something that you would like to improve with your writing, if you were >sort of< reflecting on this ((points to his written piece)) as a learner$^v$, and thinking, mm^, what do I need to do a bit better on, what would you like to improve^, d'you think// |
| 30 | Lee | //yeah |
| 31 | Cat | what would you like to improve// |
| 32 | Lee | //mm, two things, write neater and// |
| 33 | Cat | //it's not too bad though, I can read it, I have to say= |
| 34 | Lee | =and umm probably, so, have put in Little Riding Hood ((laughs)) |
| 35 | Cat | so you'd have liked to have got an extra character in$^v$= |
| 36 | Lee | =yeah$^v$ |
| 37 | Cat | and are you working^ on your paragraphing^ I notice// |
| 38 | Lee | //yea::h// |
| 39 | Cat | //I see some other things marked here// |
| 40 | Lee | //they're where paragraphs were, because I forgot to put them in |
| 41 | Cat | (2) do you get the idea^ of paragraphs yet^ |
| 42 | Lee | umm, sort of |
| 43 | Cat | when do you need^ to start a new paragraph^ |
| 44 | Lee | umm (3) I don't really know, but, after a bit, I just put a paragraph, and then, after a bit, I just put another one |
| 45 | Cat | they're hard things, aren't they$^v$, even I find that$^v$ |

understandings of the movements in and around the base Q-A pairing. Cate pauses before directly quizzing Lee on his understanding of paragraphing, and Lee pauses even longer when pressed for an answer.

Between them, Cate and Lee thus identified not only one aspect of writing that was challenging in general, as confirmed by Cate (turn 45), but also an aspect of Lee's knowledge that was causing him difficulty. The exchange is intelligible only when the talk is brought to focus on how the components of the task field and of the learner's resources interact, and how that interaction is, in this setting, noteworthy and, after deliberation (significant pauses) and effort, shared.

Here, Lee (turn 109, Table 12.10, Excerpt 4.2) listed some textual features that he took to make up his teacher's sense of what is important in writing, then directed attention to inadequacies in his own piece of writing to support the teacher's priorities. Cate then invited Lee to speculate about his teacher's satisfaction with this list of priorities in writing. Lee eventually offered a tentative suggestion, that is, ending with an interrogative (^) tone, 'asking

**Table 12.10** Excerpt 4.2 – For Us to Actually Like What We're Writing

| 108 | Cat | what do you think ((teacher's name)) thinks is im<u>por</u>tant^v^, to write well in class |
|---|---|---|
| 109 | Lee | make sure that you have paragraphs, umm full stops, whole sentences, 'cos, usually I have all this ((points to a section of his piece of writing)), then that's a, a finished sentence^v^ |
| 110 | Cat | aah, too long, the sentence^ |
| 111 | Lee | yeah^v^ |
| 112 | Cat | is there anything^, do you think that's <u>enough</u> for him, >if the punctuation is perfect<, and, >the sentences are perfect<, is that enough^, or is there something else, anything else= |
| 113 | Lee | =u:umm= |
| 114 | Cat | =that he's looking^ for= |
| 115 | Lee | =for us to actually <u>like</u> what we're writing^ |
| 116 | Cat | mm (2) so how does your teacher know how well you can write, and what to teach you next^, how does he, know what he needs to <u>teach</u> you |
| 117 | Lee | um (1) I don't know^v^ |

back', about students 'actually' liking what they are writing about. Cate unsuccessfully invited Lee to speculate about how his teacher knows about Lee's writing ability and what to teach next.

We find three phases to the questioning here: first Lee provided a detailed list of his teacher's expectations of writing; second, he speculated (with a strong questioning inflection) about what additional expectations the teacher might have; and third, he flatly indicated he did not know on what basis the teacher knows what to teach next about writing. This is another three-stage downgrade – listing, speculating, not knowing. The structure in this exchange, as in Extract 4.1 above, consists of Cate pressing for more specificity and demonstrations, and Lee's downgrading in his responses. It is therefore a question, reply and request for proof of knowledge, mimicking directly the conventional, well-documented IRE teacher–student exchange[4] (e.g. Mehan, 1979).

## Implications for Interviewing Young Learners

Here we draw some conclusions about interviews, schooling and literacy. First, regardless of an assessment of how the students and the interviewers 'performed' in the segments presented, or of how appropriate the questions and answers were, there are implications to be drawn. These include the understanding that first, the interview itself is a distinctive interactional practice. It is conducted here in the school context about school-type topics, by former classroom teachers now researchers, and turns out to resemble a version of the forms of interaction commonly observed in classroom talk – a series of IRE exchanges whereby students' responses to questions are presented publicly as provisional, as handing the floor back to the teacher for evaluative commentary, expansions, redirections and so on. The close similitude of the interview format to the lesson exchange format is notable, and so has implications for interviewing young learners, particularly with respect to a need for a heightened awareness of this interactive practice and an interviewer's role in its conduct.

Second, that, in ten years' time Gina, Harriet and Lee would likely answer these questions in a qualitatively different way, and not just somehow more accurately or truthfully, but in a way that reflected an epistemic access informed by ten more years of institutional savvy (e.g. about how teachers name the subcomponents of reading and writing as text, and as sets of abilities). Further, since learners transition across classrooms, grade levels and literacy practices, their responses may reflect particular transitional points in a way that acknowledges that they themselves would be expected to name elements of their own knowledge, skills and dispositions that might be of public interest, recognisable without being obvious.

Interviewees are routinely called on to answer the interviewer's questions in ways that reflect an epistemic access informed by this institutional savvy. They acknowledge that they themselves are expected to talk about elements of their own knowledge, skills and dispositions that might be of public interest (to the interviewer then-and-there). For these young learners, it means interacting as the self-observing individuals who are called up in an interview setting, in which

> people are being treated as being in a special epistemic position with respect to their own conduct. And not just with respect to actions and events, but causal and developmental relationships. (Potter & Hepburn, 2012: 567)

To cause–effect relationships and developmental narratives expected as learners transition across their years of schooling can be added the interviewee's special epistemic position with respect to estimates about the relationship between his or her practices, or beliefs, or goals and those of the researchers and, significantly, of other speakers in comparable settings ('is this too obvious or too outlandish, or just too idiosyncratic to mention?'). The typicality rating of the speaker's contributions might range from commonplace to bizarre, but the speaker, in this case the student, needs to make some judgement about what might be relevant, productive and noteworthy responses to questions here-and-now in the interactive flow of the interview.

There are some implications for analysis. Adding momentum to the mistake of assuming ignorance of what is left out of students' accounts is an issue that is difficult to ignore – that they are children, beginners in life and in literacy as well as in school. Commonsensically, this relevance can readily translate into an 'explanation' of their responses (reflected back then onto an explanation of the nature and appropriateness of interviewers' questions and follow-ups). This form of explanation-by-categorisation has been widely studied as a subfield of ethnomethodology (Austin, Dwyer & Freebody, 2003; Eglin & Hester, 1992; Fitzgerald, Housley & Rintel, 2017; Jayyusi, 1984).

Interviewees are assumed to be able to 'psychologise' their states and actions, to assess how similar the outcomes of that analysis might be for other people like them, and, thereby, to determine whether their states and actions amount to noteworthy contributions to this setting, the interview. Simply put, we take these students' responses to be indications as to how they were made self-reflective, cognitively aware, able to make judgements (e.g. about what they find hard, or what they like best, or how their teacher decides what to teach), to remember and analyse the questions in terms of the school context in which they were also being interviewed (Potter & Hepburn, 2012).

There are implications for interview as method. We acknowledge the role of the researcher/interviewer is quite different (obviously) from that of a teacher. Although we have made the point that the researchers are former teachers, we place stock in the detail that these interviews were also conducted in the familiar setting of their school. This matters for young interviewees adapting to the cognitive and social demands of the unfamiliarity of an interview under the familiarity of the question–answer exchange system. Within the interviews, the researchers seemed to adopt slightly different personas (to that of teacher), perhaps as recognition of the circumstances and the curriculum expectations that the differently aged students might have experienced. This potentially developed different sorts of relationships and responses. For example, to be a 'good girl' for liking reading perhaps places a certain onus on the child to continue to express her pleasure about reading.

As a final implication, like researchers generally, TRANSLIT researchers were focused on the overarching research questions on literacy and literacy transitions rather than viewing the interview itself as an interactive episode. Interviewers typically spend hours of work developing and refining their interview questions, and so interpretations of what these might mean to young literacy learners is very useful, particularly since many researchers might not consider the questions they ask from the child's perspective. For example, they would have considered what questions might elicit what they were interested in finding out; what kinds of aspects of literacy children would be aware of, as much as how they experienced literacy learning at particular points in time at school; and what they understood about children at particular stages of schooling as parents and former teachers themselves. Perhaps in the sequential flow of the interview itself, researchers implicitly adjusted their 'scripted' and 'unscripted' questions and responses in ways that positioned the interviewee as a Kindergarten, Year 2 or Year 6 student (and the assumed literacy knowledge they might have), or to take a certain role, or give a certain response, noting that their interruptions and extensions within the exchange seemed to shape the way the child responds as it does in ordinary school-type conversation.

## Conclusion

Seeking out participant perspectives and interpretations through interviews is a common research practice. Attending to the ways the interactional nature of an interview itself elicits, or not, what is known, understood or practised about the topic of concern in the interview, is not often dealt with in research reporting – this is an issue we attempt to redress in this chapter. So to conclude, in the question–answer exchange format of the interview, as in much social research, it is impossible to do justice to the artfulness and sheer doggedness of Gina, Harriet and Lee, and their fellow students who took part, as they negotiated the swarm of unpredictable questions and prompts that came their way. Their answers were appropriate in precisely the ways in which they intended them to be appropriate – they observed the procedural realities and uncertainties of schooling that bear down, visibly and forcefully, on students in their institutional circumstances, whether or not their interviewers happened to find these observations noteworthy, interesting or banal.

One way of interpreting students' differing explications of the subcomponents of reading and writing, and of their own varying levels of skills for dealing with those subcomponents, is to imagine that they reflect students' more accurate or 'mature' understandings of literacy demands vis-à-vis their own developing capabilities as they transition across the years of schooling. The developmental trend made visible in these variations can then be registered as 'data'. But the increasing tendency to use students' analyses of literacy and of themselves as learners can be taken instead to reflect their increasing ability to grapple with and formulate the institutional logistics of teaching and learning, a set of logistics of the sort that generated the interview questions and probes to begin with. That is, if the interviews are analysed on the assumption that the students' responses are in fact unmediated statements 'from the heart', and that the questions, probes, expansions and the build-up of supportive reactions provided by the interviewer simply cleared the way for those authenticities, then what has been discovered – about literacy, transitions or schooling, or this student's capabilities and preferences – was already known, precisely because it had already formed the bases of the format, the questions, probes and prompts. The data thereby simply convey an evaluation of the interview's methodology.

Analysing interviews such as these can provide, instead, an opportunity to look afresh at how students can coordinate with researchers in displaying their interpretations in the here-and-now of the researcher's guidance; how the institutional paraphernalia of reading and writing can be recruited, reshaped and worked through by the novice; and how it is those paraphernalia, trivial or even invisible to the adults in the room, that come to constitute the challenges to the students as they transition across the primary school years, and, because they do not notice them, to the teachers and researchers.

# 13

# Transitioning from Primary to High School

Emma Rutherford Vale, Helen Lewis, Honglin Chen and Pauline Jones

## Introduction

The transition from primary to high school is commonly held to be difficult for the literacy progress of many learners (Luke et al., 2003; Victorian Auditor General's Office, 2015), with consistent rates of progress for all students remaining elusive (Dinham & Rowe, 2007; Galton, Gray & Ruddock, 1999). Transition outcomes have been found to be influenced by an array of factors, including, for example, social and emotional support (Waters, Lester, Wenden & Cross, 2012), curriculum continuity (Galton et al., 1999; Vinson & Harrison, 2006) and particular dispositions towards learning (Noyes, 2006). Challenges that accompany the transition from primary to high school are brought about by changes in institutional setting, and social and learning environments (van Rens, Haelermans, Groot & Maassen van den Brink, 2018). Addressing these challenges has had mixed success, with particular aspects including continuity of curriculum and of teaching and learning pedagogy appearing less well addressed by transition programmes in Australian schools (Vinson & Harrison, 2006). The changing disciplinary demands of high school – where the curriculum embraces increasingly technical school subjects – make attention to curricular and teaching adjustments at the transition of critical interest (Hynd-Shanahan, 2013; Wyatt-Smith & Cumming, 2003). As students transition into increasingly distinct, abstract and technical bodies of knowledge, they must develop flexible language and literacy repertoires to meet new demands, both for more precise and technical writing that is becoming increasingly crafted and distinct from everyday language, and for language for generalising, abstracting and reasoning in increasingly nuanced ways (Christie & Derewianka, 2008; Humphrey, 2017; Painter, Derewianka & Torr, 2005). Changing learning demands need literacy foundations that are sufficiently robust to engage with increasingly specialised ways of knowing inscribed in distinct knowledge discourses (Birr Moje, 2008; Lo Bianco & Freebody, 1997; Wyatt-Smith & Cumming, 2003).

## Theoretical Framework

Two complementary theories inform our approach to understanding the varying experiences of the students in our study: Bernsteinian sociology of education (1975, 2000) and systemic functional theory (Halliday, 1973, 1993; Halliday & Hasan, 1985). Bernstein's work (1975, 2000), with its recognition of the centrality of educational experience in the reproduction of social inequality, gives impulse to the need to take seriously young people's accounts of their experiences with respect to changing literacy and learning demands across the middle years of schooling. Bernstein argued that pedagogic activity is a major means through which individuals are socialised to different ways of using language that have profound consequences for them in terms of social outcomes. Bernstein's (1975) distinction between *common-sense* and *uncommon-sense* or *educational* knowledge is particularly pertinent in exploring the transition to high school. Common-sense knowledge is grounded in a specific context, based on personal or shared experience, involves concrete non-technical understandings and is characterised by a 'lack of insulation between topics' (Painter, 2005: 71). Educational knowledge, in contrast, tends to be generalised, distant from personal experience, abstract and technical and characterised by increasing compartmentalisation into discrete subject areas. School literacy instruction is concerned with shifts along a continuum between the two, building on the common-sense understandings that children bring to the early years of school, over time developing their capacity to manage the more complex knowledge practices and the changing language and literacy practices associated with educational knowledge. The history of collaboration between Bernsteinian sociology and systemic functional linguistic theory in educational settings is extensive. Halliday, like Bernstein, was interested in how language is implicated in social processes. As linguists, he and colleagues

(Martin, 1984; Martin & Rose, 2008) went further and posited a systematic relationship between actual language in use and the social context in which it is used – both in terms of the institutional or broad cultural settings as well as the more immediate context of situation. A major contribution of Hallidayan linguistic theory is the description of a principled link between context and language choice (Halliday & Hasan, 1985). Halliday identified three variables in the context of situation: the field or social action, the 'what is going on' of the interaction; the tenor or the social relationships being enacted; and the mode or the way language is used to weave these meanings together into a coherent message. These three contextual variables comprise the register of the situation. The register both shapes and is realised by language choices that have evolved to make these meanings of field, tenor and mode. A learner's pathway through schooling may then be conceptualised as a progressive expansion of their 'registerial repertoire' (Matthiessen, 2009) as they encounter more specialised disciplinary fields, widening relations of tenor and increasing use of language for reflection, entailing increasingly challenging language and literacy demands (Derewianka & Jones, 2016). Changes in the context of student learning foreground the transition to high school as a critical time for successful apprenticeship into the discourses of educational knowledge (Birr Moje, 2008). This changing context is illustrated in Table 13.1.

Student experiences of the enacted curriculum form a critical apprenticeship into meanings and dispositions for successful trajectories at school (Hammond & Gibbons, 2005; Thwaite, Jones & Simpson, 2020). Our interest in this chapter, then, is in student reactions – their reflections, experiences and understandings of the different pedagogical settings encountered during the move from primary to high school.

## Methodology

This chapter reports on data collected as part of the Transforming Literacy Outcomes longitudinal study (TRANSLIT). The data consist of semi-structured interviews of approximately thirty minutes each with twenty-one Year 7 students from three high schools: two situated in a southern Sydney cluster and one in a satellite cluster of TRANSLIT in south-western Sydney.

**Table 13.1** Development of Language for School Knowledge

| An expanding language and literacy repertoire for educational meanings | | |
|---|---|---|
| **Early childhood** | **Later childhood** | **Adolescence** |
| **Language as action** 'Common-sense' and everyday meanings Familiar audiences Spoken like and flowing organisation of meanings | ⟵⟶ | **Language as reflection** 'Uncommon-sense', abstract and technical meanings A widening range of audiences – taking up the stance of discipline experts Dense, crafted and written like |
| Language embedded in everyday contexts *Mum, you feed the cat.* | Developing language for technical and abstract meanings. *Cats are **a species of small carnivorous mammal*** | Developing language to condense meanings in written forms that enable theorising. *The rate of extinction of species is **accelerating**. **Acceleration of extinction events**....* |

*Source*: adapted from Halliday (2009: 121)


**Table 13.2** Student Interview Data Sources

| School | Year | Semester | Students | Interviews[a] | Characteristics |
|---|---|---|---|---|---|
| A | 7 | 1 2 | 7 | 12 | High ICSEA[b], inner city, high-attaining cohort |
| B | 7 | 1 2 | 10 | 17 | Average ICSEA, urban including semi-rural, range of attainment levels |
| C | 7 8 | 2 2 | 4 | 2 2 | Low ICSEA, portside, higher proportion of below-average attainment levels |

[a]Discrepancies between number of students and number of interviews reflect student absences.

[b]ICSEA – Index of Community Socio-Educational Advantage. Calculated for all school cohorts in Australia drawing together information about parental education and income levels.

The schools chosen represent the range of socioeconomic and cultural diversity. Students were chosen from each school based on achievement levels, gender and cultural backgrounds to form a balanced sample. This enabled examination of how students from a range of literacy attainment levels (below average, average and above average or high[1] in Year 6) respond to literacy transitions. Table 13.2 provides an overview of student interview data.

Interviews were conducted twice – once at the beginning and once towards the end of Year 7. Students were asked to reflect on their literacy learning in the subjects English, history and science,[2] including, for example, what and how well they were learning to read and write; the kinds of texts they were using for learning; the kinds of literacy tasks they were engaged in; and changes in the level of learning challenge. All interview data were analysed thematically using qualitative data analysis software. Through inductive analysis, we identified themes pertaining to literacy, learning and change at the transition to high school. Thematic analysis was supplemented with linguistic analysis from an SFL perspective to explore more closely the way student talk construed different accounts of learning and different kinds of knowledge. Linguistic analysis draws on Hallidayan understandings that language can shape both dynamic and reflective (synoptic) perspectives on learning (see Table 13.1) and Bernsteinian distinction between common-sense and uncommon-sense forms of knowledge. In the following section, we discuss themes in relation to two key aspects of the transition: *expanding curriculum experiences and learning demands* and *learning capabilities at play in the transition to high school*, with close attention to the subjects of English and science augmented by discussion of history and geography.

# Findings

Students reported positively on the transition to high school at the beginning of Year 7, describing it as less difficult than anticipated and judging features of the new educational setting including increased specialisation of subjects, instruction from subject expert teachers and a greater sense of independence as welcome changes. That most students reported the transition as less difficult than anticipated accords with findings of large-scale transition studies (Cairney, Lowe & Sproates, 1994; Evangelou et al., 2008). A closer analysis of student accounts of transition, however, provides a more nuanced picture, suggesting that the impact of transition emerges cumulatively. Student accounts were suggestive of a 'honeymoon period' during which high school is perceived as exciting and students participate in modified 'settling in' programmes, with many reporting that the classroom teaching and learning was relatively familiar, and the level of difficulty changed only modestly at the first interview. By the end of Year 7, a more complex picture of changes in learning setting emerges, shedding light on variations in student preparedness to cope. In the following section, analysis seeks to illustrate student understandings of changes across the transition and variable student responses to these.

## Expanding Curriculum Experiences and Learning Demands

The widely acknowledged shift into more distinct disciplinary learning in high school was confirmed by student accounts, identified by students in terms of increased specialisation and technicality of lesson content and terminology; longer and more challenging reading texts; specific disciplinary conventions for presenting and organising information; and more specialised processes and practices. Disciplinary differences experienced by students in Year 7 can be exemplified in subject English where student accounts suggested a new focus on responding critically to texts using evidence, less focus on writing narrative texts, stronger focus on the literary 'canon' and a stronger focus on canonical ways of valuing and responding to texts. Students overall also described a significant increase in the length of texts and a broadening of types of response including the comparative study of texts. In the interview excerpt that follows, Liam (School C) suggests that English writing prior to transition mainly involved writing narratives, whereas in high school they are expected to write responses using a particular paragraph convention which he identifies with the acronym TXXXC (topic, explain, example, expand, conclude). The movement into specialised disciplinary knowledge was much more marked in accounts from high school A where students engaged with highly valued literary texts such as Beowulf and explored specialised literary forms. In the second extract, Nico (School A) explains they have been introduced to the literary devices of kennings and metonymy, which he finds challenging and much more difficult than the work he did in English prior to high school.

> With Mr Locke we just got on the computers and wrote like narratives and stuff ... We don't really do narratives [in high school] ... We do TXXXC's.

> The ... it's like topic sentence, like explain and like two other, I forgot what they're called but – then conclusion. (Liam, School C)
>
> Well in the writing, we're already learning about ... kennings and metonymy, and in [primary] school, all we learn is probably just similes and metaphors, something simple like that ... So for the supermarket I just wrote 'a castle of intended service' unlike the grocery store or something maybe last Year 6s would do, or the Year 5. (Nico, School A)

Shifts towards less common-sense and more valued disciplinary textual forms were evident in other high school subjects, with students describing their learning areas across the transition as more distinct, more focused on specialised knowledge and accompanied by particular practices. This included layout of textual forms specific to subjects, such as description of an artefact, how to interpret maps and legends, how to structure an argument with evidence and how to visually represent information in diagrams following conventions of the subject areas. Some students observed that the new conventions for writing and layout would have been easier if they were introduced in primary school, others commented on the vast difference between what their subjects looked like across the transition; and some students expressed satisfaction with the significant change in curriculum content.

> It's different because when I did it in primary, we didn't have to do all this sentence structure as much as we have to now. We would have to like just write the answers on the board ... on the board, but now we have to like do it by ourselves and make the sentence structure. (Alice, School C, discussing PEEL paragraph structure)
>
> It's a lot harder cause they actually use like a lot of different language and they don't just work on like – they actually work on like science .... (Amy, School B)
>
> English – they're going through the canon of literature. So they're getting books that are historically very dominant ... and we're reading through them, finding out the different parts of them and how they're made up. So kennings and metonymy ... I've been waiting for it for quite a while. I've been very happy. (Gino, School A)

Each of these accounts implies both an increase in specialisation of content and less flexibility in what defines learning of those subjects in high school.

In particular, Alice's comment points to expectation of adherence to specific literacy conventions in increasingly independent ways. The movement into increasing specialisation is particularly apparent in student accounts of their science learning, which suggest highly variable experiences prior to entry to high school. Most students described science in primary school involving engaging, activity-based experiences, which in many accounts, though, did not necessarily involve generalising to knowledge from these activities:

> You would just research something and you could do an experiment but most of the times it was just like a tornado in a bottle, stuff like that. (Zane, School B)

> If we did science it was normally quite a random though fun little experiment, like it was simple ones, like those types of little experiments that kids do and they're still fun but they're not playing with bunsen burners or mixing chemicals. (Sage, School B)

These accounts also imply gaps in experience of curriculum, with this more common-sense approach to science replaced by more formalised apprenticeship into equipment, materials and processes used to investigate areas of science knowledge once in high school. These gaps were not limited to science and English, and despite apparent continuity of learning from the early primary through to late secondary years in the official national curriculum, students' accounts of their experiences varied significantly with respect to the enacted

Table 13.3 Gaps in Curriculum Experiences

| | |
|---|---|
| Antonia (School A) | **I've done the science fairs** in primary school but that's just kind of a guess, because the teachers aren't … **that's not a subject they teach, science.** |
| Nedda (School B) | Well, because we didn't have a lab or anything, so we had to either go outside or do it in our classroom. So we couldn't do chemicals at all. All we did for science was basically learn I guess like weight and stuff and … we didn't do that many experiments but **what we learnt in science wasn't at all what we learn here.** |
| Tarni (School C) | It's different because like primary school we weren't doing that much work compared to high school where **you come here you have to go to every subject, in primary you've only just got like one**, you don't even have a subject. |
| Dejan (School C) | But then there's like history, which we never did in primary school, there's a bit of science … like geography we – I don't think we ever did geography. TM, cooking, sewing, all that kind of stuff, we never did that. |

curriculum, with the result that it was sometimes difficult for them to connect prior learning to their new subjects across the transition (see Table 13.3).

Although students from all high schools commented on discontinuities or gaps in their experience of curriculum content, those described as high-attaining students commented very positively on the increase in specialisation and accounted for practices such as wide reading, outside interests and personal attributes that they believed enabled them to easily navigate the transition.

Alongside changes in the nature of the curriculum, changes in the learning context also placed pressure on learning skills. Students at two of the three high schools reported significant increases in homework and assignment expectations, accompanied by shorter time frames and more crowded work schedules which required increasingly independent skills for prioritising tasks and monitoring learning. Some students responded very positively to the requirement for greater independence and self-organisation, viewing the increased responsibility as a form of freedom:

> Well I really like the fact that there's ... more freedom we have around the school. ... Well not really ... more responsibility to get to classes and do all the homework ... it feels very nice. (Lewis, School A)

Other students though reported feeling unprepared for the new requirement to manage demands of homework and assignments from multiple teachers. Students not identified as high attaining particularly expressed significant challenge with the changed expectations at the beginning of Year 7. Kieran (School B) is one of a small number of respondents who describe high school as a lot harder, with *a lot more assignments to do*, but high-attaining learners also comment on the extraordinary change in homework and assignment loads, with Eva noting:

> It's not as ... it's not too different from last year being Enrichment, cause we had a similar workload <u>but never due</u> ... <u>none of it was ever due the next day</u> we always had about a week to do it ...and so you're thinking, look on the timetable, oh crud, it's [due] tomorrow. (Eva, School B, emphasis original)

Alongside these pressures, other changes to the learning environment in the form of assessment (in exams and graded assignments) and the nature of teacher feedback were also suggestive of a requirement for more independent and strategic skills for monitoring learning. Sergio (School A), when asked about his approach to writing in history and whether he concentrates on each paragraph or at the level of whole text level, explains that he focuses on the body paragraphs, because the detail in there is *what gets you most marks*. His observation demonstrates an attentiveness to assessment strategies which was notable in responses from other learners in School A and to some extent from high attainers in School B. These students appeared to be attending to their learning in terms of both short- and longer term trajectories. Antonia (School A), for example, identifies the value of her current learning in terms of its future applicability to high-stakes assessment in five years' time. Her reference 'to proper techniques' is suggestive of an immediate orientation to valued disciplinary practices:

> Well recently we did a 1,000-word story in English … obviously, I've done stories before in primary school and in other classes, but it's interesting to learn the proper techniques … And since we've started essay writing, it's really interesting to go, oh this is how you actually do this, and this is what you would do in Year 12. That's definitely come up in pretty much all of our classes. (Antonia, School A)

It is also indicative of high schools having different expectations in terms of how far along the educational trajectory that students' attention should be. In *pretty much all* of her classes, Antonia reports that her attention has been directed to longer term learning trajectories and accountabilities, disposing her to view class learning as functioning to serve long-term learning goals.

Not all students accounted for such long-term outlooks on their literacy progress; indeed some students struggled to make sense of their learning progress once in high school. Tracy (School B), who begins high school very positively, expresses diminished confidence in her ability to track her learning progress over the course of Year 7. Interviewed late in term 1, Tracy noted that she had been *really worried and scared* about transition but found *it's not actually that hard, it's like easy*. Reinterviewed in term 4 though, we find Tracy has been moved to a lower streamed science class on the recommendation of her teacher who feels she needs more learning support. Asked about the feedback she receives in science Tracy explains that the teachers do not check the students' books like they did in primary school (Table 13.4). She

**Table 13.4** Tracy, School B, Interview 2

| | |
|---|---|
| Interviewer | So, do you get any feedback in [science] class on your writing ever? |
| Tracy | Teacher doesn't really check our books. They don't really look at our books, they just like take the sheets back, they don't really give them back, they don't mark them or anything they just keep them, probably chuck them out. Yeah. |
| Interviewer | So, what about in English, do you get feedback on your writing there? |
| Tracy | Not really, not really in any class, like they don't really look at our books, like mark them. Yeah. |
| Interviewer | How do you find that? |
| Tracy | Well I don't really … it doesn't bother me **but still**. |
| Interviewer | Is it different from primary? |
| Tracy | Yes, **very different**. |
| Interviewer | What did they do in primary? |
| Tracy | You used to put your books back, give them back to the teacher, she would mark them and then give them back to you the next day. Yeah but they don't really do that **they just want to see you write, they just look at it and then they say, 'Okay you've done it'**. Yeah. |
| Interviewer | So, it's more just to check that you're doing it – [yeah] – not to give you feedback, did you get feedback in primary do you think? Like how you could do better? |
| Tracy | Like they used to write down the bottom of the page like 'Good job' but this will … like fix something else or something and yeah. |
| Interviewer | So how do you know how well you're doing with your writing? |
| Tracy | **I don't. I don't think I'm going** … well **I'm not really sure.** [ellipsed interviewer reassurances] Yeah I don't really know how I'm going cause the teacher doesn't really … it … it's more like you have to wait until the end of the year to get your report back, then find out what you're like better at than what you're not good at. But yeah. |

**Bold** = language that expresses and modulates attitudes.

seems quite dissatisfied with this lack of attention to her individual work and expresses uncertainty about how to understand how she is progressing. Tracy equates feedback with individual written comments on her work and without these, she finds independently monitoring her learning more difficult in high school. Her second interview is marked by an evident drop in confidence and a less buoyant attitude to learning (see bold, Table 13.4).

It is not our contention that Tracy did not receive feedback from her teachers; in fact, at Tracy's first interview, she describes how her science teacher assisted her when she had done her assignment incorrectly. It may be that Tracy had not yet developed the independent learner disposition to judge her own progress and recognise what is required of her. However, at this point, beyond the initial positive transition process, Tracy is experiencing the high school learning context as lacking navigational points to chart her progress.

## Learner Capabilities at Play in the Transition to High School: Responses to Changes in Teaching and Learning

Tracy's account is just one of the diverse levels of preparedness to respond to changes in the learning environment. In responding to greater specialisation of content and demands for more independent learning skills, students illustrated and drew on a variety of resources. Those who reported adapting well to the changed learning environment hinted at particular personal and organisational skill sets that supported learning in the new educational setting. For example, in responding to increased homework and assignment demands, Sage reported a personal capacity to adjust: *we get a lot of homework but I've kinda got used to it now* (Sage, high attainer, School B). Others described a more strategic response explaining how they navigated the new time pressure of assignment deadlines by using planning and time management skills:

> You can still research enough if you've got a set out plan, sort of like a plan of attack, it's like okay, this night start researching, this night I'll start writing up a bit, go back to research it. (Eva, high attainer, School B)

Some students demonstrated a particular value set which helped them to adjust to high school. For example, Sergio observes that spending time on homework is *better than just sitting down and watching TV* (Sergio, high attainer, School A). Organisational skills, personal attributes and values that enabled some students to navigate the changed accountabilities of high school presented challenges for other students. Kieran (School B), described by his teacher in primary school as below average and at risk, gives a positive account of the transition but he is missing learning opportunities by failing, for example, to hand in the term assignment for science. Zane (School B) similarly has not submitted the term 1 science assignment, conceding he may have forgotten to hand it in, and Tracy (School B), although completing her homework, without more individual teacher guidance, is finding that she has misinterpreted the assessment task and must redo it.

**Table 13.5** Tarni, School C, Interview 1

| | |
|---|---|
| Interviewer | Okay so tell me about what you … the explaining you do in History |
| Tarni | We **have to write** on … so there's this magazine and **we have to open** it **and** we have to answer questions. But we have to **read** the book **first**, like say if you were on page 178, what we were doing <u>today, in my first period</u>, we had to read it and **then** answer the questions. |

Bold = verb groups; underline = expressions of time sequence

Beyond these perhaps anticipated pressures for increasingly independent learning skills impacting differently on students, qualitative differences were also apparent in the ways students accounted for their learning. Language for reflecting on learning and talking about literacy demands varied widely across the cohort. Differences were apparent in how students identified the purpose of class tasks for example, with some learners giving particularly vague or generic responses to questions about the type of texts they had written and about the takeaway knowledge from a lesson. Sophia (School B), when asked about the explanation that she has written in science, responds: *It's like a report kind of thing, like a non-fiction report type of thing, yes.* Tracy (School B) responds similarly to questions about the same task: *[it is] facts or, like, if you want to find out something. I'm not sure.* Differences were also evident in the way that students accounted for learning, with some students appearing more oriented to the activity of lessons, rather than the knowledge of lessons. In the following account Tarni (School C) is asked to expand on a comment she has made about 'explaining' in history. Her response is particularly marked by the way she gives a moment-by-moment account of the steps involved in her learning (see underline in Table 13.5).

Tarni's account is organised chronologically and focuses on the specifics of the physical context (*this magazine, on page 178*) at a particular time (*in my first period*) recounting the material processes of the lesson. Notably, she does not interpret the question as a request for the reasoning she was engaged in an historical event or for the generalised knowledge developed. An alternative account might have described how students were learning about the process of mummification or describing the ways colonisation impacted on Indigenous Australians; instead Tarni accounts for the moment-by-moment activity of her history learning. Alice (Table 13.6) similarly interprets the interviewer's question about assessment as a request for a recount of the specific steps involved

**Table 13.6** Alice, School C, Year 7, Interview 1

| Interviewer | And how would Sir assess something like that to see if you knew what you'd learned? |
| --- | --- |
| Alice | He would give us, like sometimes like one or two pages and we will just … we **would be** silent, and we **would have to do** the test and then we **would give** it to him, and he marks it. |

in an assessment event (the action of assessment) rather than generalising to the textual processes or conceptual knowledge to be assessed (the reflection of assessment). Tarni and Alice account for the common-sense activity of the lesson, that is, what was done, rather than what was learned, situating their accounts at the context-embedded end of the continuum (Table 13.1) rather than more reflection oriented.

Such common-sense accounts of learning tended to contrast with those of higher attaining learners who were more likely to connect descriptions of classroom activity to generalisations about knowledge and processes that count in discipline areas. In particular, the extent to which learners were able to move from an account of the specific action of the classroom (here and now) to generalisations about the nature of the knowledge or processes undertaken in the lesson (more abstract and synoptic) seemed indicative of different orientations to valued meanings in high school. In the example following, a higher attaining student is describing his learning in geography. He recounts the activities involved (*choose one of them, write about it*) but he links these to the more abstract geography knowledge and disciplinary processes (see bold in Gino's extract) developed through that activity. The classroom activities (the action of a lesson) are connected to understanding of geography ideas – that is, '*issues*' and '*human rights*' (the knowledge of the lesson). Gino also reasons about the purpose of one of these activities (*so that you knew why*).

> Oh yeah, we did a small project on gathering information on a certain topic to do with geography. So a certain **issue** in the world. They taught us how **all these issues correlate with geography**. So we had to choose one of them and then write about them and what the problem is and all that. So what I did was **human rights**, and then I looked up all the information, used Freedom House and then got **the most authoritarian countries**, gathered

information on them **so that you knew why it was like that**, and so on. (Gino, School A)

Similarly, when Lewis is asked about a task he has completed in English, he provides concrete examples of the activities involved in the task, but he also identifies the valued literary process of transforming texts to demonstrate interpretation of a class text (see bold). In this way he is identifying the purpose of the learning task or what his teacher values through the activity. Lewis tacitly recognises that the learning activities embedded in the classroom context represent particular processes that are valued in that subject.

> He wanted us to show how you could take information from a book and **apply it** to a newspaper article. So we were doing the book Mister Monday; with part of the book we had to write a newspaper article, and we had to take information from the book but also make up information that wasn't in the book but **make it apply to the information we already knew**. (Lewis, School A)

These accounts of student learning illustrate differences in what students take away from lessons and suggest differences in repertoires for generalising about learning and for identifying what is valued in the high school learning context. They draw attention to different preparedness to navigate learning that is becoming more abstract and which requires skills for making generalisations about knowledge (what is learned) drawing on a language of reflection.

## Discussion

> The task of school is to bridge the gap between the expectations embodied in the curriculum frameworks and the resources which children make available to schools in the way of their development and education at home. (Teese & Lamb, 2009: 10)

The findings of this study reveal the complex adjustments students must make to successfully navigate entry to high school, as well as the variable experiences and repertoires that students bring to make these adjustments. In particular, student accounts draw attention to the different resources students bring across the transition and how these provision students differently to adjust to new kinds of knowledge and increasingly independent accountabilities. Successful student transitions in the short term may not necessarily translate to successful progress in high school over the longer term, particularly for learners without sufficiently developed school repertoires and without sufficient supports in the new educational setting. Accounts detailed here suggest that transition practices as they stand are successful in ensuring that the experience of commencing high school is not as daunting as anticipated, but they may not address the ongoing effects of increasingly abstract disciplinary content and the broadening range of specialised texts and processes that meet students across the transition.

## Developing Repertoires for Disciplinary Learning

If we take up the systemic functional view that meanings are shaped by context, then we must take seriously the implications of curricular discontinuities described by learners in the enacted curriculum across the transition. Changes in the kinds of curricular knowledge and practices across the transition implicate changes in the registerial repertoires that students must develop and use to experience success in the new educational setting. A contextual view of language makes this relationship explicit:

> Developing knowledge and understanding in school subject areas and developing control of the linguistic resources that construct and communicate that knowledge and understanding are essentially the same thing. (Hasan, 2009 cited in Unsworth, 2000: 245)

Learners can only construe those meanings that are available to them, built up through numerous experiences of context through the range of pedagogic interactions in classrooms. Opportunities for students to engage with increasingly specialised, abstract and analytical meanings that foster development of their registerial repertoires for making such meanings are critical. So, when Nedda (School B) notes that science in primary school was *nothing at all* like science in high school, there is a strong possibility that she is not well prepared for the content and literacy demands of secondary science. There is a tendency to view changes and differences in subjects over the transition as a 'breath of fresh air' for Year 6 students, but differences and gaps in the enacted curriculum equate to differences and gaps in language and literacy repertoires for success beyond the transition. Over time, the welcomed specialisation of high school may become more alienating than engaging for students who find their language and literacy repertoires give them less purchase on the specialised meanings of high school. As much as these accounts raise concerns for the continuity of students' experiences with curriculum literacies, accounts of gaps and discontinuities may be as much about the way discipline knowledge is framed in primary school. Tarni's (School C) statement that we *didn't even have subjects* in primary school suggests that curricula in primary school may be much more commonsense, less 'kept apart' and thereby harder for students to connect with what they encounter after transition. If students are not to be treated as a 'tabla rasa' on arrival in high school, they need to be able to connect prior learning to the school subjects and practices that greet them across the transition. Notions of what it means to do science or history, or English should articulate across the transition.

## Addressing the Attainment Gap

Not all students reported being concerned by changes in the curriculum. Many students welcomed the more specialised forms of knowledge and remained engaged about and excited by the specialised curriculum of high school. Some students commented that the shift to greater specialisation in Year 7 was long awaited. Differences in what students bring to the new learning context then place important weight on the kinds of disciplinary apprenticeship offered on entry to high school. High schools cannot meet the varied needs of learners across the transition without close attention to 'what students bring' and to 'what students will require' for successful apprenticeship into the meaning-making practices of the curriculum disciplines. Where discontinuities in curriculum were reported, accounts from high-attaining students confirm the considerable capital that they bring to bear – from out-of-school learning, personal interests and family culture – to smoothly traverse gaps that may become risky for other students. Tarni, Alice, Tracy and Kieran, all identified as travelling less well in their learning, illustrate in their accounts developing repertoires for the reflective meanings and independent learning orientations which are valued in high school. Equally, accounts such as Sophia's and Tracy's of their writing in science suggest they are developing capacities for reflecting on their learning in the curriculum areas – its processes and textual demands. Pedagogic approaches that recognise 'literacy as an essential aspect of disciplinary learning' (Birr Moje, 2008: 99) are necessary to support students developing robust registers for the curriculum disciplines in high school. Unless teachers make the valued meanings of different subjects more visible and provide tools with which to shape them, students are left to draw on their own resources to fill these gaps.

Confounding repeated calls for more systematic apprenticeship into disciplinary literacy are long-standing challenges facing subject-specific literacy instruction in high schools. Many teachers continue to report a lack confidence and expertise to teach literacy within their areas of specialisation (Fang, 2014; Love, 2010). As a result curriculum literacies remain largely invisible in many high school classrooms, in spite of the inclusion of cross-curricular literacy capabilities in the Australian curriculum (Hannant & Jetnikoff, 2015; Wyatt-Smith & Cumming, 2003). At the same time as many high schools report lack of preparedness to apprentice students into disciplinary discourses, primary school teachers often report lack of confidence in teaching more specialised subjects (Mansfield & Woods-McConney, 2012; Paatsch, Hutchison & Cloonan, 2019). Primary schools need opportunities to engage more closely with high schools to develop shared understandings and language vis-à-vis critical disciplinary understandings and practices across the transition. There was already some evidence of such work at one primary school site in the broader TRANSLIT study where the Year 5 and 6 coordinator was carefully re-examining their English programme for the ways that it articulated to the practices valued in the high school English curriculum. Such initiatives cannot be sustained though by the work of individual teachers and point to the need for more systemic responses.

Accompanying students' reactions to the specialised content of the high school setting, we noted that they illustrated different positionings in relation to independent learning. We do not propose that this is an entirely separate set of skills and do not believe that it is a coincidence that high-attaining learners demonstrated strong skills both in dealing with changes in content and in responding to changes in demands for learner independence. Reflections and responses from high-attaining students demonstrated a disposition towards what is valued in educational contexts, what knowledge is important and how that knowledge will be rewarded in assessment. We argue that explicit understandings about what and how students are learning are tied up with increasing sensitivity to the valued knowledge and practices of different disciplines and to a capacity to read the tacit messages about what counts in the learning environment.

## Conclusion

Students' capacity to successfully navigate the transition rests on their literacy repertoires, their individual learning dispositions and the nature of the pedagogies they encounter. Failure to collaboratively address the transition from primary to high school from curricular and pedagogic perspectives will continue to impact students unevenly. Addressing persistent attainment gaps (Luke, 2010) and achieving equitable education outcomes requires better coordination so that students experience high school as a progression rather than a new beginning. Programmes at the start of Year 7 can better address the effects of transition with close attention to what young people bring with them, and to the literacy and learning repertoires needed for curricular success. The research reported here points to the need for primary and high schools to take seriously the challenge of curricular continuity and for systems to support them to do so. Such attention may gain better traction on the enduring issue of inequality of educational outcomes and do more to foster equitable outcomes (Education Council, 2019) beyond entry to high school.

# Envoi to Part III: Literacies for Successfully Navigating Transitions at School and Beyond

## Elizabeth Birr Moje

The construct of transitions is amazingly overlooked in education research, *writ large*, and as a result is understudied in literacy research. Unfounded assumptions about transitions abide, such as the idea that a child must 'learn to read' by grade three to allow for 'reading to learn' beyond that grade. Other dichotomies have travelled with the 'learn-to-read/reading-to-learn' divide, such as the sharp division between narrative and information text, or the ways that Louise Rosenblatt's (1978) theory was taken up as if the aesthetic and efferent purposes are independent of each other and tied to information (efferent reading) versus narrative (aesthetic reading), when, in fact, Rosenblatt made clear that these ways of reading are always present and in interaction with one another.

Why do so many dichotomous perspectives exist in education practice and research, and in what ways do these false dichotomies reify and contribute to our failure to identify, understand and mediate transitions for children across the developmental spectrum and school years and grades? It is worth noting that dichotomies should lead literacy researchers to investigate transitions, rather than ignore them. Perhaps it is the case that these dichotomies lull us into a false sense of transitions as abrupt moments in time, rather than as trajectories in which the challenges that present themselves in overtly transitional moments are built over time. As the authors of this volume argue, if a child builds a cumulative experience of success, in which resources to support not only success but also growth and development are readily available, then transitions are navigable. These TRANSLIT chapters both explicitly identify and allude to the dichotomies responsible for bumpy transitions.

These chapters also explore how literate identities are shaped by and enacted in response to both the popular dichotomies of literacy and the transitions that accompany them.

For example, Chapter 10, by Matruglio, reveals the dichotomy between reading for enjoyment and reading for critique and analysis that is played out as children move from primary to secondary grades. This difference between the teaching of aesthetic reading skills and efferent reading skills evokes the false dichotomies of reading narrative versus reading information, as well as the enormously problematic claims about learning to read versus reading to learn. As the author illustrates, primary grade teachers are so focused on teaching reading process that they often fail to engage learners in conversations about the content of the text they are reading.

The focus on literacy processes in primary grades is clearly evident in Chapter 11, where Mantei and Kervin demonstrate that literacy identities are established early, and in relation to the way that teachers talk about and teach literacy. If reading rapidly is important to a teacher, then children who can read rapidly are good readers, regardless of whether they have understood their reading. If writing is about handwriting (and not breaking the pencil while doing it), then the child who can master the intricate work of making letters on paper is a good writer. Worth noting in this account was that none of the children interviewed had much to say about the content of their reading or writing. None of them talked about purposes for reading or writing. And enjoyment was linked to skill, often in the instrumental dimensions of reading and writing (fluency, handwriting). As if Chapter 11 was foreshadowing Chapter 13, I found myself wondering, to what extent do these identities – marked by both the pedagogies of the classroom and the transitions the children experienced in just one year – carry forward and shape students' abilities to navigate future transitions?

In Chapter 12, Edwards-Groves and Freebody offer a novel perspective on literacy research and challenge literacy researchers to examine what they think they are learning through research interviews. As if responding to Chapter 11, Edwards-Groves and Freebody remind the reader that interviewers and interviewees – especially when the latter are young children – do not always share goals for the interview experience. The children represented in Chapter 11 were drawing on the cues available to them in their learning lives about what the interviewers wanted to know. Indeed, interviewees are rarely afforded complete knowledge of what is behind an interviewer's questions in an attempt to elicit authentic responses (i.e. to avoid 'leading' the researcher). What Edwards-Groves and Freebody suggest, however, is that attention to what children 'recruit' from their experience with literacy and share in interviews can, in fact, teach researchers a great deal, including about what we may be missing. Perhaps, in fact, children's literate identities are far more expansive than we were able to glimpse because they assumed that by asking questions of them in school, the interviewers wanted to know what school literacies are like. This is not a critique of Chapter 11 but a reminder that literacy researchers need to interrogate their methods even as they analyse their data. Researchers need to keep in mind that people – even small children – are constantly making sense of situations and contexts, and that their actions and stories are always situated in and mediated by those contexts, even the context of a research interview. Edwards-Groves and Freebody's take on research interviews reminds me of 'small stories' work (Bamberg, 2004; Georgakopoulou, 2013), which challenges constructs of identity as stable and implicates identity research in contributing to the illusion of lives lived as grand and continuous narratives.

Finally, in Chapter 13, Rutherford Vale, Lewis, Chen, and Jones describe how literacy demands shift across the primary–secondary continuum from reading about concrete things and activities available in lived experience to reading about abstract concepts and historical events not at all available in the child's lived experience. I am particularly struck by the fact that those youth 'identified as higher attaining' in the Rutherford Vale et al. chapter seemed more motivated to take on the transitional challenges than those who had not attained great heights at lower levels of schooling. I am prompted to ask: Which comes first, attainment, the identity of an attainer or the motivation to attain? I am also struck by Rutherford Vale et al.'s observation that those who seemed to struggle with transitions recounted the actions or activities they needed to complete school-based literacy activities, whereas the students who managed the transitions focused more on the substance of their learning. Indeed, I was struck by the desire that older youth represented in Chapter 13 expressed for taking on new substantive learning.

This finding reminds me of findings from a study of thousands of adolescent learners in Detroit, Michigan, United States, in which we noted that the readers who were proficient with a range of texts we put in front of them brought a purpose to each text. In reading process interviews, they would utter phrases such as 'It seems like the author wants us to ...'. In other words, they recognised that reading had a purpose, and they were able to craft that purpose even if it was not provided to them (Moje, Kim, Stockdill & Kolb, 2010). We concluded that literacy skill drew heavily on purpose and interest, and on positionalities or identities that Freebody (1992) referred to as *reader as meaning maker* and *reader as text user* (and perhaps even *reader as text critic or analyst*).

What Rutherford Vale and colleagues demonstrate is that those resources (identities, interests, purposes) seemed to be missing for the 'lower attaining' students, and that the lack of those resources had implications for how they managed the transitions they were experiencing. This finding has enormous implications for what happens across the continuum of school experience. Although the findings are noted among older learners, I cannot help but think of the classrooms described in Chapter 11, in which literacy learning was about letters and sounds and speed and handwriting. If literacy learning in school is reduced to just code-breaking resources (Freebody, 1992), then how do children learn to be meaning makers, text users and text critics? This point raises a number of important questions that could help us think about how to structure instruction to provide those resources that will support future transitions:

- What are the resources and affordances available to different types of learners for navigating new contexts? What role do the resources of purpose (value), interest, identity, self-efficacy play in navigating new demands across transitions? How does the lack of articulated or understood purpose for literacy shape later navigations? How does the singular identity of reader as code breaker insufficiently prepare learners for later transitions?
- When, if at all, do educators provide motivating texts and contexts (or activities) that invite learners to embrace transitions? To what extent do our assumptions about where motivation lies (in the learner or in our learning environments) shape how well children are able to navigate? How can we better learn about how children identify themselves and build on those identities to help them grow and navigate not just the transitions of

schooling but all the transitions they have to make every single day and throughout their lives?
- How should we think about the ways our positionings, labellings and identifications of children at very young ages shape their self-efficacy and motivation, their confidence in entering new terrain and their agency in advocating for their own needs (Learned, 2016)? The relationship between self-concept of ability or self-efficacy and motivation to persist in learning is not a new concept (Bandura, 1977; Eccles et al., 1983; Eccles, Lord & Midgley, 1991; Eccles & Midgley, 1989; Eccles et al., 1993), and yet time and time again we see children – especially racially and ethnically minoritised and/or poor children – being positioned as struggling, disengaged, even as 'behaviours' (Learned, 2016; Masterson, 2020). What will it take to change the way educators, policymakers and education researchers think about how they position children and how those positionings push children away from school literacies? What will it take for the adults in charge to recognise the literacy and cultural assets and skills children and youth bring to school as resources for engaging in the literacy and other learning tasks valued in school (Moje, Overby, Tysvaer & Morris, 2008)?

From my perspective, all the chapters in this section – and this entire volume – are about how students both learn literacies that help them navigate new contexts and about the navigating that is required to learn the new literacies required in those new contexts. Think about that for a moment: Transitioning and navigating *both require and produce* literacy skills for transitioning and navigating. We might call this idea 'necessary literacies', evoking the conundrum of 'necessary knowledge' for reading to learn (Moje & Speyer, 2014), or the idea that one must bring certain kinds of knowledge to a reading to be able to learn new knowledge from the reading. In the same way, literacy skills build on each other and allow children to navigate the learning of new literacies. A good example is the literacy skill of recognising that words have multiple meanings. We know that it is not enough for children simply to know more words (Townsend, Barber, Carter & Salas, 2020). We know that the more vocabulary breadth, depth *and flexibility* that children possess, the greater likelihood of proficient reading performance (Thompson, 2003). Readers with the ability to navigate the multiple meanings of words will also be more likely to read new texts, learn new words in those texts, ask challenging questions of those texts and navigate across the multiple texts they have to read and multiple conversations about text they must have each year of their schooling.

Thus, the richer and more multifaceted one's literacy skills become, the more likely that one can navigate, imagine multiple purposes for reading, bring a sense of purpose to their reading or imagine audiences for their writing. And the converse is true: If one is treated to a diet of skill drill that remains focused on mastering only graphophonic codes, then one is less likely to be able to deploy a range of skills necessary for agentic and empowered navigation of transitions. When teachers focus only on the literacies of code breaking, they are not building the 'necessary literacies' for transitioning to new moments of future learning. I want to emphasise here that I am not just referring to the literacy skills necessary to know how to read in later grades but also to the skills necessary for being *readers, writers and thinkers*. Children who are not developing the full range of literacy skills from an early age are not developing the full range of future learning options. The children who were shown to be struggling in Chapter 13 knew how to read, but they were not readers, writers and thinkers (at least not in the ways that gave them agency in school; had we seen them in another context, reading texts that mattered, then we might have seen very different children).

In other words, to come full circle, the 'learn to read and then read to learn' dichotomy is patently wrong. Learning to read requires developing skill in all the resources necessary for reading, from the first moment of instruction. And for some children these resources are developed but not necessarily in school. What is devastating about this conundrum is that the children who demonstrate successful robust reading skills (probably bolstered by something that happened at home before school) are the ones who get more support for developing the necessary resources of reader as meaning maker, text user and text critic, whereas the children who do not demonstrate those resources are fed a diet of code-breaking activities in school. The conundrum of the relationship between necessary and aspirational literacies (one needs the skill to attain more skill) implicates Stanovich's (1986) concept of Matthew effects, in which the rich get richer, and the poor get poorer. That certainly seems to be evident in the Rutherford Vale et al. chapter, wherein the youth who are hungry to learn 'Kennings and metonymy' succeed in school, and those who probably do not even know that they could care about the terms, struggle.

Finally, all the chapters about transitions compel me to ask the question of whether literacy researchers, practitioners and policymakers have challenged people to ask – and answer – the hard question about what is literacy for? Why do we read and write? What motivates acts of literacy? The old debates about the so-called science of reading are once again rearing their ugly heads, obfuscating the real questions that we should be asking: Are we doing enough to engage children in reading and writing for meaningful purposes? Do we care about why people read? Do we help children understand why people read and write? If we did, then we would not have to debate whether children should learn phonics *or* comprehension. We would recognise that they need both and more. We would not have to worry about teaching children to put punctuation in the 'correct' place when they write because they would be motivated to communicate in meaningful and clear ways. We would be striving to engage children in the full range of what literate activities and literate identities can *do* for them, and in that striving, we would teach the necessary literacies – or the resources – that children need to navigate not only school transitions but also the many challenging transitions (e.g. pandemics, racial injustices, political chaos) they will encounter in the multiple contexts of their lives.

# Epilogue: Ways to Transition Forward

Pauline Jones, Erika Matruglio and Christine Edwards-Groves

In this final section, we ask questions of, and make recommendations for, transition-specific theory and research, policy and practice. The work represented in this volume proceeded being mindful of the 'taken-for-granted' key transition points (preschool to early school; early school to middle primary; late primary to early secondary; and early secondary to late secondary). It offers researchers, curriculum and policy writers, teachers and teacher educators a picture of literacy development as it is experienced by participants and enacted in their educational communities. In doing so, the contributors problematise the view of literacy development as a process of transitioning from one educational point to another, suggesting that literacy development involves a multiplicity of transition points which operate on different time scales, in different spaces and with different consequences for learners and teachers alike. The book posits that there are many ways to consider transitions: the day-to-day transitions that occur in the lives of teachers and students, from activity-to-activity, subject-to-subject, year-by-year transitions that occur as young people progress through schooling, and the transitions they experience from home literacy practices to those at school. For the students whose accounts are reported in this volume, experiences of transition involve opportunities and challenges that present as particular moments and accumulate over time as trajectories which shape their literate identities. Drawing on a range of theoretical and analytical approaches, chapters in this volume offer a multi-perspective spectrum of accounts, demands and practices of literacy transitions as a necessary way forward for advancing current understandings and practices about literacy pedagogy (including the junctures and disjunctures they afford) across the years of schooling.

## The Research Questions

The following overarching research question framed the TRANSLIT study: *What is the nature of students' literacy experiences at critical transition points in schooling?*

This question was addressed in the following sub-questions: (i) What are the literacy demands at critical transition points? In other words: What literacy demands are evident in curriculum? How do teachers perceive these demands? What literacy practices are evident in classroom practice? (ii) How do students experience the literacy demands at critical transition points? In other words: How do students perceive these demands? How do students respond to these demands? (iii) What contextual factors are involved in teachers' and students' responses to these demands?

With respect to *the literacy demands of the curriculum*, elsewhere it has been argued that the curriculum presents a set of skills and understandings that follow a fairly normative developmental model (Hayes, 2018). Yet, the research base with respect to literacy development is far from complete (Weekes, Chapter 2), particularly with respect to literacy in the later years of primary school and into the secondary years, and the relations between different aspects of literacy (oral language, reading/viewing and writing/composing) in the development of individuals' literacy repertoires. If, as Derewianka (Chapter 3) points out, the interests of researchers and curriculum writers do not align, the 'more coherent developmental pathway' necessary to inform literacy curriculum and pedagogy will remain elusive. Several contributors call into question a number of the dichotomies that are tied to transitions – learning-to-read versus reading-to-learn, common-sense knowledge versus educational. These are false dichotomies because, as Moje (Envoi Part III) argues, such skills and knowledge exist in interaction with each other. Similarly, Kindenberg and Freebody (Chapter 4) remind us of Vygotsky's ([1934] 1978) view that development takes place as certain semiotic, cognitive and social functions develop and connect to other functions, scaffolded by expert guidance in the context of discipline-related activity.

We ask, therefore, how is it that curriculum is constructed on such a slim research base? It is possible to question the very idea of curriculum levels; for example, why is a language feature like passive voice prescribed for Year 9 and not Year 6 when children must engage with sequential and factorial explanation texts? Or perhaps we might delay introducing science with its complex literacy demands until the upper primary years? Should curriculum be treated as an enactment of practices in increasingly specialised disciplinary contexts rather than an idealised rendering of what students need to know and do?

There is a folk wisdom around transition that identifies key points such as preschool to the first year, third year to fourth year, and sixth year to seventh year, but these are partly a product of the institutionalisation of schooling and partly due to the formalisation of curriculum that both reflects and reinforces issues. Despite the attempt in some curricula to account for learner diversity through the division of learning into two-year stages, the national curriculum in Australia is organised into year levels. We ask whether year levels are appropriate ways of sequencing curriculum. Or, might we have three to four broad descriptions of what could constitute curriculum content for students aged five to fifteen?

*Teachers' perceptions* of the curriculum demands were often described in terms of the skills and attributes required of students for successful progression. Matruglio (Chapter 10) writes of the challenges for teachers of balancing the diversity of needs of the students in their classrooms with ensuring they are ready for the next stages of learning. Students' capabilities tended to be tied up with independence, intrinsic motivation and the ability to think critically, with the result that transition difficulties often resulted in the reinforcement of learners as particular types of learner, for example, independent, high-achieving, struggling. Poignantly, teachers' accounts of their practice often featured regret that the reality of their classrooms was not as they wished them to be. The challenges for teachers were also apparent to Mantei and Kervin (Chapter 11) who write of the pressures on early years teachers, as they face an avalanche of curriculum and policy documents, and of professional learning programmes and commercial resources, endorsed variously by district officials, professional associations, social and mainstream media. They argue for a system-based approach to resourcing literacy curriculum so that teachers can deliver the rich, coherent literacy programmes anticipated by the curriculum and policy writers.

Close examination of *the literacy practices in classroom practices* reveals some continuities, but overwhelmingly many discontinuities were reported (in particular, see Chapter 6 by Edwards-Groves, Freebody and Garoni). The contributions together demonstrate how literacy skills and dispositions specialised to curriculum disciplines are increasingly valued in school classrooms, and that this specialisation is evident from early in the primary years. In particular, the observations of classroom practice reported demonstrate the importance of attending to the unfolding interactions between teacher and students in order to understand the increasing complexity of literacy learning and teaching. At some points, pedagogic practice remained remarkably similar, but for others, the difference was marked. The researchers reveal both tacit and overt classroom practices and in doing so problematise many of the 'taken-for-granted' assumptions of literacy pedagogy. A number of contributors argue for a more explicit pedagogy: one that makes procedures, practices and the changing demands of the school curricula more explicit, while at the same time mindful of the need for movement between strongly framed teacher-fronted pedagogic moments and those more loosely framed where learners have more latitude over goings-on (Martin, 1999).

Literacy pedagogy observed by contributors differed considerably across the years from preschool to secondary school. Despite similarities in the nature of literacy experiences offered in the preschool and first year of school sites, Kervin and Mantei (Chapter 5) identify differences in the ways literacy was organised with respect to timing (duration and flexibility), interactions (degree of formality) and resources (purposes). In their detailed observations of pedagogical interactions from early primary, later primary and upper secondary classes, Edwards-Groves, Freebody and Garoni (Chapter 6) observed a distinct trajectory across literacy in English and history that progressed from knowing how to 'do' literacy lessons to 'doing literacy' (e.g. writing a narrative) to learning the 'literacy of different domains'. Chen, Lewis and Rose (Chapter 7) identify another change from early primary to middle primary years English classes evident in distinct differences in knowledge practices observable as the contexts for learning become more demanding of reasoning skills from early on in students' school trajectories. Turney and Rutherford Vale's (Chapter 9) study of students' writing in science reveals considerable shift in literacy demands across the primary–secondary school divide in terms of the genres encountered, the increased salience of image, the degree of technicality and condensation of meaning in image and language – all of which suggest that this transition point is potentially risky and that closer attention to discipline-based literacy pedagogy in both upper primary and lower secondary is warranted. The data collected during the project suggest that literacy pedagogy changes across subject contexts as well as across the years of schooling, amplifying the need for closer examination of literacy development both horizontally (across disciplines) as well as vertically (across the years).

In making a case for more explicit pedagogy, Jones, Matruglio and Rose (Chapter 8) found that pedagogic practices around literature in the upper primary and lower secondary English classrooms observed were similar in their instructional goals (i.e. to develop an informed appreciation of poetic texts). However, students in both years were not taught explicitly how to access the metaphorised meanings necessary for appreciating the themes of poetry, with the result that success remained with a few students who either intuit the means to do so or learn to outside of school.

*Students' experiences of literacy demands* are understandably difficult to investigate across the years because students are not often asked to articulate their experiences of learning to be literate. Edwards-Groves and Freebody (Chapter 12) problematise the practice of interviewing primary school students, pointing out that these are complex situations for children to reflect upon. They argue that the increasing awareness shown by students as they progress through primary school may be less a matter of becoming more mature and therefore reflexive about literacy learning, than it is a matter of students adjusting to the institutional and routinised ways of doing literacy at school.

In their focus on the shift from the primary to the secondary years, Rutherford Vale et al. (Chapter 13) report on students' accounts of how they responded to the transition experience. All of the interviewees recognised differences in the nature and volume of curriculum content, noting the different expectations of secondary school in terms of more homework, the need for better organisational skills and increased independence. Interestingly, students' experiences of transition tended to change over the course of the year; for some, the early bloom diminished with the increased difficulty and specialisation of content in the secondary years. With respect to the achievement gap, high attaining students welcomed the increased specialisation, but others required more support, thus raising questions about curricula continuity and the increasingly complex attendant literacy repertoires required to ensure smooth transitions across the primary–secondary divide. Moje's (Envoi Part III) observation that 'transitioning and navigating *both require and produce* literacy skills for transitioning and navigating' is most perceptive.

Our discussants (Rowsell, Lefstein and Moje) raise questions about *the contextual factors* involved in teachers' and students' responses to the changing nature of literacy demands. Such questions include the nature of literacy itself in contemporary classrooms and its relationship to the literacies children and young people engage with in homes and communities, contemporary debates about the nature of literacy and the narrowing of curricula to 'code-breaking' (Freebody, 1992) and the place of assessment and its role in sorting students. All three discussants raise the important issue of the selection of some literacy practices by schools and delegitimising of others, suggesting a 'mega' transition is necessary to move the current, 'retro' school-based view of literacy to one that recognises the hybrid, multimodal practices of our current milieu, and the need to equip young people with future-oriented literacies. We agree but the project described here focussed on what the teacher participants construed as literacy in a context shaped by high-stakes testing and concerns about falling standards in a highly politicised environment. The result is that outside of the use of technology for researching and publishing texts, explicit attention to digital literacy or the multimodal nature of literacy was not a high priority in the many lessons observed. Nor are such skills well represented in current Australian curricula. Until such time as the multimodal demands of literacy in different curriculum disciplines are described, teachers and schools are left to develop their own responses to what they see as their students' needs.

The issue of assessment was not within the scope of the project reported here, yet high-stakes summative assessment drove many of the practices observed in schools. Australian teachers spend time preparing their students for the national NAPLAN tests undertaken in Years 3, 5, 7 and 9, and in the state of New South Wales for the Year 12 Higher School Certificate – all of which enter into the classrooms as 'horizons of consequence'. At the time of writing, there is considerable debate about the value of these tests and there is little doubt that they do narrow the curriculum. As Macken-Horarik (2009) has argued, no matter what new possibilities a curriculum may offer students and teachers, assessment is a 'reality principle' that sorts and streams students.

In pursuing this research, we have sought to stimulate a robust discussion of school literacy development among the literacy field. In describing the differentiated, fractured and often messy nature of transition, we offer one plausible explanation for differences in literacy outcomes, providing insights into where continuities and discontinuities occur for the participants in our study and prompting examination of literacy transitions and progression more broadly.

Our research problematises grade levels (e.g. 'the grade 3 reader') which are created as objective realities but actually, they are fictional, only some children possess the attributes that constitute successful attainment of curriculum at particular levels. In this book, we offer a set of analytical tools that enable examination of how students struggle at other year levels. Further, we recognise the dangers of attributing learning characteristics to students from early in their school experiences. The problems and challenges that students' attributes present to teachers in their literacy learning can be seen as the products of problems in their literacy learning histories that can, in turn, result in the production of new problems. Such compounding of success and failure, with its 'cognitive, behavioural and motivational consequences' (Stanovich, 1986), means that the child who has had a rough transition at the beginning of the year presents with more problems at the end of the year: the history of where they've been is written on them, it is not something that they have initiated.

We make a case for deploying contributing rather than competing paradigms to consider curriculum as something beyond the 'lamination of student attributes'. We acknowledge that there is work to be done to provide the best possible explanation of literacy growth and development, to identify where and why discontinuities and disjunctions occur and to validate this research and subsequent work on the problem of inequity in literacy outcomes. To inform such renovations of curriculum and pedagogic models, we also argue the case for more longitudinal studies of students' literacy development across a number of more overtly different social, economic and geographical contexts. But above all, we need to address the conception of literacy transitions as a linear progression through discrete points in time, emphasising instead what Myhill (preface) refers to as 'the multi-faceted, pluri-dimensional nature of literacy development'.

# Appendix: Transcription Conventions

The following transcription symbols used in the transcripts have been adapted from Jefferson's notation system.

Atkinson, J. M., & Heritage, J. (1984). Jefferson's transcript notation. In J. M. Atkinson & J. Heritage (Eds.), *Structures of social action: Studies in conversation analysis* (pp. ix–xvi). Cambridge: Cambridge University Press.

**Transcription Conventions**

| | |
|---|---|
| [[ | Utterances that begin at the same time |
| [ | Overlap in speakers' talk |
| ] | Point where simultaneous talk finishes |
| = | Talk between speakers latches of follows without a break |
| () | Indicates length of silence, e.g. (0.2) |
| ::: | Indicates that a prior sound is prolonged, e.g. li::ke |
| - | Word is cut off, e.g. ta- |
| > < | Words enclosed within are said at a faster pace than surrounding talk |
| ? | Rising inflection |
| ¿ | Rising inflection but weaker than? |
| . | Stopping fall in tone |
| , | Continuing intonation |
| ! | Animated tone |
| ↑ | Marked rising pitch |
| ↓ | Marked falling pitch |
| no | Underline indicating greater emphasis |
| CA | Upper case indicates loudness |
| ° | Softness e.g. It's a °secret° |
| hhh | Aspiration or strong out-breath |
| (it is) | Words within are uncertain |
| () | Indicates that some word/s could not be worked out |
| (()) | Verbal descriptions, e.g. ((sits down)) |

Adapted from Atkinson and Heritage (1999).

# Notes

## 4 Transitions in School Literacy: Co-opting Everyday Rationalities

1 Although the focus of Christie and Derewianka's investigation was on students' written texts, their work has implications for our understanding of the shift in complexity found in the texts that students encounter over the school years, a shift paralleling the evolution of writing demands.
2 In evolutionary science, the term 'co-option' describes the fact that some existing traits and abilities of an organism may 'find their purpose' as the environment evolves, rather than being 'evolved' in response to the demands of the existing environment. Transferred to educational settings, co-option captures the notion of a 'postponed purposefulness'.
3 Two of the texts (Exhibits 1 and 2) are taken from student 'work samples' (illustrating assessment criteria) provided online by the Australian Curriculum, Assessing and Reporting Authority (ACARA), a statutory authority responsible for delivering the Australian national curriculum. Exhibit 3 is an editorial from a Swedish newspaper, translated by the first author. So these examples represent different communicative purposes, but for our analytic purposes here they are seen as representing literacy expectations at different stages of Christie and Derewianka's (2008) learning trajectory, and thus relevant to our discussion of 'co-option'.
4 The cosmic microwave background (CMB) radiation, for instance, is defined as 'a faint glow of light that fills the universe, falling on Earth from every direction with nearly uniform intensity'; this explanatory definition is then extended to include the effects and longevity of CMB.

## 5 Transition from Preschool to School: Spaces, Time, Interactions and Resources

1 An initial capital is used when referring to the first year of formal school as it is known in the NSW school system where the research was undertaken.
2 A read-aloud is an instructional practice where an educator reads a text aloud to children. Typically, this text is selected by the educator to meet an intended pedagogical purpose.

## 6 Transitions in Literacy and Classroom Interaction across the School Years

1. We note our strategic and deliberate use of the term 'cultural' in various sections of this chapter as assigning broad relevance and sensemaking to those present in the interactions; shared practices make possible mutual understandings among those of a cultural entity (like a Western cultural use of written stories is understood by members of that culture). For example, in *classroom activities* (like the patterned ways a joint reading of text is conducted, or a particular routine way of asking or answering questions is learned or expected from *the cultural activities* or *cultural work-in-progress* for those then and there), or in *objects* (like picture books or novels in lessons emerge from but return to the practice as *cultural objects* known and experienced by those who use such objects), or *logic* (like developing shared understandings or reasoning in lessons and in everyday life forms the *cultural logic* that makes sense to those who present and those who might enter into that 'shared' understanding or reasoning). Further, see the quote by James Heap (1985) in a subsequent section of this chapter.
2. Detailed descriptions of CA can be found in Schegloff (2007), Hutchby and Wooffitt (2008), and Liddicoat (2011). Collections of CA studies include Antaki (2011) and Sidnell and Stivers (2013).
3. Transcript conventions are provided in appendix.
4. Known in CA as a base adjacency pair, or base pair (Schegloff, 2007).
5. Note the IRF was first delineated by Sinclair and Coulthard (1975); the IRE by Mehan (1979).

## 7 Understanding Literacy Transitions: Pedagogic Practices in Primary Writing Classrooms

1. Figures have changed little since the data were collected.
2. These are pseudonyms to protect anonymity of the teachers.

## 8 Investigating Pedagogic Discourse in Late Primary and Junior Secondary English

1. The idea of schooling as 'apprenticeship' aligns with that of the perpetual 'practicum space' (see Chapter 6).
2. See Mercer et al. (2019) for notable exceptions including Resnick et al. and Webb et al. (dialogue in Mathematics), Tan and Tang (dialogue in Science).

3 Our emphasis here is on students' appreciation of poetry rather than its creation as our data set includes several lessons which focus solely on reading poetry.
4 In the Australian context, most children attend a preschool setting prior to entering school at approximately five to six years of age. They attend primary school until age six when they enter secondary school for grades 7–12, most students completing school at eighteen years of age. The TRANSLIT study focused on preschool to Year 9 (i.e. our participants were between four and fourteen years of age in Year 1 of the study).
5 In terms of genre, *The Rose* is a story type known as *observation*, which condenses events and concludes with a comment (Martin & Rose, 2008).
6 In Table 8.5, the teacher also directs the behaviour of one student 'Bianca, shhh, just listening'. This is an action exchange, in which the teacher demands an action, and Bianca complies non-verbally. Bianca in this case is the primary actor, or A1, while the teacher demands the action, labelled as A2.
7 In Table 8.10 the hands-up routine is analysed as students inviting evaluation and the teacher permitting one student to display for evaluation. The permission here is the primary action (A1), delayed by soliciting a display (dA1).
8 *Migrant Hostel* is an instance of the story genre *anecdote*, which recounts a remarkable event in order to share feelings.
9 See Chapter 6 for a discussion of these as 'epistemic literacies'.
10 Constructivist theories celebrate this assumption but certainly did not originate it.

## 10 Categories, Appraisals and Progress in Literacy Transitions

I gratefully acknowledge the help of Peter Freebody on this chapter. The initial framing of the chapter was developed in discussion with him and he provided useful critique and suggestions throughout the chapter's development.
1 Names of systems are rendered in SMALL CAPS in SFL.
2 All teacher names are pseudonyms to protect participants' anonymity.

## 12 Articulating Education with Primary Students

1 Transcription conventions (after Jefferson, 1984).
   - ^ ˅ mean upward and downward inflection respectively;
   - lo::ong means extended vowel;
   - ((transcriber's comment));
   - comma means brief pause, (n) means n second pause;

- underlined means emphasised;
- = = means tightly connected turns at talk;
- // // means interruption
- >said-very-rapidly<

We represent these paralinguistic features because speakers routinely show that they are relevant to how talk is interpreted when it happens, and therefore to how its transcribed form needs to be interpreted by analysts (Jefferson, 1984; Sacks, Schegloff, & Jefferson, 1974).

2 Line numbering reflects the sequence position of the segment in the overall interview.
3 As a caveat, we note that the student interviews were considered by the researchers as 'edge of seat' events in which students often appeared edgy about the experience, many looking for encouragement. In the interview itself, researchers tried a range of approaches such as sitting alongside (rather than opposite), in sandpits, and so on, to try and manage the newness of the experience for the interviewees.
4 IRE refers to the *Initiation-Response-Evaluation* teacher–student exchange structure identified by Mehan (1979) as the persistent and resistant turn structure comprising institutional talk.

## 13 Transitioning from Primary to High School

1 High-attaining students, identified by teacher assessment, are those who attained entry into a selective or top streamed class in Year 7 and who obtained an A in English or science.
2 Research in the satellite cluster focused particularly on literacy development in science.

# References

## Chapter 1

Alexander, R. (2020). *A dialogic teaching companion*. London: Routledge.

Anderson, L. W., & Krathwohl, D. R. (2001). *A taxonomy for learning, teaching and assessing: A revision of Bloom's taxonomy of educational objects: Complete edition*. New York: Longman.

Bernstein, B. (1996). *Pedagogy, symbolic control and identity*. London: Taylor & Francis.

Berry, M. (1981). Systemic linguistics and discourse analysis: A multilayered approach to exchange structure. In M. Coulthard & M. Montgomery (Eds.), *Studies in discourse analysis* (pp. 120–45). London: Longman.

Bloom, B. S., Engelhart, M. D., Furst, E. J., Hill, W. H. & Krathwohl, D. R. (1956). *Taxonomy of educational objectives: The classification of educational goals. Handbook 1: Cognitive Domain*. New York: David McKay.

Bowles, A., Dobson, A., Fisher, R. & McPhail, R. (2011). *An exploratory investigation into first year student transition to university*. Paper presented at the Research and Development in Higher Education: Reshaping Higher Education, 34 (pp. 61–71). Gold Coast, Australia, 4–7 July 2011.

Christie, F., & Derewianka, B. (2008). *School discourse*. London: Continuum.

Dewey, J., & Archambault, R. D. (1964). *John Dewey on education: Selected writings*. New York: Modern Library.

Evangelou, M., Taggart, B., Sylva, K., Melhuish, E., Sammons, P., & Siraj-Blatchford, I. (2008). *What makes a successful transition from primary to secondary school?* Retrieved from https://dera.ioe.ac.uk/8618/1/DCSF-RR019.pdf.

Feez, S. (2010). *Montessori and early childhood*. London: Sage.

Freebody, P. (2013). *Minutes of scoping meeting for TRANSLIT*. School of Education, University of Wollongong, 3 November 2013.

Garfinkel, H. (1967). *Studies in ethnomethodology*. Englewood Cliffs, NJ: Prentice Hall.

Gonski, D., Arcus, T., Boston, K., Gould, V., Johnson, W., O'Brien, L., … Roberts, M. (2018). *Through growth to achievement: The report of the Review to achieve educational excellence in Australian schools*. Retrieved from https://docs.education.gov.au/system/files/doc/other/662684_tgta_accessible_final.pdf.

Goss, P., Sonnemann, J., & Emslie, O. (2018). *Measuring student progress: A state-by-state report card*. Retrieved from https://grattan.edu.au/report/measuring-student-progress.

Halliday, M. A. K. (1991). The notion of 'context' in language education. In M. Gladessy (Ed.), *Text and context in functional linguistics* (pp. 1–24). Amsterdam: John Benjamins.

Halliday, M. A. K. (1993). Towards a language-based theory of learning. *Linguistics and Education, 5*, 93–116.

Halliday, M. A. K., & Matthiessen, C. (2014). *Halliday's introduction to functional grammar* (4th edn). London: Routledge.

Jones, P. T., Derewianka, B., Freebody, P., Turbill, J., Kervin, L., Chen, H., ... Klasson, L. (2014–18). Transforming Literacy Outcomes (TRANSLIT). University of Wollongong: Australian Govt (DEEWR), University of Wollongong.

Martin, J. R., & Rose, D. (2007). *Working with discourse: Meaning beyond the clause* (2nd edn). London: Continuum.

OECD (2018). *Equity in education: Breaking down barriers to social mobility*. Retrieved from https://www.oecd-ilibrary.org/education/equity-in-education_9789264073234-en.

Orem, R. C. (1966). *A Montessori handbook: 'Dr. Montessori's own handbook'*. New York: Putnam.

Perry, B., Dockett, S. & Petriwskyj, A. (Eds.). (2014). *Transitions to school: International research, policy and practice*. Netherlands: Springer.

Rose, D., & Martin, J. R. (2012). *Learning to write, reading to learn: Genre, knowledge & pedagogy in the Sydney School*. Sheffield: Equinox.

Sacks, H. (1972). An initial investigation of the usability of conversational data for doing sociology. In D. Sudnow (Ed.), *Studies in social interaction* (pp. 31–74). New York: Free Press.

Sacks, H., Schegloff, E. A., & Jefferson, G. (1974). A simplest systematics for the organisation of turn-taking for conversation. *Language, 50*(4), 696–735.

# Chapter 2

ACARA (2013). *General capabilities in the Australian curriculum: Literacy*. Sydney: Author.

ACARA (2019). *2019 NAPLAN results*. Retrieved from https://reports.acara.edu.au/NAP.

# References

Alexander, P. A., & Fox, E. (2010). Adolescents as readers. In M. L. Kamil, P. D. Pearson, E. Birr Moje & P. P. Afflerbach (Eds.), *Handbook of reading research* (pp. 157–73). New York: Routledge.

Alexander, R. (2008). *Towards dialogic teaching: Rethinking classroom talk*. North Yorkshire: Dialogos.

Andrews, R., Torgerson, C., Beverton, S., Freeman, A., Locke, T., Low, G., ... Zhu, D. (2006). The effect of grammar teaching on writing development. *British Educational Research Journal, 32*(1), 39–55.

Applebee, A. (2000). Alternative models of writing development. In R. Indrisano & J. R. Squire (Eds.), *Writing: Research/theory/practice* (pp. 90–110). Newark, DE: International Reading Association.

Beck, I. L., McKeown, M. G. & Kucan, L. (2013). *Bringing words to life: Robust vocabulary instruction*. New York: Guilford Press.

Beers, S. F., & Nagy, W. E. (2009). Syntactic complexity as a predictor of adolescent writing quality: Which measures? Which genre? *Reading and Writing, 22*(2), 185–200.

Bereiter, C., & Scardamalia, M. (2013). *The psychology of written composition*. New York: Routledge.

Bernstein, B. (1975). *Class, codes and control: Volume 3: Towards a theory of educational transmissions*. London: Routledge and Kegan Paul.

Bloomfield, L. ([1914] 1933). *Language*. New York: Henry Holt.

Brisk, M. E. (2015). *Engaging students in academic literacies: Genre-based pedagogy for K-5 classrooms*. New York: Routledge.

Britton, J. N., Burgess, T., Martin, N., McLeod, A. & Rosen, H. (1975). *The development of writing abilities (11–18)*. London: Macmillan.

Buckingham, J., Wheldall, K. & Beaman-Wheldall, R. (2013). Why Jaydon can't read: The triumph of ideology over evidence in teaching reading. *Policy: A Journal of Public Policy and Ideas, 29*(3), 21–32.

Castles, A., Rastle, K. & Nation, K. (2018). Ending the reading wars: Reading acquisition from novice to expert. *Psychological Science in the Public Interest, 19*, 5–51.

Chall, J. (1967). *Learning to read: The great debate*. New York: McGraw Hill.

Chall, J. (1983). *Stages of reading development*. New York: McGraw Hill.

Chambers, B., Cheung, A. C. K. & Slavin, R. E. (2016). *Literacy and language outcomes of comprehensive and developmental-constructivist approaches to Early Childhood Education: A systematic review*. Baltimore, MD: Centre for Research and Reform in Education.

Chen, H., & Myhill, D. (2016). Children talking about writing: Investigating metalinguistic understanding. *Linguistics and Education, 35*, 100–108.

Christie, F. (2010). Literacy as a theme in educational theory and policy. In F. Christie & A. Simpson (Eds.), *Literacy and social responsibility: Multiple perspectives* (pp. 9–23). London: Equinox.

Christie, F., & Derewianka, B. (2008). *School discourse.* London: Continuum.

Coch, D. (2017). Learning to read: The science of reading in the classroom. In J. Cooney Horvath, J. M. Lodge & J. Hattie (Eds.), *From the laboratory to the classroom. Translating the science of learning for teachers* (pp. 191–212). London: Routledge.

Cole, P., Jane, G., Suggett, D. & Wardlaw, C. (2016). *Gender differences in Years 6–7 literacy and numeracy transition outcomes.* Melbourne, VIC: Victorian Auditor General.

Coltheart, M., & Prior, M. (2007). *Learning to read in Australia. Policy Paper No. 6.* Canberra ACT: Academy of Social Sciences in Australia.

Coxhead, A. (2012). Researching vocabulary in secondary school English texts: 'The hunger games' and more. *English in Aotearoa (78)* (October 2012), 34–41.

Cummins, J. (2008). BICS and CALP: Empirical and theoretical status of the distinction. In B. Street & N.H. Hornberger (Eds.), *Encyclopedia of language and education. 2nd edition. Volume 2: Literacy.* New York: Springer Science + Business New Media LLC.

De La Paz, S., & Graham, S. (2002). Explicitly teaching strategies, skills, and knowledge: Writing instruction in Middle School classrooms. *Journal of Educational Psychology, 94*(4), 687–698.

de Silva Joyce, H., & Feez, D. (2016). *Exploring literacies: Theory, research and practice.* London: Palgrave Macmillan.

Dinham, S., & Rowe, K. (2008). *Fantasy, fashion and fact: Middle schools, middle schooling and student achievement.* Paper presented at the British Educational Research Association Annual Conference, Heriot-Watt University, Edinburgh.

Donovan, C. A., & Smolkin, L. B. (2008). Children's understanding of genre and writing development. In C. MacArthur, S. Graham & J. Fitzgerald (Eds.), *Handbook of writing research* (pp. 131–43). New York: Guilford Press.

Ehri, L. C. (1999). Phases of development in learning to read words. In J. Oakhill & R. Beard (Eds.), *Reading, development and the teaching of reading: A psychological perspective* (pp. 79–108). Oxford: Blackwell Science.

Ehri, L. C., Nunes, S. R., Willows, D. M., Schuster, B. V., Yaghoub-Zadeh, Z. & Shanahan, T. (2001). Phonemic awareness instruction helps children learn to read: Evidence from the National Reading Panel's meta-analysis. *Reading Research Quarterly, 36*(3), 250.

Elliott, J. G., & Grigorenko, E. L. (2014). *The Dyslexia debate*. New York: Cambridge University Press.

Fang, Z., & Schleppegrell, M. (2010). Disciplinary literacies across content areas: Supporting secondary reading through functional language analysis. *Journal of Adolescent & Adult Literacy, 53*(7), 587–97.

Flanigan, K., & Greenwood, S. C. (2007). Effective content vocabulary instruction in the middle: Matching students, purposes, words and strategies. *Journal of Adolescent and Adult Literacy, 51*, 226–38.

Flesch, R. (1955). *Why Johnny can't read: And what you can do about it*. New York: Harper and Row.

Foorman, B., Beyler, N., Borradaile, K., Coyne, M., Denton, C.A., Dimino, J., Furgeson, J., Hayes, L., & Henke, J., Justice, L., Keating, B., Lewis, W., Sattar, S., Streke, A., Wagner, R., & Wissel, S. (2016). *Foundational skills to support reading for understanding in Kindergarten through 3rd Grade (NCEE2016–4008)*. Washington, DC: National Center for Education Evaluation and Regional Assistance (NCEE), Institute of Education Sciences, U.S. Department of Education.

Freebody, P. (2013). Knowledge and school talk: Intellectual accommodations to literacy? *Linguistics and Education, 24*, 4–7.

Freebody, P., & Luke, A. (1990). Literacies programs: Debates and demands in cultural context. *Prospect, 5*, 7–16.

Fricke, S., Bowyer-Crane, C., Haley, A. J., Hulme, C., & Snowling, M. J. (2013). Efficacy of language intervention in the early years. *Journal of Child Psychology and Psychiatry and Allied Disciplines, 54*(3), 280–90.

Frith, U. (1985). Beneath the surface of developmental dyslexia. In K. Patterson, J. Marcshall & M. Coltheart (Eds.), *Surface dyslexia, neuropsychological and cognitive studies of phonological reading* (pp. 301–30). London: Erlbaum.

Funnell, E., Hughes, D. & Woodcock, J. (2006). Age of acquisition for naming and knowing: A new hypothesis. *Quarterly Journal of Experimental Psychology, 59*, 268–95.

Gibbons, P. (2009). *English learners, academic literacy and thinking. Learning in the challenge zone*. Portsmouth, NH: Heinemann.

Goodman, K. (1967). Reading: a psycholinguistic guessing game. In H. Singer & R. B. Ruddell (Eds.), *Language and literacy: The selected writings of Kenneth Goodman* (vol. 1, pp. 93–102). Boston: Routledge and Kegan Paul.

Graham, S., Bruch, J., Fitzgerald, J., Friedrich, L., Furgeson, J., Greene, K., ... Smither Wulsin, C. (2016). *Teaching secondary students to write effectively (NCEE 2017–4002)*. Washington DC: National Centre for Education Evaluation and Regional Assistance (NCEE), Institute of Education Sciences, U.S. Department of Education.

Graham, S., & Perin, D. (2007). A meta-analysis of writing instruction for adolescent students. *Journal of Educational Psychology, 99*(3), 445–76.

Graves, D. H. (1983). *Writing: teachers and children at work*. Portsmouth, NH: Heinemann Educational.

Halliday, M. A. K. (1975). *Learning how to mean*. London: Edward Arnold.

Halliday, M. A. K. ([1993] 2004). Towards a language-based theory of learning. In J. Webster (Ed.), *The language of early childhood: Volume 4 in the Collected Works of M.A.K. Halliday* (pp. 327–52). London: Continuum.

Hammer, C. S., Hoff, E., Uchikoshi, Y., Gillanders, C., Castro, D. C., & Sandilos, L. E. (2014). The language and literacy development of young dual language learners: A critical review. *Early Childhood Research Quarterly, 29*(4), 715–33.

Hanewald, R. (2013). Transition between primary and secondary school: Why it is important and how it can be supported. *Australian Journal of Teacher Education, 38*(1), 62–74.

Harpin, W. (1976). *The Second 'R'. Writing development in the Junior School*. London: Allen and Unwin.

Hill, S., Comber, B., Louden, W., Rivalland, J., & Reid, J. (2002). *100 children turn 10: A longitudinal study of literacy development from the year prior to school to the first four years of school*. Canberra: Commonwealth of Australia.

Hulme, C., Bowyer-Crane, C., Carroll, J. M., Duff, F. J. & Snowling, M. J. (2012). The causal role of phoneme awareness and letter-sound knowledge in learning to read: Combining intervention studies with mediation analyses. *Psychological Science, 23*, 572.

Humphrey, S. (2017). *Academic literacies in the middle years: Enhancing teacher knowledge and student achievement*. London: Routledge.

Jones, S., Myhill, D. & Bailey, T. (2013). Grammar for writing? An investigation of the effects of contextualised grammar teaching on students' writing. *Reading and Writing, 26*(8), 1241–63.

Kent, S. C., & Wanzek, J. (2016). The relationship between component skills and writing quality and production across developmental levels: A meta-analysis of the last 25 years. *Review of Educational Research, 86*(2), 570–601.

Kim, J. S. (2008). Research and the reading wars. In F. M. Hess (Ed.), *When research matters: How scholarship influences Education Policy* (pp. 89–111). Cambridge, MA: Harvard Education Press.

Konza, D., & Michael, M. (2010). Supporting the literacy of diverse students in secondary schools. *International Journal of Learning, 17*(7), 193–208.

Koole, T. (2011). Displays of epistemic access: Student responses to teacher explanations. *Research on Language & Society, 43*(2), 183–209.

Krakouer, J., Mitchell, P., Trevitt, J. & Kochanoff, A. (2017). *Early years transitions. Supporting children and families at risk of experiencing vulnerability: Rapid literature review.* Melbourne: Department of Education and Training Victoria.

Kucan, L., & Sullivan Palincsar, A. (2010). Locating struggling readers in a reconfigured landscape: A conceptual review. In M. L. Kamil, P. D. Pearson, E. Birr Moje & P. P. Afflerbach (Eds.), *Handbook of reading research* (pp. 349–60). New York: Routledge.

Langer, J. A. (1986). *Children reading and writing: Structures and strategies.* Norwood, NJ: Ablex.

Langer, J. A. (2001). Beating the odds: Teaching middle and high school students to read and write well. *American Educational Research Journal, 38*(4), 837–80.

Language and Reading Research Consortium, & Logan, J. (2017). Pressure points in reading comprehension: A quantile multiple regression analysis. *Journal of Educational Psychology, 109,* 451–64.

Lee, N., Mikesell, L., Joaquin, A. D. L., Mates, A. W. & Schumann, J. H. (2009). *The interactional instinct: The evolution and acquisition of language.* New York: Oxford University Press.

Lepola, J., Lynch, J., Kiuru, N., Laakkonen, E. & Niemi, P. (2016). Early oral language comprehension, task orientation, and foundational reading skills as predictors of Grade 3 reading comprehension. *Reading Research Quarterly, 51*(4), 373–90.

Loban, W. (1976). *Language development: Kindergarten through Grade Twelve. INCITE Committee on Research Report No. 18.* Washington, DC: National Council of Teachers of English; Office of Education (DHEW).

Louden, W., Rohl, M. & Hopkins, S. (2008). *Teaching for growth: Effective teaching of literacy and numeracy.* Perth: Western Australian Department of Education and Training.

Love, K., Macken-Horarik, M. & Horarik, S. (2015). Language knowledge and its application: A snapshot of Australian teachers' views. *Australian Journal of Language and Literacy, 38,* 171–82.

Luke, A., Elkins, J., Weir, K., Land, R., Carrington, V., Dole, S., … Rod Chadbourne, T. B., Donna Alverman and Lisa Stevens. (2003). *Beyond the middle.* St Lucia, Brisbane: School of Education, University of Queensland.

Martin, J. R., & Rose, D. (2008). *Genre relations: Mapping culture.* London: Equinox.

Masters, G. (2019). *Nurturing wonder and igniting passion: Designs for a future school curriculum. NSW Curriculum Review Interim Report*. Sydney: NSW Education Standards Authority.

Meiers, M., Khoo, S. T., Rowe, K., Stephanou, A., Anderson, P. & Nolan, K. (2006). *Growth in literacy and numeracy in the first three years of school: ACER research monograph; n. 61*. Melbourne: ACER.

Mercer, N., & Howe, C. (2012). Explaining the dialogic processes of teaching and learning: The value and potential of sociocultural theory. *Learning, Culture and Social Interaction, 1*(1), 12–21.

Miller, J. F., Andriacchi, K. & Nockerts, A. (2016). Using language sample analysis to assess spoken language production in adolescents. *Language Speech and Hearing Services in Schools, 47*(2), 99–112.

Moje, E. B. (2008). Foregrounding the disciplines in secondary literacy teaching and learning: A call for change. *Journal of Adolescent & Adult Literacy, 52*(2), 96–107.

Morris, D., Bloodgood, J. W., Lomax, R. G. & Perney, J. (2003). Developmental steps in learning to read: A longitudinal study in kindergarten and first grade. *Reading Research Quarterly, 38*(3), 302–28.

Myhill, D., & Jones, S. (2006). *Patterns and processes: The linguistic characteristics and composing processes of secondary school writers*. Technical Report RES-000-23-0208 to the Economic and Social Research Council.

Myhill, D., Jones, S., Watson, A. & Lines, H. (2013). Playful explicitness with grammar: A pedagogy for writing. *Literacy, 47*(2), 103–11.

Myhill, D., & Watson, A. (2014). The role of grammar in the writing curriculum: A review of the literature. *Child Language Teaching and Therapy, 30*(1), 41–62.

Nagy, W. E., & Anderson, R. C. (1984). How many words are there in printed school English? *Reading Research Quarterly, 19*, 304–30.

Nation, K., & Snowling, M. J. (2004). Beyond phonological skills: Broader language skills contribute to the development of reading. *Journal of Research in Reading, 27*(4), 342–56.

National Early Literacy Panel (2008). *Developing early literacy: Report of the National Early Literacy Panel*. Washington, DC: National Institute for Literacy.

National Reading Panel (2000). *Report of the National Reading Panel: Teaching children to read*. Washington, DC: U.S. Department of Health and Human Services.

Nippold, M. A., Mansfield, T. C., & Billow, J. L. (2007). Peer conflict explanations in children, adolescents, and adults: Examining the development of complex syntax. *American Journal of Speech-Language Pathology, 16*(2), 179–88.

Nippold, M. A., Ward-Lonergan, J. M., & Fanning, J. L. (2005). Persuasive writing in children, adolescents, and adults: A study of syntactic, semantic, and pragmatic development. *Language, Speech, and Hearing Services in Schools, 36*(2), 125–38.

Owens, R. E. (2012). *Language development: An introduction*. Boston, MA: Pearson.
Painter, C. (1984). *Into the mother tongue*. London: Bloomsbury.
Paratore, J. R., Cassano, C .M. & Schickedanz, J. A. (2010). Supporting early (and later) literacy development at home and at school. In M. L. Kamil, P. D. Pearson, E. Birr Moje & P. P. Afflerbach (Eds.), *Handbook of reading research* (pp. 107–26). New York: Routledge.
Paris, S. (2005). Reinterpreting the development of reading skills. *Reading Research Quarterly*, 40(2), 184–202.
Paris, S. G., & Luo, S. W. (2010). Confounded statistical analyses hinder interpretation of the NELP Report. *Educational Researcher*, 39(4), 316–22.
Parsons, S., Schoon, I., Rush, R. & Law, J. (2011). Long-term outcomes for children with early language problems: Beating the odds. *Children and Society*, 25(3), 202–14.
Perera, K. (1984). *Children's writing and reading: Analysing classroom language*. London: Blackwell.
Perera, K. (1985). *Grammatical differentiation between speech and writing in children aged 8 to 12*. Paper presented at the Annual meeting of the International Writing Convention, Norwich, England.
Piaget, J. (1970). *Science of education and the psychology of the child*. Harmondsworth, Middelsex: Penguin Books.
Pugh, K., & McCardle, P. D. (2009). Conclusion: Integration of methodologies in cognitive neuroscience-research, planning, and policy. In K. Pugh & P. D. McCardle (Eds.), *How children learn to read: Current issues and new directions in the integration of cognition, neurobiology and genetics of reading and dyslexia research and practice* (pp. 301–11). New York: Psychology Press.
Purdie, N., Reid, K., Frigo, T., Stone, A. & Kleinhenz, E. (2011). *Literacy and numeracy learning: Lessons from the longitudinal literacy and numeracy study for Indigenous students*. Camberwell, VIC: Australian Council for Educational Research.
Rose, D., & Martin, J. R. (2012). *Learning to write, reading to learn. Genre, knowledge and pedagogy in the Sydney School*. Sheffield: Equinox.
Rose, J. (2006). *Independent review of the teaching of early reading*. Nottingham: Department for Education and Skills.
Sanacore, J., & Palumbo, A. (2008). Understanding the fourth-grade slump: Our point of view. *Educational Forum*, 73(1), 67–74.
Scott, C. M., & Windsor, J. (2000). General language performance measures in spoken and written narrative and expository discourse of school-age children with language learning disabilities. *Journal of Speech, Language, and Hearing Research*, 43, 324–39.

Shanahan, T., & Lomax, R.G. (1986). An analysis and comparison of theoretical models of the reading – writing relationship. *Journal of Educational Psychology*, 78, 116–23.

Shanahan, T., & Shanahan, C. (2008). Teaching disciplinary literacy to adolescents: Rethinking content area literacy. *Harvard Educational Review*, 78(1), 40–59.

Skinner, B. F. (1974). *About behaviorism*. New York: Random House.

Smagorinsky, P. (1987). Graves revisted: A look at the methods and conclusions of the New Hampshire study. *Written Communication*, 14, 331–42.

Smith, J., & Elley. (1998). *How children learn to write*. London: Longman.

Snow, C., Griffin, P., & Burns, S. M. (2005). *A knowledge to support the teaching of reading: Preparing teachers for a changing world*. San Francisco, CA: Jossey-Bass.

Stanovich, K. (1986). Matthew effects in reading: Some consequences of individual differences in the acquisition of literacy. *Reading Research Quarterly*, 21(4), 360–406.

Struthers, L., Lapadat, J. C., & MacMillan, P. D. (2013). Assessing cohesion in children's writing: Development of a checklist. *Assessing Writing*, 18(3), 187–201.

Thomas, W. P., & Collier, V. P. (1997). *School effectiveness for language minority students*. Washington, DC: National Clearinghouse for Bilingual Education, George Washington University.

Thomson, S., Hillman, K., Wernert, N., Schmid, M., Buckley, S., & Munene, A. (2012). *Monitoring Australian year 4 student achievement internationally: TIMSS and PIRLS 2011*. Melbourne: Australian Council for Educational Research (ACER).

Vygotsky, L. S. (1978). *Mind in society: The development of higher psychological processes*. Cambridge, MA: Harvard University Press.

Walberg, H. J., & Tsai, S. (1983). Matthew effects in education. *American Educational Research Journal*, 20, 359–73.

Westerveld, M. F., & Moran, C. A. (2011). Expository language skills of young school-age children. *Language, Speech & Hearing Services in Schools*, 42(2), 182–93.

Whitehurst, G. J., & Lonigan, C. J. (1998). Child development and emergent literacy. *Child development*, 69, 848–72.

Wilkinson, A., Barnsley, G., Hanna, P. & Swan, M. (1980). *Assessing language development*. London: Oxford University Press.

Wray, D., & Medwell, J. (2006). *Progression in writing and the Northern Ireland Levels for Writing: A research review undertaken for CCEA*. Warwick: University of Warwick.

Xue, Y., & Meisels, S. (2004). Early literacy instruction and learning in Kindergarten: Evidence from the early childhood longitudinal study

– Kindergarten class of 1998–1999. *American Educational Research Journal, 41*, 191–229.

# Chapter 3

Alamargot, D., & Fayol, M. (2009). Modelling the development of written composition. In R. Beard, D. Myhill, M. Nystrand & J. Riley (Eds.), *Handbook of writing development* (pp. 23–47). London: Sage.

Andrews, R., Hoffman, J. & Wyse, D. (2010). Implications for research, policy and practice. In D. Wyse, R. Andrews & J. Hoffman (Eds.), *The Routledge international handbook of English, language and literacy teaching* (pp. 531–8). Oxon: Routledge.

Andrews, R., & Smith, A. (2011). *Developing writers: Teaching and learning in the digital age*. UK: McGraw Hill.

Applebee, A.N. (1981). *Writing in the Secondary School: English and the content areas*. Urbana, IL: National Council of Teachers of English.

Bazerman, C. (2004). Speech acts, genres, and activity systems: How texts organize activity and people. In C. Bazerman & P. Prior (Eds.), *What writing does and how it does it: An introduction to analyzing texts and textual practices* (pp. 309–40). London: Routledge.

Bazerman, C., Applebee, A. N., Berninger, V., Brandt, D., Graham, S., Matsuda, P. K., Murphy, S., Rowe, D. W. & Schleppegrell, M. (2017), Taking the long view on writing development. *Research in the Teaching of English, 51*(3), 351–60. United States: National Council of Teachers of English.

Beard, R., Myhill, D., Nystrand, M. & Riley, J. (2009). General Introduction. In R. Beard, D. Myhill, M. Nystrand & J. Riley (Eds.), *The SAGE Handbook of Writing Development* (pp. 1–5). London: SAGE.

Bereiter, C. (1980). Development in writing. In L. W. Gregg & E. R. Steinberg (Eds.), *Cognitive processes in writing* (pp. 73–96). Hillsdale, NJ: LEA.

Bereiter, C. & Scardamalia, M. (1987). *The psychology of written composition*. Hillsdale, NJ: Lawrence Erlbaum Associates.

Berninger, V. (1996). *Reading and writing acquisition: A developmental neuropsychological perspective*. Colorado: Westview Press.

Bernstein, B. (1990). *The structuring of pedagogic discourse*. London: Routledge.

Britton, J.N., Burgess, T., Martin, N., McLeod, A. & Rosen, H. (1975). *The development of writing abilities (11–18)*. Urbana, IL: National Council of Teachers of English.

Burtis, P.J., Bereiter, C., Scardamalia, M. & Tetroe, J. (1983). The development of planning in writing. In C. G. Wells & B. Kroll (Eds.), *Explorations of children's development in writing* (pp. 153–74). Chichester, England: John Wiley.

Case, R. (1985). *Intellectual development: Birth to adulthood*. New York: Academic Press.

Christie, F. (2010). The ontogenesis of writing in childhood and adolescence. In D. Wyse, R. Andrews & J. Hoffman (Eds.), *The international handbook of English, language and literacy teaching* (pp. 146–58). London: Routledge/Taylor and Francis.

Christie, F., & Derewianka, B. (2008). *School discourse: Learning to write across the years of schooling*. London: Continuum.

Derewianka, B., & Jones, P. (2016), *Teaching language in context* (2nd edn). South Melbourne, Australia: Oxford University Press.

Flower, L., & Hayes, J.R. (1981). Cognitive process theory of writing. *College Composition and Communication, 32*(4), 365–87.

Garcia-Debanc, C., & Fayol, M. (2013). About the psycholinguistic models of the writing process for a didactics of written production. *Repères* [En ligne], Hors-série, http://journals.openedition.org/reperes/505. doi:10.4000/reperes.505.

Graves, D. (1983). *Writing: Teachers and children at work*. Exeter, NH: Heinemann.

Haas, C. (2013). *Writing technology: Studies on the materiality of literacy*. New York: Routledge.

Hayes, J. R., & Flower, L. S. (1980). Identifying the organization of writing processes. In L. W. Gregg & E. R. Steinberg (Eds.), *Cognitive processes in writing* (pp. 3–30). Hillsdale, NJ: L.E.A.

Hyland, K. (2001). Bringing in the reader. *Written Communication, 18*(4), 549–74.

Hyland, K. (2011). Issues in theory, research and pedagogy. In R. M. Manchón (Ed.), *Learning-to-write and writing-to-learn in an additional language*. Amsterdam: John Benjamins.

Jacobs, G. M. (2004). A classroom investigation of the growth of metacognitive awareness in kindergarten children through the writing process. *Early Childhood Education Journal, 32*(1), 17–23.

Langer, J. A. (1986). *Children reading and writing: Structures and strategies*. Norwood, NJ: Ablex.

Martin, J. R. (2009). Genre and language learning: A social semiotic perspective. *Linguistics and Education, 20*(1), 10–21.

Myhill, D. (2009). Becoming a designer: Trajectories of linguistic development. In R. Beard, D. Myhill, J. Riley & D. Nystrand (Eds.), *Handbook of writing development* (pp. 402–14). London: Sage.

Myhill, D., & Chen, H. (2020). Developing writers in primary and secondary school years. In H. Chen, D. Myhill & H. Lewis (Eds.) *Developing writers across the Primary and Secondary Years: Growing into writing.* London: Routledge.

Nystrand, M. (1989). A social-interactive model of writing. *Written Communication,* 6(1), 66–85.

Perera, K. (1984). *Children's writing and reading: Analysing classroom language.* Oxford: Blackwell.

Scardamalia, M., & Bereiter, C. (1985). Fostering the development of self-regulation in children's knowledge processing. In S. F. Chipman, J. W. Segal & R. Glaser (Eds.) *Thinking and learning skills: Research and open questions* (pp. 563–77). Hillsdale, NJ: LEA.

Sitko, B. (1998). Knowing how to write: Metacognition and writing instruction. In D. Hacker, J. Dunlosky & A. Graesser (Eds.) *Metacognition in educational theory and practice* (pp. 93–116). Hillsdale, NJ: Erlbaum.

Wray, D., & Medwell, J. (2006). *Progression in writing and the Northern Ireland Levels for Writing: A research review undertaken for Council for the Curriculum, Examinations and Assessment (CCEA), Northern Ireland.* Warwick: University of Warwick.

# Chapter 4

Abbott, A. (2001). *Chaos of disciplines.* Chicago: University of Chicago Press.

Australian Curriculum, Australian Reporting and Assessment Authority (ACARA, n.d., a). *Work sample portfolio science year 5 above satisfactory.* Australian Curriculum. https://docs.acara.edu.au/curriculum/worksamples/Year5_Science_Portfolio_Above.pdf.

Australian Curriculum, Australian Reporting and Assessment Authority (ACARA, n.d., b). *Work sample portfolio science year 10 satisfactory.* Australian Curriculum. https://www.australiancurriculum.edu.au/resources/work-samples/samples/mysterious-universe-at/.

Bernstein, B. (1975). *Class, codes and control, Vol. 3: Towards a theory of educational transmissions.* London: Routledge and Kegan Paul.

Bernstein, B. (1999). Vertical and horizontal discourse: An essay. *British Journal of Sociology of Education,* 20, 157–73.

Biesta, G. (2014). Pragmatising the curriculum: Bringing knowledge back into the curriculum conversation, but via pragmatism. *Curriculum Journal,* 25, 29–49.

Carlgren, I. (2020). Powerful knowns and powerful knowings. *Journal of Curriculum Studies,* 52, 323–36.

Christie, F., & Derewianka, B. (2008). *School discourse*. London: Continuum.

Davydov, V. V. (2008). *Problems of developmental instruction. A theoretical and experimental psychological study*. New York: Nova Science Publishers.

Garfinkel, H. (1960). The rational properties of scientific and commonsense activities. *Behavioral Science, 5*, 72–83.

Garfinkel, H. (1967). *Studies in Ethnomethodology*. Englewood Cliffs: Prentice Hall.

Haack, S. (1993). *Evidence and inquiry: Towards reconstruction in epistemology*. Oxford: Basil Blackwell.

Halliday, M. A. K. (1993). Towards a language-based theory of learning. *Linguistics and Education, 5*, 93–116.

Halliday, M. A. K. (1999). The notion of 'context' in language education. In M. Ghadessy (Ed.), *Text and context in Functional Linguistics* (pp. 1–24). Philadelphia, PA: John Benjamins.

Husserl, E. ([1900/1901] 2001). *Logical Investigations*, 2nd edn. D. Moran (Ed.). 2 vols. London: Routledge.

Lynch, M. (1993). *Scientific practice and ordinary action: Ethnomethodology and social studies of science*. Cambridge: Cambridge University Press.

Macbeth, D. (2011). Understanding understanding as an instructional matter. *Journal of Pragmatics, 43*, 438–51.

MacDonald, S. P. (1994). *Professional academic writing in the Humanities and Social Sciences*. Carbondale, IL: SIUP.

McLennan, D. A. (2008). The concept of co-option: Why evolution often looks miraculous. *Evolution, Education, and Outreach, 1*, 247–58.

Martin, J. R., & White, P. R. (2005). *The language of evaluation*, Vol. 2. London: Palgrave Macmillan.

Ruggerone, L. (2013). Science and the life-world: Husserl, Schutz, Garfinkel. *Human Studies, 36*, 179–97.

Schütz, A. (1943). The problem of rationality in the social world. *Economica, 10*, 130–49.

Schütz, A. (1953). Common sense and scientific interpretation of human action. *Philosophy and Phenomenological Research, 14*, 1–38.

Sharrock, W. (2004). What Garfinkel makes of Schütz: The past, present, and future of an alternate, asymmetric, and incommensurable approach to Sociology. *Theory and Science, 5*, 1–13.

Värmby, G. (2020, February 7). Dags för mer realism i klimatfrågan [It's time for a more realist view on the climate issue]. Göteborgsposten. https://www.gp.se/ledare/dags-för-mer-realism-i-klimatfrågan-1.23553979.

Vygotsky, L. S. ([1934] 1978). *Mind in society: The development of higher psychological processes*. M. Cole, V. John-Steiner, S. Scribner, & E. Souberman (Eds.). Cambridge, MA: Harvard University Press.

Yates, L., & Young, M. (Eds.). (2010) Special issue on 'knowledge, globalization, and curriculum'. *European Journal of Education, 45*, 1.

# Envoi to Part 1

Arreaza, A., Robertson, B. & Ruben, J. (2020). Generation COVID: Children have been hit from all sides, and they need help now. https://www.theguardian.com/commentisfree/2020/aug/03/generation-covid-coronavirus-children-help. *The Guardian*, 3 August 2020 Retrieved on 18 November 2020.

Barton, D., & Hamilton, M. (1998). *Local literacies: Reading and writing in one community*. London: Routledge.

Bloom, A. (2018). Schools failing to prepare pupils for social media cliff edge. https://www.tes.com/news/schools-failing-prepare-pupils-social-media-cliff-edge. Retrieved on 18 November 2020.

Compton-Lilly, C. (2016). *Reading students' lives: Literacy learning across time*. New York: Routledge.

Cope, B., & Kalantzis, M. (2000). Multiliteracies: The beginning of an idea. In B. Cope & M. Kalantzis (Eds.), *Multiliteracies: Literacy learning and the design of social futures*(pp. 3–8). London: Routledge.

Jack, A. (2020). Exams and lockdown: How the pandemic threatens social mobility at university. https://www.ft.com/content/ad50c7c0-7682-4613-ab64-cb7658e69681 12 August 2020 and retrieved on 18 November 2020.

Kress, G. (2010). *Literacy in the new media age*. New York: Routledge.

Kuby, C. R., Gutshall Rucker, T. & Kirchhofer, J.M. (2015). 'Go be a writer': Intra-activity with materials, time and space in literacy learning. *Journal of Early Childhood Literacy, 15*(3), 394–419.

Kuby, C. R., Spector, K. & Thiel, J. J. (Eds.). (2018). *Posthumanism and literacy education: Knowing/becoming/doing literacies*. New York: Routledge.

Leander, K. M., & Boldt, G. M. (2013). Rereading 'a pedagogy of multiliteracies': Bodies, texts, and emergence. *Journal of Literacy Research, 45*(1), 22–46.

Leander, K. M., & Sheehy, M. (2004). *Spatializing literacy research*. New York: Peter Lang.

Leander, K., & Ehret, C. (Eds.). (2019). *Affect in literacy teaching and learning: Pedagogies, policies, and coming to know*. New York: Routledge.

Lemke, J. (2000). Across the scales of time: Artifacts, activities, and meanings in ecosocial systems. *Mind, Culture, and Activity*, 7(4), 273–90.

Marsh, J., Kumpulainen, K., Nisha, B., Velicu, A., Blum-Ross, A., Hyatt, D., Jónsdóttir, S. R., Levy, R., Little, S., Marusteru, G., Ólafsdóttir, M. E., Sandvic, K., Scott, F., Thestrup, K., Arnseth, H. C., Dýrfjör›, K., Jornet, A., Kjartansdóttir, S. H., Pahl, K., Pétursdóttir, S. & Thorsteinsson, G. (2017). *Makerspaces in the early years: A Literature review*. University of Sheffield: MakEY Project, 1–139.

Mills, K. A., & Comber, B. (2015). Socio-spatial approaches to Literacy Studies: Rethinking the social constitution and politics of space. In J. Rowsell & K. Pahl (Eds.), *The Routledge handbook of literacy studies* (pp. 91–103). London: Routledge.

Rowsell, J. (2013). *Working with multimodality: Rethinking literacy in a digital age*. London: Routledge.

Rowsell, J. (2017). Passing through: Reflecting on the journey through Community Arts Zone. *Pedagogies: An International Journal*, 12(1), 1–3.

Rowsell, J. (2020). 'How emotional do I make it?': Making a stance in multimodal compositions. *Journal of Adolescent & Adult Literacy*, 63(6), 627–37. https://doi.org/10.1002/jaal.1034.

# Chapter 5

Bauman, R., & Briggs, C. C. (1990) Poetics and performance as critical perspectives on language and social life. *Anthropological Review*, 19: 59–88.

Bernstein, B. (1975). *Class, codes and control: Vol. III. Towards a theory of educational transmissions*. London: Routledge & Kegan Paul.

Bernstein, B. ([1996] 2000). *Pedagogy, symbolic control and identity: Theory, research, critique*. Rev. edn. London: Rowman & Littlefield.

Bloome, D., & Katz, L. (1997). Literacy as social practice and classroom chronotypes. *Reading & Writing Quarterly: Overcoming Learning Difficulties*, 113, 205–22.

Campbell, S., Torr, J., & Cologon, K. (2012). Ants, apples and the ABCs: The use of commercial phonics programmes in prior-to-school children's services. *Journal of Early Childhood Literacy*, 12(4), 367–88.

Campbell, S., Torr, J. & Cologon, K. (2014). Pre-packaging preschool literacy: What drives early childhood teachers to use commercially produced phonics programs in prior to school settings. *Contemporary Issues in Early Childhood*, 15(1), 40–53.

Comber, B., & Kamler, B. (2004). Getting out of deficit: Pedagogies of reconnection. *Teaching education*, *15*(3), 293–310.

Department of Education, Employment and Workplace Relations (DEEWR) (2009). *Belonging, being and becoming: The early years learning framework for Australia*. Retrieved from https://docs.education.gov.au/documents/belonging-being-becoming-early-years-learning-framework-australia.

Dyson, A.H. (2001). Where are the childhoods in childhood literacy? An exploration in outer (school) space. *Journal of Early Childhood Literacy*, *1*(1) 9–39.

Heap, J. L. (1985). Discourse in the production of classroom knowledge: Reading lessons. *Curriculum Inquiry*, *15*, 245–79.

Kervin, L., Comber, B. & Baroutsis, A. (2019). Sociomaterial dimensions of early literacy learning spaces: Moving through classrooms with teacher and children. In H. Hughes, J. Franz & J. Willis (Eds.), *School spaces for student wellbeing and learning: insights from research and practice* (pp. 21–38). Singapore: Springer.

Kervin, L., Turbill, J. & Harden-Thew, K. (2017). Invisible to visible: Mapping the continuum of literacy learning experiences in an early years setting. *Journal of Early Childhood Literacy*, *17*(4), 465–84.

Mantei, J., & Kervin, L. (2018). Examining literacy demands for children during teacher-led episodes of reading aloud across the transition from Preschool to Kindergarten. *Australian Journal of Language and Literacy*, *41*(2), 82–93.

NSW Department of Education and Training (2009). *Best start kindergarten assessment: Administration guide*. Sydney, Australia: NSW Department of Education and Training.

Rowe, D. W. (1989). Author/audience interaction in the Preschool: The role of social interaction in literacy learning. *Journal of Reading Behavior*, *21*(4), 311–49.

Taylor, L. (2019). Discursive stance as a pedagogical tool: Negotiating literate identities in writing conferences. *Journal of Early Childhood Literacy*, *21*(4), 1468798419838596.

Zubrick, S. R., Taylor, C. L. & Christensen, D. (2015). Patterns and predictors of language and literacy abilities 4–10 years in the longitudinal study of Australian children. *PLoS One*, *10*(9), e0135612.

# Chapter 6

Allender, T., & Freebody, P. (2016). Disciplinary and idiomatic literacy: Re-living and re-working the past in senior school history. *Australian Journal of Language and Literacy*, *39*, 7–19.

# References

Antaki, C. (2011). *Applied Conversation Analysis: Intervention and change in institutional talk*. London: Palgrave Macmillan.

Austin, H., Dwyer, B. & Freebody, P. (2003). *Schooling the child: The making of students in classrooms*. London: Routledge.

Christie, F., & Derewianka, B. (2008). *School discourse*. London: Continuum.

Drew, P. (1997). 'Open' class repair initiators in response to sequential sources of troubles in conversation. *Journal of Pragmatics, 28*(1), 69–101.

Drew, P. (2018). Epistemics in social interaction. *Discourse Studies, 20*(1), 163–87.

Edwards-Groves, C. (2017). Teaching and learning as social interaction: Salience and relevance in classroom lesson practices. In P. Grootenboer, C. Edwards-Groves & S. Choy (Eds.), *Practice Theory perspectives on pedagogy and education: Praxis, diversity, and contestation* (pp. 191–214). Singapore: Springer.

Edwards-Groves, C., Anstey, M. & Bull, G. (2014). *Classroom talk: Understanding dialogue, pedagogy and practice*. Newtown, Sydney: Primary English Teaching Association Australia.

Edwards-Groves, C., & Davidson, C. (2017). *Becoming a meaning maker: Talk and Interaction in the dialogic classroom*. Newtown, Sydney: Primary English Teaching Association Australia.

Edwards-Groves, C., & Grootenboer, P. (2017). Learning spaces and practices in the primary school: A focus on classroom dialogues. In K. Mahon, S. Francisco & S. Kemmis (Eds.), *Exploring education and professional practice: Through the lens of practice architectures*, (pp. 31–48). Singapore: Springer.

Freebody, P. (2013). School knowledge in talk and writing: Taking 'when learners know' seriously. *Linguistics in Education, 24,* 64–74.

Freebody, P. (2019). What kind of knowledge can we use? Scoping an adequate program for literacy education. In R. Cox, S. Feez & L. Beveridge (Eds.) *The alphabetic principle and beyond: Surveying the landscape* (pp. 32–47). Newtown, NSW: Primary English Teaching Association of Australia.

Freebody, P., & Luke, A. (1990). 'Literacies' programmes: Debates and demands in cultural context. *Prospect: A Journal of Australian TESOL, 11,* 7–16.

Garfinkel, H., (1967). *Studies in Ethnomethodology*. Englewood Cliffs, NJ: Prentice Hall.

Garoni, S. K. (2019). *The Social Accomplishment of Transition: Investigating classroom talk practices as students move from primary to secondary school*. Doctoral thesis. Charles Sturt University. Wagga Wagga, Australia: Charles Sturt University.

Goodwin, C., & Heritage, J. (1990). Conversation analysis. *Annual Review of Anthropology, 19,* 283–307.

Heap, J. L. (1977). Toward a phenomenology of reading. *Journal of Phenomenological Psychology, 8,* 103–13.

Heap, J. L. (1985). Discourse in the production of classroom knowledge: Reading lessons. *Curriculum Inquiry, 15*, 245–79.

Heritage, J. (1984). *Garfinkel and Ethnomethodology*. Cambridge: Polity.

Hutchby, I., & Wooffitt, R. (2008). *Conversation analysis*, 2nd edn. Cambridge: Polity.

Koole, T. (2012). Conversation analysis and education. In C. A. Chapelle (Ed.), *The Encyclopedia of Applied Linguistics* (pp. 977–82). Oxford: Blackwell.

Lee, Y.-A. (2007). Third turn position in teacher talk: Contingency and the work of teaching. *Journal of Pragmatics, 39*, 180–206.

Liddicoat, A. J. (2011). *An introduction to Conversation Analysis*. London: Continuum.

Macbeth, D. (2000). Classrooms as installations. In S. Hester & D. Francis (Eds.), *Local Education Order* (pp. 21–72). Amsterdam: John Benjamins.

Macbeth, D. (2011). Understanding understanding as an instructional matter. *Journal of Pragmatics, 43*, 438–51.

McHoul, A. (1978). The organization of turns at formal talk in the classroom. *Language in Society, 7*, 183–213.

Mehan, H. (1979). *Learning lessons*. Cambridge, MA: Harvard University Press.

Pomerantz, A. (1980). Telling my side: 'Limited access' as a 'fishing' device. *Sociological Inquiry, 50*, 186–98.

Pomerantz, A. (1988). Offering a candidate answer: An information seeking strategy. *Communication Monographs, 55*, 360–73.

Sacks, H. (1992). *Lectures on conversation, Volumes I & II*. G. Jefferson (Ed.). Oxford: Blackwell.

Schegloff, E. (2007). *Sequential organization in interaction*. Cambridge: Cambridge University Press.

Sidnell, J., & Stivers, T. (2013). *Handbook of Conversation Analysis*. Oxford: Blackwell.

Sinclair, J. M., & Coulthard, M. (1975). *Towards an analysis of discourse: The English used by teachers and pupils*. London: Oxford University Press.

ten Have, P. (2007). *Doing Conversation Analysis: A practical guide*, 2nd edn. London: Sage.

# Chapter 7

ACARA (2019). *NAPLAN achievement in reading, writing, language conventions and numeracy: 2017 national report*. Retrieved from http://www.nap.edu.au/results-and-reports/national-reports.

Baker, C., & Luke, A. (1991). *Towards a critical sociology of reading pedagogy.* Amsterdam: John Benjamins.

Bernstein, B. (1990). *The structuring of pedagogic discourse: Class codes and control* (Vol. IV). London: Routledge & Kegan Paul.

Chall, J. S., & Jacobs, V. A. (2003). The classic study on poor children's fourth-grade slump. *American Educator.* Retrieved from https://www.aft.org/periodical/american-educator/spring-2003/classic-study-poor-childrens-fourth-grade-slump.

Chen, H., & Vale, E. R. (2020). Developing confident writers: Fostering audience awareness in primary school writing classrooms. In H. Chen, D. Myhill & H. Lewis (Eds.), *Developing writers across primary and secondary years: Growing into writing* (pp. 131–53). Milton Park: Routledge.

Christie, F. (1995). Pedagogic discourse in the primary school. *Linguistics and Education, 7,* 221–42.

Christie, F., & Derewianka, B. (2008). *School discourse.* London: Continuum.

Claxton, G., & Carr, M. (2004). A framework for teaching learning: The dynamics of disposition. *Early Years, 24*(1), 87–97.

Derewianka, B., & Jones, P. T. (2016). *Teaching language in context.* Oxford: Oxford University Press.

DfE (2017). *National curriculum assessments at key stage 2 in England, 2017 (SFR 69/2017).* Retrieved from https://www.gov.uk/government/uploads/system/uploads/attachment_data/file/667372/SFR69_2017_text.pdf.

Flower, L. S., & Hayes, J. R. (1981). A cognitive process of theory of writing. *College Composition and Communication, 32*(4), 365–87.

Freebody, P. (1991). Remarks on cognitive-psychological and critical-sociological accounts of reading. In C. Baker & A. Luke (Eds.), *Towards a critical sociology of reading pedagogy* (pp. 239–55). Amsterdam: John Benjamins.

Graves, D. (1983). *Writing: teachers and children at work.* Portsmouth, NH: Heinemann.

Halliday, M.A.K. (1978). *Language as a social semiotic: The social interpretation of language and meaning.* London: Arnold.

Humphrey, S. (2017). *Academic literacies in the middle years: A framework for enhancing teaching knowledge and student achievement.* London: Routledge.

Martin, J. R., & Rose, D. (2007). *Working with discourse: Meaning beyond the clause* (2nd edn). London: Bloomsbury.

Martin, J. R., & Rose, D. (2008). *Genre relations: Mapping culture.* London: Equinox.

McNaughton, S. (2020). *The literacy landscape in Aotearoa New Zealand.* Retrieved from Auckland, New Zealand. https://cpb-ap-se2.wpmucdn.com/blogs.auckland.

ac.nz/dist/f/688/files/2020/01/The-Literacy-Landscape-in-Aotearoa-New-Zealand-Full-report-final.pdf.

Myhill, D., & Chen, H. (2020). Developing writers in primary and secondary school years. In H. Chen, D. Myhill & H. Lewis (Eds.), *Growing into writing: Developing writers across primary and secondary years* (pp. 1–18). Milton Park: Routledge.

NCES (2017). *The Nation's report card*. Retrieved from https://nces.ed.gov/nationsreportcard/writing/.

Noyes, A. (2006). School transfer and the diffraction of learning trajectories. *Research Papers in Education*, *21*(1), 43–62.

Painter, C., Derewianka, B. & Torr, J. (2007). From microfunction to metaphor: learning language and learning through language. In R. Hasan, C. Matthiessen & J. Webster (Eds.), *Continuing discourse on language: A functional perspective* (Vol. 2, pp. 563–88). London: Exquinox.

Rose, D. (2014). Analysing pedagogic discourse: An approach from genre and register. *Functional Linguistics*, *1*(11), 1–32.

Rose, D. (2018). Pedagogic register analysis: Mapping choices in teaching and learning. *Functional Linguistics*, *5*(3), 1–33.

Rose, D. (2019). Building a pedagogic metalanguage I: Curriculum genres. In J. Martin, K. Maton & Y. Doran (Eds.), *Accessing academic discourse: Systemic functional linguistics and legitimation code theory* (pp. 236–67). Abingdon: Routledge.

Rose, D., & Martin, J. R. (2012). *Learning to write, reading to learn: Genre, knowledge, and pedagogy in the Sydney school*. Sheffield: Equinox.

# Chapter 8

Alexander, R. (2020). *A dialogic teaching Companion*. London: Routledge.

Austen, H. (1993). Verbal art in children's literature: An application of linguistic theory to the classroom. *English in Australia*, *103* (March): 63–75.

Australian Curriculum Assessment and Reporting Authority (ACARA) (2015). *The Australian Curriculum: English Vers 8*.1. Australian Curriculum and Reporting Authority (ACARA) https://acara.edu.au/curriculum.

Bernstein, B. (1990). *The structuring of pedagogic discourse*. London: Routledge

Christie, F. (2005). *Classroom discourse analysis: A functional perspective*. London: Bloomsbury.

Christie, F., & Derewianka, B. (2008). *School discourse*. London: Continuum.

Christie, F., & Martin, J. R. (Eds.). (1997). *Genre and institutions: Social processes in the workplace and school.* London: Cassell.

Edwards Groves, C., & Davidson, C. (2017). *Becoming a meaning maker: Talk and interaction in the dialogic classroom.* Primary English Teaching Association (PETAA).

Goldman, S., Britt, M. A., Brown, W., Cribb, G., George, M., Greenleaf, C., Lee, C., Shanahan, C. & Project READI, (2016). Disciplinary literacies and learning to read for understanding: A conceptual framework for disciplinary literacy. *Educational Psychologist, 51*(2), 219–46.

Hasan, R. (1985). *Linguistics, language and verbal art.* Geelong: Deakin University Press.

Macken-Horarik, M. (2006). Hierarchies in diversities: What students' examined responses tell us about literacy practices in contemporary school English. *Australian Journal of Language and Literacy, 29*(1), 52–79.

Martin, J. R. (1992). *English text: System and structure.* Amsterdam: Benjamins.

Martin, J. R. (1996). Evaluating disruption: Symbolising theme in junior secondary narrative. in R. Hasan & G. Williams (Eds.), *Literacy in Society.* London: Longman Applied Linguistics and Language Study, 124–71.

Martin, J. R. (2006). Metadiscourse: Designing interaction in genre-based literacy programs. In R. Whittaker, M. O'Donnell & A. McCabe (Eds.), *Language and Literacy: Functional Approaches* (pp. 95–122). London: Continuum.

Martin, J. R., & Rose, D. (2005). Designing literacy pedagogy: scaffolding asymmetries. In R. Hasan, C. M. I. M. Matthiessen & J. Webster (Eds.), *Continuing Discourse on Language* (pp. 251–80). London: Equinox.

Martin, J. R., & Rose, D. (2007a). *Working with discourse: Meaning beyond the clause.* London: Continuum (1st edn, 2003).

Martin, J. R., & Rose, D. (2007b). Interacting with text: The role of dialogue in learning to read and write. *Foreign Languages in China, 4*(5): 66–80.

Martin, J. R., & Rose, D. (2008). *Genre relations: Mapping culture.* London: Equinox.

Maton, K. (2014). *Knowledge and knowers: Towards a realist sociology of education.* London: Routledge.

Matruglio, E., & Jones, P. T. (2020). Writing their futures: Students' stories of development and difference. In H. Chen, D. Myhill & H. Lewis (Eds.), *Growing into writing: Developing writers across primary and secondary school years* (pp. 173–93). London: Routledge.

Mehan, H. (1979). *Learning lessons: Social organisation in the classroom.* Cambridge, MA: Harvard University Press.

Mercer, N., Wegerif, R. & Major, L. (2019). *The Routledge handbook of research on dialogic education*. London: Routledge.

Moje, E. B. (2008). Foregrounding the disciplines in secondary literacy teaching and learning: A call for change. *Journal of Adolescent & Adult Literacy, 52*(2), 96–107.

NESA (2020). *NSW Curriculum Review: Final Report*. Sydney: Education Standards Authority (NSW).

NSW Board of Studies (2012). *English K-10 Syllabus*. Sydney: Board of Studies NSW.

Nuthall, G. A. (2005). The cultural myths and realities of classroom teaching and learning: A personal journey. *Teachers College Record, 107*(5): 895–934.

Resnick, L., & Schantz, F. E. (2015). Re-thinking intelligence: Schools that build the mind. *European Journal of Education, 50*(3): 340--9.

Rose, D. (2007). Towards a reading based theory of teaching. Plenary paper in L. Barbara & T. Berber Sardinha (Eds.). *Proceedings of the 33rd International Systemic Functional Congress*, São Paulo: PUCSP, 36–77. ISBN 85-283-0342X http://www.pucsp.br/isfc/proceedings/.

Rose, D. (2015). New developments in genre-based literacy pedagogy. In C. A. MacArthur, S, Graham & J. Fitzgerald (Eds.), *Handbook of writing research*, 2nd edn (pp. 227–42). New York: Guildford.

Rose, D. (2016). Genre, knowledge and pedagogy in the 'Sydney School'. In N. Artemeva (Ed.), *Trends and Tradition in Genre Studies* (pp. 299–338). Ottawa: Inkwell.

Rose, D. (2018). Pedagogic register analysis: Mapping choices in teaching and learning. *Functional Linguistics, 3*(5), 1–33, Springer Open Access, http://rdcu.be/HD9G.

Rose, D. (2019). Building a pedagogic metalanguage I: Curriculum genres and Building a pedagogic metalanguage II: knowledge genres II. In J. R. Martin, K. Maton & Y. J. Doran (Eds.), *Accessing academic discourse: Systemic functional linguistic and legitimation code theory* (pp. 236–302). London: Taylor & Francis.

Rose, D., & J. R. Martin (2012). *Learning to write, reading to learn: Genre, knowledge and pedagogy in the Sydney School*. London: Equinox.

Shanahan, C., & Shanahan, T. (2014). Teaching disciplinary literacy to adolescents: Rethinking content-area literacy. *Harvard Educational Review, 78*(1), 40–59.

Sinclair, J.McH. & Coulthard, R. M. (1975). *Towards an analysis of discourse: The English used by teachers and pupils*. London: Oxford University Press.

Thwaite, A., Jones, P. T., & Simpson, A. (2020). Enacting dialogic pedagogy in primary literacy classrooms: Insights from systemic functional linguistics. *Australian Journal of Language and Literacy, 43*(1), 33–46.

Universities Admissions Centre (2020). *Report on the Scaling of the 2019 NSW Higher School Certificate*. UAC: Sydney.

Williams, G. (1995). *Joint book-reading and literacy pedagogy: A socio-semantic interpretation*. Unpublished PhD dissertation. School of English, Linguistics and Media, Macquarie University (available as CORE 19: 3 and 20: 1).

# Chapter 9

Australian Curriculum Assessment and Reporting Authority (ACARA) (2016). *The Australian Curriculum: Science Version 8.3* (pp. 1–96). https://www.australiancurriculum.edu.au/download/.

Bezemer, J., & Kress, G. (2010). Changing text: A Social Semiotic analysis of textbooks. *Designs for Learning*, 3(1–2), 10. https://doi.org/10.16993/dfl.26.

Christie, F. (2012). *Language education throughout the school years: A Functional perspective*. Sussex: Wiley-Blackwell.

Christie, F., & Derewianka, B. (2008). *School discourse*. London: Continuum.

Christie, F., & Maton, K. (2011). Why disciplinarity? In F. Christie & K. Maton (Eds.), *Disciplinarity: Functional linguistic and sociological perspectives* (pp. 1–9). London: Continuum.

Danielsson, K., & Selander, S. (2016). Reading multimodal texts for learning – a model for cultivating multimodal literacy. *Designs for Learning*, 8(1), 25–36. https://doi.org/10.16993/dfl.72.

Doran, Y. (2019). Building knowledge through images in physics. *Visual Communication*, 18(2), 251–77. https://doi.org/10.1177/1470357218759825.

Fang, Z. (2014). Preparing content area teachers for disciplinary literacy instruction. *Journal of Adolescent & Adult Literacy*, 57(6), 444–8. https://doi.org/10.1002/jaal.269.

Fang, Z., & Schlepegrell, M. (2008). Technicality and reasoning in science: Beyond vocabulary. In Z. Fang & M. Schlepegrell (Eds.), *Reading in secondary content areas: A language-based pedagogy* (pp. 18–38). Michigan: University of Michigan Press.

Fang, Z., Schleppegrell, M. J. & Cox, B. E. (2006). Understanding the language demands of schooling: Nouns in academic registers. *Journal of Literacy Research*, 38(3), 247–73. https://doi.org/10.1207/s15548430jlr3803_1.

Feez, S., & Quinn, F. (2017). Teaching the distinctive language of science: An integrated and scaffolded approach for pre-service teachers. *Teaching and Teacher Education*, 65, 192–204. https://doi.org/10.1016/j.tate.2017.03.019.

Ge, Y. P., Unsworth, L., Wang, K. H., & Chang, H. P. (2018). What images reveal: A comparative study of science images between Australian and Taiwanese junior high school textbooks. *Research in Science Education*, *48*(6), 1409–31. https://doi.org/10.1007/s11165-016-9608-9.

Goldman, S. R., Britt, M. A., Brown, W., Cribb, G., George, M., Greenleaf, C., Lee, C. D., Shanahan, C. & Project READI. (2016). Disciplinary literacies and learning to read for understanding: A Conceptual framework for disciplinary literacy. *Educational Psychologist*, *51*(2), 219–46. https://doi.org/10.1080/00461520.2016.1168741.

Halliday, M. A. K. (1978). *Language as a social semiotic*. London: Edward Arnold.

Halliday, M. A. K. (1993). Towards a language-based theory of learning. *Linguistics and Education*, *5*(2), 93–116. https://doi.org/10.1016/0898-5898(93)90026-7.

Halliday, M. A. K. (2004). *The language of science (Collected works of MAK Halliday Vol. 5)*. London: Continuum.

Halliday, M. A. K., & Martin, J. R. (1993). *Writing science: Literacy and discursive power*. Bristol: University of Pittsburgh Press.

Hao, J. (2018). Reconsidering 'cause inside the clause' in scientific discourse – from a discourse semantic perspective in systemic functional linguistics. *Text and Talk*, *38*(5), 525–50. https://doi.org/10.1515/text-2018-0013.

Harlen, W., & Holroyd, C. (1997). Primary teachers' understanding of concepts of science: Impact on confidence and teaching. *International Journal of Science Education*, *19*(1), 93–105. https://doi.org/10.1080/0950069970190107.

He, Q., & Forey, G. (2018). Meaning-making in a secondary science classroom: A systemic functional multimodal discourse analysis. In K. Tang & K. Danielsson (Eds.), *Global developments in literacy research for science education* (pp. 183–202). New York: Springer International. https://doi.org/10.1007/978-3-319-69197-8_12.

Hood, S. (2008). Summary writing in academic contexts: Implicating meaning in processes of change. *Linguistics and Education*, *19*(4), 351–65. https://doi.org/10.1016/j.linged.2008.06.003.

Kress, G., Jewitt, C., Ogborn, J. & Tsatsarelis, C. (2001). *Multimodal teaching and learning: The rhetorics of the science classroom* (1st edn). London: Continuum.

Kress, G., & van Leeuwen, T. (2006). *Reading images: The grammar of visual design*. London: Routledge.

Lemke, J. L. (1990). *Talking science: Language, learning and values*. New Jersey: Ablex.

Lemke, J. L. (1998). Multiplying meaning: Visual and verbal semiotic in scientific texts. In J. R. Martin & R. Veel (Eds.), *Reading science: Critical and functional perspectives on discourses* (pp. 87–113). London: Routledge.

Love, K. (2010). Literacy pedagogical content knowledge in the secondary curriculum. *Pedagogies*, 5(4), 338–55. https://doi.org/10.1080/15544 80X.2010.521630.

Martin, J. R. (1992). *English text: System and structure*. John Benjamins.

Martin, J. R., & Rose, D. (2008). *Genre relations: Mapping culture*. Equinox.

Murphy, C., Neil, P. & Beggs, J. (2007). Primary science teacher confidence revisited: Ten years on. *Educational Research*, 49(4), 415–30. https://doi.org/10.1080/00131880701717289.

Rothery, J. (1989). Learning about language. In R. Hasan & J. R. Martin (Eds.), *Language development: Learning language, learning culture*. New Jersey: Ablex.

Royce, T. (2002). Multimodality in the TESOL classroom: Exploring visual-verbal synergy. *TESOL Quarterly*, 36(2), 191. https://doi.org/10.2307/3588330.

Shanahan, C., & Shanahan, T. (2008). Teaching disciplinary literacy to adolescents: Rethinking content-area literacy. *Harvard Educational Review*, 78(1), 40–59.

Tang, K. S. (2016). How is disciplinary literacy addressed in the Science classroom?: A Singaporean case study. *Australian Journal of Language and Literacy*, 39(3), 220–32.

Unsworth, L. (2020). Intermodal relations, mass and presence in school science explanation genres. In M. Zappavigna & S. Dreyfus (Eds.), *Discourses of hope and reconciliation: On J. R. Martin's contribution to systemic functional linguistics* (pp. 131–51). London: Bloomsbury Academic.

Unsworth, L., & Chan, E. (2009). Bridging multimodal literacies and national assessment programs in literacy. *Australian Journal of Language and Literacy*, 32(3), 245–57.

# Chapter 10

Boyatzis, R. E. (1998). *Transforming qualitative information: Thematic analysis and code development*. London: Sage.

Cohen, L., Manion, L. & Morrison, K. (2007). *Research methods in education* (6th edn). New York: Routledge Falmer.

Cremin, T., & Chappell, K. (2019). Creative pedagogies: A systematic review, *Research Papers in Education*, DOI: 10.1080/02671522.2019.1677757.

Fontana, A., & Frey, J.H. (2000). The interview: From structured questions to negotiated text. In N. K. Denzin & Y. S. Lincoln (Eds.), *Handbook of qualitative research* (2nd edn, pp. 645–72). London: Sage.

Langdridge, D. (2004). *Research methods and data analysis in psychology*. Harlow, England: Pearson Education.

Martin, J. R., & White, P. R. R. (2005). *The Language of evaluation: Appraisal in English*. Hampshire: Palgrave.

Masters, G. (2019). *Nurturing wonder and igniting passion. Designs for a future school curriculum. NSW Curriculum Review Interim Report*. Sydney: NSW Education Standards Authority.

New South Wales Department of Education (2020). Diversity and Inclusion. Retrieved from https://education.nsw.gov.au/teaching-and-learning/learning-from-home/teaching-at-home/diversity-and-inclusion.

Rose, D., & Martin, J. R. (2012). *Learning to write, reading to learn: Genre, knowledge and pedagogy in the Sydney School*. Sheffield: Equinox.

# Envoi to Part II

Alexander, R. J. (2001). *Culture and pedagogy: International comparisons in Primary Education*. Oxford: Blackwell.

Jackson, P. W. (1968). *Life in the classrooms*. New York: Rinehart and Winston.

Street, B. (1993). The new literacy studies: Implications for education and pedagogy, *Changing English*, 1(1), 113–26.

# Chapter 11

Australian Curriculum, Assessment and Reporting Authority (ACARA) (2014a). *Foundation to Year 10 curriculum*. Canberra, ACT: Commonwealth of Australia. http://www.australiancurriculum.edu.au/english/curriculum/f-10.

Australian Curriculum, Assessment and Reporting Authority (ACARA) (2018) *National Literacy Learning Progression*. Accessed at https://www.australiancurriculum.edu.au/resources/national-literacy-and-numeracy-learning-progressions/national-literacy-learning-progression/.

Buchholz, B. A. (2016). Dangling literate identities in imagined futures: Literacy, time, and development in a K–6 classroom. *Literacy Research: Theory, Method, and Practice*, 65(1), 124–40.

Campbell, S. (2019). Putting the jigsaw together: Reading and teaching of phonics in the early years. In Annette Woods and Beryl Exley (Eds.), *Literacies in Early*

Childhood: Foundations for Equity and Quality (pp. 68–81). Oxford: Oxford University Press.

Compton-Lilly, C. (2006). Identity, childhood culture, and literacy learning: A case study. *Journal of Early Childhood Literacy*, 6(1), 57–76.

Dyson, A. H. (2003). *The brothers and sisters learn to write: Popular literacies in childhood and school cultures*. New York: Teachers College Press.

Dyson, A.H. (2019). Ethnography upside down. In N. Kucirkova, J., Rowsell, G., & Falloon, (Eds.), *The Routledge international handbook of learning with technology in early childhood* (pp. 74–90). London: Routledge.

Gee, J. (1990). *Social linguistics and literacies: Ideology in discourses*. New York: Falmer Press.

Harste, J., Woodward, V. & Burke, C. (1984). *Language stories and literacy lessons*. Portsmouth, NH: Heinemann.

Heath, S. B. (1983). *Ways with words: Language, life, and work in communities and classrooms*. New York: Cambridge University Press.

Kervin, L. (2016). Powerful and playful literacy learning with digital technologies. *Australian Journal of Language and Literacy*, 39(1), 64–73.

Martens, P., & Adamson, S. (2001). Inventing literate identities: The influence of texts and contexts. *Literacy, Teaching and Learning*, 5(2), 27.

NSW Department of Education (2017). *Literacy and Numeracy Strategy 2017–2020*. Accessed online at https://education.nsw.gov.au/teaching-and-learning/curriculum/literacy-and-numeracy/literacy-and-numeracy-strategy-2017-2020.

NSW Education Standards Authority (2012). *English K-10 Syllabus and Support Materials*, NESA: https://educationstandards.nsw.edu.au/wps/portal/nesa/k-10/learning-areas/english-year-10/english-k-10.

Sfard, A., & Prusak, A. (2005). Telling identities: In search of an analytic tool for investigating learning as a culturally shaped activity. *Educational Researcher*, 34(4), 14–22.

Sumara, D. J. (1998). Fictionalizing acts: Reading and the making of identity. *Theory into Practice*, 37(3), 203–10.

Taylor, L. (2019). Discursive stance as a pedagogical tool: Negotiating literate identities in writing conferences. *Journal of Early Childhood Literacy*, April, 1–22.

Vasudevan, L., Schultz, K. & Bateman, J. (2010). Rethinking composing in a digital age: Authoring literate identities through multimodal storytelling. *Written communication*, 27(4), 442–68.

Yoon, H. S. (2016). 'Writing' children's literate identities: the meaning of language in multilingual, multicultural contexts. *Multicultural Education Review*, 8(2), 65–82.

# Chapter 12

Austin, H., Dwyer, B. & Freebody, P. (2003). *Schooling the child: The making of students in classrooms*. London: Routledge.

Edwards-Groves, C. (2003). *On task: Focused literacy learning*. Sydney: Primary English Teachers Association (PETAA).

Edwards-Groves, C. (2017). Teaching and learning as social interaction: Salience and relevance in classroom lesson practices. In P. Grootenboer, C. Edwards-Groves & S. Choy (Eds.). (2017). *Practice Theory perspectives on pedagogy and education: Praxis, diversity, and contestation* (pp. 191–214). Singapore: Springer.

Edwards-Groves, C., & Davidson, C. (2017). *Becoming a meaning maker: Talk and interaction in the dialogic Classroom*. Primary English Teachers Association Australia, Sydney, NSW: PETAA.

Eglin, P., & Hester, S. (1992) Category, predicate and task: The pragmatics of practical action. *Semiotica*, 3, 243–68.

Fitzgerald, R., Housley, W. & Rintel, S. (2017). Membership categorisation analysis: Technologies of social action. *Journal of Pragmatics*, 118, 51–5.

Freiberg, J., & Freebody, P. (1995). Analysing literacy events in classrooms and homes: Conversation-analytic approaches. In P. Freebody, C. Ludwig and S. Gunn (Eds.), *Everyday literacy practices in and out of schools in low socio-economic urban communities* (pp. 185–372). Brisbane, Australia: Griffith University.

Gardner, R. (2019). Classroom interaction research: The state of the art. *Research on Language and Social Interaction*, 52, 212–26.

Groundwater-Smith, S. (2005). Learning by listening: student voice in practitioner research. In P. Ponte and B.H.J. Smit (Eds.), *International Practitioner Research & Collaborative Action Research Network (CARN) Conference*. Utrecht, The Netherlands: Fontys University of Professional Education.

Jayyusi, L. (1984). *Categorisation and the moral order*. London: Routledge and Kegan Paul.

Jefferson, G. (1984). Transcript notation. In J. M. Atkinson and J. Heritage (Eds.), *Structures of social action: Studies in conversation analysis* (pp. ix–xvi). Cambridge: Cambridge University Press.

Macbeth, D. (2000). Classrooms as installations: Direct instruction in the early grades. In S. Hester & D. Francis (Eds.), *Local educational order: Ethnomethodological studies of knowledge in action* (pp. 21–71). Amsterdam, Netherlands: John Benjamins.

Mehan, H. (1979). *Learning lessons: Social organization in the classroom*. Cambridge, MA: Harvard University Press.

Pires Pereira, Í. S., & González Riaño, X. A. (2018). Elementary students' perspectives on a curriculum for literacy education. *Research Papers in Education*, *33*, 89–112. DOI:10.1080/02671522.2016.1270999.

Potter, J., & Hepburn, A. (2012). Eight challenges for interview researchers. In J. F. Gubrium, J. A. Holstein, A. Marvasti & K. McKinney (Eds.), *The Sage Handbook of Interview Research, Second Edition* (pp. 555–70). London: Sage Press.

Sacks, H., Schegloff, E., & Jefferson, G. (1974). A Simplest Systematics for the Organization of Turn Taking in Conversation. *Language, 50*, 696–735.

Schegloff, E. A. (2007). *Sequence organization in interaction: A primer in Conversation Analysis* (Vol. 1). Cambridge: Cambridge University Press.

# Chapter 13

Bernstein, B. (1975). *Class, codes and control: Towards a theory of educational transmissions* (Vol. 3). London: Routledge and Kegan Paul.

Bernstein, B. (2000). *Pedagogy, symolic control and identity: Theory, research, critique*. London: Taylor and Francis.

Birr Moje, E. (2008). Foregrounding the disciplines in secondary literacy teaching and learning: A call for change. *Journal of Adolescent and Adult Literacy, 52*(2), 96–107.

Cairney, T. H., Lowe, K. & Sproates, E. (1994). *Literacy in transition: An evaluation of ilteracy practices in upper primary and junior secondary schools*. Retrieved from http://www.gu.edu.au/school/cls/clearinghouse.

Christie, F., & Derewianka, B. (2008). *School discourse*. London: Continuum International Publishing Group.

Derewianka, B., & Jones, P. (2016). *Teaching language in context* (2nd edn). South Melbourne, Victoria: Oxford University Press.

Dinham, S., & Rowe, K. (2007). *Teaching and learning in middle schooling: A review of the literature*. Retrieved from Victoria: https://research.acer.edu.au/tll_misc/11/.

Education Council (2019). *Alice springs (mparntwe) education declaration*. Retrieved from Victoria: https://docs.education.gov.au/documents/alice-springs-mparntwe-education-declaration.

Evangelou, M., Taggart, B., Sylva, K., Melhuish, E., Sammons, P., & Siraj-Blatchford, I. (2008). *What makes a successful transition from primary to secondary school?* Retrieved from https://ro.uow.edu.au/sspapers/2430/.

Fang, Z. (2014). Preparing content area teachers for disciplinary instruction. *Journal of Adolescent and Adult Literacy, 57*(6), 444–8. doi:doi:10.1002/JAAL.269.

Galton, M., Gray, J. & Ruddock, J. (1999). *The impact of school transitions and transfers on pupil progress and attainment* (Research Report No 131). Retrieved from United Kingdom: https://www.semanticscholar.org/paper/The-Impact-of-School-Transitions-and-Transfers-on-Galton-Gray/acf4c0eebedfb47034a62fbc3870e1d161bdc13b.

Halliday, M. A. K. (1973). *Explorations in the functions of language*. London: Edward Arnold.

Halliday, M. A. K. (1993). Towards a language-based theory of learning. *Linguistics and Education, 5,* 93–116.

Halliday, M. A. K. (2009). Grammatical Metaphor. In J. J. Webster (Ed.), *The Essential Halliday*. London: Continuum.

Halliday, M. A. K., & Hasan, R. (1985). *Language, context and text: Aspects of language in a social-semiotic perspective*. Victoria: Deakin University.

Hammond, J., & Gibbons, P. (2005). Putting scaffolding to work: The contribution of scaffolding in articulating ESL education. *Prospect, 20*(1), 7–30.

Hannant, K., & Jetnikoff, A. (2015). Investigating a disciplinary approach to literacy learning in a secondary school. *Literacy Learning: the Middle Years, 23*(3), 28–37.

Humphrey, S. (2017). *Academic literacies in the middle years: Enhancing teacher knowledge and student achievement*. London: Routledge.

Hynd-Shanahan, C. (2013). The challenge of teaching disciplinary literacy. *Journal of Adolescent and Adult Literacy, 57*(2), 93–8. doi:10.1002?JAAL.226.

Lo Bianco, J., & Freebody, P. (1997). *Australian literacies, informing national policy on literacy education* (Vol. 1). Melbourne: Language Australia.

Love, K. (2010). Literacy pedagogical content knowledge in the secondary curriculum. *Pedagogies: An International Journal, 5*(4), 338–55. doi:10.1080/1554480X.2010.521630.

Luke, A. (2010). Will the Australian curriculum up the intellectual ante in primary classrooms? *Professional Voice, 8*(1), 41–8.

Luke, A., Elkins, J., Weir, K., Land, R., Carrington, V., Dole, S., … Stevens, L. (2003). *Beyond the middle: A report about literacy and numeracy development of target group students in the middle years of schooling*. Retrieved from https://espace.library.uq.edu.au/view/UQ:84090.

Mansfield, C. F., & Woods-McConney, A. (2012). "I didn't always perceive myself as a "science person"": Examining efficacy for primary science teaching. *Australian Journal of Teacher Education, 37*(10): 37–52.

Martin, J. R. (1984). Language, register and genre. In F. Christie (Ed.), *Children writing: A reader*. Geelong: Deakin University Press.

Martin, J. R., & Rose, D. (2008). *Genre relations mapping culture*. London: Equinox.

Matthiessen, C. (2009). Meaning in the making: Meaning potential emerging from acts of meaning. *Anniversary Issue of Language and Learning*, 59, 211–35.

Noyes, A. (2006). School transfer and the diffraction of learning trajectories. *Research Papers in Education*, 21(1), 43–62. doi:10.1080/02671520500445441

Paatsch, L., Hutchison, K., & Cloonan, A. (2019). Literature in the Australian English curriculum: Victorian primary school teachers' practices, challenges and preparedness to teach. *Australian Journal of Teacher Education*, 44(3), 61–76.

Painter, C. (2005). Preparing for school: Developing a semantic style for educational knowledge. In F. Christie (Ed.), *Pedagogy and the shaping of consciousness* (pp. 66–78). London: Bloomsbury.

Painter, C., Derewianka, B. & Torr, J. (2005). From microfunction to metaphor: Learning language and learning through language. In R. Hasan, C. Matthiessen & J. J. Webster (Eds.), *Continuing discourse on language* (Vol. 2, pp. 562–88). London: Equinox.

Teese, R., & Lamb, S. (2009). *Low achievement and social background: Patterns, processes and interventions*. Retrieved from Melbourne: https://www.researchgate.net/scientific-contributions/Stephen-Lamb-2009338712.

Thwaite, A., Jones, P. & Simpson, A. (2020). Enacting dialogic pedagogy in primary literacy classrooms: Insights from systemic functional linguistics. *Australian Journal of Language and Literacy*, 43(1), 33–46.

Unsworth, L. (2000). Investigating subject-specific literacies in school learning. In L. Unsworth (Ed.), *Researching language in schools and communities: Functional linguistic perspectives* (pp. 245–74). London: Continuum.

van Rens, M., Haelermans, C., Groot, W. & Maassen van den Brink, H. (2018). Facilitating a successful transition to secondary school: (how) does it work? A systematic literature review. *Adolescent Research Review*, 3, 43–56. doi:10.1007/s40894-017-0063-2.

Victorian Auditor General's Office. (2015). *Education transitions*. Retrieved from Victoria: https://www.audit.vic.gov.au/sites/default/files/20150318-Education-transitions.pdf.

Vinson, T., & Harrison, J. (2006). *Good transitions: Through the eyes of primary and secondary principals*. Paper presented at the Cornerstones: A conference for public education, The Wesley Centre, Pitt St, Sydney.

Waters, S., Lester, L., Wenden, E., & Cross, D. (2012). A theoretically grounded exploration of the social and emotional outcomes of transition to secondary school. *Australian Journal of Guidance and Counselling*, 22(2), 190–205.

Wyatt-Smith, C. M., & Cumming, J. J. (2003). Curriculum literacies: Expanding domains of assessment. *Assessment in Education: Principles, Policy and Practice, 10*(1), 47–59.

# Envoi to Part III

Bamberg, M. (2004). Talk, small stories, and adolescent identities. *Human Development, 47*(6), 366–9.

Bandura, A. (1977). Self-efficacy: Toward a unifying theory of behavioral change. *Psychological Review, 84*, 191–215.

Eccles, J. S., Adler, T. F., Futterman, R., Goff, S. B., Kaczala, C. M., Meece, J. L., & Midgley, C. (1983). Expectancies, values, and academic behaviors. In J. T. Spence (Ed.), *Achievement and achievement motivation* (pp. 75–146). San Francisco: W.H. Freedman.

Eccles, J. S., Lord, S. & Midgley, C. (1991). What are we doing to early adolescents? The impact of educational contexts on early adolescents. *American Journal of Education, 99*, 521–542.

Eccles, J. S., & Midgley, C. (1989). Stage/environment fit: Developmentally appropriate classrooms for early adolescents. In R. E. Ames & C. Ames (Eds.), *Research on motivation in education* (Vol. 3, pp. 139–85). New York: Academic Press.

Eccles, J.S., Midgley, C., Wigfield, A., Miller-Buchannan, C., Reuman, D., Flanagan, C. & MacIver, D. (1993). Development during adolescence: The impact of stage-environment fit on young adolescents' experiences in schools and families. *American Psychologist, 48*, 90–101.

Freebody, P. (1992). A socio-cultural approach: Resourcing four roles as a literacy learner. In A.J. & A. M. Badenhop (Ed.), *Prevention of reading failure* (pp. 48–60). Ashton- Sydney: Scholastic.

Georgakopoulou, A. (2013). Building iterativity into positioning analysis: A practice-based approach to small stories and self. *Narrative Inquiry, 23*(1), 89–110. https://doi.org/https://doi.org/10.1075/ni.23.1.05geo.

Learned, J.E. (2016). 'The behavior kids':Examining the conflation of youth reading difficulty and behavior problem positioning among school institutional contexts. *American Educational Research Journal, 53*(5), 1271–309. https://doi.org/10.3102/0002831216667545.

Masterson, J. E. (2020). Reading in 'Purgatory': Tactical Literacies in a Remedial Reading Class. *Reading Research Quarterly*. https://doi.org/https://doi.org/10.1002/rrq.373.

Moje, E. B., Overby, M., Tysvaer, N. & Morris, K. (2008). The complex world of adolescent literacy: Myths, motivations, and mysteries. *Harvard Educational Review, 78*, 107–54.

Moje, E. B., Kim, H.-J, Stockdill, D., Kolb, C. (2010, April). Examining youth reading and writing from many angles: What multiple theories and methods reveal about who young people are as literate beings. Paper presented at the annual meeting of the American Educational Research Association, Denver, CO.

Moje, E. B., & Speyer, J. (2014). Reading challenging texts in high school: How teachers can scaffold and build close reading for real purposes in the subject areas. In K. Hinchman & H. Thomas (Eds.), *Best practices in adolescent literacy instruction* (2nd ed., pp. 207–31). New York: Guilford.

Rosenblatt, L. (1978). *The reader, the text, and the poem: The transactional theory of the literary work*. Carbondale: Southern Illinois University Press.

Stanovich, K. E. (1986). Matthew effects in reading: Some consequences of individual differences in the acquisition of reading. *Reading Research Quarterly, 21*, 360–407.

Thompson, C. A. (2003). *The oral vocabulary abilities of skilled and unskilled African American readers* [Unpublished Dissertation] Michigan, University of Michigan: Ann Arbor.

Townsend, D., Barber, A.T., Carter, H., & Salas, R. (2020). More than words: Older adolescents' linguistic resources in the context of disciplinary achievement and academic risk. *Reading Psychology, 41*(8), 778–802. https://doi.org/10.1080/02702711.2020.1782291.

# Epilogue

Freebody, P. (1992). A socio-cultural approach: Resourcing four roles as a literacy learner. In A. Watson & A. Beadenhop (Eds.), *Prevention of reading failure* (pp. 48–60). Sydney: Ashton Scholastic.

Hayes, D. (2018). New research shows what makes a difference and why 'evidence-based' is not enough. *EduResearch Matters: A voice for Australian educational researchers*. Australian Association for Research in Education.

Macken-Horarik, M. (2009). Multiliteracies, metalanguage and the protean mind: Navigating school English in a sea of change. *English in Australia, 44*(1), 33–43.

Martin, J.R. (1999). Mentoring semogenesis: 'genre-based' literacy pedagogy. In Francis Christie (Ed.), *Pedagogy and the Shaping of Consciousness: Linguistic and Social Processes* (pp. 123–55). London: Continuum.

Stanovich, K. E. (1986). Matthew effects in reading: Some consequences of individual differences in the acquisition of reading. *Reading Research Quarterly, 21*, 360–407.

Vygotsky, L.S. ([1934] 1978). Mind in society: The development of higher psychological processes. In M. Cole, V. John-Steiner, S. Scribner & E. Souberman (Eds.). Cambridge, MA: Harvard University Press.

# Index

abstraction 19, 25, 56, 69, 120, 146, 155, 160, 185
ACARA 15, 27, 60, 119, 145, 164, 171, 186, 230, 273
achievement gap 19, 202, 285
adjacency pair 98–104, 235–45, 291
aesthetic reading 273, 274
agency 6, 11, 13, 93, 178, 211, 212, 277
Alexander's generic model of teaching 73, 210
analytical thinking 203
Appraisal theory/framework 63, 194–6, 205, 207
aspects of literacy 10, 14, 28, 109, 114, 229–51, 282
aspirational literacies 278
assessment 27, 78–81, 92, 103, 116, 119, 161, 173, 190, 201, 210–11, 218, 231, 271, 286–7
  as activity/reflection 266
  high stakes 262
audience 24

basal readers 93, 224–5
benchmarking 221–31
Bernstein, B. xviii, 6, 7, 17, 29, 55, 57, 58, 59, 68, 81, 84, 91, 93, 122, 152, 166, 168, 254, 257
Bloom's taxonomy 6

capabilities
  general 169
  learning 257
  literacy 199, 270
  student 117
case study/ies 9, 123, 130, 147, 218–19, 223, 227, 230
Christie, F. 21, 24–7, 35, 51, 55–7, 62, 63, 68, 116, 120–3, 146–8, 169, 172, 254
classroom groupings 200

commitment (of meaning) 176, 181
comprehension 21–3, 31, 92, 100, 106, 114, 210, 217, 222, 226, 279
contemporary literacy theory 72
context xviii, 6–9, 15, 17, 21, 23–6, 31, 32, 33, 44, 52, 60–5, 78, 80–90, 91, 93, 98, 115, 121–3, 130, 132, 173, 174, 183–9, 191, 199, 211, 215–31, 249, 250, 254, 256, 261, 265–9, 271, 275–9
  of culture 255
  of situation 255
continuum
  common-sense/uncommon-sense xviii, 10, 57, 58, 60, 65, 140, 171, 178, 179, 254, 257–60, 266, 282
  context-embedded/reflection 266
conversation analysis 7, 12, 96–8, 233
co-opting 68, 69
creativity 90, 92, 203
criticality 202–3
cross sector instruction 73
cultural objects 104
curricula continuity 286
curriculum
  demands 35, 169, 193, 283
  enacted 255, 268–9
  formal 83, 95, 209
  hidden 209
  literacies 269, 270
  national 14, 260, 283
  reform 15, 79, 216, 232
  science 12, 56, 169, 171–7, 183–6, 189, 190, 210, 244, 257–9, 260–70, 283
  specialised 269
curriculum disciplines 14, 269, 286

Detailed Reading 166–7
Derewianka, B. 6, 10, 24–7, 35, 37, 55–7, 62, 63, 68, 72, 116, 120, 121, 146, 169, 172, 254, 255, 282

differences in attainment 173, 256, 269, 271, 275, 287
differentiation 191, 222
discontinuities 92, 95–6, 117, 168, 209, 261, 269, 283, 287
dispositions 11, 77, 116, 164, 204, 220, 242, 249, 253, 255, 271, 284
disciplinary
  apprenticeship 269
  discourses xviii, 270
  gaze 146, 157, 165, 186
  learning 258, 268, 270
  silos 73
  subjects xvii
discipline xix, 3, 14, 22, 39, 50, 69, 92, 108, 110, 114, 115, 146, 169, 171, 190, 234, 256, 266, 269, 282–6
discipline specific literacies 71, 114, 169, 171, 189
dialogic basis of 146
diversity 11, 13, 28, 46, 173, 192–201, 204, 205, 256, 283
doing literacy 102, 284, 285

educational phases 210
educator xvii, 4, 5, 15, 53, 70, 71, 73, 78–82, 84, 86, 87, 89–93, 232
efferent reading 273
epistemic literacies 77, 79, 82, 86, 96, 113, 115, 121, 293
English
  curriculum 145, 146, 163, 211, 216, 270
  primary 168
  secondary 161
  syllabus 30, 48, 50, 92, 217, 230
envoi 71, 209, 273, 282, 286
entities 96, 101, 163, 173, 175, 181–9, 215–19, 229–32, 274–5, 276, 279, 281
ethnomethodology 7, 97, 250
evaluation processes 191
everyday rationalities 55, 65–9, 113
exchange xviii, 10, 11, 12, 56, 84, 95, 98–107, 110, 115, 116, 122–41, 148–57, 163, 190, 234–51, 266–77, 282, 284
exchange structures 56, 96, 98, 116, 152, 238
explicit pedagogy/instruction 11, 52, 81, 121, 165, 166, 172, 212, 218, 231, 284, 285
explicitness 183, 184, 212

false dichotomies 273, 274, 282
feedback 40, 43, 46, 47, 52, 101, 148, 262–3
fluency in reading 217, 224, 226
foregrounding 163
Four Resources model 21, 115
fourth grade slump 27

Garfinkel, H. 7, 58–9, 65–8
generalisation 42, 56, 140, 142
genre 37, 39, 43, 48, 106, 108, 109, 115, 183
  canonical/non-canonical 180
  curriculum 148, 151, 158, 165
  explanation 36, 37, 165, 180–8, 283
  information report 177–9
  knowledge 148
  stages 177–88
group discussions 38, 149–58

Halliday, M. A. K. xviii, 6, 17, 18, 55, 121, 172–5, 254–6
handwriting 25, 41, 48, 52, 83, 100, 224, 228, 229, 274, 276
Hasan, R. 145, 163, 254–6, 268
Heap 85, 92, 95, 100
home-school connection 229, 243
horizons of consequence 13, 192, 194, 201, 286

ideologies 29, 78, 80, 91, 168
image/s 43, 44, 49, 56, 63, 73, 122, 127, 140, 148, 172–86, 189
  everyday/technical 175
  photographic 177–9
inequality of access 165
interaction/s 31, 210, 237, 241, 247, 249, 255
  classroom 56, 95, 97, 98–117, 166
interactional norms 209
interview/s xix, 13, 80, 81, 83, 120, 124, 192–5, 200, 218, 219, 233–52, 256–8, 263, 265, 266, 274, 275
IRE, IRF 101, 103, 113, 148, 152, 248, 249

knower
  primary 122, 125, 151
  secondary 151
knowledge 113, 115, 116, 117, 120–42, 146, 148–52, 155, 160–7, 169, 171, 177, 180, 186, 189, 190, 209, 210, 216,

217, 218, 220, 222, 230, 234, 235, 238, 240, 242, 243, 247, 248, 249, 251, 253, 254, 255, 256, 257, 258, 259, 260, 265, 266
common-sense/uncommon-sense xviii, 10, 57, 58, 60, 65, 140, 171, 178, 179, 254, 257–60, 266, 282
conceptual 180, 266
educational xviii, 5, 10, 254, 255
exchange 10, 122, 124, 125, 130
forms of xviii, 7, 12, 57, 95, 96, 116, 117, 257, 269
practices 254, 284
specialisation 169, 259, 260, 261, 264, 269, 270

L3 (Language, Learning & Literacy) program 218
language
  evaluative 196
  everyday 181, 253
  features 17, 25, 44, 47, 172, 223
  of science 171
  technical 172
learner/s
  capacities/capabilities 13, 17, 43, 82, 117, 169, 192, 199, 200, 201, 204, 216, 229, 239, 243, 252, 257, 264, 270, 273
  diverse group of 191
  EAL/D (English as an Additional Language or Dialect) learners 200, 205
  future-oriented 286
  independent/ce 196, 198, 199, 205, 206, 222, 263, 283
learning
  as apprenticeship 163, 171, 255, 260, 269, 270
  cumulative 3, 14, 83, 146, 147, 190, 273
  disciplinary 7, 102, 109, 258, 268, 270
  intentions 83, 97, 124, 131, 220–3
  tasks 122, 133, 141, 148, 277
learning to read/reading to learn 273, 274, 282
lesson/s 7, 8–12, 83, 92, 95–7, 100, 101–4, 110, 116, 124, 128, 135, 139, 145–8, 157, 158, 162–6, 180, 183, 192, 200, 204, 209, 220, 232–8, 267, 284, 286

as activity/as knowledge 265
history 209
stages 125, 127, 132
literacy
  aspects of 10, 15, 16, 19, 22, 23, 28, 109, 114, 229, 238, 251, 282
  as 'doing' 230
  as a general capability 169–71
  debates 279–86
  demands xviii, 3, 4, 8, 11, 12, 13, 55, 85, 104, 117, 191–3, 252, 255, 265, 268, 275, 282–6
  development xvii, 4, 5, 9–12, 14, 15–20, 26–8, 30, 53, 55, 56, 67, 96, 116, 119, 120, 191–4, 205, 217, 281, 282, 285, 287
  digital 286
  disciplinary literacy 96, 173, 185, 270
  dispositions 77, 220
  experiences 3, 8, 77–92, 102, 120, 147, 223, 227, 282, 284
  leadership 219, 221
  multimodal 171, 176, 183, 190
  progression 10, 29, 48, 217, 287
  repertoires 253, 269, 217, 282, 286
  skills 3, 21, 92, 93, 120, 142, 217, 277, 278, 284, 286
  as social practice 84
  task-based approach to 227
  teaching 82, 102, 217, 218
  testing 22, 28, 119, 204, 286
  'the basics' of 198, 222
  trajectory/ies 3, 10, 29, 51, 55–65, 68, 83, 191, 194, 284
  turns 71
literacies
  school 275, 277
literate identities 215–19, 229, 230, 274, 275, 279, 281
literature 12, 145, 149, 155, 157, 163, 166, 210, 231, 259, 285
  as verbal art 145

Martin, J. R. 121, 122, 145–8, 151, 152, 157, 163, 166, 172, 174, 194, 198, 255, 284
Matthew effect 19, 278
meaning cues 166
meaning making resources 169, 171

# Index

meaning/s/meaning making xviii, 6, 7, 16, 17, 18, 22, 24, 26, 31, 33, 42–9, 84, 87, 88, 112, 121, 122, 140, 142, 145, 146, 148, 152, 155, 156, 166, 169, 171–90, 232
  evaluative 193
  figurative vs literal 166
  first order 145, 163, 164
  second order 145, 166
  scientific 169, 182
  thematic 62, 145, 148, 152, 153–9, 162–8
media 174
metafunctions
  ideational 174
  interpersonal 174
  textual 174
metaphor 42, 68, 145, 155, 160, 162, 166
  patterns of 167
metalanguage 130–5, 153
  literary 158, 160, 161, 168
modelling 25, 121, 128, 130–6, 141, 142, 152, 165, 167, 212
'moral sympathy' 235
motivation 110, 197, 204, 206, 222, 275–7, 283
multimodal 43, 48, 50, 71, 122, 169, 170, 171, 172, 173, 286
  ensembles 176, 183, 189
  meaning-making 48, 174
  practices 176, 183, 185, 186, 190, 286
multimodal communicational practices 71
  design and multiple modes 73
  modalities 72, 122, 125, 139, 148

NAPLAN (National Assessment Program-Literacy and Numeracy) 119, 286
National Literacy and Numeracy Progressions 217
necessary literacies 277–99
New South Wales Department of Education 17, 199
nominalisation 172, 178, 181, 182

oral language xvii, 15, 24, 28, 71, 224, 282
  development 10, 17–19

participation structures 10, 106, 149, 195
proficient reading 277

pedagogy 4, 6, 7, 9, 11, 68, 79, 95, 96, 114–16, 120, 162, 163, 168, 191–3, 199, 211, 216, 253, 281–5
  co-opting 69
  critical 164
  direct instruction 79
  explicit 165, 172, 218, 285
  liberal progressivist 164
  meaning-based 22
  models of 22, 48, 78, 287
  visible/invisible 12, 80–1, 164
  writing 12, 25, 51, 121
pedagogic
  discourse 7, 141–3, 145
  dialogue 168
  interactions 284
  practices 284
  strategies 205
pedagogic register analysis 120, 122–3, 135–41, 151, 155
personal response 164
phase 152
phonics 16, 21, 83–4, 217–18, 220–1
phonological awareness 217
poetry 145
  appreciation 147
  poetics 147
  symbolism in 149, 153
primary literacy 209
proficient reading 277
purposeful participation 215

questioning 97–8, 110, 238, 248

read-aloud 291
reading 215, 245, 275, 276
  achievement 19
  and disciplinarity 22
  development 19–23
  joint 86–7, 111–13
  proficiency 222, 227
  relationship to writing 22–3
  skills 20, 21
reasoning practices 146, 172
recontextualization 29, 80
register
  curriculum 122, 148, 164
  pedagogic 122, 148

register variables 148
   field/s of social activity 148, 174, 255
   modes of meaning making 148, 174, 255
   tenor of social relations and values 148, 174, 255
registerial repertoires 255, 268
representations 157, 171
Rose, D. 146, 148, 166, 296, 299, 301, 303, 314, 315, 317, 320, 321, 325
Rosenblatt's theory of reading 273

Sacks 7, 294, 313, 324
scaffolding 165–6
schooling 72
   middle years 169, 254
   primary years 215–18, 233
science 171
   inquiry skills 170
   primary/secondary 190
   language of 171
   skills 171
   text 210
secondary 145
semiotic resources xviii, 6, 11–12, 171–3, 180, 189–90
skills 164, 217
   development 224
   foundational 223
   independent 265
sociocultural xviii, 16, 18, 23–7, 121
   paradigm 215
social semiotic theory 121, 173
sociocultural approaches to literacy pedagogy 17
   modelling 25, 121, 128, 130–8, 141, 165, 167, 212
   guided practice 121
   independent writing 43, 121, 125, 132
Stanovich 278, 287
student
   experiences 190, 255, 285
   gifted and/or talented 221
   high attaining 261, 266, 269, 270, 271, 275, 285
   identity 216
   low attaining 270, 276
success criteria 220
substantive learning 275

symbolic articulation 145
symbolic resources 168
systemic functional linguistics/semiotics 174–5, 193, 257

teacher
   accounts 191
   interviews 195, 205
   perceptions 193, 283
   talk 129, 194
technicality 146, 185
text/s
   infographic 189
   literary 258
   mediating 149
   multimodal 169, 174
   types of 223, 265
   visual/verbal 178–81
   written 178
thematic analysis 193, 257
thinking skills
   analytical 202–4
   critical 202–5
   'lower order' 203
trajectories 262–3
transcript conventions 292
transition xvii, 68–9, 82, 216
   challenges, transitional 191, 194, 205, 275
   gaps, transitional 72
   to Kindergarten 210
   points, literacy xvii, 26–7, 28, 35, 37, 50, 117, 191, 193, 233, 237, 254, 281
   to primary school 210, 273
   primary/secondary point of 147
   to secondary school 169, 210, 253, 275
TRANSLIT xvii, 123, 147, 173, 218, 233, 255, 282, 293

visual grammar 171
Vygotsky 17, 69, 282

word recognition 217
writing
   achievement 27
   development 23–6, 29, 37, 41, 50–3, 62–3, 173
   demands 253, 259, 291

genres 17, 24, 35, 50, 148, 169, 174, 189, 209, 284
lessons 100, 124, 209
modelled 221, 225
NAPLAN tests of 27
pedagogy, approaches to

cognitive 24, 32, 37, 41, 52, 121
process 16, 43, 121
text-based 17, 121
process 72
purpose 32, 35, 132
science 182

www.ingramcontent.com/pod-product-compliance
Lightning Source LLC
Chambersburg PA
CBHW052142300426
44115CB00011B/1485